MILESTONES 1:
THE MUSIC AND TIMES OF MILES DAVIS TO 1960

JACK CHAMBERS

Milestones 1: The Music and Times of Miles Davis to 1960

BEECH TREE BOOKS
WILLIAM MORROW
New York

TO SUSAN
for all the good reasons
and then some

The author is grateful to Jack Maher and Deborah Kelly of
Down Beat and to Frank Driggs for their help with the
photographs in this volume, and to Louise and Dale
Dickson for their hospitality in Chicago. Every effort has
been made to identify and acknowledge the photographers
whose work is presented here.

Copyright © 1983 by University of Toronto Press

Library of Congress Catalog Card Number: 85-70574

ISBN: 0-688-02635-4

Printed in the United States of America

First U.S. Edition

1 2 3 4 5 6 7 8 9 10

The word "book" is said to derive from *boka,* or beech.
The beech tree has been the patron tree of writers since ancient times and
represents the flowering of literature and knowledge.

Contents

Miles Davis at the Newport Jazz Festival, 1955; from left, Percy Heath, Thelonious
Monk, Zoot Sims, Davis, Gerry Mulligan, and Connie Kay (Robert Parent, courtesy of
Down Beat)

Preface

You can't judge Miles on *Relaxin'* and *Cookin'* only and not on *Miles Smiles* and not on *Bitches Brew* or just on *On the Corner*. You look at the man's work and you see *Sketches of Spain*, a string orchestra, the quintet, a rock date. That to me is what an artist does, he gets interested in many areas over his life, which is all related by a single thread, which is his sound.   Dave Liebman

For the final chapter of her book *Jazz People*, the English photographer and journalist Valerie Wilmer chronicled her meeting with Miles Davis. The entire interview consists of the following three lines of dialogue:

Later!
But Mr Davis ...
Look, baby, when I said 'later' I meant LATER!

A reader approaching Wilmer's interview with no preconceptions about Miles Davis – that is, a reader who happens to be the highest lama of Tibet or the lowest mutant of the Ozarks – might simply wonder what his hurry is all about. But most people have preconceptions about Miles Davis and will find the interview revealing, because it shows him to be what they already believe him to be – prickly, private, angry, rude, arrogant, and caustic. It is surprising that so many people in the world should 'know' all this about a man who has revealed so very little of himself, at least offstage. On stage, of course, Davis has given us one of the best-defined and most personal images in the history of jazz. For the first twenty-five years of a career that began in earnest in 1945, and perhaps also in the still poorly understood years preceding and following his retirement from 1975 to 1981, in both his spontaneous improvisations based on standard themes and his own composed themes, Davis has consistently shown himself to be wary, brooding, introverted, wry, gentle, and sensitive.

The discrepancy between the character revealed on stage and offstage has not, of course, escaped attention. The novelist James Baldwin calls him "a miraculously tough and tender man" and claims that "Miles's disguise would certainly never fool anybody with sense, but it keeps a lot of people away, and that's the point." But if he has succeeded in keeping people away from him in his private life, he has never even attempted to keep them away from his music. He has persistently worked his way into the forefront of modern jazz movements, never shying away from the leader's role and never hesitating to dictate the course of the music. His career swings through the entire post-war history of jazz, crystallizing its main currents all the way from bebop to jazz-rock.

In Nat Hentoff's definition, "Jazz is a continual autobiography, or rather a continuum of intersecting autobiographies." The autobiographies are told in music, and the music – as Davis has reminded us several times – speaks for itself. But the "autobiography" of Davis – his music – is already so rich and varied that even his most diligent listeners are in danger of losing their way. There is a need for a guide to the music as it has unfolded, and also, I trust, for a biography of the "miraculously tough and tender man" who has provided the music. In the end, the man and his music are one and the same. In spite of Davis's recalcitrance with would-be chroniclers, he has left enough clues along with his music, albeit sprinkled far and wide, for the story to come clear. It has its contradictions, and it is vague at some points, but no more so than many biographies of much more willing subjects. In fact, it is so complete that it might surprise Davis himself, who takes some pride in the fact that he does not "give stories."

"It's nothing personal," Davis once told Joe Goldberg, "but I don't give stories. If Jesus Christ himself came down from the cross and asked for a story, I'd say, 'I'm sorry, I don't have the time.' You have to write it, that's your business, so just write about the music, about whether you like it or not. Write what you know, or what you don't know, like everybody else." As a statement of policy, Davis's words are clear and unequivocal. There is little doubt that he means them, and he has been more or less consistent about holding to them throughout his career. Valerie Wilmer was neither the first nor the last prospective interviewer whom Davis rebuffed.

However, he has not been absolutely rigid. As might be expected of a man who has been one of the most prominent musicians in the world for over thirty-five years, he has often been asked for interviews, and he has occasionally consented – or perhaps relented. There are at least fifteen interviews in existence, all of them longer than the one with Valerie Wilmer and some of them quite extensive, including even a "self-portrait" (1957) – a press release from Columbia Records in Davis's own words, which were culled from a taped interview with George Avakian. There are also, of course, many smaller items, such as Leonard Feather's "blindfold tests" with Davis for *Down Beat* magazine and reminiscences by Michael Zwerin, Max Gordon, and others.

The quality of these sources, naturally, varies enormously. In some of the interviews, Davis's distaste for the whole affair is almost palpable, and the information he surrenders is largely opaque: for instance, when Harriet Choice of the *Chicago Tribune* asks him how he knows which musicians are right for his bands, he answers, "The same way I know what girl I want to screw." Even some of the long interviews have their problems. The best known is the 1962 *Playboy* interview, because it inaugurated the highly touted series of interviews in that magazine, and perhaps also because the interviewer, Alex Hailey, later became a celebrity with the publication and television adaptation of his book *Roots*. But that interview is not all it is cracked up to be. In at least a couple of instances, there is a curious similarity between what Hailey puts into the mouth of Miles Davis and what Marc Crawford elicited from Davis's father for *Ebony* magazine the year before. One point of similarity is shown in this parallel text:

CRAWFORD

Davis's father: When he was in high school he played trumpet. In school competitions he was always the best, but the blue-eyed boys always won first and second prizes ... The officials, Miles and everybody else knew he should have had first prize.

HAILEY

Davis: In high school, I was the best in the music class on the trumpet. I knew it and all the rest knew it – but all the contest first prizes went to the boys with blue eyes.

There can be little doubt that Hailey ransacked Crawford's article in order to find some of the words that Davis speaks in the *Playboy* interview, rather than vice versa, not only because Crawford's article ante-dates Hailey's, but also because of textual evidence. In at least one instance Hailey has taken Crawford's quotation from Davis's father and put it in the mouth of Davis himself, where it comes out as gibberish:

CRAWFORD

Davis's father: Historically, way back into slavery days, the Davises have been musicians and performed classic works in the homes of the plantation owners. My father, Miles the first, was born six

HAILEY

Davis: The slave Davises played classical string music on the plantation. My father, Miles the first, was born six years after the Emancipation. He wanted to play music, but my grandfather years after the Emancipation and forbade me to play music because the only place a Negro could play then was in barrel houses.

wanted him to be more than an entertainer for white folks.

Any assertion by Miles Davis that *his* father was Miles Davis the first and that he was born six years after the Emancipation is utter nonsense, and Miles Davis would know that better than anyone, except perhaps his own father, whose father in turn these facts concern.

The *Playboy* interview is neither the most revealing nor the most interesting interview with Davis, despite the publicity it received. Several of the others contend for that honor: Nat Hentoff's may reveal more about Davis's music of the time (1958) than any other, and Sy Johnson's may reveal more about his character at the time (1976) than any other, but my personal favorite is probably the interview with Julie Coryell, in her book *Jazz-Rock Fusion* (1978), which is long and chatty and full of fresh topics.

In any event, there exists a fair amount of first-person information on Davis – almost enough to make an autobiography, by assembling Davis's own words from the various sources – almost, but not quite. I have done that wherever possible, letting Davis speak for himself.

Along with the various interviews, the most useful source has been Jorgen Grunnet Jepsen's *A Discography of Miles Davis* (1969), which provides a listing of the studio recordings and recorded performances of Davis up to May 1968, as far as they were known at the time. Like all of Jepsen's discographies, this one provided a wonderful foundation for the rest of us to work from. My copy now contains hundreds of corrections, most of them on miniscule details, as well as the dozens of additions to the known works prior to May 1968 that have become known more recently, and also, of course, the dozens of additions since 1968. Michel Ruppli's discography finally provided a successor to Jepsen's when it appeared in *Jazz Hot* in 1979. Brian Priestley's discography, appended to Ian Carr's *Miles Davis: A Biography*, updates the entries to 1981 and also clears up some old mysteries. My own discography below updates and corrects some of the main entries but omits the discographical freight of master numbers and complete issues, readily available for those who want them in Jepsen's and Ruppli's listings. I am grateful to Jan Lohmann for letting me hear some of the more important private recordings in his collection and for helping me with information about the discographically difficult period 1970–5.

There are four earlier book-length studies of Davis. *Miles Davis*, by the English reviewer Michael James, was published in 1961 and reviews all of Davis's recorded works that James had access to. Although the list of works has more than quintupled since then, James's little book remains a very useful guide to the music that it covered. *Miles Davis: A Musical Biography*, by Bill Cole, was roundly condemned by its reviewers when it appeared in 1974, mainly because it contains errors galore, beginning with the incorrect birthdate. (Most authors err by one day, copying the mistake from Leonard Feather's *Encyclopedia of Jazz*; Cole errs by three weeks.) Cole's book cannot really be counted among the sources. Ian Carr's *Miles Davis: A Critical Biography* appeared in England early in 1982 and in the United States several months later (with its subtitle inexplicably shortened to *A Biography*). Carr, a British jazz trumpeter, highlights his narrative of the main events of Davis's life with his sensitivity to jazz style and trumpet technique, especially when dealing with Davis's fusion music of the late 1960s, the main influence on Carr's own music. *'Round about Midnight: A Portrait of Miles Davis*, by Eric Nisenson, also appeared in 1982. A paperback categorized by its publisher as a celebrity biography, it is less concerned with Davis's music than with his style and less concerned with his life than with his image, and Nisenson portrays both the style and the image succinctly.

My book is organized in two volumes, which subdivide Davis's long and extraordinarily productive career into its main phases. *Milestones I* traces the emergence of the teenaged Davis from East St. Louis, Illinois, into post-war New York City, where he joined the ranks of the bebop revolutionaries, worked out his individual style, and took his place in the forefront of jazz music by late 1959. Davis's activities during this period are covered in two main movements: the first, under the heading "Boplicity," details his apprenticeship, first in his hometown and later under the aegis of Charlie Parker and Dizzy Gillespie, culminating in his first masterwork with the short-lived experimental nonet of 1948; the second, titled "Miles Ahead," concerns his creative recess during his years of heroin addiction and his dramatic return to form in the 1950s, culminating in the years of the first great quintet and the sextet. *Milestones II* takes up his music and his times from 1960, also in two main movements: it begins, in "Prince of Darkness," with his formal reorganization of bebop in the second great quintet and continues in "Pangaea" with his restless search for further formal expansions, leading to fusions with free form, rock, and other music.

The book thus presents Davis to the reader in the variety of personae – bebop prodigy, hipster, fashion plate, autocrat, activist, rock star – he has offered for public consumption and his music in the shifting guises he has chosen as his medium. Through all the personae and the guises, all these surfaces, shines the single, expansive, encompassing spirit that is Miles Davis. The business of a biographer is to present the surfaces as faithfully and as comprehensively as he can and hope that the spirit is ultimately recoverable by his readers from them. That has seemed a tall order, when the subject is Miles Davis and the surfaces comprise so many lifestyles, itineraries, associations, bands, recordings, and all the rest. Yet those of us who have lived through a fair amount of the history that this book documents have managed to see through all the diversity with which Davis's career has presented us to the spirit pervading it, and so I can hold out some hope that my readers will be able to do the same when it is compressed into print.

I am beholden to Colette Copeland, Dale Dickson, Bernard Lecerf, Jan Lohmann, Dan Morgenstern, and Chuck Netley, for sundry favors which made this book better than it would otherwise have been. No financial assistance was sought or received for the research and writing of *Milestones I* and *II*.

ABBREVIATIONS

The following standard abbreviations have been used in the discographical entries:

arr	arranger	gtr	guitar
as	alto saxophone	perc	percussion
b	bass	pno	piano
bs	baritone saxophone	ss	soprano saxophone
clnt	clarinet	tba	tuba
comp	composer	tbn	trombone
cond	conductor	tpt	trumpet
dms	drums	ts	tenor saxophone
flt	flute	vcl	vocal
frh	french horn	vib	vibraphone

PART ONE
BOPLICITY

The history of both jazz and jazzmen is that of creative purity gradually corrupted by success. In his youth, the great jazz musician has to struggle to impose his art; if he succeeds in doing so, he must struggle daily *against* his own success. How many men have won *this* struggle? Charlie Parker undoubtedly did, because he never reached the peak of success and because he died at the age of thirty-five. [Thelonious] Monk and Miles Davis may win it, either because of their tough, incorruptible characters, or because they took Pascal's advice and fled success rather than try to stand up to it.   André Hodeir (1962)

The Charlie Parker Quintet at the Three Deuces, 1948; from left, Tommy Potter, Parker, Max Roach (behind Parker), Miles Davis, and Duke Jordan (William Gottlieb, courtesy of *Down Beat*)

1

Tune-up
1926–44

Music is the song I love,
And nothing comes between.
Melodies are à la carte,
But they reach my selfish heart.
  Miles Davis (February 1976), quoted by Julie Coryell (1978)

"Childhood? Who wants to remember that?" asked Miles Davis in 1981. And he added, "I was born like this."

At the time he had just turned 55, and he was sitting uneasily for an interview with George Goodman, Jr, of the *New York Times*, part of the promotional hullabaloo surrounding his imminent return to the concert stage after more than five years of retirement. He was garbed in a white cap, a red jump suit, and cowboy boots, the kind of ultramodish attire that he had been affecting for more than a decade, ever since the average age of his audience was halved by his appearances at rock emporiums. Even so, his appearance seemed thoroughly unfamiliar because he wore a moustache for the first time in almost thirty years and a goatee for the first time ever. It was, to that extent, a new face that Davis had prepared for the public after so many years out of sight, and for the part of his public with any memories at all it would be one more rebirth to reckon with. His altered appearance as well as his disdain for discussing his childhood – or, for that matter, anything else that had happened to him more than a few months ago – was part and parcel of the same Davis creed: the refusal to look back, to pay any homage at all to the past or even to waste much time deploring it, and the utter absence of nostalgia. It is a creed that Davis professes consistently, so that from a distance his career and his life seem suffused by a Heraclitan obsession with change and flux. In truth, Davis's creed has less to do with Heraclitus than with Charlie Parker, and it is less a philosophical stance than a gut reaction to growing up black in mid-century America. It is middle-aged hipsterism, more articulate and reasoned than in the hip youth of the bebop revolutionaries, when it meant merely mumbling and turning away, but its highest values remain much the same – a cool, detached, unfeeling, impersonal response to the vagaries of life, whether good or bad. Expressions of sentiment are considered signs of weakness. Talking openly about the past invites the flow of feeling, and so Davis has avoided talking about it as far as he can. But just as in his art Davis has never been successful in submerging his feelings, no matter how cool and detached the surface of the music, so in his life he has not been able to avoid talking about the past entirely. Over the years he has offered details that, together with the recollections of other, less reluctant witnesses, can be pieced together to make a surprisingly coherent and far from unrevealing collage of his middle-class upbringing in the American Midwest. If he has stopped well short of giving us what Holden Caulfield called "all that David Copperfield kind of crap," he has revealed more of his childhood and adolescence than he ever imagined that he would, and certainly more than anyone had any right to expect.

Miles Dewey Davis III was born in Alton, Illinois, on 26 May 1926. His father, a dentist with ambitions that went well beyond even the comfortable limits enjoyed by most men of his profession, came to realize, at the very moment that his first son came into the world, that his ambitions required an urban arena, and he moved his family 25 miles south to East St. Louis when young Miles was only one. In East St. Louis he divided his energies between his dental practice in the city and a two-hundred-acre farm in the countryside near Milstead, Illinois. Miles Davis's mother, Cleota Henry Davis, was a taciturn woman, whose social ambitions almost matched her husband's business ambitions. Besides Miles, the Davises had a daughter, Dorothy, two years older, and in 1929, after they had been settled in East St. Louis for two years, their third child, Vernon, was born.

According to Miles's father, who was known locally as Doc Davis, his oldest son's musical ability and his leadership were inherited directly from the Davis side of the family. "By genetics and breeding Miles is always going to be ahead of his time," he told Marc Crawford in 1961. "Historically way back into slavery days, the Davises have been musicians and performed classic works in the homes of the plantation owners. My father, Miles I, was born six years after Emancipation and forbade me to play music because the only place a Negro could play then was in barrel houses. My father was the most efficient double entry bookkeeper in Arkansas before the coming of the adding machine and white men came to his home under cover of night for him to fix their books. He was later driven from his extensive holdings." "My grandfather made a hundred dollars a day during the Depression," Miles Davis told Julie Coryell. "When his kids got old, he gave them land." Those land holdings no doubt provided the collateral for the comfortable conditions in which Doc Davis's family was raised.

There was nevertheless a price to be exacted from a black man who was too successful in Arkansas at the turn of the century. So Davis's grandfather was removed from his land, probably because his holdings outstripped too conspicuously those of his white neighbors or perhaps because his bookkeeping jobs made him too knowledgeable about the business dealings of the whites. For whatever reason, Miles Davis's grandfather lived much of his adult life under the threat of violence from white men. One of his sons, Frank, who inherited less business acumen from his father than did Doc Davis, served as his father's bodyguard. The experience of white antagonism thus became part of the patriarch's legacy no less important than his worldly ambition, and it was passed down to his sons, and to his grandsons, just as forcibly.

Besides Frank, Doc Davis also had a second brother, Ferdinand, who is warmly remembered by his nephew. Unlike Frank, the bodyguard, and even more than Doc Davis himself, Ferdinand was a man of culture and a citizen of the world. "My uncle went to Harvard and studied in Berlin," Davis told Julie Coryell. "He was the editor of *Color* magazine. He used to tell me everything ... He talked to me about Caesar and Hannibal ... He was a brilliant guy. He made me feel dumb." Ferdinand seems to have been more than willing to fill in the gaps in his nephew's education, but there were some gaps that Miles Davis's mother felt were better left unfilled. His association with his uncle Ferdinand became a minor source of conflict between Miles and his mother. Davis recalls, "My mother said, 'Oh God, Ferd and you together!' (He had a suite downtown.) I said, 'We're the only ones in the family with any brains' – Ferd, me, and my father."

If Doc Davis could hardly compete with his brother's flair in the eyes of his son, he still had credentials of his own that were impossible for his son to undervalue. He graduated from Arkansas Baptist College, Lincoln University in Pennsylvania, and Northwestern College of Dentistry, making up at least in quantity what he may have lost in his son's eyes by not going to Harvard. "Three degrees," his son points out, "and he finished when he was twenty-four." Besides that, he alone inherited the bent for business, his father's business sense sitting less easily on his brothers. "My father told them to always count their money," Davis says. Counting his own money became increasingly difficult for Doc Davis during young Miles's youth and adolescence. In East St. Louis he began to specialize in dental surgery in the city and in special breeds of pork on the farm, with great success in both. "My father is worth more than I am," Davis claimed in 1962, when he himself was earning a six-figure salary. "He's a high-priced dental surgeon with more practice than he can handle – because he's good at his business – and he raises hogs with pedigrees. It's a special breed of hogs with some funny name I would tell you, but I never can remember it."

Of his mother, Davis has had much less to say, and not much that is positive. Mother and son seem to have had a fairly stormy relationship, and they certainly did not share any confidences. He had been away from home living in New York for about ten years before he discovered that she knew any music at all. "I didn't know until after I'd gone back there for a visit a few years ago that my mother even knew one note of music," he told Nat Hentoff. "But she sat down one day and played some funky blues. Turned out my grandmother used to teach organ. I was surprised my mother could play because she always looked as if she'd hit me everytime I played my horn." He has occasionally conceded, as he did to Cheryl McCall, that "she was a very beautiful woman," but he qualifies even that praise: "My mother was pretty and very blank-faced ... *no expression*. She looked at me when I played the trumpet. She'd say *When are you gonna play something that I can understand?*" Mrs Davis was only participating in a form of hypocrisy that was widespread among bourgeois blacks all over America for most of the century following Emancipation. Its source was a deep-seated dread among black parents that their own children would be sucked back into the social vortex of barge-toting and bale-lifting from which they had worked against great odds to free themselves. Rightly or wrongly, they believed that the surest way for their offspring to slip backward was by playing any of the forms of black music – ragtime, marches, dance tunes – the parents had left behind in their scramble up the social ladder. Thousands of middle-class black youngsters felt the parental pressure. Doc Davis received it as an edict from his own father in Arkansas around the turn of the century, and in succeeding decades the same pressure was exerted – unsuccessfully, thank God – on Duke Ellington in Washington, Earl Hines in Pittsburgh, Fats Waller in New York, Hampton Hawes in Los Angeles, and countless other sons and daughters on whose shoulders lay the burden of upward social mobility.

It must nevertheless have been clear to Davis that his mother was not dead set against *all* music. His sister and his brother also studied music as children, and his sister did so with their mother's blessing. "My sister Dorothy studied music for ten years – she says her mother wanted to keep her off the streets," he told Julie Coryell. "My brother Vernon went to the Roosevelt Conservatory in Chicago for three years. He went to Howard University too. He played trumpet and piano." Davis claims that he taught his brother to play the trumpet so he could join him in the high school marching band. For Vernon, as for their sister Dorothy, music became an avocation, not a profession.

The city where the Davis children were raised, East St. Louis, sits on the east bank of the Mississippi River, as does the town of Alton, where Miles Davis and his sister were born. The river at this point coincides with the state line, separating Illinois on its east bank from Missouri on its west. The river also forms a natural city limit for East St. Louis, but the urban landscape does not simply end there. Indeed, it seems to erupt across the river, the site of St. Louis, Missouri, the biggest city to be found within hundreds of miles in the Midwest. In spite of the physical barrier of the river and political barrier of the state lines, East St. Louis is really just an appendage of metropolitan St. Louis, as its name implies. The urban sprawl of St. Louis takes on the appearance of an urban oasis amid a vast expanse of corn and cattle country. Kansas City, the nearest urban center of comparable size, is 246 miles away to the west; Chicago is a little further, 278 miles due north; New York is 930 miles to the east, and Los Angeles is twice as far away, to the southwest.

Apart from the fact that it is the place where Miles Davis was raised, for jazz buffs the main distinction of East St. Louis comes from the title of the Bubber Miley-Duke Ellington composition *East St. Louis Toodle-oo*, the theme song of the Ellington orchestra in the late 1920s and a staple in its repertoire for many years. The composition has nothing to do with East St. Louis. Ellington told Stanley Dance that the tune was born when the band traveled to New England and saw a sign advertising Lewando Cleaners. Someone in the bus sang out *"Oh, Lee – wan – do!"* and every time the bus passed the sign after that the musicians set up a chorus. The chorus grew into the arrangement that eventually became known as *East St. Louis Toodle-oo*. At the time of its first recording by the Ellington band in 1927 it featured a solo by the St. Louis trumpeter Louis Metcalf. Metcalf's prominence probably accounts for the title. Years later Ellington mused, "It would have been better if we had called it *Lewando* and got some advertising money from it."

"East St. Louis was so bad," Davis told Leonard Feather, "that it just made you get out and do something." That impression was no doubt formed after the Davis family moved into a white neighborhood, when Miles was in elementary school. "About the first thing I can remember as a little boy," he said later, in a story repeated endlessly by jazz journalists, "was a white man running me down the street hollering, 'Nigger! Nigger!' My father went hunting him with a shotgun." Doc Davis has told the same story, adding, "I got my shotgun, but I could never find him." And he concluded, sadly, "I don't think Miles, a sensitive boy, ever forgot it, or our troubles." The incident was a malevolent ripple on what would have been, for a white child, a smooth surface. "You're going to run into that Jim Crow thing regardless of how wealthy you are," Davis has said. "I can't buy no freedom. Having money has helped me once in a while, but I'm not looking for help ... There's no excuse for being poor anyway. You see, you're not supposed to wait on anybody to give you nothing. My father taught me that."

Davis learned the lessons of his father very well, from the beginning: "I have never been what you would call poor. I grew up with an allowance, and I had a big newspaper route. I saved most of what I had except for buying records." The newspaper route is obviously a source of pride to him, because he has mentioned it to interviewers several times. He was ten years old when he started working on it, and soon "it got bigger than I could handle because my customers liked me so much. I just delivered papers the best I could and minded my business, the same way I play my horn now." He was beginning to discover other strengths in his personality, especially at the farm. "He liked long walks in the country," his father remembers, "and hunting and fishing. He was an excellent horseman and if he was ever thrown he'd remount immediately and master his mount." That steel resolve would show up even more forcefully in a few years, when he began playing trumpet on 52nd Street beside such technical wizards as Charlie Parker and Dizzy Gillespie.

There was increasing friction between his mother and father, and very often it seems to have centered around young Miles. "When I was eleven, my mother said, 'Spank Miles.' And my father would say, 'For what?' She'd say, 'He's crazy.' He'd say, 'Remember that.'" The friction, which would eventually lead to a legal separation, was aggravated by Cleota Henry's inclination to pit her own wishes against those of her eldest son and then to call in her husband to arbitrate. She seemed doomed to lose, for Clark Terry, who knew the Davis family before he left St. Louis, has said, "Doc Davis was the type of guy who believed his son could do no wrong."

For Miles's thirteenth birthday, his mother talked about getting him a violin, but his father decided that he should have a trumpet instead. According to Davis, "Once my father was fixing a music instructor's teeth, who said, 'Send Miles around. I go to the grade school every Wednesday. Buy him a trumpet.'" That conversation was apparently enough to convince Doc Davis, and his son went along with him. "My mother said, 'Why don't you play the violin!' I said, 'If I take a violin out on the streets, I'll have more knockouts than I have now.'" Looking back on the incident, Davis sees it as a kind of power struggle between his parents: "My mother wanted to give me a violin for my birthday, but my father gave me a trumpet – because he loved my mother so much!" That same year saw a deeper disruption of his relations with his mother: "Me and my mother fell out when I was thirteen. We were close at one time; we could talk to each other, but you know, I wasn't going to take none of that shit from her just because she was my mother ... It was a matter of either talk straight to me or not at all. When she did, we became real tight ... [My father] just told my mother to leave me alone." From that time he seems to have reacted against her every wish, but that did not deter her from expressing her views.

The one positive recollection Davis has of his mother stems from her bringing jazz into the house. "My mother bought two records – Duke Ellington and Art Tatum," he says. "She hit on the right thing, didn't she?" Her choices seem altogether out of character from everything else we know of her.

Young Miles seems to have taken immediately to the trumpet he received for his birthday, although the lessons given by the itinerant school teacher were far from inspiring. "Once a week we would hold notes," Davis recalls. "Wednesdays at 2:30. Everybody would fight to play best." Learning to play the trumpet soon came to occupy more of his time than the school schedule allotted to it: "I used to spit rice to school every day and back, or spit half a pea – it makes you used to playing the trumpet." For Davis, the monotony of the school lessons was soon relieved, again through the intercession of his father. "Lucky for me, I learned to play the chromatic scale right away," Davis says. "A friend of my father's brought me a book one night and showed me how to do it so I wouldn't have to sit there and hold that note all the time."

Soon after, he began to take private lessons. Again, the choice of teacher was dictated by the fact that Doc Davis was doing some dental work for a trumpet teacher, but the choice was excellent. Elwood Buchanan had recently returned from a stint in the trumpet section of some touring dance bands, including Andy Kirk's orchestra. He steered Davis toward jazz music: "He used to tell us all about jam sessions on the showboats." St. Louis was visited regularly by showboats traveling the Mississippi, bringing musicians from New Orleans and other ports. When he got a little older, Davis spent some time on the showboats, sometimes joining in the jam sessions and always learning directly from the old pros, but Buchanan gave him the taste for jazz on the showboats from the beginning.

Buchanan also directed Davis's attention toward certain players whose styles were to have an abiding influence on his own mature style – Bobby Hackett and Harold Baker. Hackett, a white cornetist from New England, was only eleven years older than Davis, but he had been playing professionally around New England and New York since 1929, when he was fourteen. Indentified as a disciple of Bix Beiderbecke, Hackett played with a spare, singing tone that swung gently but insistently. In 1939–41, when Buchanan was telling Davis about him, Hackett's reputation was still largely a local one on the eastern seaboard, but because of Buchanan's exposure to Hackett's work when he was on the road, he became a formative influence for Davis. Almost a decade later, when Davis was firmly entrenched as a member of the bebop revolution and Hackett was entrenched in the opposing swing establishment, Hackett surprised some of his cohorts by remarking, "The other night I started to think I was sounding like Miles Davis, and I liked it." Tit for tat.

Harold Baker, a St. Louis native, known throughout his career as Shorty, was a member of some of the best bands in the land during the 1930s, including those of Don Redman, Teddy Wilson, and Andy Kirk. Although Baker had played in the Duke Ellington orchestra for part of 1938, his long tenure with Ellington (1943–51, 1957–9) was still to come when Buchanan was telling the young Miles Davis about him. Once described by Ben Webster, Baker's colleague in the Ellington band, as "the greatest unrecognized trumpet player in the world," Baker had a masterly technique that gave him complete control of the horn at all tempos but was most effective when he played ballads, later the forte of Davis as well. Although he was never the featured soloist in Ellington's trumpet section, over the years he produced a significant body of recorded solos that consistently shine in their lyrical embellishments of the melody. His tone is bolder than Hackett's, but still sharp and clear. It survives in the work of Miles Davis. "I recall how often, when Miles first came on the New York scene," says songwriter Mort Goode, "the men in Duke's band, Johnny Hodges and countless others, pointed up the similarities and the warmth." Mary Lou Williams, the pianist and arranger who was married to Baker, says, "Harold Baker was terrific when he played a slow tune and Miles always said, I heard him say: 'Oh, if I could only play as sweet as Harold Baker.'"

Buchanan's choice of models for his student went against the grain at the time, when the most influential trumpet styles derived from Louis Armstrong's hot, ebullient playing. Armstrong's lessons had been carried into the swing bands in several highly personal versions, by the likes of Charlie Shavers, Buck Clayton, Rex Stewart, and Roy Eldridge. These men and almost all the other top trumpeters of the day shared Armstrong's energy and verve, and sought his great range and bold tone. For most young trumpeters, those elements were essential, and by the time Miles Davis arrived in New York those essentials would be transliterated very successfully into the bop idiom by Dizzy Gillespie.

Partly because of Buchanan's influence, the hot trumpet tradition would be much less important for Davis. Buchanan was directing his attention toward an alternative tradition, much less fashionable, featuring a lighter tone, a narrower range, and a more lyrical bias. The patriarch of this tradition is Leon (Bix) Beiderbecke, a Midwesterner from Davenport, Iowa, who died in 1931 when he was only twenty-eight, leaving behind just a few recordings that show his style to any advantage and several others that, however prized by his admirers, mainly reveal his propensity for recording with mediocre bands. Compared to the incomparably corporeal Armstrong at the head of the other tradition, Beiderbecke seems a mere wraith. In the years of Miles Davis's early adolescence, Beiderbecke's memory survived best in a few mythic anecdotes on the theme of alcoholic self-destruction. The few trumpeters who claimed to be following him included only a couple of Chicagoans whose technical competence was openly doubted and the up-and-coming Hackett.

Harold Baker's style obviously shared the main features of Beiderbecke's, but it probably never occurred to him that he might be considered Beiderbecke's descendant, however indirect. Instead, Baker was an exponent of the distinctive style of trumpet-playing that had been heard in St. Louis for years. A curious *Kulturbund* makes St. Louis a wonderful, and inexplicable, breeding ground for lyrical jazz trumpeters. The list of St. Louis trumpeters is long, and everyone on it shares (to a greater or lesser extent) the essential features that are so handsomely realized in Baker's style, even when the men belong to different generations. Clark Terry, six years older than Davis, is another St. Louis trumpeter and, except for Davis, probably the best known. Terry admits the influence of the older players in his hometown, listing among them some who are virtually unknown beyond the city limits. He offered the following list in an interview with Stanley Dance: "Levi Madison, who I think played one of the prettiest trumpets I ever heard. He was older than Shorty Baker, but he had a very similar tone. Then there were Dewey Jackson, George Hudson, Crack Stanley, Mouse Randolph, Bobby Merrill, Sleepy Tomlin, who was with Jimmy Lunceford at one period, and Joe Thomas, who lives in New York now." The list can be extended by adding the names of Louis Metcalf, Charlie Creath, Ed Allen, and, of course, Elwood Buchanan. All of them were the precursors of Clark Terry and Miles Davis, but the list does not end with Terry and Davis. The most prominent St. Louis trumpeter since Davis is Lester Bowie of the Art Ensemble of Chicago. As a player of free form music, Bowie is seldom heard in a context where one can make comparisons with his St. Louis forebears, but the sound is clearly there. In a telling instance, the drummer Lenny White listened to an unidentified record as part of a blindfold test in *Down Beat*, and while he failed to identify either the Art Ensemble or Bowie, he commented, "The trumpet player's been listening to Miles Davis." He heard the sound of St. Louis in Bowie's playing.

For Miles Davis, the sound of St. Louis and the sound of the Beiderbecke tradition came together in Buchanan's taste, and they were crystallized in his teaching: "'Play without any vibrato,' he used to tell us. 'You're gonna get old anyway and start shaking,' he used to say. 'No vibrato!' That's how I tried to play," Davis recalls. "Fast and light – and no vibrato."

Buchanan encouraged Davis even when he seems to have been incapable of putting together a lesson. "I used to make a lot of noise, but my instructor liked me 'cause he liked the way I played," Davis told Julie Coryell. "He used to say, 'Little Davis, come here.' I'd say, 'What do you want?' He'd say, 'Do nothing 'til you hear from me; pay no attention to what's said –' Every time he'd get drunk, that's what he'd sing – that song." The song, *Do Nothing 'til You Hear from Me*, was a popular hit for Duke Ellington and lyricist Bob Russell in 1943; its melody was Ellington's *Concerto for Cootie*, written as a solo showcase for trumpeter Cootie Williams three years earlier.

Around 1943, Davis was clearly outstripping the teachings of Buchanan and was set to move on. However, he never found a better teacher, apart from the musicians he hung out with when he first arrived in New York, and he never forgot the lessons he learned from him, including even his attitude toward the instrument. "The approach to the trumpet by my instructor in St. Louis, Elwood Buchanan, is so slick," he told Don DeMicheal years later. "You can't help but play fast if you approach the trumpet like he does. He approached the trumpet like he was really going to play it – and he did."

Davis had made excellent progress under Buchanan's tutelage. Only the recognition was sometimes missing. "In high school I was the best in the music class on the trumpet," Davis says. "I knew it and all the rest knew it – but all the contest first prizes went to the boys with blue eyes." Doc Davis recalls the same situations: "Miles always had to settle for third prize. The officials, Miles and everybody else knew he should have had first prize. You can't treat a kid like that and tell him to come out and say the water isn't dirty." Young Miles saw the dirt all right and resolved to avenge himself by working twice as hard. "It made me so mad," he says, "I made up my mind to outdo anybody white on my horn. If I hadn't met that prejudice, I probably wouldn't have had as much drive in my work. I have thought about that a lot. I have thought that prejudice and curiosity have been responsible for what I have done in music ... I mean I always had a curiosity about trying new things in music – a new sound, another way to do something, things like that."

He was also finding musicians closer to his own age who shared his curiosity. "My best friend was a man named Duke Brooks," he says. "We used to have great days. He was a real genius. He played piano like Bud Powell although he never saw or heard him." Another friend, identified by Davis simply as Bruz, seems to have done his share in imparting the values of St. Louis trumpet-playing to him. "I'd say, 'Man, you really sound bad,' and Bruz would laugh. He was one of the baddest of the bad. He would play very few notes – a man of few, but choice, statements – musically, I mean. I learned a lot of shit from him." Bruz was probably Irving Wood, a trumpeter a few years older than Davis whose nickname is elsewhere recorded as Broz.

Davis's second teacher, Gustav, the first trumpet with the St. Louis Symphony Orchestra who is identified by Davis as Gustat and by Clark Terry as Gustaph, emphasized technique and probably complemented Buchanan's emphasis on style as a result. "Gustat could run chromatic scales in two octaves," Davis says, "seventeen times in one breath." Their first meeting was not very promising. "I went to Gustat and played one note. He said I was the worst trumpet player he ever heard in his life. I said, 'That's why I'm here – I'm the pupil, you're the teacher.'" In spite of his prickly manner, the new teacher obviously had a heart. Clark Terry remembers, "I could never afford the famous St. Louis teacher, Gustaph, but I would go and ask him questions and he would never turn me down.

He knew who I was, a kid from a poor neighborhood, and he helped me with my problems." Another of Gustav's students was Levi Madison. Davis echoes Terry's praise for Madison, calling him "one of Gustat's best students": "He'd play all those pretty notes. Boy, we used to have fun. God damn! maybe 'cause we were at home." Unfortunately, Madison chose to stay at home, and as a result his playing went unrecorded.

Like Elwood Buchanan, Gustav also made a lasting impression on Miles Davis, although in a much less personal sense. He has remained a reference point to whom Davis could turn after he moved away from St. Louis. He has also directed other trumpeters to him, including Dizzy Gillespie. "When Dizzy got fucked up in the mouth, I told him to go to Gustat," Davis recalls. "He sent him to a doctor who gave him a shot inside of his mouth." Gustav also gave Davis the mouthpiece that he has used since he was a teenager. "Someone told me to have it copied," he said recently, and he was lucky in taking the advice. "As soon as I did, Jim Rose, my road manager, lost it [the original one]."

Around 1941, Davis met Clark Terry for the first time. It was not an auspicious meeting, but the irony of the situation clearly delights Terry, and he has told the story many times. "I was with a band led by a one-legged piano player named Benny Reed," Terry says. "We were playing at a Carbondale, Illinois, night club known as the Spinning Wheel. One afternoon we were engaged to play at a picnic grounds where there was an athletic competition between various southern Illinois high schools. There were several school bands in attendance with their teams. One of the bandleaders, who had the East St. Louis outfit, was an old friend of mine." In other accounts, Terry has identified the East St. Louis bandleader as "an old drinking buddy." He continues, "He wanted me to meet a little trumpet player he admired very much and eventually brought the kid over to introduce us. The kid started right in asking questions – how did I do this, or that?" Terry remembers that the young Davis was simply eager, but not at all pushy or aggressive in his queries. "He came up to me very meekly," Terry says, "and said, 'Pardon me, Mr. Terry, but would you tell me something about the horn? I'd like to know how you do certain things.'" "We talked," Terry says, "but my mind was really on some girls dancing around a Maypole." "And I was so preoccupied with all the beautiful schoolgirls around that I said, 'Why don't you get lost – stop bugging me,' which is something I never normally do." "I kind of fluffed the kid off," Terry adds. If the incident had happened a few years later, Terry might well have earned an enemy for life, but as it happened, Davis was young and apparently willing to accept being "fluffed off" in order to learn. His own account of his meeting with Terry shows no hard feelings – far from it. "Around that time I met Clark Terry," he says. "He was playing like Buck Clayton in those days, only faster. I started to play like him. I idolized him."

Soon after that meeting, when Davis was only sixteen, he began playing professionally around St. Louis. His precocious career was helped, no doubt, by the fact that many of the older, more experienced musicians were leaving town with the armed services, as the United States geared up for and then joined the Second World War. Davis's first regular job as a trumpet player was exactly the one that he most desired at the time, and he landed it through a combination of audacity and sheer luck. In a bull session with some of his friends he had been denigrating some of the local St. Louis bands and lauding Eddie Randle's Blue Devils, calling them "the only band in town," when some of his friends decided to call his bluff and dared him to ask Randle for a job. "You know how I take dares," he told Julie Coryell. "I called him and he said, 'Come on over.'" Davis was hired, and he worked with the band for three years.

Very little is known about the band because it stayed so close to home, which was one of the reasons that it could be the working band for a high school sophomore. Its members definitely included some musicians who deserved to be heard further afield, according to Davis. He has said that the band's saxophonist, Clyde Higgins, "played like Bird and could read anything, but Jimmy Lunceford wouldn't hire him 'cause he was too black. They only wanted to hire handsome cats." The band's book seems to have been made up mainly of what would later be known as rhythm and blues. In 1969, Davis told an interviewer, "You don't have to be a special kind of player to play rock. That's what we were playing when I first started playing with Eddie Randle's Blue Devils in St. Louis – played the blues, *all* the time."

Playing regularly in the band accelerated his development. Clyde Higgins's wife, Mabel, who played piano with the Blue Devils, helped him, and he became more and more preoccupied with what he could learn from instructional books. "I used to buy a lot of books on theory," he says. "Also, people would show me different things – like Mabel Higgins, who showed me some things on piano – a great woman; she was fat but great. I spent a lot of time learning this shit – reading a lot of books, canceling on a lot of people I thought I liked." And, of course, he was playing in public regularly and learning in a practical way, for which there has never been a substitute in the education of a jazzman.

In a very short time, he came a very long way. Clark Terry again supplies the telling details: "I was used to going up to the Elks Club in St. Louis to jam," he says. "One night, as I was climbing the long flight of stairs, I heard a trumpet player flying about on his horn in a way I couldn't recognize. Eddie Randle had the band, and I knew everyone in it but this little trumpet player. After I got over by the stand it dawned on me I'd seen the fellow before. As I said, 'Aren't you –?', he broke in with, 'Yeah, I'm the kid you fluffed off in Carbondale.'" The incident took place within a year of their first encounter in Carbondale.

Terry befriended him, and for the year remaining before Terry was drafted into the navy and stationed in Chicago, he opened up the doors of the St. Louis jazz scene for him. Davis recalls: "He'd come over to my house and ask my father if I could go with him, you know, and he'd take me to a session. Man, we'd play from six o'clock to six the next morning." In no time at all their sessions together at a club called the Moonlight Inn were important local events. "When Clark Terry and I were friends, in order to get inspiration, he would play with me. He could play real fast. People would hear that we were playing and the place would be full. I wasn't drinking or anything then ... Clark used to play so fast 'cause he played out of a clarinet book, and I used to play out of a piano book and a French book on clarinet. I'd play a whole page in one breath. He'd play everything down the scale. Sometimes, just to tease him, I'd play what he'd play. We had a ball."

Terry joined the navy in 1942 and stayed until 1945, serving most of that time as a member of the navy band in Chicago, where he could make it back to St. Louis on leave if he wanted to. After the war, he returned to St. Louis and played locally for a while, but by then Davis had left for New York. "I tried to get him to come to New York," Davis says, "but I couldn't. He came three years later." By the time Terry arrived in New York, Davis was already recognized as one of the young stars.

Terry has defended the character of his young friend against his later critics. "He was a nice, quiet little kid then, and I think the changes in him are a cover-up. Deep down, basically, he's a beautiful cat ... If he seems to go to great lengths to conceal it, he's probably been given a hard time by people who've mistreated him and he feels he doesn't have to accept these things any more."

The jam sessions that Terry introduced him to were often on the showboats, the ones that Davis had heard about from Elwood Buchanan. "The boat would stop in St. Louis and Clark would call me up and say, 'Let's go to the session.' I had to get the okay from my father. So we'd go to a session; we'd jam all night. Guys would drink whiskey, change drums. Drummers would do all kinds of tricks with their sticks; trumpet players doing different shit – playing high notes, changing keys. They didn't care what you wanted to play – 'Let's play!'" Some of the men who impressed him are now dim legends in the early annals of the music. "Fats Pichon was a fat cat who played piano; Stanley Williams was just a little lighter than me, with straight black hair. They could swing like a mother-fucker – those funky meters, the way they play today. I said, 'Oh, shit, that's how bad I want to be.'"

Not all the players Davis met were from New Orleans; some were from Kansas City, which had replaced New Orleans as the incubator of jazz style in the previous decade, and some were from Oklahoma. Davis remembers two trumpeters particularly: "Alonzo Pettiford was one of the best trumpet players I've ever heard; he could play real fast. But my main man used to play sax and trumpet. His name was Charlie Young. All those guys who came from Kansas City and Oklahoma, they were playing eastern music," meaning the music of New York City. It was probably the other way around; the musicians in New York were absorbing the lessons of the Midwesterners, who were gravitating there all the time. Alonzo Pettiford's brother, Oscar, a superb bassist and also one of the few men capable of playing jazz on a cello, had left for New York before Miles Davis made it to the showboats.

The greatest player to come out of Kansas City before Charlie Parker, tenor saxophonist Lester Young, nicknamed "the President" by Billie Holiday and known as Prez to the other musicians, was also based in New York by this time. Several commentators have noted the stylistic similarities between Lester Young and Miles Davis, even though none of them was aware of the close encounters the two had in St. Louis. Sadik Hakim, Young's pianist, who was known at the time by his Christian name, Argonne Thornton, recalls: "One of the things I guess people don't realize is that Lester contributed much to the way Miles plays. When I first went with Lester Young, we used to go to St. Louis quite a bit when we traveled; it was one of the cities we stopped in and played in frequently. I remember Miles used to come and listen to Shorty McConnell [the band's trumpeter], and he used to come and bring his horn and play. He was very young, of course. But he'd sit in and he really dug Prez at the time and I think much of his style, if you listen to him closely, was from Prez. He took many of the things Prez did and transferred them to his style, which we know as the cool style, which Miles is famous for."

Another musician who provided a valuable lesson for Davis was Fats Navarro, then an almost unknown young trumpeter. Davis's recollection links Navarro with the music of New Orleans, but Navarro was not from the center of creole culture at all but from Florida. "Fats Navarro was in a band with Andy Kirk and Howard McGhee that played in town," Davis remembers. "He started that whole style from New Orleans. Fats is a creole; nobody ever mentions him. He's one of the greatest trumpet players I ever heard. He could also play saxophone like Coltrane. He didn't imitate anybody – he had his own style, he created it." For Davis, Navarro's example reinforced the importance of developing an individual style.

His early exposure to good musicians, established ones as well as unknowns, leads Davis to disparage the usual view that bebop started in New York in the early 1940s. "Nobody started a style," he said, "it just happened. It happened when I was thirteen. Everyone who came from Oklahoma, Kansas City, New Orleans, and St. Louis played like that." Undeniably, however, New York became the focal point for the experiments with aggressive rhythms and innovative harmonies known as bebop, and the style spread outward from there.

Inevitably, Davis's precocious contact with touring musicians contributed to more than his musical education. "Music was easy," he has said, and it could not occupy all of his time. "I was fascinated by the musicians, particularly guys who used to come up from New Orleans and jam all night. I'd sit there and look at them, watch the way they walked and talked, how they fixed their hair, how they'd drink, and of course how they played." He quickly came to realize that a man's style was not confined to his music. More than that, in music he found that he could support the lifestyle to which he was attracted. Because the other members of Eddie Randle's band held day jobs in the steel mill and elsewhere, Davis became the band's "musical director," charged with setting up and rehearsing the music for the acts they accompanied. The responsibilities brought him a pay raise. "When I was about sixteen, I was making $85 a week with Eddie Randle's band," he recalled, although on other occasions he has raised the remembered salary to $100 and $125, and lowered the remembered age to fifteen. "I was driving my father's car and I had ten suits. I got them from the pawnshop. I'd get them down to $20 a suit – Brooks Brothers and so on." At the age of sixteen he was already on his way to the lifestyle that would someday encompass Ferraris and the best-dressed list of *Gentleman's Quarterly*.

By contrast, Clark Terry at about this same age, a few years before Davis, had found himself in totally different circumstances. "I worked myself up on a paper route, and another for hauling ashes and tin cans, even going out of my neighborhood, maybe a mile away," Terry recalled. "I worked in a bowling alley setting pins. Every night and weekends I'd be working. Eventually, out of my savings, I bought a $15 bike – $10 down and a dollar a month." It seems a far cry from wearing Brooks Brothers suits and driving your father's car, but the contrast does not end there. The hard-earned bicycle turned out to be, as Terry said, "my undoing. We were supposed to hand over the money we earned and when my father found out about it he was furious. 'Whoever sees him first,' he told the others, 'tell him now he's got a bike to keep riding on it!' He meant it, definitely, and it seems I've been riding on it ever since, because I never went home from that point on." Part of the difference between Terry and Davis, but only part, was a matter of timing; Terry's adolescence was spent in the Great Depression but Davis was just young enough that he could spend most of his in the years of full employment brought on by the war.

As Davis's sense of style in other matters blossomed, so did his sense of style in music. He started to get noticed by visiting musicians by the time he was sixteen. Incredible though it seems, Kinney Dorham, another aspiring young trumpeter living in Austin, Texas, heard about Davis while they were both high school students, through a neighbor who spent some summers in St. Louis. Sonny Stitt, only two years older than Davis, arrived in St. Louis touring with Tiny Bradshaw's band. In between sets at the club where he was playing, he dropped into the Rhumboogie nightclub where Randle's Blue Devils were accompanying the floor shows and his attention became fixed on Miles Davis. Davis says that Stitt approached him at intermission and said, "You look like a man named Charlie Parker and you play like him too. Come on with us." Stitt then went back to his boss and coaxed him to make Davis an offer. "The fellows in the band had their hair slicked down, they wore tuxedos, and they offered me $60 a week to play with them," Davis says. "I went home and asked my mother if I could go, but she said no, I had to finish high school. I didn't talk to her for two weeks." Later on, in 1943 and 1944, Davis had similar offers from Illinois Jacquet, whose band toured out of Houston, and from A.J. Sulliman, whose band, McKinney's Cotton Pickers, was a final attempt at reviving one of the most popular recording bands of a decade before. All of them were told that they would have to wait until he graduated from high school.

That day was not far off. Davis maintains that his work at Lincoln High School was not a particular problem for him because he possesses a photographic memory: "See, if I had a book, I could look at it and remember the whole page. It came to me like that. I can remember anything – telephone numbers, addresses. Even today I can just glance at them and remember. That's the reason I used to take care of band payrolls; I could remember all the tabs and shit." The school regimen, as he remembers it, was easy, even though he was out playing music most of the night. "I was awake until five in the morning, then in class at nine, talking about Shakespeare. Miss Johnson, my teacher, was too hip – she saw me with a girl and said, 'That bitch ain't nothing.' I didn't fuck until I was eighteen. I made all As, and I got out of school and said, 'Fuck it!' I didn't make my own graduation. My father didn't care. He just said, 'Anything you're going to do, do it well.'"

His parents were now separated, and Davis's growing independence was matched by a growing sense of responsibility, especially for his sister, Dorothy. He claims that he taught her mathematics even though she was two years ahead of him in school. He also claims to have paid for part of her education at Fisk University, in Nashville, Tennessee, starting when he was sixteen. Around the time that Davis moved to New York to start his own further education, Dorothy graduated from Fisk as a qualified teacher.

As might be expected of a young dude in a Brooks Brothers suit, Davis was soon attracting attention for reasons other than his music. His account of Miss Johnson's advice to him in high school, although it is couched very much in the idiom of Davis himself, no doubt has its basis in fact. He has described another early encounter as well: "Ann Young, Billie Holiday's niece, said, 'Let me take you to New York and buy you a new horn.' But I was making $125 a week and buying slick suits in pawnshops, and I had just bought a horn, and I wasn't fucking." These references to the age at which he "started fucking" are curious. They crop up, apparently unsolicited, in several interviews he gave in the 1970s, and usually, though not exclusively, when his interviewer is female. That might suggest that he is tossing them into the conversation for their shock value – especially when, as in the interview with Harriet Choice for the *Chicago Tribune*, he makes an outlandish remark and then asks, "You gonna print that?" Moreover, his claims seem to have no basis in truth. His claim that "I didn't fuck until I was eighteen" is pure fiction, because almost two years before that, in 1943, he was already an expectant father. He was probably married that year, at the age of sixteen (although the *New York Times* primly referred to the arrangement as a "relationship" in contrast to his later marriages). His young wife, Irene, gave birth to a daughter, Cheryl, in 1944, and to his two sons, Gregory in 1946 and Miles IV in 1950. Davis became a grandfather in 1968, at the age of forty-two.

In June 1944, when he was graduating *in absentia* from high school, Davis left St. Louis for the first time with a band, Adam Lambert's Six Brown Cats. Lambert's band, an obscure New Orleans group playing a modern swing style, had finished a long engagement at the Club Silhouette in St. Louis, where Joe Williams, who much later became the featured vocalist with Count Basie's orchestra, was their singer. As they were about to leave for a two-week engagement at the Club Belvedere in Springfield, Illinois, their trumpet player, Tom Jefferson, grew homesick and decided to return to New Orleans. Davis was recommended to replace him. He recalls, "There was a school teacher in St. Louis who was a hell of a trumpet player. They needed someone in Springfield, Illinois, who could read and he told them about me. That's where I made my first hundred dollars. Sometimes we'd play for strippers, then a guy would come in and tell jokes." After the two weeks in Springfield, Lambert's Brown Cats moved on to Chicago but Davis returned home.

His return to St. Louis put Davis in the right place for what would be the best musical experience of his St. Louis years. The Billy Eckstine orchestra was scheduled to play for two weeks at the Riviera in St. Louis that July. Although the public would not know it for another year or so, most musicians in the United States already knew that the Eckstine band was a collection of the finest young jazz talent in the country. The band provided the steady jobs for many of the insurgents who were leading the bebop revolution in New York. In the summer of 1944, the band had just been formed, and the two weeks at the Riviera proved to be crucial for its development. Art Blakey joined the band there as its drummer, filling a chair that had been suspect before he arrived. In New York most of the musicians were preoccupied with playing after-hours and with other diversions, and the engagement in St. Louis allowed the band to work together with some concentration of effort. Eckstine says, "That is where we really whipped the band together – in St. Louis. We used to rehearse all day, every day, then work at night."

According to Dizzy Gillespie, the band's musical director and lead trumpet player, they were originally scheduled to play at the Plantation Club instead of the Riviera. Gillespie recalls the strange set of circumstances leading to the change of venue: "The Plantation Club in St. Louis was a white club," he points out. "They fired Billy Eckstine's band because we came in through the front door. We just walked right in with our horns, in front. And the gangsters – St. Louis was a stronghold of gangsterism – said, 'Them guys got to go.' So we changed jobs with George Hudson. He came over and played for them. Clark Terry was with that band. We went over to work at another place." If Gillespie's memory is correct, the band seem to have made a good deal for themselves out of the situation, for the Riviera, where the Eckstine band played in July 1944, is described by Clark Terry as "a big, plush sort of place where Ellington swears he originally wrote *Sophisticated Lady*."

Miles Davis, who had turned eighteen that spring, ended up playing with the Eckstine band during their stay. He recalls the events leading up to his temporary engagement this way: "A friend and I went to see them. I had my horn with me; we'd just left rehearsal. As soon as I walked in, this guy runs up to me and says, 'Do you have a union card?' It was Dizzy. I didn't even know him. I said, 'Yeah, I have a union card.' 'We need a trumpet player. Come on.' I wanted to hear him. I could always read, so I got on the bandstand and started playing. I couldn't even read the music at first from listening to Dizzy and Bird. The third trumpet man was sick; I knew the book because I loved the music so much, so I played with the Eckstine band around St. Louis for about three weeks. After that, I knew I had to go to New York." These events were reconstructed a little differently by Eckstine. "Miles used to follow us around in St. Louis," he says. "He used to ask to sit in with the band. I'd let him so as not to hurt his feelings, because, then, Miles was awful. He sounded terrible, he couldn't play at all." Later he added, "You couldn't hear him past the reed section."

The two accounts are irreconcilable, but there are probably elements of truth in both. The teenaged Davis was no doubt a less accomplished musician than the New York pros with whom Eckstine was used to working, but if Davis were as utterly incompetent as Eckstine suggests, he would certainly not have been received so enthusiastically by Gillespie and Parker when he turned up in New York a few months later. Eckstine's version may have been revamped in the telling, perhaps to add a touch of irony to his early encounter with the trumpeter

Eddy Randle's Blue Devils at the Rhumboogie Club, St. Louis, 1943; Miles Davis, age 17, in the far right of the back row (courtesy Frank Driggs collection)

Billy Eckstine and Charlie Parker at the opening of Birdland, August 1949 (courtesy of *Down Beat*)

who would soon be heralded as a rising star. In any event, Davis was recruited by Gillespie to replace an ailing regular. Buddy Anderson, the third trumpeter in the section, discovered that he had tuberculosis soon after the band arrived in St. Louis. He returned home to Oklahoma City and retired from music altogether. Davis filled his chair while the band was in St. Louis, and when it moved on to its next engagement at the Regal Theater in Chicago, Gillespie recruited Marion Hazel to replace Davis.

Davis's brief stint with the Eckstine band was his first brush with the leaders of the jazz vanguard of the day. It sharpened his urge to leave East St. Louis for New York, a move that had been a matter of considerable controversy within his family ever since his graduation from high school. His mother wanted him to join his sister at Fisk. "You know how women are," Davis shrugs. "She said they had a good music department and the Fisk Jubilee Singers." Davis responded by taking home the latest edition of the *Esquire Jazz Book* and brandishing it at her. "I looked in the book, and I asked my mother, 'Where's all this?'" "That's where I wanted to go," he says. Finally, to settle the dispute, "I got hold of my father, and got permission to go to New York, where I enrolled at Juilliard." His intention to attend the Juilliard School of Music should have assuaged his mother, but there is no indication that it did.

When Miles Davis left East St. Louis in 1945, the war was still raging in the Pacific, although there was a growing hope that its end was finally in sight. In the next decade, Davis would visit his family fairly frequently, and after that, his returns to the area would be surrounded by the aura of triumph, with a hail of advance publicity for his club dates and concerts, and line-ups around the block for reserved seats. His father would grow in stature in the post-war boom, running for state representative but losing, and increasing his wealth until his son, when he was perhaps the best-paid jazz musician in the history of the music, could point to him with filial pride and say, "He's worth more than me." Of his mother, Davis has had little more to say than this of her remaining days: "When my mother was sick I went to see her in the hospital. I knew she was dying of cancer. But when she died I didn't go to the funeral." Miles Davis sums up his roots in East St. Louis by declaring, "I don't believe in families. Like, if I die, my money ain't going to go to people just because they're close relatives. The people that are closest to me are the ones that helped me to do what I do, not just because somebody's my brother. If I had a lot of money, I wouldn't leave everything to my brother or sister just because they're related to me." Looked at dispassionately, that view of the family is perhaps very rational, and one might even imagine the pragmatic Doc Davis beaming at his first-born son for expounding it. Miles Davis put East St. Louis behind him irrevocably when he boarded the train for New York. He would return fairly frequently, but always as a visitor.

Davis's move to New York, like so many of his moves, was perfectly timed, thus making it much easier for him to cut off his ties with the place where he had spent a secure and relatively comfortable youth. The new sound of bebop was just moving out of the Harlem night spots where it took shape and was settling into the downtown jazz clubs on 52nd Street – *The* Street, it was called. Within a few years it would be everywhere, even on Broadway, where it would have its own clubs. Bebop gradually displaced both the swing bands and the traditional Dixie-landers, who fought a tough rearguard action to keep it out. In the bebop explosion, many young unknowns would rise to prominence in jazz. Miles Davis would eventually be the foremost among them, and he had been well prepared for his rise to the top by what he had learned in St. Louis. He recognized that himself. "When I got to New York, I thought everybody knew as much as I did," he said, "and I was surprised. Wasn't nobody playing but Dizzy and Roy [Eldridge]. The guys who *were* playing, you didn't even know or hear of. Same way in my home-town. I was fifteen and guys would come to hear me play because they heard about me." Now, three years later, at eighteen, he was on his way to New York, where almost no one had heard about him. Three years after *that*, when he turned twenty-one, everyone in the world who knew anything about the music at all would have heard about him.

2

52nd Street Theme
1945–6

I used to make the rounds and play many places – Victoria at 141st and Seventh, the Harlem Club on 116th between Lenox and Seventh, places on Eighth Avenue. There were about fifteen places where we'd go … It was a wonderful time. But 52nd Street was better. Uptown we were just experimenting. By the time we came down our ideas were beginning to be accepted. Oh, it took some time, but 52nd Street gave us the rooms to play and the audiences … 52nd Street was a mother. I say mother – and I don't mean motherfucker, though it was that, too.   John Birks 'Dizzy' Gillespie

Miles Davis traveled to New York City with another aspiring young trumpeter from St. Louis, a young man remembered only by his first name, Henry. He too was planning to enrol at the Juilliard School of Music, but he apparently did not share Davis's ulterior motive of making his way into the thriving jazz scene that was then in full bloom in Harlem – which even to Davis must have seemed a faint hope. The first hurdle was to pass the audition at Juilliard so that they could be admitted into the summer semester. "There was an entrance exam," Davis recalled for Julie Coryell. "I played a song called *Youth Dauntless* – I don't know what that means, but it was very fast. My best friend Henry was taking the exam too. He said, 'If I don't get in, my mother will kill me!' I said, 'What are you gonna play?' He said, 'Clyde McCoy's *Sugar Blues*.' We both got in but he just couldn't play – he turned out to be a good writer. He was pretty cool, but he just looked wrong playing the trumpet."

As soon as the entrance exam was passed, Davis started searching for Charlie Parker, the alto saxophonist whom he had listened to in awe when he was sitting in with Billy Eckstine's orchestra the summer before. Parker was known to his friends as Bird, an abbreviation of Yardbird, the nickname he sported from his hometown days in Kansas City because of his prodigious appetite for fried chicken. He already carried an underground reputation as the best young jazz player alive, but that reputation would not begin to surface for a few more months, when his recordings of *Groovin' High* and *Shaw Nuff* with Dizzy Gillespie for Savoy Records (made in February 1945) became available. For the time being, his reputation was confined mainly to the Harlem habitués of Clark Monroe's Uptown House, Minton's Playhouse, and the other night spots that featured jam sessions with the young upstarts, and to the handful of young blacks who had been aware enough to seek out the Billy Eckstine orchestra, as Miles Davis had, when it made its inaugural tour.

In 1945, Parker was still close enough to anonymity to be hard to find. "I spent my first week in New York and my first month's allowance looking for Charlie Parker," Davis recalls. He finally caught up with him at a jam session at a place called the Heatwave in Harlem. If the search seemed difficult, its result must have made Davis feel that it was all worthwhile. Parker not only recognized Davis, but he greeted him expansively and hung out with him for the rest of the night. When he finished playing for the night, Parker packed up his horn and went with Davis back to his rooming house, where they talked some more and finally caught some sleep. The next day, when Davis returned from his classes, Parker was still there, and they decided to share the apartment on a regular basis. Charlie Parker had moved in.

The immediate attraction of the guru of the jazz vanguard for the untried Juilliard student begs for an explanation, but it will probably remain a mystery. Apart from the music they played, the two men had almost nothing in common. Parker was twenty-four and Davis was eighteen. Parker had been educated on the streets of Kansas City and had been enmeshed in night life since the age of fifteen, when he moved out on his widowed mother; she had doted on his every whim and supported his every indulgence from the day he was born, even though it meant abject poverty for her. Davis had been exposed to the rawest elements of the night but had to return home to a family that took some pains to impress upon him that he was expected to bear its high standards. Parker had gluttonous appetites for food and drink and sex, and the appetites were usually visible – the dregs of his indulgences accumulated on his clothes until the suit finally wore out and he could beg or borrow a replacement. Davis, already a father, drank a little but was not very interested in it, and he was proud of the small closetful of suits he owned. Parker began using heroin when he was little more than a boy and was addicted to it by the time he was fifteen; Davis knew some heroin addicts in the St. Louis nightclubs but was not interested in it himself – not yet. Apart from their music, the two had little in common.

An uncynical view of Parker's attraction to Davis and the attention he gave him would simply claim that Parker saw in Davis the promise of remarkable musicianship, which of course he later realized. Probably no one has ever taken that view seriously, because too much is known about the character of Parker. In the personality of an abysmally spoiled youngster growing into an insatiable adolescent junkie, regardless of his musical genius, there is hardly room for sponsoring a young disciple. Parker was notoriously selfish in almost every close relationship throughout his entire life, whether with musicians who idolized him, fans who worshipped him, or women who adored him. Parker's story includes countless tales of his borrowing another musician's saxophone when his was pawned, playing a job with it, and then pawning the borrowed one; or of women nursing him back to health from a narcotic or alcoholic stupor and then waking to find him gone, sometimes with their silverware, fur coats, and money. As the poet Ted Joans puts it, "He took from those he loved as well as from those he had only just met." The wonder is that Parker never ran out of dupes, and many people allowed him to work his con on them more than once. But then, he was not just a psychopath, but also a genius. He stands as one of the greatest improvisers in the history of jazz. He possessed a gift so enormous that it prevailed through most of the health and personality problems that wracked him. Because of Parker's genius, almost no one has ever thought to ask why the young Miles Davis should have admitted a character like Parker so easily into his private life – the question has always been about Parker allowing Davis into *his* life. Davis arrived in New York with rooms for Parker to live in and an allowance of $40 a week for Parker to spend. Although Parker, throughout his adult life, was notorious for singling out his young idolators and treating them with cruel condescension – making them carry his saxophone case, hold doors for him, run trifling errands, and otherwise demean themselves – nothing we know about Davis suggests that he would play that role. The point that Parker saw in Davis someone who was relatively well fixed has more credibility, and Parker did take some of his money and pawn some of his belongings. Davis was willing enough to share his allowance with Parker and his other new friends. "I blew it takin' care of Bird ... and all them guys," he told Cheryl McCall. "They didn't have any money, *I* had the money. Got so bad I used to tell them, just keep some of it, 'cause those guys asked me for money."

For Parker, rooming with Davis may or may not have meant that he had ready access to the money he needed to support his appetites, but it certainly also meant the companionship of a young musician who respected his abilities and gave him some cause for self-respect. For Davis, the arrangement meant ready access to the vital music scene in which Parker was already a leader, and a conspicuous entry into it.

Just a few months earlier, the burgeoning new style of the young blacks in Harlem had moved downtown, to fabled 52nd Street, where its thunderstruck white audience would christen it bebop or rebop, eventually shortened to just bop.

The surfacing of the new music would soon send up a clamor that would some-times end in fist fights over the relative merits of bop versus the traditional two-beat music that originated in New Orleans. The Street had itself been the nightclub center for more traditional jazz styles, especially swing, during the preceding decade. But the wartime clientele of servicemen from all over the country were moved less by swing music than were the more genteel downtowners they were crowding out of the clubs; several of the managers on 52nd Street had switched to striptease and pop vocalists to keep the audiences coming in. The switch away from jazz did not, however, sit well with some of the managers, probably because the girlie shows brought in crowds that were tougher to handle but also, according to Arnold Shaw in *The Street That Never Slept*, because some of the managers were genuine music fans. The Onyx, at 57 52nd Street, tried bringing in a bop band as an alternative to striptease. The first bop band on The Street was a quintet led jointly by Dizzy Gillespie and bassist Oscar Pettiford, with Don Byas on tenor saxophone, George Wallington on piano, and Max Roach on drums. To the managers, the business proved good enough to warrant a second look. After that, bop groups began working at the Three Deuces and the Spotlite, across the street from the Onyx, as well.

The real birth of bop as a 52nd Street fixture happened in the winter of 1944–5 when Parker and Gillespie led a quintet, with Al Haig on piano, Curly Russell on bass, and Stan Levey on drums, at the Three Deuces. The audacious melodies and breakneck rhythms had the jazz fans agog. For the next three years, until the jazz clubs moved a few blocks away to Broadway, there was always at least one bop band playing somewhere on The Street as long as the clubs were not darkened by the periodic clean-ups of the vice squad. When Parker was not working in the band, he was usually there sitting in with them. Starting in the spring of 1945, Miles Davis was often at his side. "I used to follow him around, down to 52nd Street, where he used to play," Davis says. "Then he used to get me to play. 'Don't be afraid,' he used to tell me. 'Go ahead and play.'" Sometimes Davis could over-come his nerves and get up on the bandstand, but even then his efforts were wary. "I used to play under him all the time," he says. "When Bird would play a mel-ody, I'd play just under him and let him lead the note, swing the note. The only thing that I'd add would be a larger sound. I used to quit every night when I was playing with that guy. I'd say, 'What do you need me for?' That man could swing a whole band. One of the record companies should have recorded him with a good big band. Then you would have heard something!"

Parker's insistence that Davis get up and play is one piece of evidence that his interest in the young trumpeter was not entirely self-serving. He had himself been through a period when his talent was less than fully formed and the older musicians had given a rough ride. He had refused to give in. Now, he was refusing to allow Davis to give in. Budd Johnson, the tenor saxophonist whom Parker had succeeded in the Earl Hines band and was with him now in Eckstine's band, saw the parallel: "Well, when Charlie started to play the saxophone in Kansas City, when the cats would see him come around, they'd say, 'Oh no, not this cat again, man! I mean, look –' And they did the same thing with Miles Davis on 52nd Street. 'If this cat's gonna get on the stand, I'm not gonna play, man.' That's how bad he sounded." Johnson's comment is one of the few direct statements that corroborates Eckstine's criticism of Davis in St. Louis. Far from quitting now, Davis was putting himself through the paces that would bring him up to The Street's standards before much longer. And he was doing a lot more than just forcing himself to get up on the bandstand. "Every night I'd write down chords I heard on matchbook covers," he says. "Everybody helped me. Next day I'd play those chords all day in the practice room at Juilliard, instead of going to classes."

Then suddenly, and certainly prematurely, Davis found himself in a recording studio with a band led by a reedman named Herbie Fields. Under other circumstances, it might have proven to be a break for the young trumpeter, a chance to be heard by a wider public before his career had properly started. However, he played almost as if he were trying to be inaudible. It was, to put it mildly, a forgettable recording debut. The recordings were made by Savoy, an aggressive independent label, and the details are as follows:

Herbie Fields' Band with Rubberlegs Williams
Miles Davis, tpt; Herbie Fields, as, ts; unknown rhythm section; Rubberlegs Williams, vcl. New York, 24 April 1945
That's the Stuff You Gotta Watch (Savoy 564); *Pointless Mama Blues* (Savoy 564); *Deep Sea Blues* (Savoy 5516); *Bring It on Home* (Savoy 5516)
Jepsen and Ruppli both list John Mehegan, pno; Al Casey, gtr; Slam Stewart, b; and Lionel Hampton, dms; Priestley lists Teddy Brannon, pno; Leonard Gaskin, b; and Eddie Nicholson, dms.

Davis's recording debut, a month before his nineteenth birthday, catches him in the uncertain mood that he described when he played beside Parker on 52nd Street. (These sides have never been reissued, and the originals are very hard to find, and so I have heard only *That's the Stuff You Gotta Watch* and *Pointless Mama Blues*; even if there is a marked improvement in his playing on the other pieces, it will still probably raise the level only to the pedestrian.) On both of the first tunes, Davis uses a mute except for the opening ensemble of *Pointless Mama Blues*, and he sounds as if he is facing away from the microphone. By contrast, the vocalist, Rubberlegs Williams, is a bawler, and Herbie Fields, playing tenor saxophone on both pieces, displays a raucous, rough tone, very much in the rhythm-

and-blues idiom. Davis can barely be detected playing wispy obbligatos on the vocal choruses, and he lays out entirely when Fields solos. The earliest discographies listed Snooky Young as the trumpeter on these sessions, but since then Davis has admitted that he was the trumpeter. He confessed, "I was too nervous to play, and I only performed in the ensembles, no solos." Still, if one concentrates on the trumpet line, it is possible to pick out typical little figures played by Davis occasionally, especially at the close of the vocal choruses on *Pointless Mama Blues*.

Rubberlegs Williams is credited in some accounts as a blues shouter, but that calling seems much too generous on the evidence of these recordings. He comes off instead as a comedy singer, making weird vocal noises and slyly underlining the mild innuendos of his jive lyrics. The records were clearly an attempt by the small Savoy label to get a hit with a novelty song, a genre the public had recently shown they would buy when other labels put out such cornball items as *Open the Door Richard* and *Cement Mixer (Putt-ee Putt-ee)*. Williams, a show-business veteran who performed low comedy in minstrel costume and dresses, had been approached earlier by the producers of Continental records for a similar project. The song for Continental, recorded in January, was called *I Want Every Bit of It*, and it seems to have met with the same lack of success that these Savoy sides were to have. On *I Want Every Bit of It*, Williams's accompanists included Dizzy Gillespie and Charlie Parker as well as several other top musicians. Probably Gillespie was invited to play on the Savoy date and declined, suggesting Davis as his substitute.

The leader of the recording session, Herbie Fields, remains a shadowy figure. Considered at the time to be a rising star on 52nd Street, he was, as it turned out, very close to the peak of his career instead. He had returned to New York in 1943 from the army, where he was a bandleader, and at the time of these recordings was featured with Lionel Hampton's band. Fields's return to civilian life was followed almost immediately by one of the few triumphs of his career, as he was awarded the *Esquire* New Star for alto saxophone in 1945. One of the few recollections of Fields from these times comes from Jimmy Heath, the tenor saxophone player, who complained that "the cool school was an effeminate kind of playing; they were the ones who didn't try to swing hard," and then added, as if by way of explanation, "Herbie Fields used to put pancake make-up on his face to travel with Lionel Hampton." As a white man in a black band, Fields used to darken his complexion artificially, but there was certainly no hint of effeminacy in Fields's playing, and no coolness either. In any event, after his promising start in the mid-1940s, Fields soon disappeared from jazz altogether. He committed suicide in 1958.

Not surprisingly, Davis's studies at Juilliard were not going very well. Diverted by making his recording debut and concerned with surviving on 52nd Street, he paid little attention to the Juilliard program, which increasingly seemed simply irrelevant to him. "I didn't believe it," he told Julie Coryell. "They showed me some things I already knew when I was fourteen about theory and all that shit." When he did leave the practice room to work on the program, he found it less than challenging: "I did Juilliard summer school in one night – Mozart's *Requiem in E-flat*; I took it apart musically, with Hindemith's *Kleine Kammermusik* for an introduction." Inevitably, he soon concluded, "All that shit they were teaching wasn't doing me a damn bit of good." He persisted, however, for about a semester and a half, probably out of deference to his father, who had gone out on a limb to send him there.

It is often assumed that Charlie Parker was mainly responsible for the music that Davis was learning, probably because of their shared accommodation in the first year and Davis's stint in the Parker quintet later on, in 1947–8. Ross Russell, who recorded Davis with Parker in four sessions during 1946–7, says, "Parker's music was the alpha and omega of Miles Davis's trumpet style and musical system." But Russell's statement could apply equally well to dozens of musicians Davis's age, on whom Parker's influence was undeniably great. That influence touched Davis no less than it touched virtually all of his contemporaries, and also no more. Parker was a teacher solely by his example. "He never did talk about music," Davis has said. More important to his development were the musicians who did talk about music with him during these crucial years, and the first – and perhaps the most important – was Dizzy Gillespie.

No less than Parker, John Birks Gillespie seems to have been interested in Davis's development from the moment he arrived in New York. Gillespie, who was saddled with the nickname Dizzy because of his crazy antics whenever he was onstage, has always been a comparatively stable and reliable individual among jazzmen, despite the nickname. If Parker was the spirit of the bop movement, Gillespie was its head and its hands. He looked out for the interests of the younger players who were yearning to join in, and he seems never to have given a thought to the fact that he and Davis, who was nine years younger, might someday be seen as contenders or rivals by a fickle jazz audience. Gillespie's long and distinguished career has been sullied somewhat by his neglect in the superficial popularity polls conducted annually by such magazines as *Down Beat*, *Esquire*, and, later on, *Playboy*, in which top awards went to Davis rather than Gillespie year after year; it was not until 1956 that Gillespie was voted top trumpeter in the *Down Beat* readers' poll, and the only other years he was so voted came in 1977 and 1979, when Davis was in temporary retirement. Fortunately, the musicians are more likely to assign such contests their true value, which is nothing at all. If, in the view of a segment of their listeners, Gillespie has spent much of his career in Davis's shadow, that is a strange irony, for no one spent as many hours discussing music and working out technicalities with Davis in these formative years. It is only since 1979, with the publication of Gillespie's memoirs (with Al Fraser), *To Be or Not to Bop*, that the early involvement of the two trumpeters became widely known.

While Davis was sharing his apartment with Parker, Gillespie's house was the daytime gathering place of the boppers. "My house was full all the time," Gillespie says. "Miles used to stay there. He didn't have a bed there because there was no room to have a bed for him. But as soon as he'd get up – boom, he was over there. Kinney Dorham, Max [Roach], everybody. Any one of the guys of that era – Monk, all of them – came by my place, which was a clearinghouse for our music." It was Gillespie who urged Davis to learn to play the piano. "Miles ... used to ask me, 'Man, where do you get them notes?' 'Off the piano,' I'd say. 'That's your ass if you don't play the piano, you can't find them. You might luck up on them sometimes, but if you play the piano, you'll know where they are all the time. You might get lucky and find one every now and then just from playing your own instrument, but if you know the piano you'll know where they are all the time. You can see them.'"

Davis learned Gillespie's lessons quickly, and their relationship soon became useful to both. In Gillespie's memoirs, the two men remembered Davis coming upon an Egyptian minor scale in a theory book and going immediately to Gillespie's house to show it to him. "Egyptian minor scale, that's right," Gillespie recalled. "He was going to Juilliard then. You see, music is so vast, like rhythms and harmonics in our music. Imagine, if you just study that, and study what it has done. And it's infinite." The lesson that Gillespie appears to be proudest of was the playing of minor harmonics in a chord, the so-called flatted fifth, taken to be one of the hallmarks of bebop. Gillespie points out, "It wasn't considered a 'flatted fifth' then, it was considered a half step ... That's what Rudy [Powell] taught me [in 1938], and that has governed my playing ever since. And that's one of the distinctive things about Miles Davis, that he learned from me, I'm sure. Because I showed him on the piano the pretty notes in our music." He adds, "There are some nice notes in a chord, man, so now Miles knows how to hold one note for hours. That's how Miles got all those pretty things he plays. It resolves all the time, that one note. To find out where the notes resolve, you don't have to play every chord. You can hold one note and it'll take care of three chords, because it's in all of them. And pretty notes, too." Gillespie is generally credited with introducing the flatted fifth into bebop as a major stylistic device, and it became a feature of every bopper's style, not just Davis's. But Davis learned it directly while most other musicians were forced to pick it up from Gillespie's records and performances. "We used to hang out together, man, every night," Davis says, "so the shit, you know, rubbed off."

Naturally, much of the discussion between the two centered on their individual styles. In one well-known exchange, they reveal their essential differences. "I asked Dizzy, 'Why can't I play high like you?' 'Because you don't hear up there,' he said, 'you hear in the middle register.' And that's true. There are times when I can't even tell what chords Dizzy is working on when he's up high, and yet he'll tell me what he's playing is just an octave above what I do." Dave Burns, a trumpeter in Gillespie's big band later in the 1940s, sums up the relationship by saying, "If there wasn't a Dizzy Gillespie, there wouldn't have been a Miles Davis. He wouldn't have played that way because he wouldn't have heard Dizzy." Even though their mature styles are poles apart, Burns is probably right. Davis's mature style is not in any meaningful sense derived from Gillespie's, and their technical abilities differ markedly, with Gillespie one of the most gifted pyrotechnicians on his instrument in the history of jazz (or any other genre), but the harmonic basis of their music and their use of rhythm mark their school tie. The influence was by no means one-sided. "I used to tell Dizzy, 'Play in the low register 'cause your low register is out of tune,'" Davis recalls. "See, he and I could talk. Nobody else could tell him. Dizzy's like a relative."

Gillespie was not alone in working with Davis. The musical world Davis entered when he sought out Charlie Parker was a free school. "Monk would write out chords for me, Tadd Dameron, and Dizzy, who advised me to study piano, which I started to. I had some background in understanding progressions from a book I'd bought in St. Louis, *Georgia Gibbs Chord Analysis*." The book, written by a pop singer and picked off the rack of a St. Louis music shop, seems to have been more useful than the training he was supposed to be getting at Juilliard.

As the summer session came to a close and the fall semester got under way, Davis found that he was being accepted more readily by the older musicians on The Street, and as a result he became more involved than ever in the clubs. He had developed his own nightly routine, and he usually showed up without Parker at his side. Coleman Hawkins was playing an extended run at the Downbeat Club, at 66 52nd Street, and his trumpeter, Joe Guy, frequently failed to show up. Davis became a regular substitute, although he still worked free. Around this time, Davis recently told George Goodman, Jr, Hawkins hired him as a kind of non-playing musical director for one of his recording sessions. Davis's job was to spot mistakes Hawkins's sidemen made when they played his arrangements in the studio. Generally, Hawkins seems to have filled the role of patron for Davis. "He would buy a coat for $300 and sell it to me for $15," Davis says.

A few doors away from the Downbeat Club, another tenor saxophonist, Eddie Davis, known as Lockjaw, led a group at the Spotlite that included Rudy Williams on alto, and if Joe Guy was on the stand with Hawkins that night, Davis knew he was welcome to sit in at the Spotlite. According to one report, he accepted a job with Eddie Davis at the Spotlite around this time and played regularly for a month. If so, it was his first paid job in New York.

As often as not, when Davis showed up on The Street he was with Freddie Webster, a trumpeter with the Benny Carter and Jimmy Lunceford bands, among others. Already twenty-eight, Webster was still waiting for the break that would help to publicize his talent, by recording a featured solo or leading a group on 52nd Street. It was a break that never came. In the meantime, he was not bothered much by personal ambition, satisfied to know that other trumpeters recognized his talent for what it was. Even Dizzy Gillespie said that "Freddie Webster probably had the best sound on a trumpet since the trumpet was invented – just alive and full of life." And everyone on The Street knew, as Sadik Hakim put it, that "Miles Davis definitely thought a lot of Freddie Webster and wanted his tone and was influenced by his style." Unfortunately that tone and that style were never documented satisfactorily before Webster died, suddenly and mysteriously, in Chicago in 1947, when he was only thirty. According to George Hoefer, when Webster was a fixture on the New York scene in 1945 he "frequently played at Minton's. Webster had a singing tone with a beauty that especially appealed to Davis. Musicians still talk about the shows at the Apollo when Webster was playing with the Jimmy Lunceford band. When the band played *Stardust*, Webster would be featured in a solo played from the balcony." Davis was not the only trumpeter affected by Webster's sound. Years later, in a blindfold test for *Down Beat* magazine, Thelonious Monk identified a record by Gillespie as characterizing the Webster sound. "That was the Freddie Webster sound, you know, that sound of Dizzy's," he told Leonard Feather, later adding: "Well, if that's not Diz, it's someone who plays just like [Webster]. Miles did at one time too ... Yes, that's the Freddie Webster sound." Webster's influence on Gillespie has seldom been mentioned, but his influence on Davis often is, although it can never be fully appreciated because of the sparsity of recorded evidence from Webster. If we take Davis literally, probably the best recorded instance of Webster's tone and style is heard in Davis's solo in *Billie's Bounce*, recorded in November 1945, a solo that Davis says he likes just because he sounds like Webster.

The little that is known about Webster suggests that he was a complex character. Born in Cleveland, Ohio, in 1917, he grew up with the composer-pianist Tadd Dameron, who was born there in the same year. He worked in Chicago and elsewhere in the Midwest before joining up with the touring bands that would eventually take him to both coasts. Art Pepper, the Los Angeles alto saxophonist, toured with him in Benny Carter's band in 1942. "Freddie Webster was a nice looking, kind of strange looking, little cat," Pepper says. "I had a strong affection for him. He was a little man who could back up the little man complex. His playing was incredibly beautiful. And he always carried an automatic pistol. He felt that because he was black and because of his size, somebody was going to push him into a corner and he'd need an equalizer." Davis may have responded to

Webster's style in more ways than one. Pepper's suggestion of Webster's abrasive personality no less than his beautiful trumpet-playing might well have described the Miles Davis of a few years later.

For Davis, another great virtue of Webster's playing was its economy. "Freddie didn't play a lot of notes," Davis told Nat Hentoff. "He didn't waste any. I used to try to get his sound. He had a great big tone, like Billy Butterfield, but without a vibrato. Freddie was my best friend. I wanted to play like him. I used to teach him chords, everything I learned at Juilliard. He didn't have the money to go. And in return, I'd try to get his tone." Davis's admiration for Webster's self-editing in his playing, a trait that even Gillespie lacked, harks back to his training from Elwood Buchanan and comes up time and again throughout his career. The musicians who earn Davis's highest praise are always those who articulate melodies by a few carefully placed notes rather than by virtuoso runs at great speed. That sensitivity to economy that he heard in Webster signals the beginning of a break from his first 52nd Street models, although it would take a few years to integrate the economy he admired into his own style.

While Webster took over as Davis's main colleague and collaborator in the intensive learning program he was going through, for both of them Gillespie stood out as the master. "Freddie Webster and I used to go down every night to hear Diz," Davis recalls. "If we missed a night, we missed something. Stand up at the bar, throw a quarter, and name the note that it came down on. That shit be going down so fast, and we'd be testing ourselves." Later on he recalled: "We really studied. If a door squeaked, we would call out the exact pitch. And every time I heard the chord of G, for instance, my fingers automatically took the position for C sharp on the horn – the flatted fifth – whether I was playing or not." The tests at Juilliard seemed more and more superfluous.

About Juilliard, Davis says, "Originally I went there to see what was happening but ... I found out nothing was happening." He earned a chair in the student orchestra, but even that proved tedious. "Up at Juilliard I played in the symphony, two notes, 'bop bop,' every ninety bars, so I said let me out of here and then I left." Any conflict he had felt back in East St. Louis about where his musical future lay had been resolved by the head-to-head confrontation of the jazz clubs and academe. "I realized I wasn't going to get in any symphony orchestra," he says. "And I had to go down on The Street at night to play with Bird or Coleman Hawkins, so I decided to go that way – all the way." There remained, of course, the awkward job of telling Doc Davis about his decision. Even with a father who had been so supportive in every decision he had taken so far, this one had an ominous feel to it. It was certainly not the kind of discussion that could be carried out on the telephone, and Davis did not even let his father know that he was on his way home. He just appeared.

In a conversation with Dizzy Gillespie and Al Fraser some thirty-four years later, Davis remembered the confrontation. "My father looked up one day and I was back in St. Louis. 'What the fuck're you doing here?' he said. I said, 'I'll explain. A guy named Dizzy Gillespie and Charlie Parker, Yardbird –' 'Yardbird Parker and Dizzy Gillespie?' he said. 'What're they doing?' 'Well, they're playing a new kind of music, and I can't get that – I can't learn that at Juilliard.' Because everything at Juilliard, I knew."

His father's response, he has reported elsewhere, was gratifying. "Okay – just do it good," he said. "If you need a friend, call me." Davis quit Juilliard as soon as he returned to New York, probably in October 1945.

If it seems obvious to us that Davis's disaffection for Juilliard was basically because they were training musicians for a kind of music that he did not want to play, that realization seems never to have entered his mind. "I was allowed to quit Juilliard," he has said, "because they stretch everything out there, and I did improvisation, and I had imagination." In his view, the trumpeters who stayed behind and eventually graduated "haven't got tones good for anything – they have a legit sound, and it's a white sound." He has even, on one occasion, proposed his own alternative education system for training musicians, and, not surprisingly, individuality gets top priority. As an educator, he told Don DeMicheal, "I'd have different guys for different things. Get Dizzy for the freedom in music, and a white guy who's stricter on tradition and form, and learn both of them. Then you go your own way ... Let it come out the way it comes out, not the way you [the educator] want it to be." Although Davis would almost certainly deny it, his own musical education in 1945 very nearly measured up to the system he propounded as an ideal to DeMicheal. He had Gillespie, of course, and also Parker, Hawkins, Webster, and all the others, helping him to discover the "freedom" in music, and he had his instructors at Juilliard, "stricter on tradition and form," as well.

Once he had cut himself loose from Juilliard, Davis worked in various groups all over the city. Since he was well connected on The Street, there was probably even a choice, perhaps slim, of jobs for which he could try. Away from The Street, his friend Freddie Webster was playing with John Kirby's band at the Café Society Downtown, giving him a link there, and of course there were always the clubs in Harlem. The prospects looked good, but because of some very lucky timing his prospects turned out to be better than ever. As it happened, Charlie Parker found himself in need of a trumpet player at almost the very moment Davis found himself in need of a job.

The move downtown for the new music was already a year old, and the exposure had done wonders. While the jazz periodicals were laced with hate mail and caustic critical comment, a few younger writers, among them Barry Ulanov and Leonard Feather, the co-editors of *Metronome*, were coming forward with spirited defenses. Neither the amount of publicity, even if it was mainly bad, nor the distaste of the older fans – the reactionaries, who would soon be branded 'moldy figs' – had done the club owners any harm. Young people, many of them just back from the armed services, were flocking to the clubs, anxious to be part of the new movement. White musicians such as the clarinetist Tony Scott, pianist George Wallington, and drummer Shelly Manne were beginning to catch on, too, and swelling the ranks of the initiates. The 52nd Street clubs even had the luxury of line-ups when Charlie Parker and Dizzy Gillespie were fronting a quintet. Parker was becoming an idol. Everywhere he played, he was followed around by a coterie of fans, some of them lugging Wollensak wire recorders, the predecessors of tape recorders, to catch what they could of his playing on those cumbersome outfits. There were also the women of the street willing to meet him in the musicians' room in the twenty minutes between sets, the errand boys of the dope peddlers, and sometimes even the big-time peddlers themselves, pushing samples on him, and of course there were the musicians, addicts, pimps, salesmen, students – they all turned up. Their adulation came as no surprise to Parker, and their gifts aroused no particular gratitude. He accepted both with cool detachment, as if he had been a seigneur all his life. But all the attention was not doing his health much good, or his reliability. Often he did not show up to play at all, and sometimes when he did he was in terrible condition. Gillespie sat him down every chance he got and tried to get him to sort out his priorities, and when Parker was in his more coherent moods he readily agreed to a basic arrangement that involved his showing up, playing every set, and staying sane until the night's work ended. And then he would miss the next set or fail to show up the next night. As the co-leader of their quintet, Gillespie had to face the crowds that had been promised both Gillespie *and* Parker, to scuffle to find a pick-up player to fill in for him, and to negotiate with the irate club owners about the docked payrolls and the broken contracts. Eventually Gillespie had had enough. He knew that he could sustain the jobs with his own name. He and Parker agreed that they would carry on making records together when the chance came, but they would split up the quintet as a working unit and go their separate ways in the clubs.

The word about Gillespie and Parker's split-up spread among the club managers, and when Parker went looking for work he took Davis with him. "He used to talk to people about work and they'd say, 'You don't have a trumpet player,'" Davis recalls. "And he'd say, 'Here's my trumpet player right here.'" As a result, Parker moved into the Three Deuces for a short engagement in October 1945, leading a quintet with Davis, Al Haig, Curly Russell, and Stan Levey. The rhythm section was the same one that the Parker-Gillespie quintet had used in the same club earlier. Later that month, Parker moved over to the Spotlite, keeping Davis and Levey with him but picking up Sir Charles Thompson on piano and

Leonard Gaskin on bass. That engagement might have settled into a long run if the police had not closed down the Spotlite along with some of the other clubs on The Street in early November.

At first, the musicians and everyone else assumed that the closing was temporary, just one of the police department's periodic clean-ups of the area. This time, however, The Street remained closed for several weeks, and the pressure from the police when it did reopen kept it from ever fully recovering its status. It was the beginning of the end for the jazz clubs on 52nd Street, although no one could know that at the time.

Almost as soon as the Spotlite closed, Parker simply moved his quintet uptown, to Minton's in Harlem, and they kept right on playing. Davis gained confidence every night. The crowds were usually noisily partisan to Parker, but every night Davis noticed more of the listeners obviously attentive to his solos as well, and some of them looked for him between sets, wanting to talk about the music and, especially, wanting to hear him talk about *his* music. He was still struggling with some of the trumpet parts – especially on the tough lines of such tunes as *Cherokee* and Gillespie's *Night in Tunisia*, which Gillespie maneuvered through with such élan – but only a handful of listeners, including Freddie Webster and Gillespie when they were there, knew that he was faking them.

It was probably between sets at Minton's that Teddy Reig, the producer for Savoy, approached Parker about a recording session. They agreed to record some of Parker's tunes and set the date for 26 November, a Monday, which was a day off from Minton's. The pay was set at union scale, which was more than Savoy usually paid, but the union stewards were watching the little label closely, suspecting that they were taking too many liberties in some of their sessions.

The circumstances surrounding the recording session were straight out of a Sennett comedy, even if the stewards were watching. Fortunately, external circumstances never seemed to bother Parker, and the session resulted in some superb bebop. For Davis, now nineteen, the recordings gave his career the kind of fillip that would make him one of the best known of the young boppers. Ross Russell, who would later record some of Parker's best work for his own independent label, Dial, calls this Savoy date "the definitive session toward which bop had been striving." The details are as follows:

Charlie Parker's Reboppers
Miles Davis, tpt; Charlie Parker, as; Dizzy Gillespie, pno (on *Billie's Bounce* and *Now's the Time*); Sadik Hakim, pno (on *Thriving on a Riff*); Curly Russell, b; Max Roach, dms. New York, 26 November 1945
Billie's Bounce (five takes); *Now's the Time* (four takes); *Thriving on a Riff* (three takes) (all on Savoy S5J 5500; master takes only on Savoy 2201; alternate takes on Savoy 1107)

Thriving on a Riff has sometimes been issued as *Thriving from a Riff*; the former title was on the original release on 78 rpm. The other titles recorded at this session, with Gillespie instead of Davis on trumpet and Hakim on piano, are *Warmin' up a Riff*, *Ko Ko* (two takes), and *Meanderin'*; all are issued as above.

The first problem arose over finding a piano player. It was long believed that the piano player was supposed to be Thelonious Monk, who could not be found. However, Teddy Reig recalls that Bud Powell was supposed to play and that Parker knew in advance that Powell would not be able to make it; according to Sadik Hakim, Powell had gone home to Philadelphia. Reig says, "See, in those days you didn't just tell a guy, 'Like, we're gonna have a date at four o'clock,' and he'd show up. You had to go round him up, from about one o'clock on. When I finally got to where Bird was, around Dewey Square and Seventh Avenue, he had Dizzy with him. I say, 'What the hell is he doing? Where's he going? You coming down with us, John?' And he said something about he was gonna play piano, seeing that Bud couldn't make it." The problem of the missing piano player, then, seemed to be solved, until they picked up Davis. They started to talk about what they would record, and Parker named *Ko Ko*, a melody based on the chord changes of *Cherokee*. Davis balked, saying he did not play it well enough to record it, but Parker insisted on keeping it in, probably because he had already accepted Reig's $300 advance to provide four original compositions for this session. When Parker remained adamant, Davis told him that Gillespie would have to play the trumpet part, which meant that they would still need another piano player for *Ko Ko*. Someone finally found Sadik Hakim at a place called Hector's Cafeteria. (It is largely because of Hakim's presence that the complicated personnel shifts finally got sorted out; fifteen years later, when students of jazz were locked in debate about who played what, Hakim came along to settle the debates, saying, "All anybody had to do to find this out was ask me." He was hardly an obvious candidate to ask, however, because his name did not appear on the studio sheets; neither he nor Parker was a member of the New York local at the time, and union rules stipulated a non-union quota of one for recording sessions. Hakim was listed as Hen Gates on the original labels.)

Even if Gillespie and Hakim had not been conscripted, they would probably have found their way to the studio. Word of the session, which was Parker's first as a leader, had spread outward from Minton's, and the recording studio bulged with Parker's regular complement of hangers-on. All kinds of characters were circulating through the studio, and Parker would occasionally dispatch one or more of them on some errand, sending them out for hamburgers and whiskey. The session, as might be expected, lasted much longer than the three-hour union limit.

The first take of the opener, *Billie's Bounce*, a medium blues named for Billie Miller, the personal secretary of Parker's manager, Billy Shaw, showed the promise that the session would finally fulfil, even though Davis faltered on the lead behind Parker near the end of the theme statement and Parker was bothered by a squeaky reed on his solo. Following Parker's solo, Davis enters with a strong broad tone, surprising to hear after his tentative playing on the opening, and Max Roach, the drummer, raises his level behind him, providing a little lift for the soloist. It is a masterful piece of drumming, probably Roach's best showing until the two takes of *Ko Ko* at the end of the day, and it shows off Davis neatly. The second take ends abruptly because of reed problems during Parker's solo, but the third take is complete, and it features a very bold solo by Davis, his best on the open horn all day. As luck would have it, Parker stumbles opening his own solo by being too adventuresome and then suffers through more squeaks, with the result that this take, showing off Davis so well, was not released at the time. Parker also aborted the fourth take during his solo, but the fifth one was completed and became the master take, featuring a very blue solo by Parker but also catching Davis fluff a note in the ensemble and build his solo, which is adequate, on some distinctly Gillespie-like phrases. Davis later said that he counted his solo on *Billie's Bounce* among his favorites "because the trumpet sounded like Freddie Webster"; he was probably referring to his superior solo on the first take, which was released as the alternate. The resemblance to Webster may reside in more than just the open tone. Benny Bailey, a trumpeter who knew Davis well soon after this in California, says: "I happen to know for instance that on the recording of *Billie's Bounce* which Miles made with Charlie Parker in Los Angeles [sic], his solo was exactly the one Freddie played for this particular blues. Evidently Miles said he was nervous on the date and couldn't think of anything to play so he did Freddie's solo note for note." If Davis was following Webster's model, that might explain why his solo on takes 1 and 3 are played with so much confidence.

Now's the Time, another blues, has been discussed reverentially in recent years because its militant title came to be seen as an intimation of the black nationalism behind the bop movement, which had to be covert then. The first take ends almost as soon as it begins because Davis enters late in the theme statement, and the second take struggles through an inept statement of the theme by both horns before stopping, probably on a signal from Reig in the control booth. The third and fourth takes are both complete. The third, issued as the alternate, is weak for all soloists: Parker plays a series of blues clichés, Davis toils over long, awkward lines and seems to slow down the tempo, and Curly Russell, the bassist, thumps out a wooden chorus. It is thus remarkable – and one of the real joys of listening to these takes in succession – to hear how all the looseness falls away on the very next take, which became the master. Davis's solo again features a broad tone, but Parker's solo preceding him is so dazzling, with its flashing runs, that it seems to echo well after it has ended anyway. Still, Davis's solo on the master turned out to be his best effort on *Now's the Time*, and it did his reputation no harm when it was released soon afterward.

Billie's Bounce and *Now's the Time* are so firmly entrenched among the classic recordings of jazz that it is difficult to imagine the impact they had when they were made available to the largely unsuspecting jazz public outside New York. Every jazz buff who heard them reacted strongly – whether positively or nega-tively – to their unsettling harmonies and tough rhythms. Frank Sanderford, a Chicago journalist who later became a close friend of Parker, describes his own reaction this way: "My jazz tastes then were rather old – Lester Young was the last innovation. I had listened for a few times to a couple of Bird records. The first time I heard *Now's the Time* I wondered if the musicians were 'birding' me, if they were having a private little joke of their own. Of course, I later found out that that was an important part of the whole thing. But aside from any wry humor and sardonic wit, there emerged a beautiful sadness, tinged with anger at times, all clothed in an exactness of craftsmanship that had never before been expressed in jazz." Not all the fans with "old" tastes were so open-minded. The reviewer of *Billie's Bounce* and *Now's the Time* for *Down Beat* (22 April 1946) was scathing: "These two sides are excellent examples of the other side of the Gillespie craze – the bad taste and ill-advised fanaticism of Dizzy's uninhibited style ... The trumpet man, whoever the misled kid is, plays Gillespie in the same manner as a majority of the kids who copy their idol – with most of the faults, lack of order and meaning, the complete adherence to technical acrobatics ... Good, bad or indifferent, the mass of Gillespie followers will love these sides, for even bad music is great if it's Diz. This is the sort of stuff that has thrown innumerable impressionable young musicians out of stride, that has harmed many of them irreparably. This can be as harmful to jazz as Sammy Kaye." Clearly, the battle lines were drawn. To follow Gillespie, according to the moldy figs, was to court disaster.

With the advantage of hindsight and the perspective afforded by having the alternate takes as well as the masters available, it is possible to detect the germ of Miles Davis's individualism in these recordings. Even so, it is little more than a hint, and the dominant impression of Davis on these records derives a bit uncom-fortably from Gillespie. Even as good a listener as Whitney Balliett could only hear Gillespie's influence in what the nineteen-year-old Davis played on this day; Balliett wrote in *The New Yorker* in 1958, "Davis's debut, some twelve years ago, with such musicians as Charlie Parker and Max Roach, was wobbly. His approach consisted largely of an awkward blotting up of the work of Dizzy Gillespie. He had a shrill, mousy tone, he bungled more notes than not, and he always sounded as if he were playing in a monotone." But there is something in the style that is distinct from Gillespie. It may or may not be "an awkward blotting up" of Freddie Webster, but it certainly does nothing to devalue Parker's recording debut as a leader.

The third number on which Davis plays, *Thriving on a Riff*, is built on the changes of *I Got Rhythm* and was better known at live performances later on as *Anthropology*. Davis is muted on all three takes and seems to have no problems steering through the peppy theme. Only the first take has both an opening and closing ensemble by the horns. The second and third takes open instead with a solo by Davis, and the second ends soon after it begins. The order of the parts on the first take is the same as for *Billie's Bounce* and *Now's the Time*, with an ensemble, a long solo by Parker, a shorter one by Davis, and the ensemble again. Parker plays well, but Davis gets involved in a long line during his solo and breaks it off abruptly when he runs out of breath. On the other complete take, the third, issued as the master, the arrangement has been altered to allow Hakim to solo: it begins directly with Davis's solo, moves to Parker's, and then to Hakim's before the closing ensemble. In order to stay within the three-minute limit of 78 rpm recordings, something had to be sacrificed to allow Hakim his solo space, and the opening ensemble went. It might have been more merciful to sacrifice Davis's solo instead, because he was clearly rattled by opening directly with his solo, and he struggles near the beginning at the point where he had stopped completely on the previous take. The solo is otherwise quite attractive, but the opening mistake is completely exposed. It is a little hard to believe – again, with the advantage of hindsight – that there could have been serious debate for so many years about whether the trumpeter on *Thriving on a Riff* was Gillespie or Davis. The aural evidence is clear, and most listeners guessed correctly that it was Davis. A British discographer advanced the following argument: "The trumpet, in addition to being a little off-mike (intentionally?), appears to be either unfamiliar with, or unable to play the theme, and misses a good many notes ... Dizzy is unlikely to have been fazed by the relative simplicity of *Anthropology*, of which he is credited as co-composer. In short, while the *Thriving* solos don't sound at all like Gillespie, they clearly *could* be by Miles."

This first Savoy session with Parker was hardly an unalloyed triumph for Davis, and it was not even as successful as it might have been if things had gone just a little differently – if take 3 or even take 1 of *Billie's Bounce* had been released before take 5, if the original arrangement of *Thriving* had been pursued instead of the one that forced him into an opening solo, and so on. And there was still the matter of Davis having to surrender his trumpet to Gillespie on *Ko Ko*, in full view of the assembled fans. By the time that happened, however, most of the fans, and most of the musicians too, were oblivious to the change. Between *Thriv-*

ing and *Ko Ko* there was a long delay while someone went eight blocks away searching for Parker's Rico #5 reeds, to eliminate the squeak once and for all. During the delay, the party in the studio continued, and by the time the recording resumed, Davis was asleep on the floor, completely unaware of Gillespie's facile manipulation of the trumpet part that had stumped him. Almost thirty-five years later, Davis just shook his head at the recollection of that introduction that he could not master. "That's the damnedest introduction I ever heard in my life," he told Gillespie and Al Fraser. For Gillespie it was no problem at all. He sailed through it in the recording studio.

The police shutdown of 52nd Street continued after Parker's engagement at Minton's ended. The piano player in Parker's group at Minton's, Sir Charles Thompson, was hired to stay on with a trio afterward, and he hired Davis. The third member was drummer Connie Kay. The odd instrumentation – trumpet, piano, and drums – did not bother Thompson, who seemed to live with contradictions most of the time. Originally from the Midwest like so many of the other 52nd Street veterans, Thompson had conferred his knighthood on himself, probably to give jazz another rank to go along with its dukes, counts, and kings. He spent most of his career in the company of swing players such as Buck Clayton, Illinois Jacquet, and Roy Eldridge, who valued his Basie-style piano, but that piano style also included echoes of Bud Powell, and Thompson kept busy by working with the boppers as well. He knew very well that at Minton's he did not have to worry about showing up on the bandstand with unusual or awkward instrumentation, because the working members of the band were never alone on the bandstand for very long. Connie Kay remembers the parade of players very well: "We'd play one set and generally that was it. The rest of the evening it would be people sitting in – Charlie Parker and Dizzy Gillespie, Milt Jackson, Georgie Auld, Red Rodney. I remember when Ray Brown first came there. Freddie Webster came in all the time and showed Miles how to get those big oooh sounds, those big tones Miles uses now."

When Thompson's gig ended, Coleman Hawkins took over the bandstand at Minton's, and he also hired Davis. Probably Sir Charles Thompson stayed on with Hawkins as well, and perhaps Tommy Potter was the bassist. Davis was teamed for the second time with Hawkins, the first master of the tenor saxophone, this time for pay. Hawkins, from St. Joseph, Missouri, near Kansas City, was only forty-one in the late fall of 1945, but he was revered as the first man to prove that the tenor could be used as a solo horn in jazz. Until he made his first records with the Fletcher Henderson orchestra in the early 1920s, the tenor was seldom used as anything but an ensemble instrument; once Hawkins showed the way, tenor soloists popped up all over the place, and the tenor soon became the most common wind instrument in jazz. The style that Hawkins pioneered featured a broad, breathy tone, carried over from the days when the instrument's function was to give depth to the ensemble, but his brilliance came from his ability to modulate the barrel-house tone with great delicacy. He was a great interpreter of ballads, and his recording of *Body and Soul* remains one of the most celebrated ballad performances ever. It is no coincidence that Davis had a close connection with Hawkins during this first, formative year in New York. "I learned to play ballads from Coleman Hawkins," he has said. "He plays all the chords and you can still hear the ballad." For Davis, Hawkins was one more of the great teachers that The Street provided.

Around the time that Davis was playing with Hawkins in Harlem, his living arrangement with Parker ended. Parker had met a waitress named Doris Sydnor, a young woman with an apparently fathomless maternal feeling toward him, and he moved into her apartment at 411 Manhattan Avenue, where Sadik Hakim was also boarding. Davis was thoroughly fed up with Parker's problems off the bandstand. "I used to put him to bed sometimes with the needle still in his arm and him bleeding all over the place," Davis says. There were other problems too. "Bird was really selfish," Davis said later. "If you had some dope, he'd want all of it. If you had some food, he'd want all of *that*." Parker was treating Davis the way he treated most of his friends and acquaintances, but as long as they were sharing living space Davis was especially vulnerable. "He used to pawn my suitcase and take all my money," Davis says. "He was a dirty motherfucker, man. I loved to listen to him, but he was so fucking greedy. Just greedy – you know how greedy people are. But he had a hell of a mind." In spite of Parker's behavior and Davis's blunt reactions to it, the two men somehow remained full of respect for one another and their professional association continued unchanged.

As soon as Parker moved out, Freddie Webster moved in with Davis, and their informal seminars on the music of The Street carried on night and day. Davis tried to supplement his education on the The Street with more formal training. He sought out William Vachiano, a respected teacher of advanced students in New York, but the experience only soured him further on formal instruction. "Vachiano, my teacher in New York, would always say, 'Play *Tea for Two.*' The motherfucker wouldn't teach me," Davis complained to Julie Coryell. "I'd say, 'Man, I'm paying you – teach me something!'" Davis's battles with the celebrated Vachiano later grew into a minor legend among New York musicians. Marc Levin, a multi-instrumentalist who plays jazz-based experimental music, studied with Vachiano in 1958 and heard the rumors then. "Everybody studied with William Vachiano," Levin says. "Miles Davis studied with Vachiano, but I heard at the time that Vachiano had a lot of trouble with Miles Davis." And vice versa, apparently.

It was not only in the more formal educational context that Davis balked at what he was hearing. Mary Lou Williams, then a fixture in the Café Society Downtown, recalls, "I knew a guy who taught me all the sounds of [John] Coltrane in the 40s. His name was Milton Orent and he knew so much that he couldn't play. He was going to learn jazz and then I learned from him, writing and sounds and things. When Sarah Vaughan and people would come up, Milton would sit at the piano and play some way-out changes. Miles used to come up too and he .didn't like it. Milton played way-out sounds like Coltrane and that was when I was in the Café Society." In the late 1950s, Davis would foster Coltrane's development in much the same way as his own was fostered by Parker, but this contact with the unknown piano player whom Mary Lou Williams insists on comparing to Coltrane left him cold – perhaps because he "knew so much that he couldn't play." For all his efforts, Davis's schooling was always more successful when it was in the hands of practicing musicians.

Davis was also forming alliances with musicians closer to his own age, and they would soon direct bebop toward the next stage of its development. One of his closest friends was Max Roach, the Brooklyn-born drummer, who was just over a year older than Davis. Roach was already being touted as Kenny Clarke's successor as the top bop percussionist. Together, Davis and Roach were fast becoming a clique within the clique surrounding Parker, and Parker knew it. Tony Scott remembers an incident that must have happened at the Three Deuces or the Spotlite that fall, although it is not certain when Roach was in these bands, the drummer of record being Stan Levey. As Scott recalls it, "One night he was playing The Street with Miles and Max, and I took out my clarinet and started to assemble it, when Miles turned to me and said, 'Bird don't like no one to play with him.' 'Okay,' I said, and sat down. After a set, Bird spotted me and said, 'Tony, what's the matter with you? Do I have to give you an engraved invitation every time? Come and play a few with us.' I told him what Miles had said. He said, 'Miles and Max have been bugging me lately. I'm gonna fire those guys.' And he did. But such a magnificent combination could not be separated for long. They went to California," Scott says, soon after that, but not together.

The Street remained closed throughout November, and there was no indication that it might reopen in December or for a long time after that. Unlike the sporadic clean-ups in the past, this one was instigated not only by the vice squad but also by the military authorities, who were annoyed by continual reports about servicemen who were rolled, beaten, or conned there on overnight leave. The musicians soon began to feel the pinch. It was all very well for them to sit in at Minton's and the other Harlem clubs for a few nights, but none of them could survive for long without pay. Whenever they got together now, there was talk about leaving New York for a while to find some work, and California came up often in the conversation. Finally, Gillespie took the idea of a California tour to his agent, Billy Shaw, who liked it and got on the phone to an acquaintance in Los Angeles, a nightclub-owner named Billy Berg. Shaw convinced him that the new music would be a sensation in his club and promised to send him the all-star band with Parker and Gillespie that had packed the Three Deuces off and on since late 1944. Berg agreed, offering the band eight weeks at his club starting the second week of December. When Shaw passed the news along to Gillespie, however, he found him less than pleased about having to put up with Parker on the bandstand again, but neither Shaw nor Berg would consider leaving Parker out. Gillespie had to settle for a compromise, keeping Parker in the band but adding Milt Jackson, the vibraphonist from Detroit, to give the band an extra solo voice on nights when Parker failed to show up. The deal was confirmed, and the sextet, with Al Haig, Ray Brown, and Stan Levey as the rhythm section, left for California by train the first week of December.

Davis headed home to East St. Louis soon after that, arriving in time to spend Christmas with his family. He was still there in January when Benny Carter brought his big band into the Riviera in St. Louis, and Davis joined the band's trumpet section. Carter's band were a rarity, along with Stan Kenton's, because they used Los Angeles as their home base rather than New York. When Davis joined, the band were scheduled to work their way back to the west coast by late February or early March. As soon as he found that he would be traveling to Los Angeles, Davis phoned Parker there to tell him the news. Parker, who was lining up a recording date with Ross Russell of Dial Records, began promising him that he would be able to include the young trumpeter in his band as soon as he arrived.

The Carter band returned to Los Angeles to play an engagement at the Orpheum Theatre, and after that they broke up temporarily. Carter took a smaller group from the band to play local engagements during the lay-off, and he included Davis, along with trombonist Al Grey and tenor saxophonist Bumps Meyers. This small band played on a radio broadcast from Los Angeles on Sunday 31 March, and a tape that exists in some private collections catches them running through the standards *Just You Just Me*, *Don't Blame Me*, and *Sweet Georgia Brown*.

By the time of the broadcast, Davis had already made contact with Parker and begun playing with him at an after-hours spot called the Finale Club, where Parker had been hired as the contractor for the house band. Parker had landed at the Finale Club when Gillespie and the other members of his New York band returned home after the engagement at Billy Berg's, in the first week of February. Gillespie had doled out airline tickets to each of the men but Parker failed to show up at the airport. A venerable legend says that Parker cashed in his ticket almost as soon as Gillespie was out of sight in order to buy narcotics, but Ross Russell points out that during his last weeks at Berg's Parker had been toying with the idea of settling in California and may not have intended to catch that flight. He had persuaded Foster Johnson, the retired vaudevillian who managed the Finale Club, to put him in charge of hiring the club's musicians. The venture was so short-lived that it would probably have been completely forgotten if Parker had not been associated with it and if Russell, a documentor of early bop in general and of Parker in particular, had not been among its clientele. It was at 115 South San Pedro Street, in the section of the city then known as Little Tokyo but already being annexed to the nearby black neighborhood. Its low ceiling was a reminder that it had formerly housed a Japanese club, but under Johnson's management it had been turned into a bottle club that was supposed to be used only by members, who could bring in their own liquor and buy ice and mix from the club. The private memberships cost $2 at the door and were in effect for one night only. The club lasted no more than three months. Russell says, "It was closed by the vice squad of the Los Angeles Police Department just as it had established itself as *the* after hours rendezvous for resident and visiting jazz musicians."

Davis was fined by the local musicians' union soon after he arrived in Los Angeles for doubling at the Orpheum with Benny Carter and the Finale Club with Charlie Parker. Forced to make a choice between the two groups, he chose to resign from Carter's band and stay with Parker.

One musician who sometimes visited the Finale Club after his own job was over, trumpeter Art Farmer, remembers the band that Parker assembled and also recalled their uneasy reception by the local press: "Bird had a group consisting of Miles Davis on trumpet; my brother Addison [Farmer] on bass; Joe Albany, piano; and Chuck Thompson, drums ... Some chick who was writing for a Negro newspaper came down one night to review the group. She was escorted by Dootsie Williams, a trumpet player who acted as some sort of musical consultant. It was their considered opinion that Bird was saying nothing. What's more, his manner was arrogant and he was not too approachable. He had with him, she wrote, a little black, wispy trumpet player who had better technique than Bird. The bass player, she graciously said, had an indefatigable arm. But Bird just played flurries of notes without any content." Farmer continues, "I showed the paper to Bird not knowing what to expect, perhaps great indignation. He just gave a bitter little grin and said, 'She's probably all right, but the wrong people got to her first.'"

The Finale Club band made a radio broadcast, probably in early March, with the personnel that Farmer remembers there. The performance was preserved on acetate lacquer discs, a direct-to-disc process used before magnetic tape became widely available. Although the lacquers inevitably suffered over the years, they were cleaned up as far as possible and transferred to vinyl almost thirty years later, by Tony Williams of Spotlite Records. The details are as follows:

Charlie Parker Quintet
Miles Davis, tpt; Charlie Parker, as; Joe Albany, pno; Addison Farmer, b; Chuck Thompson, dms. The Finale Club, Los Angeles, probably March 1946
Anthropology [Thriving on a Riff]; Billie's Bounce; Blue 'n' Boogie; All the Things You Are; Ornithology
(all on Spotlite SPJ123 [side 2])

The first two compositions are carried over from the repertoire that Parker and Davis played at Minton's and recorded for Savoy in the fall. Beneath the surfaces of the lacquers, it is easy to pick out a much more relaxed Davis, relieved of the pressures of a recording studio and a restless audience of New York musicians. Surprisingly, at the Finale Club he plays everything with a muted horn – even *Billie's Bounce*, which he originally recorded with a broad, open sound. The other three tunes, recorded by Davis here for the first time but not the last, are all framed in arrangements a little more interesting than the conventional first two, which simply state a theme, line up solos by Parker, Davis, and Albany in turn, and close out with the theme again. On *Blue 'n' Boogie*, a Gillespie composition, Albany solos first, presumably to get him out of the way before the horns take up the riff-style arrangement. At the start of Parker's solo and at the end of his first chorus, the trumpet and alto punctuate the break with a four-bar unison passage, and after Davis's first and second choruses they do the same, using a completely different riff. After a short bass solo by Farmer, the two horns play an extended duet passage, leading into the out chorus. The relative complexity of this arrangement and its flawless execution suggest that it had been a staple for the two hornmen for some time, probably back in New York. *All the Things You Are* is also carefully arranged, with the alto saxophone stating a three-note motif before and during the trumpet statement of the melody; at the bridge, the alto takes over the melody line, picking up its motif again at the end of the bridge. It is different from a later treatment, featuring Davis when he was with the Tadd Dameron band and recorded in May 1949, which is based on John Lewis's arrangement for Dizzy Gillespie's big band; but the prominence of Davis here in the theme statement and the basic device of framing the melody with a motif both suggest that the 1946 arrangement might well be Davis's own. The remaining tune is *Ornithology*, which would be recorded again for Dial later in the month.

The Finale Club sessions featured a variety of players, many of them musicians who had moved to Los Angeles from the Midwest a few years earlier, such as

Howard McGhee from Detroit, the Farmer brothers from Iowa, and Sonny Criss from Memphis, as well as the cream of the local talent, including bassist Red Callender and Callender's protégé, Charles Mingus. Mingus was smitten by the genius of Parker and only slightly less impressed by Davis. In his autobiography, *Beneath the Underdog*, Mingus recalls a session that took place apparently soon after Davis arrived in Los Angeles. Like the rest of Mingus's autobiography, the scene mixes fantasy and fiction with fact, but it does provide a novel impression of the young trumpeter. The session included Parker, Davis, tenor saxophonist Lucky Thompson, reedman and flutist Buddy Colette, pianist Dodo Marmarosa, Mingus, and drummer Stan Levey. It opens with an announcer welcoming Davis: "And will all you people give Miles Davis a hand – Miles is just in from New York. Come on now, everybody – Miles Davis! Give him a good California welcome!" As the band proceeds to play *Billie's Bounce*, Parker calls out the names of the soloists in their turn: "Blow, Miles." After his chorus, Davis says, "I done blew, motherfucker. Now you got it, cocksucker. Blow, Lucky." A little later, he turns to the other horn players and says, "When are you motherfuckers going to stop talking and start playing, instead of just Dodo and Stan over there jacking off?" To which Mingus replies, "Miles, you're so vulgar," and Davis says, "I want to hear Bird blow, not all this dumb-ass conversation." A little later, he directs his ire at the audience which is also talking instead of listening: "Ladies and gentlemen, will you all shut up and just listen to the motherfucker blowing!" Mingus chides him: "Careful, man, you can't say that." "Schitt [sic], man," Davis replies, "I put my hand over the mike on 'motherfucker.'" Whatever its truth, Mingus's portrait shows Davis confidently aggressive among his peers even at this time.

Soon after Davis got settled in, Parker set the date for his recording session with Dial. Ross Russell had contacted Parker and the other members of the New York sextet when they first started at Billy Berg's, hoping to get them to record for Dial. The musicians were willing, and Parker made it to the chaotic rehearsal session but failed to show up at the recording session the next night. A few days later, he went to Russell at his office in the Tempo Music Shop on Hollywood Boulevard and suggested they try again, this time with Davis. Parker and Russell signed an informal agreement, dated 26 February, binding Parker to Dial Records for a year. The first recording session was set for 1 p.m. on 28 March. Parker's hand-picked septet were supposed to rehearse the night before at the Finale Club, but they ended up arguing bitterly and nothing much was accomplished. At the studio the next day, the men drifted in nursing grudges as well as hangovers. They took more than an hour setting up their instruments and getting in place, but the session produced the first of a series of recordings for Dial that are generally conceded to contain the very best of Parker's recorded work. The details are as follows:

Charlie Parker Septet
Miles Davis, tpt; Charlie Parker, as; Lucky Thompson, ts; Dodo Marmarosa, pno; Arv
Garrison, gtr; Victor McMillan, b; Roy Porter, dms. Los Angeles, 28 March 1946
Moose the Mooche (takes 1, 2, 3); *Yardbird Suite* (takes 1, 4); *Ornithology* (takes 1, 3, 4);
A Night in Tunisia (takes 1, 4, 5)
(all on Spotlite 101, except take 3 of *Moose the Mooche*, on Spotlite 105; master takes on
Archives of Jazz 503)
Other takes from this session are lost. Take 3 of *Ornithology* was originally issued as *Bird
Lore*; take 1 of *A Night in Tunisia* was originally issued, and is still commonly referred
to, as *Famous Alto Break*.

The recording session went on until 9 p.m., despite the union limit of three hours.
Russell remembers "Miles Davis, wooden and deadpanned, not playing much on
his solos but warming the ensemble parts with his broad tone." He says also that
the numerous flawed takes "were in all cases the fault of the sidemen, especially
Miles Davis, who was slow to learn new material." Russell's recollections may be
slightly jaded – he and Davis were never very friendly. Nothing in the surviving
recorded evidence supports his claim that most of the ruined takes were Davis's
fault or that he did not play well on his solos. It was largely because of what he
played on the master takes that he won *Down Beat*'s New Star award for trumpet
in 1946 and Thompson and Marmarosa won the same citations for their instruments.
   Moose the Mooche is an uptempo romp named by Parker for his Los Angeles
connection, a character identified by Russell in *Bird Lives!* as Emry Byrd, to
whom Parker signed over half of his composer's royalties from the corporation
that Dial was setting up on his behalf. That deal turned out to be a windfall for
the connection, especially because *Yardbird Suite*, a graceful, hip melody, became
something of an anthem for boppers. Davis, muted as he is on all these sides, plays
a stunning solo on the master take (the fourth), helped more than a little by the
fact that the arranger, presumably Parker, has him play sixteen bars, lay out while
Lucky Thompson plays eight, and return for eight more before giving way to
Thompson again. The contrast between Davis's muted sound and Thompson's
robust, breathy tenor saxophone works superbly, bringing to mind the contrast
that Davis would later exploit when he played alongside the saxophonists John
Coltrane and Julian Adderley in his peak years, 1955–9. *Ornithology* succeeds
almost as well as *Yardbird Suite*, although the composition lacks the polish. On *A
Night in Tunisia*, Dizzy Gillespie's best-known composition, the three horns
make an orchestral setting, with Davis flawlessly negotiating the melody in the
opening and closing ensembles. Compared to his work on the Savoy session only
four months earlier, Davis seems to have made a quantum advance, but then,

even the playing of Parker is much more polished and sure here, suggesting that the conditions of the production more than the individual development deserve the credit. Indeed, Parker's playing shines so consistently on these sides that it fairly blinds one to the achievements of his sidemen, as excellent as their playing often is. The first release from this session, a 78 rpm pairing of *Ornithology* and *A Night in Tunisia*, was rushed through production and released within a month. Almost everyone who heard it recognized it as a significant event in the development of jazz.

In California, Davis soon found that he was being sought out by the younger musicians, the men his own age or just slightly older. Having put in a year on The Street absorbing the lessons that are only available from more experienced jazzmen, Davis owned knowledge that the California musicians had not come across before, and he shared it with them as freely as the men on The Street had shared it with him. "Miles was giving me quite a bit of help musically," Benny Bailey recalls. "The first time I heard them playing was on *Lady Be Good*, just an old standard, but what they did with the chords I thought was amazing, and very confusing to me. They were adding chords and, you know how bebop was going then with the minor sevenths and flatted fifths, well I didn't understand that and Miles was really the first guy to pull my coat to what to do, how to get the most out of a tune by changing the chords." A few years later, Bailey joined the trumpet section of Dizzy Gillespie's superb big band.

In April, Davis appeared with Parker in a concert at the Carver Club, on the campus of the University of California at Los Angeles. The other players included Britt Woodman on trombone, as well as Lucky Thompson and Arv Garrison, both holdovers from the Dial session. The fact that Woodman was in the band suggests that the bassist was probably Charles Mingus, his best friend.

In spite of the Dial recordings and the steady work at the Finale Club and other places, by the spring the jazz scene in California was definitely clouding over. Parker was very heavily in debt to his connection, who obviously had not been moved to kindness by the dedication of *Moose the Mooche*. Parker was also getting burned on some of the dope he was injecting. He was incapacitated quite often, and he was ballooning in size. The storm clouds settled in when the musicians showed up for work one night and found the Finale Club padlocked. Foster Johnson claimed he had been shaken down by the police once too often and he simply closed up the place. Parker disappeared immediately and was located only after a long search by Howard McGhee, who found him living in a garage in the heart of the ghetto and subsisting on local port wine, which he drank from gallon jugs. Eventually, McGhee and his wife persuaded Johnson to let them reopen the Finale Club, and for a few days Parker was back at work there, in a quintet with McGhee, Marmarosa, Red Callender, and Roy Porter. Then Parker's connection was arrested and jailed. In an effort to clean himself up, Parker gave up heroin, but he also began to drink awesome quantities, first gallons of cheap port and later whiskey by the quart. Some kind of disaster seemed inevitable when he appeared for his second Dial recording session on Monday 29 July with a band organized by McGhee. Parker could hardly play, and his tortured attempt at playing *Lover Man* was later described by Russell as "the raw notes of a nightmare." Later that night he set fire to the bed in his hotel room and was arrested wandering around naked; he was eventually confined to Camarillo State Hospital in a rehabilitation program. He would stay there for seven months.

Through all of these goings-on, Davis's position as Parker's trumpeter had been taken over by Howard McGhee. By the summer, Davis was working in bands that usually included Charles Mingus. In August, he was featured in a band fronted by Lucky Thompson at the Elk's Ballroom on Central Avenue, the main thoroughfare of the Watts district in Los Angeles. Thompson leased the Ballroom three nights a week, running advertisements that announced "the brilliant young trumpet player, Miles Davis, last heard here with Benny Carter." Mingus was the bassist. The engagement lasted only a few weeks, however, and then Thompson left the city with Boyd Raeburn's band.

Probably during the Elk's Ballroom engagement, Davis and Thompson took part in a recording venture led by Mingus under the sobriquet Baron Mingus. The details, as far as they are known, are as follows:

Baron Mingus and His Symphonic Airs
Probably Miles Davis, Vern Carlson, tpt; Henry Coker, tbn; Boots Mussulli, as; Lucky
Thompson, ts; Buddy Colette, ts, flt; Herb Carroll, bs; Buzz Wheeler, pno; Charles
Mingus, b; Warren Thompson, dms; Herb Gayle, vcl (on *He's Gone*). Los Angeles,
probably August 1946
He's Gone (Fentone 2002); *The Story of Love* (Fentone 2002, Rex-Hollywood 28002);
Portrait (unissued)

The release details are taken from Jepsen's 1969 listing, but some sources claim that none of these titles was ever issued. They would be among the very rarest jazz records if they ever were available. The spectacle of the large, gifted Mingus passing himself off as the baron of jazz, thus hauling himself into the ersatz but celebrated royal family of jazz, seems ludicrous but is not at all out of character. Davis recalls the Mingus panache with undisguised admiration. "Mingus is a *man*," he says. "He don't do nothin' half way. If he's gonna make a fool of himself, he makes sure he makes a damn fool of himself." In the summer of 1946, when Davis was just becoming known and Mingus was still entirely unknown outside his home area, the two men gravitated toward one another. "Mingus and I

were really *close*," Davis says. "We used to rehearse all the time in California."
No jazzman can survive on rehearsals alone, of course, even if he is working
out the skills and the style that will eventually carry him to the forefront of his
art, but Davis's days of rehearsing with Mingus and scuffling for jobs in Los
Angeles helped him to pass the time until he could earn his ticket back to
The Street.

For Davis, it was another instance of being in the right place. Billy Eckstine's
band arrived in Los Angeles in the fall, probably September, to play some local
engagements. As luck would have it, Eckstine needed a trumpeter to fill his solo
chair in California, and Davis was already there, ready and waiting. The vacancy
came about because Fats Navarro, who had taken over Dizzy Gillespie's chair in
the band when Gillespie left New York for California, wanted to complete his
tenure in the New York local of the musicians' union and was unable to leave the
city. Eckstine says, "When we went out as far as California, he decided he wanted
to stay in New York and work his card out. So I got in touch with Miles Davis; he
was out there working in a group with Bird, who also had left me by then." Even
though Eckstine had lost several of his leading players from the original band, his
touch for finding excellent young musicians had not left him. The 1946 orchestra
that Davis joined included saxophonists Sonny Stitt, Gene Ammons, and Cecil
Payne, and it was still buoyed by the rhythm section of Linton Garner, Errol's
brother, on piano, Tommy Potter on bass, and drummer Art Blakey. As far as
Eckstine was concerned, this band just carried on the strong individual talents he
had assembled in the spring of 1944 and had kept together despite the considerable economic odds against it. After two and a half years, he realized that this
western tour would determine once and for all whether he was going to continue
his quest for success as a bandleader as well as a vocalist. By now, there was no
doubt at all about his ability to succeed as a vocalist. He was already very close to
the top of that field, a star whose record sales and popularity put him in the league
with Bing Crosby, Frank Sinatra, Dick Haymes, Jo Stafford, and Dinah Shore.
They owed their start to the big bands just as he did, for the bands put them
before the public in the first place. Only Eckstine, however, still clung to his roots
as a band singer, all the others having put the big bands behind them as soon as
they could make it on their own. Eckstine loved leading a band, considered himself a musician rather than a star, and felt comfortable in the company of jazz
players, but he must have realized that his vocalizing subsidized his bandleading,
and that choosing to go with the former alone made good sense financially for
him. He may have seen the Hollywood sojourn as the final effort to vindicate his
career as a bandleader.

Besides playing in ballrooms and supper clubs, the orchestra with Davis also
recorded some of Eckstine's hit songs in Hollywood. The details are as follows:

Billy Eckstine and His Orchestra
Miles Davis, Hobart Dotson, Leonard Hawkins, King Kolax, tpt; Walter Knox, Chippy Outcalt, Gerry Valentine, sometimes Eckstine, tbn; Sonny Stitt, John Cobbs, as; Gene Ammons, Arthur Samson, ts; Cecil Payne, bs; Linton Garner, pno; Connie Wainwright, gtr; Tommy Potter, b; Art Blakey, dms; Billy Eckstine, vcl. Los Angeles, 5 October 1946
Oo Bop Sh'Bam (two takes) (both on Savoy SJL 2214 [1976]); *I Love the Loveliness* (Savoy SJL 1127 [1979]); *In the Still of the Night* and *Jelly Jelly* (Savoy SJL 2214)

Similar personnel, perhaps including Ray Linn, tpt, plus strings. Los Angeles, 6 October 1946
My Silent Love; Time on My Hands; All the Things You Are; In a Sentimental Mood (all on Savoy SJL 2214)

All these titles were originally released as 78 rpm pairings on the long-forgotten National label, Eckstine's recording company from the beginning of the days with his own band in 1944. The recording session of 5 October includes some of the best big-band playing ever documented in a studio by a band of Eckstine's. Eckstine's marketability had nothing to do with his band's swinging, a fact that becomes painfully obvious to any jazz listener after the most cursory review of his National recordings. Still, on *Oo Bop Sh'Bam*, a bebop riff with a line of nonsense syllables for a vocal refrain, written by Dizzy Gillespie and Gil Fuller when they were with Eckstine in the Earl Hines orchestra, the band cut loose and Gene Ammons takes an effective solo. *Jelly Jelly*, a blues written by Eckstine and Hines that was Eckstine's very first vocal hit (in the Hines orchestra's recording), also works well for Ammons and allows the sections to swing. The remaining tracks offer little of jazz interest. Occasionally, as on *My Silent Love*, one can pick out a few bars of a trumpet lead that are possibly Davis's work, but ironically the only extended trumpet solo, lasting eight bars in the middle of *Time on My Hands*, features an orthodox player sticking close to the melody. Three decades after the recording, Eckstine identified the trumpeter as Ray Linn, a veteran of the touring bands who had settled into the Hollywood studios by this time.

Eckstine's band must have been allowed more playing room at personal appearances or his lineup of top-flight jazz players would surely have drifted away. The gap between the band's jazz potential and their invariably staid recordings is enormous. Art Blakey, in an interview with Arthur Taylor years later, bemoaned what the record company missed in studio sessions with the orchestra. "Nobody got to hear it," he said. "They didn't get recorded, and the records they did make were sadder than McKinley's funeral. Even the horses cried. Because it wasn't recorded right; they recorded a big band on two mikes, which was very unfair. They weren't interested in the band. They were interested in Billy Eckstine.

Later on they wished they had recorded the band right, because the biggest stars in jazz were playing in it." A persistent rumor maintains that Eckstine holds a collection of taped performances by his band; every jazz fan hopes that they will show the band's mettle when they are finally made public. Presumably the experience of those live performances kept Davis interested, along with the discipline of playing in a well-drilled big band. His assumption of the solo chair formerly held by Gillespie and Navarro stands as a symbolic coming of age for the young trumpeter. His success must have been all the more satisfying because Eckstine had been sharply critical of his ability two years earlier. Now Eckstine had to change his opinion. "By the time we got to California," he said, "he had blossomed out. He'd been going to Juilliard, and playing with Bird, so he came in and took over the same book, the solo book which was originally Dizzy's. Miles stayed with me until I broke up, which was in 1947."

Also in October an all-star sextet from the band recorded four titles with two vocalists who worked the Central Avenue bars. The music has never been issued on record, but the sextet included Davis and Ammons, the band's best soloists, along with their rhythm section, and they played three takes of each of the four unidentified songs, two of which were sung by Earl Coleman and two by Ann Hathaway. Hathaway remains unknown, but something is known of Coleman from two songs he recorded with Charlie Parker a few months later, soon after Parker was released from Camarillo. Ross Russell had lined up a large band of local musicians for Parker to record with on a Dial session marking his return to active playing, but Parker showed up with Coleman at his side and insisted that the singer should be allowed to record two of his songs, *This Is Always* and *Dark Shadows*. Russell finally had to give in, and then he sat back helplessly as the singer, an Eckstine sound-alike, fumbled take after take, finally getting satisfactory versions of the songs after two hours and twenty minutes. Unlike the recordings with Davis and the other members of Eckstine's band, Coleman's recordings with Parker were issued (all five complete takes of the two songs are on Spotlite 102). They reveal a hefty baritone voice and an extravagant phrasing that seem to parody Eckstine's style. Coleman's vibrato often quavers right into the next bar, and his songs with Parker come out as paeans from a trembling lover. There is little hope that his songs with the band that included Davis will be any more interesting, if they are ever unearthed.

The Billy Eckstine orchestra, including Davis, made their way back toward New York late in 1946. Chicago, naturally, was one of the stops along the way, and it was probably the last stop before the band broke up temporarily for Christmas. Davis stayed in Chicago for a while, playing an engagement at the Jumptown Club with his bandmates Gene Ammons and Sonny Stitt. For Davis, this Chicago stopover at Christmas was the first in what would become a career-long pattern. Except for a few years when his health or personal problems made the Chicago trip impossible, he has arranged his schedule so that he plays in a club or a concert there around Christmas every year. Davis's sister Dorothy lives there, teaching in a Chicago public school and, since her marriage to Vincent Wilburn, raising her family. Ever since his first Christmas away from East St. Louis, Davis has made sure that he would be in the vicinity during the holiday season.

The Eckstine orchestra reassembled in New York in the new year to finish off their commitments for January and February. After that, Eckstine disbanded permanently and struck out on his own as a featured vocalist. The disbanding put an end to Eckstine's aspirations as a bandleader and also cut off the relatively secure jobs that the band had provided for so many of the rising stars of the bebop revolution. Unencumbered by his band, Eckstine headed back to California in April, where he made his final recordings for the National label with a studio orchestra, including the hit records *Blues for Sale* and *Solitude*. (Jepsen's discography and other sources list this session as taking place in New York before disbanding and include Davis in the orchestra, but Eckstine corrected the listing when the sides were reissued in 1976 on Savoy SJL 2214.) After that, he signed with MGM Records, turning out a string of commercially successful records over the next five years, when the appeal of his highly mannered singing began to wane.

Thanks to Eckstine, Miles Davis was back in New York, and back on 52nd Street, where the music was again being played. The Street had remained shut down for several weeks in 1946, and then it had begun to show signs of life again, as first one club and then another was allowed to reopen. Now, almost a year later, there was a fair amount of night activity although it was still not bustling as it had before the shutdown. Some of the clubs remained dark, and in the ones that had reopened the managers were keeping closer tabs on their trade, as the police department also was. Hopes were high that The Street would eventually recover its old panache, but the new strictures were never to be fully relaxed, and the anarchy of the night life it had supported for so long was gone for good.

Much of the excitement among the musicians on The Street still centered around Dizzy Gillespie, who was experimenting with bebop in a big-band format. His experiment was lauded as the next logical step in the progress of bop, and he showed uncanny sense in enlisting Walter Gil Fuller, a writer for the Eckstine band, as his musical director right from the beginning. As straw boss and composer-arranger, Fuller took the responsibility for hiring musicians and compiling a book as seriously as Gillespie did, and the band generated excitement among musicians and jazz listeners almost immediately. Part of the musical activity on The Street consisted of watching for developments coming out of the Gillespie

band and participating in working them out further. One of Davis's first jobs after
the Eckstine band folded came from an attempt by Illinois Jacquet and Leonard
Feather to produce some big-band bebop. The details are as follows:

Illinois Jacquet and His Orchestra
Miles Davis, Joe Newman or Russell Jacquet, Marion Hazel, Fats Navarro, tpt; Gus
Chappel, Fred Robinson, Ted Kelly, Dicky Wells, tbn; Ray Perry, Jimmy Powell, as;
George Nicholas, Illinois Jacquet, ts; Bill Doggett or Leonard Feather, pno; Al Lucas, b;
Shadow Wilson, dms. New York, March 1947
For Europeans Only; Big Dog; You Left Me Alone; Jivin' with Jack the Bellboy
(All originally Aladdin [78 rpm]; reissued on Imperial LP 9184)

The recording session brings together Davis and Navarro, whom Davis had
replaced in Eckstine's orchestra. As habitués of 52nd Street, their paths had
crossed many times and would again on several occasions before Navarro's death
three years later. Ted Kelly, George Nicholas, and probably some of the others in
the band were members of Gillespie's band at the time and had returned not long
before this from that band's inaugural tour, a whirlwind trip through the southern
states during which they played sixty one-night stands.

In the south, the Gillespie band had been received with a lot of befuddlement
and some outright hostility, but now that they were back in the city, things were
looking up. Billy Shaw, the manager, arranged a week's booking at the McKinley
Theater in the Bronx for early April. Gillespie and Fuller saw the engagement as
their best chance to make a breakthrough with the band and win over an audience that would be large enough and enthusiastic enough to keep the band
together full-time. They were taking no chances with the players, hiring the best
men around, bar none. Max Roach, the band's drummer on the southern tour as
well as at the McKinley Theater, shakes his head in disbelief when he recalls
Gillespie's original New York band: "When Dizzy had his first big band, here's
the kind of brass section we had. He had Freddie Webster, Kinney Dorham, Miles
Davis, Fats Navarro. That's the trumpet section." With Gillespie added, that
section must rank among the most powerful of all time. Just as the rehearsals
were getting under way, the band seemed to get an unexpected boost by the
reappearance of Charlie Parker. He had been released from Camarillo in February, and after hanging around on Central Avenue and recording two separate
sessions for Dial in Los Angeles, he made his way back to the east coast by train,
stopping over in Chicago and playing with some local bands along the way. Fuller
hired Parker as soon as he arrived. After all, Parker's sound was part of the fabric
of the band itself. "We wanted it to sound like what Dizzy and Bird were doing,"

Fuller explains, "but the sound had to be translated into a big band sound." With Parker in the band, joining the best boppers on The Street, Fuller and everyone else expected to hear a glorious realization of that goal.

Parker lasted only one night. Although he had only been out of Camarillo for about six weeks, he was involved with narcotics as heavily as ever by the time he got to New York. Gillespie, feeling the pressure to make his big band succeed, was in no mood to tolerate the same old nonsense he had to put up with from Parker in the past. Fuller remembers the band's opening night at the McKinley: "Charlie Parker came in the place and had this shit in him and sat up there through the whole thing till his solo comes, and when his solo comes, Bird puts his horn in his mouth and [plays] 'doodle-loo-deloodle-loo,'" Fuller says. "And Dizzy, on stage with people in the audience, said, 'Get that mothafucka off my stage!' Because he didn't want the whole band tagged as a bunch of junkies, you know. He wouldn't let me put him in there anymore; he just wasn't gonna have that. Because Bird would always get high, man, and start nodding right on the bandstand. And you're playing the whole thing with no first saxophone player."

Gillespie remained adamant about keeping the band clean, or at least making it appear to be clean, and to him that meant keeping Parker out of it. Fuller went to him to plead Parker's case, no doubt passing along all kinds of promises that Parker had made, but Gillespie had heard it all before and would not give in. "That was a helluva band," Fuller says, "but again, we wanted Charlie Parker for writing the tunes. And I told Dizzy, 'Shit, man, it'd be worthwhile just to give him a hundred dollars a week and let him write tunes for us than be worried with him.' But we didn't have the money at that time. There was nobody putting the money up." They would just have to get along without Parker, and they could, as Gillespie knew very well.

No matter how savagely Parker abused himself, he seemed to come back full of strength. This time, though he could not have predicted it, he did not even have to reach down very deeply to tap those mysterious resources, because the conditions were all in his favor. While he was relaxing at Camarillo, out of circulation, he was not forgotten. His Dial recordings, especially *Yardbird Suite* and *Ornithology*, were the sensations of 1946. The new audience for bop, once a coterie but now growing by leaps and bounds, could not hear them often enough. Parker's seven months of inactivity added an aura of mystery that did nothing to diminish his audience. And now The Street was open again, and the managers were looking for small bands that might be able to bring the crowds back. To some club owners, Parker looked like the man to do that.

And so, in April 1947, Charlie Parker assembled a small band. He hired Tommy Potter from the defunct Eckstine band to play bass and Duke Jordan to play piano. As soon as the Gillespie orchestra finished its engagement at the

McKinley Theater, Parker enlisted Max Roach as his drummer and Miles Davis as his trumpeter. Together, they comprised the Charlie Parker Quintet, Parker's first working unit and the only one that would ever have any semblance of permanence. The quintet immediately became the most influential small band of the day.

3

Ornithology
1947–8

Once upon a time, my time, a few years ago now ...
There was a young cafe-au-lait colored bird, who blew
sax, and his earth name was Charles Parker
    Ted Joans

The first and the best of the Charlie Parker quintets was formed in April 1947, soon after Parker returned to New York from California. Their first engagement was at the Three Deuces, the setting for many of Parker's past successes and a fitting site for his triumphal return. They were originally booked to play opposite the Lennie Tristano Trio for two weeks, but their engagement was extended beyond that, and then beyond that again, until their billing read that they were there "indefinitely." The Three Deuces thus became home base for the group for the rest of the year, with occasional tours outside New York to Philadelphia, Washington, Baltimore, Boston, Detroit, Chicago, Milwaukee, and St. Louis. When they finally left the Three Deuces and moved over to a new jazz club called the Royal Roost, it was not so much a shifting of allegiance from one club to the other as it was shifting away from 52nd Street to the new home for New York's jazz clubs, Broadway.

As jazz bands large and small go, the first Charlie Parker Quintet had a fairly stable and settled personnel for the next twenty months. The piano chair seemed to be a problem at first. Everyone in the group wanted Bud Powell as the pianist, and their first recordings, less than a month after getting together, included Powell, but everyone knew that he could not keep up the nightly pace that was required because of chronic mental problems, which were categorized in the jargon of the time as "nervous breakdowns." Powell's history of unreliability made even Parker's record look good. Later, the group used John Lewis, Gillespie's piano player in the big band, on a recording session, and Tadd Dameron and Al Haig, who played some club dates with them. One reason for the vacillation over the piano player was that Miles Davis did not think highly of the playing of the man whom Parker chose for the job, Duke Jordan. Jordan, whose given names were Irving Sydney but who was known only as Duke to musicians and fans alike, came from Brooklyn, like Max Roach, and had been around Monroe's Uptown House at the time of the first significant bop experiments and later worked on The Street in several bands. Davis may have played beside him earlier in one of Coleman Hawkins's groups, since Jordan sometimes found work with Hawkins. Jordan's own recollection is that he was recruited by Parker for the quintet in "late 1946," which cannot be right because Parker was still in Camarillo; even though he did not record with the quintet until October 1947, he was probably its original working pianist, beginning in April. Despite playing around New York for several years before this, Jordan had never met Parker until the night he was hired by him, when he was playing at the Three Deuces in a trio led by guitarist Teddy Walters. He remembers it happening like this: "I was working down at the Three Deuces with a guitarist. Charlie Parker came in one night and he said, 'Wow, listen to that guy playing,' and when the set was over he asked me would I like to play with his band. He was forming a new band and as I had heard of Charlie Parker I naturally said yes, and it turned out that it was the band with Tommy Potter, Max Roach, Miles Davis and myself."

The bassist, Tommy Potter, had been with the Billy Eckstine orchestra in California, along with Davis. Like Jordan, he too was replaced during the working life of the first quintet, when Curly Russell took over as bassist in the fall of 1948, but Potter returned soon after and eventually stayed with Parker into 1949, after the first quintet had broken up.

The working life of the first quintet is measured by the time that the other two members, Miles Davis and Max Roach, stayed with it. Both joined at the beginning and both left together as well, in December 1948. With Parker, they formed the nucleus of the quintet which is respected as one of the great small bands in the history of the music. Their importance in the band is reflected in the pay scale, although not very decisively: at the Three Deuces, Parker received $280 a week, Davis and Roach $135 a week each, and Jordan and Potter $125 a week.

Parker's hiring of Davis to fill the second horn chair has sometimes elicited some mild criticisms, usually from Parker fans who consider that the pyrotechnics of someone such as Gillespie might have complemented Parker's style better than the more subdued and cerebral style that Davis was rapidly developing. The criticisms often mention that Fats Navarro was also available at the time, on the assumption that Navarro's style was closer to Gillespie's, which may be true, and that he was technically more accomplished than Davis, which is probably false, although he was better technically than Davis showed at the time of his 1945 recordings with Parker on Savoy. What is always missing from such criticisms is any justification for the premise that Parker might have been heard advantageously beside someone who reflected Gillespie's style more closely. Parker recorded most of his finest work beside Davis, not beside Gillespie, and that was probably not accidental. The stylistic similarity of Parker and Gillespie had to be artistically stifling with any concentrated contact. "They played the same chords, they played the same chords," Davis emphasized later. "Dizzy and Bird played the same thing. They used to play lines together just like each other. You couldn't tell the difference." Parker and Davis provided a play of contrasts, with Parker making bold variations and Davis making understatements, Parker playing triplets and Davis leaving spaces, Parker gushing and Davis tentative. They were complementary rather than competitive. One of the first critics to point out the crucial importance of Davis to Parker's music was André Hodeir, who noted: "Miles Davis is the only trumpeter who could have given his music the intimate character that is one of its essential charms." Parker must have been aware of that, if only intuitively, because Ross Russell recalls that Davis was "Charlie's first and only choice on trumpet."

It is probably worth wondering why Davis and Roach and the others so willingly joined up with Parker. By the time he reached New York on Easter Monday, 7 April, he was saddled with a heroin habit again. His attempt at playing with the Gillespie band that first week gave no hope whatever for his settling into even a minimally stable lifestyle. Perhaps the members of the quintet expected no more than two weeks employment, the term of the original deal Parker made at the Three Deuces. And perhaps they had very few options in the shrinking market for jazz musicians. But both Davis and Roach could have found places in the Gillespie band, which was playing an exciting book and gaining support rapidly. Neither man seems to have entertained thoughts of joining Gillespie or anyone else once Parker made his offer, and the reason was almost certainly that Parker was the greatest musician of the day. The music they produced with him would more than make up for the mundane problems of working for him. Barry Harris, the pianist from Detroit who sat in with Parker's band during this period, sums up the feeling: "It wasn't frightening at all to play with him – just the opposite – he was the one to make you feel relaxed. That's why you take all the musicians who played with Charlie Parker, who played their best with Charlie Parker. They haven't played better since. Most of them. Miles and all of them. Because he was the leader. And he had that quality, that charisma they call it nowadays. It was a life force thing." Harris undeniably overstates the case: Davis and Roach went on to make individual marks that would eventually overshadow their playing with Parker, although Jordan, Potter, and members of later quintets such as Kinney Dorham, Red Rodney, and Walter Bishop probably never played better than they did with him. For Davis and Roach no less than the others, however, their playing was elevated by the standards of his performance; if they had not gone on to other achievements their work beside Parker would have guaranteed their mark in the history of the music. They might not have gone beyond that level if they had not had his extraordinary talent so constantly in view throughout these years.

Within a month after forming the quintet, Parker was in the recording studios making four sides for Savoy. He was still under contract to Dial, and Russell was trying to work out the details for fulfilling his contract by long distance, but contractual obligations never impressed Parker. On 8 May, a Thursday, Parker assembled his All Stars, with Bud Powell on piano, for the session:

Charlie Parker All Stars
Miles Davis, tpt; Charlie Parker, as; Bud Powell, pno; Tommy Potter, b; Max Roach, dms. New York, 8 May 1947
Donna Lee (five takes); *Chasin' the Bird* (four takes); *Cheryl* (two takes); *Buzzy* (five takes) (all on Savoy s5j 5500 and on byg 529 130 and byg 529 131; master takes on Savoy 2201; alternate takes on Savoy 1107)

For the first time, Davis contributed a composition. All these titles were credited to Parker on the original 78 rpm issues, and the mistake was perpetuated on numerous reissues, but *Donna Lee* is the work of Davis (although even its most recent issue, on Savoy 2201, lists Parker as its composer on the label, even while correcting the mistake in the album notes). *Donna Lee* provides the first hint of Davis's growing interest in composition. The information that he, not Parker, is the composer came not from either of them but from Gil Evans, who approached Parker and was directed to Davis when he wanted to pick up the lead sheet for *Donna Lee* in order to write an arrangement of it for Claude Thornhill's orchestra. The suspicion that Davis wrote this piece was felt even before Evans volunteered the information. Med Flory, the alto saxophonist who wrote arrangements based on many of Parker's most famous solos for the saxophone section known as Supersax in the 1970s, heard *Donna Lee* as part of a blindfold test in *Down Beat* and remarked, "It doesn't sound like a Parker chart. It sounds like Miles wrote it." The confusion over authorship has not been helped by the fact that *Donna Lee* is named for bassist Curly Russell's daughter whereas *Cheryl*, written by Parker, is named for Davis's daughter, but these titles were assigned, apparently quite arbitrarily, by producer Teddy Reig. *Donna Lee* features very long unison lines by the two horns, based on the chord changes of *Indiana*. Neither Parker nor Davis preserves the structure of the opening melody in his solo, and Parker's solos on all takes consist of several short phrases strung together, a distinct contrast to the unbroken phrases of the written ensemble.

A more distinctive composition from this session is *Chasin' the Bird*, based on *I Got Rhythm*, in which Parker and Davis play the melody as a canon, Davis introducing his statement one bar after Parker has begun. The effect is very distinctive, and possibly unique in the jazz of the day. The structure of the round – the "chase" of the title – is repeated for two choruses and then broken by an improvised chorus and repeated again. Parker plays the improvised break in the introduction, but in the out-chorus it is taken, with some difficulty, by Powell on the first two takes; on the successful third take, Davis rather than Powell comes in to improvise the break on the out-chorus.

The other two tunes, *Cheryl* and *Buzzy*, are relatively straightforward blues variations. The first take of *Cheryl* is a false start, and after that the band needed only one complete take to be satisfied, a notably unusual occurrence in a Parker recording session. The other blues, *Buzzy*, went to the opposite extreme and required five takes. Coming at the end of the session, the number of takes seems to have taken a toll on the players. On the fifth take, released as the master, Parker's and Davis's lack of interest is quite audible, although Powell's chorus and Potter's walking bass line are very attractive. Davis's solos especially are much better on the early takes than on the fifth.

The recording session, which gave Davis better exposure than anything he had recorded in the previous ten months with Billy Eckstine and others, supplies further proof that his distinctive style was rapidly developing. The fiery phrases of Gillespie and the liquid tone of Freddie Webster, which both seemed to be calques on his style, are largely eliminated, even though he plays an open horn through-out. Barbara Gardner comments: "By 1947 Davis had filtered from his heretofore Gillespieish playing all that was not natural to himself." In some ways, the dis-tinctiveness of his sound put him at a slight disadvantage with the fans of the day who had grown to accept the Gillespie style as the standard for trumpeters. Med Flory says, "Like a lot of guys, I didn't dig Miles at the beginning when he replaced Diz. It didn't sound like Miles had any chops ... At the time, I thought Miles ruined a lot of trumpet players who tried to imitate him instead of Diz, but I realize now that those guys were never gonna play like Diz anyway, so at least Miles gave them a shot at something to hang on to. Miles is a totally musical guy, which I didn't appreciate at the time." Indeed, the other trumpet players and then the listeners began to alter their appreciation of how a jazz trumpet should sound during Davis's tenure with the Parker quintet, to the extent that Whitney Balliett could claim, a few years later, that "nine out of ten modern trumpeters are true copies of Dizzy Gillespie or Miles Davis."

In all his recording sessions with Parker, including this one, Davis was unlucky because his own solos never determined which take of a composition would be released as the master. Very often, his best solo occurs on the earlier takes, a fact that was generally recognized only years later, with the release of collations of all the existing takes. The reviewer Ronald Atkins notes that Davis often "could not retain his form over several takes, although he often managed a confident, organically developed solo at his first or second try, for instance on *Cheryl*. On later versions his tone lost some of its resonance, and, being unable or unwilling either to play around with the same phrases or to invent new structural relationships, his solos became disjointed. One can follow this process on *Donna Lee*, *Barbados* and *Perhaps*. Because so few of his best solos were issued at the time, Davis's reputation suffered. The good ones that were put out – *Blue Bird*, *Cheryl*, *Another Hair-Do* – were all early takes." In the 1950s, when he was approaching his peak both as a soloist and as a leader, Davis began recording everything in a single take, a practice that seemed to everyone around him to be reckless; looking back at his superiority on the early takes with Parker, one sees his later method as a custom-made accommodation of his own limitations.

At the Three Deuces, the audience always included a number of musicians, and part of the attraction for them was the chance that they might be invited to get up on the stand and play with Parker on some of the later sets. Parker remained receptive to the practice of sitting in, a practice he had grown up with in Kansas City and kept up in Harlem, but Davis and Roach and perhaps some of the others were less than happy with it. Dave Lambert, the bop singer, remembers going to hear Parker and being uncertain about who his regular band members were. Lambert says, "Sometimes when I went to hear Bird, he'd be on the stand with a group of about four men, and there'd be another four or five waiting to sit in and jam. Bird was never discourteous to a musician. He never told them verbally to get off the stand; instead he would call a number – *All the Things You Are*, in the key of E – and start off *pow* in a ridiculous tempo and in a tough key, and the guys would just walk off the stand ... The musicians just petered off, and the men were separated from the boys." The practice of excluding amateurs by playing difficult pieces probably increased as Davis and Roach made their objections clearer to Parker.

A glimpse of the clique that was developing in Parker's band comes by way of Jimmy Heath, the tenor saxophonist and composer, who in his early days also played alto and other saxophones and was tagged with the nickname Little Bird. In 1947–8, Heath played with Howard McGhee in a quintet that modeled its style on Parker's quintet. They were often booked into the Three Deuces when Parker was on tour, and Heath has frequently recalled an occasion when Parker's quintet were scheduled to take over from McGhee's at the Deuces. "Milt Shaw of the Shaw agency called me and said, 'Charlie Parker's not going to make the gig tonight, and you're Little Bird, so can't you come in and play for Bird?' Now, Miles and Max were in this band. I went through the floor, because in those days it wasn't like today when young musicians don't have that much respect for the older cats – they just come right up and try to blow you out. But in those days there was some respect happening, so I just told the guy, 'Look, I can't be playing in Charlie Parker's band, in his place.' And I didn't go." Heath refers to Davis and Roach as "older cats" but they were only a few months older than he was. Such was the rank, perhaps, conferred on them by their positions in the quintet.

For Davis, another advantage of his high profile in Parker's band was the chance to lead his own recording session for Savoy, which happened during the summer. "Miles was ready," Teddy Reig says. "Give Miles credit, he had to put up with a lot working with Bird and really, like, we owed him this date because of all the shit he took." Reig also saw the date as an opportunity to display Parker's talent on the tenor saxophone, which he had played in Earl Hines's band in 1943. But the session was by no means just a Parker date under the nominal leadership of Davis. Davis took the leader's role seriously, and as a result the recording became a milestone in his personal development. He wrote and arranged four compositions for it and called two rehearsals at Nola Studios on Broadway prior to entering the recording studio. For the first rehearsal, Parker nonchalantly stopped off at a bar where musicians hung out and borrowed a tenor saxophone from a man named Warren Luckey. "I had to watch out for that tenor to make sure Bird didn't hock it," Reig recalls. Parker also borrowed an instrument on short notice for the other rehearsal and for the recording session. Apart from the two rehearsals, he did not work on his tenor technique at all. Not surprisingly, at the recording session he starts out very tentatively; on *Milestones*, the first composition recorded that afternoon, he plays very little. More surprisingly, by the end of the session he plays the bigger horn like one of its masters; he seems to gain confidence with each take played, until he finally seems to be completely in control. Parker's metamorphosis into a tenor master comes as a surprise to fans who associate him only with the alto, but it was obviously expected by Davis, who selected him for the band and made no special concessions for his unfamiliarity with the new instrument in writing the arrangements. All the members of the band Davis assembled for his debut as a leader have his personal stamp of approval: the two favored members of the quintet, Parker and Roach; John Lewis, a university-trained pianist and composer whose extended work, *Toccata for Trumpet and Orchestra*, would be played by the Gillespie band in concert later in the year; and bassist Nelson Boyd, only nineteen years old, from the Tadd Dameron band. The details are as follows:

Miles Davis All Stars
Miles Davis, tpt; Charlie Parker, ts; John Lewis, pno; Nelson Boyd, b; Max Roach, dms.
New York, 14 August 1947

Milestones (three takes); *Little Willie Leaps* (three takes); *Half Nelson* (two takes);
Sippin' at Bell's (four takes)
(all on Savoy S5J 5500 and on BYG 529 131; master takes on Savoy 2201; alternate takes
on Savoy 1107)
There is a fourth take of *Little Willie Leaps*, apparently released under the title *Wailing
Willie*, but it is not available.

There has been confusion about the composer credits on this session, especially
for *Milestones*, for which Parker has often been credited (as he is on the BYG
release listed above, though not on Savoy, beginning with the releases listed
above), but Davis is its composer. The character of the music differs strikingly
from the sessions under Parker's leadership. Generally, Davis places more emphasis upon the arranged sections, in spite of the three-minute time limit for 78 rpm
issues. The tempos, too, are more restricted, staying within the bounds of medium
tempo.
   Milestones is a mellow original, unrelated to Davis's better-known composition with the same title recorded in 1958. It is ironic that this tune should have
been incorrectly attributed to Parker for several years, because none of the compositions is more unlike his style, or, perhaps better, none is more like the style
that Davis would bring to the fore a year and a half later, the 'cool' reaction to
bebop. Its arrangement also breaks up the solo pattern typical of the recordings
under Parker's leadership, by having Parker play after Davis (and also after Lewis)
instead of at the beginning.
   The careful preparation and rehearsal prior to the recording session show especially in the few takes that were required: each composition gets only two complete takes, the extra one on *Little Willie Leaps* being a false start, and the extra
one on *Sippin' at Bell's* aborting during the opening solo by Parker. *Little Willie
Leaps*, built on the changes of *All God's Children Got Rhythm*, receives two very
different treatments in its two takes. The first is played at a slower tempo and
features a relaxed solo on the open horn by Davis. The second is faster, perhaps
because the first was considered long at just over three minutes, but probably
because the producer wanted more variety of tempo for purposes of coupling up
the tunes in the 78 rpm release. Although the faster second take was released as
the master, all the players sound a bit uncomfortable on it compared to the first.
   Half Nelson is similar to Tadd Dameron's better known *Lady Bird*, which was
still unrecorded when Davis's session took place; its title suggests that Nelson
Boyd, who was Dameron's regular bassist, had a hand in working out the composition, but Davis alone is credited as the composer. Parker constructs excellent
solos on both takes, showing technical facility on the tenor saxophone that almost
rivals his wizardry on the alto. Sonny Rollins acknowledged the influence of

Parker's tenor-playing on his own style, and it must surely be his work on *Half Nelson* that impressed Rollins. *Sippin' at Bell's*, a blues that pays homage in its title to a Harlem bar, is a faster-paced tune notable for the controlled, understated solos by both Davis and Lewis. Their similarity in approaching their solos on this tune shows clearly why Davis advocated Lewis's piano style during this period.

The critical reactions to this debut for Davis as a leader have, with the advantage of hindsight, given them a central place in charting his development. As usual, critic Martin Williams's account is very incisive and well worth quoting at length. "The atmosphere of these performances is more relaxed, the themes are more fluent and more legato, and, although Davis had clearly learned from Parker and Dizzy Gillespie, he seemed to be reaching back to the easy, introverted phrasing of Lester Young," Williams wrote. "Davis's themes ... have a built-in harmonic complexity. *Sippin' at Bell's*, for example, is a twelve-bar blues, but it is so written that the soloist has to find his way through an obstacle course of some eighteen assigned chord changes in a single chorus. And the shifting structure of *Little Willie Leaps* ... almost throws so able a man as John Lewis. There is an effective tension on these recordings between the surface lyricism of Miles Davis's solo melodic lines and the complexity of their underlying harmonic outline. The wonder of it is that a man who plays with such apparent simplicity as Miles Davis would have wanted such technical challenges. But he did, and he learned a great deal from the experience. And once he had learned it, he showed an artist's wisdom in forgetting, but still knowing, what he had learned." This recording session marks the first time that Davis was not dwarfed by the mastery of Parker beside him: "In these fresh surroundings, at medium tempos over complex and fast-changing chords, Davis' melodic gift bloomed," J.R. Taylor noted. "For once, he matched Parker's work instead of complementing it."

When the recordings were released, the critical perception of Davis's work by both reviewers and fans was still somewhat jaded by the fact that Davis's style was different from the faster, tougher style of Gillespie and of his disciples Navarro and Dorham. However, the tide was changing, especially as Davis gained control of the elements of his style, which removed it even further from Gillespie's. He was finding adherents among other trumpet players and fans wherever he was heard and, in the Parker quintet, he was heard widely. The attraction toward Davis's style was first felt only by insiders but it soon became public knowledge. The first significant notice of it was given by Ross Russell in an article for the *Record Changer* the following year, 1948. Russell's comments seem a remarkable prognostication. "There is a mounting body of evidence," he wrote, "that Davis is leading the way or even founding the next school of trumpet playing. Nothing could be further from the Eldridge-Gillespie school than the Miles Davis trumpet. He plays a 'soft' horn. He has consistently been overlooked by critics because he lacks the virtuosity of his contemporaries. Davis seldom uses the upper register, preferring to play almost wholly 'within the staff.' His tone is broad and warm. Davis's sound, and his sense of chord changes and rhythm suspensions, are very close to the Charlie Parker alto style – he has played much with Parker in the past three years. As an idea man and influence, Miles Davis has just come into his full powers. If his grasp of the instrument still leaves something to be desired, he has shown considerable improvement ... since his first record (Billie's Bounce), and is certainly the trumpet to watch."

Apart from the music they played, Charlie Parker and the members of his first quintet also developed a particular approach to the presentation of their music. Unlike Gillespie, who sometimes wore funny hats and danced on the bandstand while keeping up a constant patter with his audience, the Parker quintet had no interest whatever in the compromises of show business. Their presentations revolved around inside jokes and private gestures – what Frank Sanderford called 'birding' the outsiders. Parker led the assault on conventional stage manners, and from him it soon spread outward until it became one of the hallmarks of the bebop revolution. "It was the bebop tradition to freeze out strangers," Coleridge Goode recalls. "It was their tradition. I think it stemmed from hearing that Parker would turn his back [on the audience]. So it was wear shades and turn your back and shut yourself off from the people. And just play." Parker's stage manner became a set routine, and it has been described countless times, with approbation or resentment, depending upon the disposition of the describer. But the routine was the same. Ross Russell says, "Charlie worked from a set of stock remarks considered hilarious by the cognoscenti, but less well understood by the public and sometimes resented by them, not to mention night club owners. These were delivered in a George Arliss voice and couched in stilted, stiff-collar phrases. As the set opened, the crowd would be told: 'Ladies and gentlement, the management of —— Club has gone to enormous expense to bring you the Charlie Parker Quintet.' The weighting of the word made the management sound like pikers ... When enthusiastic applause followed a good performance he would tell the audience, 'Thank you, ladies and gentlemen, ordinary applause will suffice.' The groundwork for later patronization of the public, to be made a fine art by Miles Davis, was being laid." Parker was, in spite of his stage manner, an extrovert; Davis, an introvert, would eventually cut off all communication with the audience beyond the playing of his music and in doing so would arouse such controversy that it sometimes threatened to distract all attention from what he was playing.

Early in the life of the quintet, August Blume, an avid fan, witnessed a unique entrance staged by Parker. "I was struck by the presentation at the Apollo Theater in 1947. There was a big banner proclaiming Buddy Johnson and his

Band, and, in little letters, Charlie Parker's Quintet. The Apollo Theater in Harlem really gave you your money's worth. I saw two African movies, with people running around in headdresses, and then came the live show. On a rolling stage, the resplendent Buddy Johnson Band emerged. When they finished, the curtain came down, and you could hear the clatter and noise of backstage changing. I was eagerly awaiting Bird and his group. The curtain rose, but the stage was bare. Then the guys came out pushing their instruments before them like prop men. Duke Jordan rolling out the piano, Max Roach with his drums on a little platform on wheels, Tommy Potter dragging his bass, Miles Davis shuffling out, and then Bird with his horn. Yard simply walked over to the microphone, announced the number, tapped his foot three times, and detonated a musical powder keg." The grand entrance of the Buddy Johnson Band, needless to say, was erased from memory by the time the quintet played their first notes.

If the members of the quintet were self-contained in their stage manner, they were equally wrapped up in the music they made. The legend persists that they once played on while a fire smoldered in the club where they were working. "The customers stumbled out through the smoke-filled vestibule as firemen lugged their hoses in through the doorways," Alun Morgan claims. "Apparently unaware of the mass exodus Parker, Davis, Jordan, Tommy Potter and Max Roach continued their way through a number which had started before the fire warning."

While 52nd Street and Harlem were the main venues for presenting the music, Brooklyn became a new scene for hanging out. Max Roach and Duke Jordan had been raised there, and several younger musicians were emerging from there and would soon be heard outside their borough. One of these was Randy Weston, who was only a few months younger than Davis but took a few years to decide that he wanted to play piano professionally. In the meantime, he manned a luncheonette called Frank's, one of four owned by his father in Brooklyn, and he specialized in catering to the boppers after hours. "We had the hippest juke box anywhere in New York," he says. "Cats would finish a gig in Manhattan and take the subway down for a cup of coffee and a hamburger. We had Stravinsky and Bird on that juke box, man, and the conversation was heavy every night." Among the regulars that Weston recalls were Davis and Roach, Dizzy Gillespie, Leo Parker, and Bud Powell.

In 1947, Davis finally recorded with his old mentor, Coleman Hawkins. The result, for listeners interested in the development of Davis, was disappointing, because he and the other young musicians in Hawkins's pick-up band are relegated to the background, playing chords behind Hawkins's rich tenor in much the same way as they might have for a featured vocalist. The music has none of the easy egalitarianism that Davis enjoyed playing beside Parker, who might have taken a star turn just as Hawkins does here, but never did. The details are as follows:

Coleman Hawkins All Stars
Miles Davis, tpt; Kai Winding, tbn; probably Howard Johnson, as; Coleman Hawkins, ts;
Hank Jones, pno; probably Tommy Potter or Curly Russell, b; probably Max Roach,
dms. New York, June–November 1947
Bean-A-Re-Bop; Phantomesque; The Way You Look Tonight; Isn't It Romantic
(all on Queen-disc Q-038)
The recording company was a small independent label, Aladdin.

All the titles are carefully arranged. *Phantomesque*, an original ballad by Hawkins, features Ellingtonian voicings behind Hawkins's lead, and the other two
ballads, *The Way You Look Tonight* and *Isn't It Romantic*, have simpler and
more subdued contributions from the band. On *Bean-A-Re-Bop*, a jump tune
credited to Hawkins and his piano player Hank Jones, Hawkins joins the ensemble after a fashion but his huge sound dominates it almost as if he were playing
the lead. Only on this title do Davis and Winding get heard, splitting a chorus
between them after Hawkins's solo chorus. Perhaps the lack of solo space was a
blessing, since Winding comes off laborious and struggling in his sixteen bars, and
Davis is hardly any better in his. The session was thus completely dominated by
its leader, as were so many others in his long and prolific career.

By the fall of 1947, Ross Russell had worked out the details for getting Parker
to fulfill his contract with Dial. Russell moved to New York and carefully laid out
the scheme for recording sessions that would be the apex of Parker's career. All
the sessions were held at the WOR Studios, with the technical details in the hands
of Doug Hawkins. "The working conditions over there were always very good,"
Russell says. "Hawkins sometimes seemed as important as another musician
because he was so fine technically. He was a Juilliard graduate, and he also had a
great deal of patience and understanding of what jazz musicians are trying to do."
Instead of bringing in outsiders for the recording sessions, such as Bud Powell on
the earlier Savoy session and John Lewis and Nelson Boyd on Davis's Savoy session, Russell insisted on recording the regular quintet, which made an important
difference. "The most important thing about the records we made in New York, I
think, is that they were made by a working band, Bird's own band, men that he
had selected by choice, and a rhythm section that would be hard to surpass even
today," Russell says. "There was almost complete one-mindedness among the
musicians, so that everything they played had a lot of cohesion and was very
subtle."

Russell organized three sessions, all to take place within the relatively short
span of about eight weeks. The first, on a Tuesday evening in October, began
ominously. Parker showed up early, appearing nervous and irritable, and demanded
$50 from Russell. As soon as Russell gave it to him, he turned it over to a man
who had been watching in the background and went into the washroom to pre-

pare the heroin he had bought. But by the time the rest of the quintet arrived he was settled and ready to get started. The session turned out to be a model of efficiency, requiring only fifteen takes over a four-hour span to complete six titles (instead of the usual four) – four originals by Parker and two ballads:

Charlie Parker Quintet
Miles Davis, tpt; Charlie Parker, as; Duke Jordan, pno; Tommy Potter, b; Max Roach, dms. New York, 28 October 1947
Dexterity (two takes); *Bongo Bop* (two takes); *Dewey Square* (three takes); *The Hymn* (two takes); *Bird of Paradise* (three takes); *Embraceable You* (two takes)
(all on Spotlite 104)
A third take of *Dexterity* was recorded at this ession, but has since been lost. In numer-
ᴗ ᴊs issues and reissues, these sides have had various titles: take 1 of *Bongo Bop*: *Charlie's Blues*; take 1 of *Dewey Square*: both *Prezology* and *Air Conditioning*; both takes of *The Hymn* have appeared as *Superman*, and take 1 of *Bird of Paradise* as *All the Things You Are*.

Among the originals, *The Hymn* ranks as one of the finest examples of Davis's playing as well as being a superlative example of Parker's genius. Parker assigns himself the unenviable task of opening the tune directly with his solo, at a fast tempo, before he and Davis state the theme at half-tempo. In the ensemble passages and during most of Davis's solo, the piano lays out, a device that lightened the group sound and that Davis frequently employed with his own bands during the next two decades. *Bird of Paradise* is played first as a straightforward version of *All the Things You Are*, in the arrangement recorded at the Finale Club in Los Angeles. On the second and third takes, it is transformed into an original melody based on the chord changes of *All the Things You Are*, with only oblique hints of the original melody. Because of the transformation, of course, Parker could take composer credit, and royalties, for *Bird of Paradise*. One might wonder, however, why the same process did not happen on *Embraceable You*. This slow ballad, one of Parker's finest improvisations on a ballad, is played with such invention that the original melody is heard only in fragments, apart from the eight bars played as a coda by Davis and Parker.

The title *Dexterity* refers to Dexter Gordon, the Los Angeles tenor saxophonist whom Parker and Davis had got to know during their stint in California the year before. He had arrived in New York earlier in 1947 and was active in the clubs of 52nd Street. During a period of inactivity for the Parker quintet, both Parker and Davis worked as sidemen with Gordon. "I worked with Bird at a place called the Spotlite with my sextet, with Miles and Bird, Stan Levey, Bud Powell, Curly Russell and Baby Laurence," Gordon recalls. "Laurence was the show but he was really part of the band ... He danced bebop. The way those cats danced, man, was just like a drummer. He was doing everything that the other cats were doing and maybe more. Blowing eights, fours and trading off. He just answered to the music. There were several cats at that level but he was the boss. Baby Laurence. Fantastic." Parker probably based the melody of *Dexterity* on a theme played by Gordon at that time.

The title *Dewey Square* refers to the area on 117th Street where Parker lived in a hotel after returning from California. He lived there for about a year, with Doris Sydnor, who devoted herself to nursing him and generally trying to coax him into better health. She seems to have received little reward for her efforts. Budd Johnson recalls a visit to Parker's apartment: "One day Bud [Powell] and Miles ran into me and told me that Bird was laying up at the Dewey Square hotel with pneumonia. We all went up to visit him, the boys first bringing the patient a fifth of Seagrams. When we got there, he was lying with water running off his face like a faucet. He had just polished off a bottle of wine with some person, and his wife Doris was frantic with worry. Our visit produced a burst of energy in him, and he arose and embraced us including the bottle. When his wife told him to get into bed, he put her out of the room."

The second New York recording session for Dial, just one week after the first, on Tuesday 4 November, again produced excellent results. Parker was late, but efficient when he arrived. He again recorded six compositions and took only a little more than three hours. Three of the tunes were standard ballads, requiring no elaborate ensembles or difficult tempos. The details are as follows:

Charlie Parker Quintet
Miles Davis, tpt; Charlie Parker, as; Duke Jordan, pno; Tommy Potter, b; Max Roach, dms. New York, 4 November 1947
Bird Feathers (one take); *Klakt-oveeseds-tene* (two takes); *Scrapple from the Apple* (two takes); *My Old Flame* (one take); *Out of Nowhere* (three takes); *Don't Blame Me* (one take)
(all on Spotlite 105; master takes of the last four titles are on Archives of Jazz AJ 503)
Thirteen takes were recorded; missing are the first two of *Bird Feathers* and the first of *Scrapple from the Apple*. *Bird Feathers* has also been released under the title *Scnourphology*, and the first take of *Out of Nowhere* as *Nowhere*.

The title *Klakt-oveeseds-tene* (given here in Parker's spelling, as it is listed on the Spotlite release) is a set of nonsense syllables, written out for Russell without comment when he requested a title. The composition is an ingenious march cadence on which Davis, muted, plays a line over Parker's low harmony. The ensemble resembles Dexter Gordon's *The Chase*, a well-known tenor saxophone duel between Gordon and Wardell Gray recorded earlier by Dial in Los Angeles. The fact that no one is certain whether Parker or Gordon and perhaps Gray originated the line shows the scant attention that composition was given during this period; the tenormen know that they started playing *The Chase* while Parker was hanging around Central Avenue the year before, and all three of them may have had a hand in developing the theme that eventually became well known by two different titles.

The three ballads are structured the same way. Parker opens, playing the melody with embellishments and then improvising two choruses before Davis is heard at all; Davis then plays a chorus and restates the melody, with Parker in the background, to end it. *My Old Flame* and *Don't Blame Me* were completed in one take each, and *Out of Nowhere* would have been too, except that Jordan was alloted a chorus between Parker and Davis on the first take and the playing time ran to almost four minutes. The second take eliminated Jordan's chorus altogether but somehow managed to cut only eleven seconds off the recording time, and it was necessary to play it again with a shorter allotment of space for Davis. Parker plays superbly on all three takes, and astonishingly distinctively, but for all the other players, the overlong first take is probably the best.

By the second half of 1947, the success of the Gillespie orchestra and the Parker quintet was being widely felt and was spilling over onto musicians who had been obscure figures in the original movement and to younger players coming up. One result of the success was an increase in opportunities to play, especially in one-night, all-star settings. Jackie McLean, fifteen years old and a mere beginner on the alto saxophone that would soon put him on the bandstand, remembers one all-star concert at Lincoln Square, a large ballroom that occupied the site where New York's Lincoln Center sits now. McLean had raised the $1.50 admission fee but was denied entry because he was under age and had to persuade Dexter Gordon to take him in through the stage door. "I'll tell you who was on the bill that day," McLean says. "Art Blakey, Kenny Clarke, Max Roach, Ben Webster, Dexter Gordon, Sonny Stitt, Red Rodney, Charlie Parker and Miles Davis. But Miles didn't even play with Bird on that set. Bird was playing with Ben Webster and Dexter Gordon and Freddie Webster on trumpet. Fats Navarro was playing with Sonny Stitt. Miles was playing with Bud. All this on one day." It was up to the audience to convert the dance hall into a concert hall, McLean recalls. "You could bring up folding chairs – they had rows of folding chairs close to the bandstand and near the back, away in the back, there was an open area to pass around in. People could dance if they wanted to, but most people used to take their folding chairs and move them up near the front to be near the music. That's what they were there for, not dancing." The presence of Freddie Webster at this concert must mark one of his final appearances in New York. He died in Chicago before the year ended.

Soon after the November recording session, the Charlie Parker Quintet traveled to Detroit for an engagement at a club called El Sino. The engagement, which resulted in a cancellation, illustrates the kinds of situations that seemed to be part of the lives of Parker and his men and also, incidentally, explains why Parker would show up for the next Dial recording session, in December, with a new and superior saxophone to play. As often happened when Parker had to move away from his New York contacts, he had some problems in Detroit in making the connections for his heroin supply. He showed up at the club one night hardly able to play and after a noisy argument with the management stomped out of the club. Back in his hotel room, in a fit of rage, he threw his saxophone onto the street below, smashing it. When these incidents were reported to Billy Shaw, he threatened to abandon Parker for good but, as he had done before and would do again, he eventually gave in to Parker's pleading and gave him one more chance, buying him a new Selmer saxophone into the bargain.

Back in New York, the final Dial session took place in the same studio, WOR, with Doug Hawkins again at the controls. On the evening of Wednesday 17 December, when the recording was scheduled, Ross Russell was suffering from influenza. However, he had attended the rehearsals leading up to the recordings, which were necessitated by the addition of trombonist J.J. Johnson to the regular quintet. Including Johnson had been Russell's idea: "I was always interested in the trombone, and I thought that J.J. Johnson was just the end. I liked the idea of getting him into a date, and Bird thought it was a pretty good idea." This time Parker set up a real challenge for the band, calling for five originals and only one ballad, but the band responded by completing the session under the union limit of three hours:

Charlie Parker Sextet
Miles Davis, tpt; J.J. Johnson, tbn; Charlie Parker, as; Duke Jordan, pno; Tommy Potter, b; Max Roach, dms. New York, 17 December 1947
Drifting on a Reed (three takes); *Quasimado* (two takes); *Charlie's Wig* (three takes); *Bongo Beep* (two takes); *Crazeology* (three takes); *How Deep Is the Ocean* (two takes) (all on Spotlite 106)
Several takes, probably amounting to little more than false starts, have been lost, including the first and third takes of *Drifting on a Reed* and *Charlie's Wig* and the first take of *Bongo Beep*. Alternative titles abound: *Drifting on a Reed* was introduced by Parker in his club dates as *Big Foot* and is probably at least as well known by that title; its first take was released as *Giant Swing*, and the second take as *Air Conditioning*; the second take

of *Quasimado* (of which all takes have sometimes been referred to as *Quasimodo*) was released as *Trade Winds*; and *Bongo Beep* has had a rough history, being mistakenly issued as *Bird Feathers* and as *Dexterity* on different occasions.

For some reason, the music recorded at this session is not quite up to the consummate standards of the two previous Dial sessions. Although the addition of the trombone gives the ensemble passages of *Quasimado* a little extra awkwardness, this minor ballad, based on *Embraceable You*, would not have been significantly more attractive played by the quintet alone. Elsewhere, it is impossible to find fault with J.J. Johnson, who fits in well and executes his difficult parts on such fast numbers as *Charlie's Wig* and *Bongo Beep* with characteristic ease. Davis's playing on the earliest available take of *Drifting on a Reed* seems nervous, as he plays many more notes than is usual for him and threatens to slip into the style of Gillespie again, which he otherwise seems to have put behind him. More than anything specific, the whole session is marked by a lack of spirit. Only *Crazeology*, which is a tune usually known as *Little Benny* after its composer, Benny Harris, features risk-taking in the solos, but solo space is alloted to all six players and no one gets much room to move.

Only a week before Christmas, the quintet left New York again for Detroit, to fulfill the broken contract at El Sino. This time Parker made it through the engagement without incident. Among the musicians who sat in with the quintet in Detroit was Betty Carter, the bop singer who left Detroit soon after this with Lionel Hampton's orchestra. Carter, in what is definitely a minority opinion from this time, remembers Davis still struggling with his technique. "I sat in with him in Detroit before he had even learned to play the trumpet," she says, "when his notes were really tit for tat. I had to have the experience of sitting in with Charlie Parker and those guys. When they came to town, I'd be the first one there standing in line – a real fan, but a musician too. Because music was growing on me – it was magnetizing me." She was not the only one in Detroit, which was then showing the first signs of becoming a flourishing jazz community. Aspiring young musicians always turned out there for performances by the Parker quintet, making a good audience and a convivial atmosphere.

While in Detroit, Parker was approached quietly by Teddy Reig to make another recording for Savoy. Parker had been told in no uncertain terms by Billy Shaw that once his obligation to Dial was complete he was to leave the independent labels in favor of a contract with one of the giants of the recording industry. However, Parker and everyone else knew by now that the American Federation of Musicians, in a show of strength under the tough leadership of James D. Petrillo, was calling for a recording ban starting on the last day of 1947, just a little more than a week away. For Parker and the others, the opportunity for quick cash from recording dates looked unlikely in the months to come, and they readily agreed to Reig's offer. The Savoy session, with the regular quintet, took place on the Sunday before Christmas:

Charlie Parker Quintet
Miles Davis, tpt; Charlie Parker, as; Duke Jordan, pno; Tommy Potter, b; Max Roach, dms. Detroit, 21 December 1947
Another Hair-Do (four takes); *Blue Bird* (three takes); *Klaunstance* (one take); *Bird Gets the Worm* (three takes)
(all on Savoy S5J 5500; master takes on Savoy 2201; alternate takes of *Blue Bird* and *Bird Gets the Worm* on Savoy 1107)

The session has all the marks of a quickie production. The arranged material is at an absolute minimum: *Another Hair-Do* opens and closes with a simple riff; *Blue Bird* has twelve bars of a standard blues played by Davis at the opening; and both *Klaunstance* and *Bird Gets the Worm* open with very fast improvisations by Parker and have no themes at all. The whole affair is just a blowing session and probably took no more than two hours to complete. Duke Jordan is saddled with a piano badly in need of tuning. Yet in spite of all the adversities, the music recorded is always interesting. A good example is provided by Duke Jordan's solo on the final take of *Bird Gets the Worm*, in which he avoids exposing the untuned piano any more than is necessary by halving the time of this recklessly fast piece, thus playing relatively few notes but still making a solid contribution that is one of the highlights of the day's work. The whole session consists of solos loosely strung together, but they are generally excellent.

When the engagement at El Sino ended, Parker left for California, where he joined Norman Granz's Jazz at the Philharmonic (JATP) for a concert tour of the southwest. The other members of the quintet went their separate ways for the Christmas break, with Davis probably heading to Chicago. They reassembled in New York early in the new year to resume their booking at the Three Deuces.

Charlie Parker returned from his JATP tour full of the confidence that came with star billing in such an assemblage of jazz players. On tour he had even slipped off to Mexico and married Doris Sydnor, missing a concert unannounced to do so and arousing the ire of Norman Granz as a result. The January issue of *Metronome* magazine named him the best alto saxophonist of the year, his first win ever in the periodicals. Both his JATP billing and his *Metronome* award drew more attention to the quintet, by now already well established as a working unit and as a drawing card in the clubs. But in spite of all these favorable portents, a cloud seemed to hang over Parker, and it had nothing whatever to do with the recording ban, which would last eleven months. Instead of reaching out to grasp the success that was now so close at hand, Parker seemed compelled to avoid it altogether, or, perhaps more accurately, he seemed predisposed to sit back and wait for success to envelop him rather than to make any effort at grasping it. The more adulation he felt, the more disdain he showed. The more attention he drew, the more private he became. To some extent, his unorthodox response worked wonders for him, building his legend among the hipsters who worshipped him from the front-row seats, but it took its toll among those who were closer to him, his sidemen and managers, who had to contend with a lot more than his music if they hoped to stay in contact with him.

For one thing, the exposure to narcotics was constant. Duke Jordan says, "Wherever we would be, the pushers were with us. The grapevine, as far as drugs is concerned, is very quick, very swift, and as soon as Bird hit town, someone would contact him. 'I know where something really good is,' they would say, sometimes calling the hotel at five or six in the morning, and Bird would go with them." When he returned, sometimes as much as twelve hours later, he was often incapable of playing.

During an engagement at the Argyle Show Bar in Chicago, the problems seemed to be endless. Sadik Hakim, scheduled to play with Lester Young in Chicago the next week, traveled there early "to hear Bird and Miles." One evening he accompanied Parker to the club and watched as he received an ominous reminder that he had an overdue debt to his heroin connection. "Bird came in, early for once – no one else in his band was there," Hakim recalls. "He had left his horn at the club. Now Bird had very good connections in Chicago, but this time he apparently forgot to pay them. He opened his horn case to find all the keys torn off or broken."

Frank Sanderford heard Parker in person for the first time during this engagement at the Argyle, an expensive club, and remembers it vividly. His recollection provides an insight into the closed circle that the quintet maintained. "The place was packed but somehow I managed to get a seat at the bar, directly facing the band," Sanderford recalls. "Bird was tired, only occasionally playing a short solo. A few times it seemed to me he might fall over backwards. The fellows with him would shoot side glances his way, look quickly at one another with guilt not quite being covered by hastily formed masks of derision. It was difficult to tell if they were concerned or fearful and, if so, for themselves or their leader." Somehow, Parker caught Sanderford's eye and signaled to him to make his way to the musicians' room at the end of the set. Sanderford continues, "I managed to squeeze through the crowd to a small, dark room where the musicians lounged. As I came in, they looked surlily at me. It was hot, the musicians whispered among themselves, I heard snickers." What Parker wanted him for, it turned out, was to run out and pick up a hamburger for him. Parker's request was condescending and brought sneers from the others, but Sanderford ran the errand. When he returned with the hamburger, the musicians had hardly changed their expressions. The scene was finally disrupted by the management. "Suddenly, the manager appeared and demanded in querulous tones for their return to the stand," Sanderford says. "Slowly, resentfully, they went out."

But being "tired" and unsteady on his feet was only part of Parker's Argyle adventure. Duke Jordan picks up the story: "Bird came in one night, late and drunk. He couldn't play. He was too juiced. So the quartet, me, Max, Miles and Tommy finished out the evening. The club owner figured that he could get away without paying the band. Bird went up to the union to see if he could get money for the sidemen at least. He was in the office of the colored president of the local. A deal must have been cooked up between the club owner and this official, because the man suddenly whipped out a gun and said to Bird, 'Get the hell out of here or I'll shoot you up your ass.' Charlie left, saying, 'I'll be back.' He was about to make good his promise when I stopped him downstairs from the guy's office and told him not to be foolish, that the man would not hesitate to use his gun. He took my advice. We didn't get any money, but our leader was alive." Eventually Parker got his revenge, after a fashion. In an incident that Ross Russell calls "the jazz scandal of 1948," one night at the Argyle Parker set down his saxophone and strode off the bandstand, with all eyes in the lounge on him, and into the lobby, where he entered a telephone booth and proceeded to urinate at great volume and length – "as from a stallion," in Russell's phrase. The pool of urine flowed out of the booth and onto the carpet, and then Parker emerged, smiling broadly as he buttoned up. It is interesting to think that "the jazz scandal of 1948" should not be the withholding of wages from Parker's sidemen by the manager of the Argyle, and not the collusion and armed threat of a union official, but a sophomore prank by Parker that failed to touch the core of any issue – even if it did afford some comic relief.

As winter turned to spring, jazz musicians were bothered increasingly by two problems. One was, of course, the recording ban, which continued with no sign of a let-up. For jazz, a performer's medium rather than a composer's, the recording ban had especially damaging implications. The other problem was the general decline of 52nd Street as a venue for jazz. The Street had never recovered from the shutdown of November 1946. The real offences that brought it about – the murphy men, the prostitution, the mugging of drunks, the narcotics peddling – continued, and the police were applying pressure on the managers for both real and imagined infractions, adding to the managers' woes and probably to their under-the-counter payments as well. It was a bleak time, and virtually all the jazz that was played at the time evaporated as it bounced off the smoke-stained walls of a few clubs. The Charlie Parker Quintet fared a little better than most other bands. In New York it played regularly in the few clubs that still booked jazz, especially the Onyx and, of course, the Three Deuces. Moreover, some home-made tapes of the quintet's performances at both clubs survived the buffeting of the years – although just barely – and provide a glimpse of what it was playing in live performances:

Charlie Parker Quintet
Miles Davis, tpt; Charlie Parker, as; Duke Jordan, pno; Tommy Potter, b; Max Roach, dms. Probably the Onyx Club, New York, ca spring 1948
Theme [52nd Street Theme]; *Shaw Nuff*; *Out of Nowhere*; *Hot House*; *This Time the Dream's On Me*; *A Night in Tunisia*; *My Old Flame*; *52nd Street Theme*; *The Way You Look Tonight*; *Out of Nowhere*; *Chasin' the Bird*; *This Time the Dream's On Me*; *Dizzy Atmosphere*; *How High the Moon*; *Theme* [52nd Street Theme]
(all on Prestige PR 24009)

Same personnel, plus Kenny Hagood, vcl (on *All the Things You Are*). Three Deuces, New York, ca March 1948
52nd Street Theme; *Dizzy Atmosphere*; *My Old Flame*; *All the Things You Are*; *Half Nelson*; *52nd Street Theme*; *52nd Street Theme*; *Big Foot* [Drifting on a Reed]
(all on Spotlite SPJ 141 [1979])

These recordings are not from complete sets or probably even from the same evenings, but are a conglomeration of pieces played by the quintet at various times. They were made from radio broadcasts using a hand-held microphone with a wire recorder, and the sound is barely listenable. The men who made the tapes, Bob Guy and Jimmy Knepper (who later played trombone with Charles Mingus's band and others), were Parker fanatics who edited the transcriptions by shutting off the machine during the performances whenever Parker was not playing. No title is a complete performance. But in spite of the heavy editing and the terrible sound reproduction, the tapes fill a gap in the material from 1948.

Judging from the titles recorded, the nightly repertoire of the quintet includes surprisingly few of the compositions recorded for Dial and Savoy the previous year. Only *Chasin' the Bird*, *Drifting on a Reed*, Davis's *Half Nelson*, and the ballads *Out of Nowhere* and *My Old Flame* show up. Where, one wonders, are *The Hymn*, *Donna Lee*, *Milestones*, *Bongo Bop*, *Scrapple from the Apple*, and all the others? Instead of playing the original works of the working quintet, Parker tends to call for the best works of a short-lived earlier quintet, the one that he and Dizzy Gillespie had fronted on 52nd Street in 1945: *Shaw Nuff*, *Dizzy Atmosphere*, and *A Night in Tunisia*, all by Gillespie, *Hot House* by Tadd Dameron, and the bop chestnut *How High the Moon*. Davis is heard best on *The Way You*

Look Tonight, *Dizzy Atmosphere*, and *How High the Moon*, because he states the theme and trades fours with Parker and sometimes Roach, contributions that the men running the recording machine could not eradicate. On all the tunes, the editors cut him off abruptly less than a bar into his solo.

How recordings such as these came to exist belongs to ornithology. The butchery of the tapes resulted from devotion so ardent that it blinded Guy and Knepper to the talents of all other musicians. In 1981, Knepper just shook his head at the recollection: "When Bird came along, the musicians in my circle were enchanted by him. The effect was that we couldn't listen to anybody else. People that played with Bird – even Diz – sounded silly. They sounded like they were children, playing the game that he was master of. Whoever was on those early records with him would sound childish. That kind of stunted my diversification, my catholic tastes. It was only years later that I could appreciate what Diz and others did."

Knepper and Guy were only two of several amateur recordists of Parker's music. Unfortunately, most of the others lost themselves and their caches of wire recordings in the next decade. These were the hipsters who worshipped Parker. Many of them were, like him, heroin addicts, and most of them gloried in his antics – the George Arliss announcements, the nodding onstage, the Argyle Club urination – almost as much as they admired his genius. Chief among the ornithologists was Dean Benedetti, who aspired to be a jazz alto saxophonist until the first time he heard Parker play; according to legend, he immediately discarded his own saxophone and thereafter followed Parker wherever he went or preceded him wherever he was going and set up his wire recorder on the spot. He recorded Parker from the washroom at Billy Berg's, the basement at the Onyx, and anywhere else he could find an electrical outlet where Parker was playing. Like Guy and Knepper, who probably learned from him, he is said to have recorded only Parker, not his sidemen. He died, again according to the legend, in mysterious circumstances in Sicily in the late 1950s. Intensive searches for his trunkful of Parker solos have always come up empty.

The phenomenon of the Parker fanatic has no precursor or successor in the history of jazz, and it becomes more difficult to grasp as it recedes in time. Bob Dorough was a music student in New York when it was happening, and, happily, is an articulate lyricist as well as a singer and piano player. He captures something of the spirit of the time in his notes for the album reissuing his vocal version of *Yardbird Suite* (Bethlehem BCP-6023). "Oh, it was *crazy* how we dug Bird," he says. "We'd give up pork chops for beans to have cab fare and admission to Birdland (cheep). We'd follow him whenever we could, session-gig-or-concert. And you'd give up a night's work when word came 'round that Bird was playing at the William Henry – a jam session with the cats, all the Bird-lovin', ordinary, jazz-blowin' cats. I mean, even tho' we thought of Bird as a sort of god, it seems he was occasionally induced to visit and blow with lesser mortals ... We'd all crowd into this basement pad at 136th and Broadway, bringing provisions and contributions, wine, pot, snacks, just to hear and be there – and, sometimes, *you'd get to play two or three tunes with Bird!* Wow! DONNA LEE! CONFIRMATION! HALF-NELSON! And it was *taped*. Even if you weren't there that night you could listen over and over again. Not content to buy his every recorded solo we collected tapes and exchanged them – and *listened* to them. We loved every note he played. We loved the squeaks of his reed. We loved other people too, especially the giants and the survivors, Diz, Miles, Thelonious – but we really dug Bird – it was like idolatry – it was crazy. I tried to keep my head up; make my 8:00 o'clocks, do my homework, make a little money, experience some of the vast musical scene (non-jazz) going on in New York City, etc. But my cold-water flat family gang was eggin' me on and we were Bird-happy, Bird-struck, and Bird-bent – and mostly tryin' to learn to blow a little. Small wonder that, sitting in a musicology class one day at Columbia University, I suddenly realized that the musicologists were out *there*, man, following Bird around with the Wollensack, recording every note he played – *that* was musicology-in-the-field; collecting the work of a genius who would soon sing his last song. A few days later I quit school." Dorough went on to work as a singer-pianist in Europe and then back home, setting the kind of low-key personal standards that would lead Miles Davis, improbable though it may sound, to commission a song from him in 1962. He is one of the survivors himself, like Jimmy Knepper but unlike most of their "Bird-happy, Bird-struck and Bird-bent" cohorts and, of course, unlike Bird himself.

At the same time that Parker's coterie was gathering, an epidemic of narcotics addiction began to spread among the jazz musicians. Narcotics have long been part of the night-life subculture, endemic to pimps and prostitutes, petty and grand thieves, and the fringe of outsiders who make up the night people. Jazz musicians have been members of that subculture ever since their music was installed as a diversion in the bordellos of New Orleans, and they were charter members by the time jazz spread to the American heartland as an entertainment in Prohibition speakeasies. Most jazz musicians were exposed to drugs, many of them experimented with them, and some became hard users as far back as the 1930s, including Charlie Parker. Now, in the late 1940s, as bebop was elevating jazz to the status of concert music instead of pop entertainment or dance music, addiction became more widespread. Paradoxically, one cause of the spread was the new status of jazz, which gave the musicians rank as artists instead of mere entertainers in the eyes of their peers. Parker was certainly influential, being lauded as a genius and emulated as an addict. Howard McGhee, the trumpeter who was close to Parker in California, describes the new exposure of musicians such as himself in this way: "The era that we came up in, with Dizzy and Miles and all those cats, everybody was trying to be tight with us because they liked us and dug what we were doing. They said, like, 'McGhee's my friend,' but the cat might not even realize that he was more of an enemy by turning me on. Nowadays I know, because I'm a little different than I was then, but the average cat figures that he's doing you a favor by making stuff available. Every day he's there and you just get deeper and deeper until pretty soon he's gone and you're asking where *he*'s at. They leave you out there on a limb."

The Street played a role in the narcotics trade as well. Tony Scott, who had gone there to sit in as a serviceman throughout the war, was back there as a working musician after his discharge, and he watched the decline. "The Street started to slow down after the war ended, after V-J Day," he says. "But while everybody was coming back, for another year anyway, things were pretty flush. There was always a bad element, but it got worse and worse after the war and into the late forties. It was a hotbed, for example, for narcotics. Marijuana was the main thing then. The bad element used to take especial advantage of out-of-towners and soldiers and sailors. The police started to make some arrests, and warnings were given, and things were made harder and harder on the club owners, and every once in a while something bad would happen. There began a move away from The Street." Scott feels that the problem was not only with the habitués of the clubs themselves, but also in the attitudes of the owners. "It seemed like the feeling just went out of the smaller clubs on 52nd Street," he says. "The war had ended and it was more profitable for the club owners to switch to all-girlie shows. And so The Street gradually became a place for strip joints. I remember Bud [Powell] had left The Street to take a group into the Roost on Broadway with Miles Davis, who had come onto the scene. The last jazz club folded by about 1948. And The Street was no more."

"I got off The Street about that time," Monte Kay recalls. Kay, a publisher who was also an avid jazz fan, had been running weekly jam sessions at Kelly's and elsewhere on The Street since 1942. He too became disillusioned with the aura surrounding the jazz clubs there. "It had developed a clip-joint attitude that was rough on the kids, including myself," Kay says. "If you stayed for more than fifteen minutes, they hustled you for another drink. But I was convinced there was an audience for bop." Kay started the move away from 52nd Street to Broadway, just around the corner, where jazz had never before been featured prominently. He remembers the circumstances that opened up Broadway to bop: "One night – it was a Saturday – I went into the Royal Roost, a chicken joint on Broadway and 47th Street owned by Ralph Watkins. Jimmy Lunceford was playing. Though he had an outstanding band, the place was practically empty. Watkins was skeptical about the modern stuff. But I managed to talk him into letting me and Symphony Sid produce a concert on an off night. He picked Tuesday, and we did a concert with Bird, Tadd Dameron, Miles Davis, Fats Navarro and Dexter Gordon." Kay also started the policy of admitting minors and others into a non-drinking section of the club, where for 90¢ they could sit and listen without being harassed or jostled by waiters; the idea of the non-drinking section, called the bleachers, was later adopted by another Broadway club, Birdland, which became even better known than the Royal Roost and survived much longer. After the success of Kay's Tuesday-night bop concerts, the Roost began billing bop bands regularly and Tadd Dameron, who was managed by Kay, was hired to front the Roost house band. For 52nd Street, the shift of jazz to Broadway was another serious blow in its protracted decline.

While the music played by Parker's quintet revealed new strengths the longer it worked as a unit, personal differences among its members surfaced more forcefully as it entered its second year of existence. Part of the problem came from Parker's remoteness; he was never available to take the initiative when a decision had to be made or to smooth out differences when they came up. "We all know what Bird's habits were because he'd had them since he was fourteen years old," Ray Brown says. "That preoccupied a lot of his time off the bandstand; it took up most of his social life; it dictated the type of friends that he was to have. Unfortunately, he was relegated to just dealing and running in certain areas to get what he wanted to get, to keep up with his needs." The leader's role was assumed more and more by Davis, not always with the full approval of the others. Davis saw it simply as a necessity, because of Parker's absence.

"He never did talk about music," Davis complained. "I always even had to show Duke Jordan, the pianist in the band, the chords." Davis was never satisfied with Jordan's playing and agitated to have him replaced by someone with a stronger theoretical background. Jordan, with typical gentleness, remembers the awkward situation he found himself in: "The group got on very harmoniously except for slight altercations with Miles. He and Max formed sort of a little clique. They were both getting $135 a week, ten more than me and Tommy. Miles was making it at Juilliard, and he was tight with John Lewis, and he wanted Bird to substitute John for me in the group. But Bird silenced him by quietly and firmly saying that he chose the guys and Miles could form his own outfit if anything displeased him. That was all that was heard from Miles." Jordan's recollection that Davis was "making it at Juilliard" reflects on what Jordan considers to be at the root of Davis's disaffection for his playing, since Juilliard was well in the past by now. John Lewis, who had been Davis's choice on his own Savoy date a year earlier, had a more successful university career, having graduated from the University of New Mexico in 1942. Lewis was in the eye of a similar storm over the replacement of a piano player in 1946, when Dizzy Gillespie chose Lewis to replace Thelonious Monk in his orchestra over the objections of Gil Fuller. The two situations, so similar in their essentials, underline the changing perception of their music by certain jazz musicians, who were beginning to realize that the new complexity of the music demanded some training beyond merely surviving in jam sessions.

As the tensions within the quintet grew, they were exacerbated by Parker's erratic behavior, which caused all the members grief. Even when the quintet were booked for a long engagement, the sidemen had to worry about getting paid. "At some clubs Bird was actually paid by the set, it was that risky a thing that he would show," says guitarist Jimmy Raney. "His horns presented a problem – they were in hock so often. At the Three Deuces, the porter had a job assigned to him, to go to the pawnshop every day and get Bird's horn for the job, and then return it to the shop after the job."

In spite of the unpredictability of the leader and the hard feelings between Davis and Jordan, the personnel had remained the same for sixteen months. By the late summer of 1948 that stability grew too precarious to last much longer. Someone, presumably Parker, had to make a decision: either Davis and Roach had to go, or Jordan and Potter had to go. In spite of Jordan's recollection of Parker's support for him against Davis, it was he and Potter who left. Davis and Roach were emerging as important musicians in their own right, and they drew an audience wherever they played; this latter consideration must have weighed heavily with Billy Shaw, if Parker consulted him. If the arrangement was intended to restore personal cohesion among the members of the quintet, it failed. Davis and Roach were fed up with Parker's vagaries and, armed with the confidence that they could move out on their own and be successful, were less tolerant when Parker's behavior robbed them of their pay and made havoc of their music. They remained with Parker somewhat uneasily.

Jordan was replaced by John Lewis for the one recording session of the year, in September, clearly a nod in Davis's direction, and by Tadd Dameron, another close associate of Davis's, for a Royal Roost date in September, when Dameron filled in temporarily while doubling as the piano player in his house band. Jordan's permanent replacement was Al Haig, who joined Parker in December and stayed until mid-1950. Haig was almost certainly Parker's choice rather than Davis's. He had been with Parker in the first bop quintet on 52nd Street and in the sextet that traveled to Los Angeles. He was also, like Jordan, a piano player schooled in the clubs, with very little academic training. Potter's replacement was Curly Russell, but in December, just before Davis and Roach left the quintet for good, Potter was rehired. The timing of Potter's return and of the departures of Davis and Roach is probably not accidental.

While Haig and Russell were in the group, the quintet played at the Three Deuces again – probably for the last time. Parker seemed quite unmoved by the occasion. Guitarist Tal Farlow, who played opposite the quintet in a band led by vibraphonist Margie Hyams, recalls Parker at the Three Deuces with a sense of awe because of his playing and with a sense of disbelief because of his antics. One night, Farlow remembers, "Bird came storming into the club after a lengthy absence. The management tried to get him up on the stand immediately. He wouldn't be rushed. We were standing in the rear of the place. Margie, Miles Davis, Al Haig, Curly Russell and I watched the comedy unfold. Bird had some sardines and crackers, and was eating them with a sense of relish, while the management pleaded with him to come to the stand. They got to the point where they were cajoling and begging him. He kept offering them sardines and crackers. We laughed 'til our sides hurt. Finally he came out and played."

Starting in September, the quintet usually played on Broadway. One of the advantages of playing at the Royal Roost was a weekly radio broadcast. Remote broadcasts similar to the one from the Roost had been an integral part of the swing era in the 1930s, popularizing the big dance bands, especially Benny Goodman's, and creating an audience for them far from the big urban centers where the broadcasts originated. They had also been important for the small swing bands during the heyday of 52nd Street, and they were expected to work as well for the bop bands at the Roost. The Roost remotes were instigated by Symphony Sid Torin, Monte Kay's co-promoter, who hosted a popular rhythm-and-blues program on station WHOM in the early 1940s and was the first broadcaster to promote bebop on the air when he played, and touted, the first records by Gillespie and Parker in 1945. During the recording ban of 1948, the Roost remotes were doubly significant, providing listeners with one of the few sources of current music outside the clubs themselves. Whenever a transcription of one of the remotes has been preserved, by wire recorder or disc recording or, increasingly, the new-fashioned tape recorders, its value in filling in the development of the music during the ban is inestimable. Many of the remotes were traded back and forth among fans over the years; some of them have been transferred onto records more recently, sometimes licensed by the producers for limited issues and sometimes marketed as unauthorized or bootleg albums.

From September until December, when he left the quintet for good, Davis appears on several broadcasts from the Royal Roost, sometimes with Parker and sometimes with a band of his own. Only those broadcasts with Parker are discussed in this chapter, and those without Parker will find their place in the next chapter. The Roost broadcasts by Davis with his own band belong to a different phase from the one chronicled in this chapter. The two phases are clearly separable. Davis was, in these final months with Parker, moving in two different musical directions – introducing an influential reaction to bebop and wrapping up his own involvement beside Parker in the main current of bebop.

Davis's first broadcast from the Roost with the quintet took place on a Saturday in September. Parker's quintet, as has been indicated above, takes on an unfamiliar look for the occasion, with Tadd Dameron and Curly Russell in place of Jordan and Potter:

Charlie Parker All Stars
Miles Davis, tpt; Charlie Parker, as; Tadd Dameron, pno; Curly Russell, b; Max Roach, dms. Royal Roost, New York, 11 September 1948
52nd Street Theme; Ko Ko
(*Ko Ko* issued on Le Jazz Cool JC 101)
Jepsen (1969) lists the date of this broadcast as 4 September, but several Parker discographies correct it as shown.

Le Jazz Cool issued three albums based on Parker's broadcasts from the Royal Roost and elsewhere, some of them with Davis and some without, several years ago. They are now unavailable.

Just a week after this, while Davis was engaged at the Royal Roost with his own band, a nonet, which would make its broadcasting debut that same night, Davis spent the afternoon in a recording studio with the Parker quintet, for the first time in almost nine months. The recording ban was still in force, and the recording had to be done clandestinely. Herman Lubinsky of Savoy had contacted Parker and set the recording dates with him. Why he chose to violate the ban is not clear. Possibly he knew that Davis and Roach were set to leave Parker's band and he wanted to record the quintet before it broke up. Or perhaps he was simply fed up with waiting for the end of the strike which by now looked interminable. He and Parker agreed to record eight titles, all of them originals by Parker, in two sessions, the first on Saturday 18 September, and the second the following Friday:

Charlie Parker All Stars
Miles Davis, tpt; Charlie Parker, as; John Lewis, pno; Curly Russell, b; Max Roach, dms. New York, 18 September 1948
Barbados (four takes); *Ah-Leu-Cha* (two takes); *Constellation* (five takes)
(all on Savoy S5J 5500; master takes on Savoy 2201; alternate takes on Savoy 1107)
Davis does not play on the fourth title recorded at this session, *Parker's Mood* (five takes).

Same personnel and place, 24 September 1948
Perhaps (seven takes); *Marmaduke* (eight takes); *Steeplechase* (two takes); *Merry-Go-Round* (two takes)
(all on Savoy S5J 5500; master takes on Savoy 2201; alternate takes on Savoy 1107)
For several years the dates of these two sessions were listed incorrectly as 29 August and

August-September, respectively, but the Savoy company ledgers have now confirmed the dates listed above.

These recordings, the last ones made for Savoy by either Parker or Davis, rank among the best the two men made together. It is worth comparing them with the first recordings they made together, also for Savoy, in November 1945. There, the fumbling young Davis had to give way to Dizzy Gillespie because he could not master the introduction to *Ko Ko;* here, he dispatches the intricate heads of *Barbados* and *Marmaduke* with apparent ease, and he solos confidently at all tempos. On listening to the fast *Constellation* from this session, Med Flory noted: "This was 1948, and by this time, Miles was playing very well, way up high, very fast, as together as anybody can get." For most listeners, *Parker's Mood,* a soulful blues played by Parker backed only by the rhythm trio, is the highlight of these final Savoy sessions, and it is hard to argue with that opinion when Parker, one of the greatest blues players, is so near the top of his form. Of the other sides, all by the quintet, *Ah-Leu-Cha* remains a striking performance of an interesting composition. Structurally, it is identical to *Chasin' the Bird,* recorded for Savoy in May 1947, with the two horns playing simultaneous counter-melodies for sixteen bars and then Parker playing the release alone for eight bars before the two horns restate the counter-melodies for the final eight. If one listens to *Chasin' the Bird* right after *Ah-Leu-Cha,* the maturity attained by the first Charlie Parker Quintet becomes obvious: *Chasin' the Bird* is, by comparison, a ragged ensemble, with the two horns seeming to miss the timing of the counter-melodies perceptibly, if only by a millisecond. On *Ah-Leu-Cha,* the horns are in phase, and the melody sounds rich and full. *Ah-Leu-Cha* has been relatively neglected among the compositions Parker recorded with the first quintet, but unjustly so. One of the few recordings of it since the original one is by Davis and his first quintet with John Coltrane, made several years after this one, in October 1955, a few months after Parker died. It is the only Parker composition to be recorded by Davis after leaving Parker's quintet.

Soon after the clandestine Savoy sessions, Parker left New York again to tour as a featured soloist with Norman Granz's Jazz at the Philharmonic. By the time he returned to fill an engagement with the quintet at the Royal Roost, the recording ban had finally ended. The settlement between the American Federation of Musicians and the recording companies came in November, and the companies began tooling up for the new season. Billy Shaw got Parker to sign an exclusive contract with Mercury Records, where Norman Granz was the jazz producer, but there was no immediate move by the company to record the quintet.

The documentation for the final weeks of the quintet's existence comes instead from the surviving Roost broadcasts, with their home-made sound and radio production. Davis made three broadcasts with Parker in December, two of them on Saturdays – 11 and 18 December – and the other on a Sunday – 12 December:

Charlie Parker All Stars
Miles Davis, tpt; Charlie Parker, as; Al Haig, pno; Tommy Potter, b; Max Roach, dms.
Royal Roost, New York, 11 December 1948
Groovin' High; Big Foot [Drifting on a Reed]; Ornithology; Slow Boat to China
(all on ESP-Bird-1; *Groovin' High* and *Ornithology* on Le Jazz Cool JC 101; *Big Foot* on Le Jazz Cool JC 102)

Same personnel and place, 12 December 1948
Hot House; Salt Peanuts; Half Nelson; White Christmas; Little Willie Leaps
(*Hot House* on Le Jazz Cool JC 103; other titles unissued)
The unavailable titles from this broadcast should not be confused with the broadcast of 25 December, when the same titles were played. The later broadcast had Kinney Dorham on trumpet replacing Davis.

Same personnel and place, 18 December 1948
Chasin' the Bird; Out of Nowhere; How High the Moon
(all on MEEXA 1776; *Chasin' the Bird* and *Out of Nowhere* on Le Jazz Cool JC 102)

The broadcast versions of the various compositions have a refreshingly spontaneous quality, as might be expected. Some of them are given perfunctory performances, as *Groovin' High* is here, with Parker idly attempting to leap an octave instead of sticking to the harmony on the out-chorus. Others are surprising because of the transformations they have undergone since their earlier recorded performances; here, *How High the Moon* is played over a latin beat, and *Out of Nowhere* is played at a fast tempo. Davis and Roach set up a pattern on several of these tunes (*Big Foot, Ornithology,* and *Chasin' the Bird*) in which Davis plays four-bar phrases in a descending scale and Roach thumps the bass drum at the conclusion of each phrase; the effect is bumptious, even if it was obviously enjoyed by the two players. The repertoire is expanded by comparison with the Onyx recordings earlier in the year. The most satisfying performances are versions of Parker originals recorded the previous year, *Big Foot, Ornithology,* and *Chasin' the Bird*. The quintet's repertoire also included at least two of Davis's originals from the previous year, *Half Nelson* and *Little Willie Leaps*.

Five days after the last of these broadcasts, on 23 December, Davis quit the band for good. "Miles and Bird were hardly speaking," says Ross Russell. "Christmas week the internal tensions within the group came to the surface. Complaining to me that 'Bird makes you feel one foot high,' Miles Davis stalked off the stand, not in an ordinary huff, but never to return. Max Roach quit the same night." But Roach was persuaded to stay on for at least two more nights, until his replacement, Joe Harris, who had recently left the Gillespie orchestra, could take over. Roach appears on the broadcast from the Roost the next Saturday, Christmas day, but the trumpeter in the band is Kinney Dorham (whose given name, McKinley, is sometimes rendered as Kenny). As soon as Davis quit, Parker dispatched a handsome young singer who was appearing with his band at the Roost, an unknown named Harry Belafonte, to Dorham's apartment on Sugar Hill with the message that the job in Parker's band was available. Dorham, a Texan, had played in several modern bands, including Russell Jacquet's, Billy Eckstine's, and Dizzy Gillespie's, but his main ambition was to join Parker's group. He was proud to state: "I took Miles Davis's place. He recommended me for the spot."

Russell claims that "events had proved that the presence of Miles in the same band with Charlie presented insoluble personality conflicts." Maybe so, but it is easy to overemphasize the differences between the two men. Certainly they remained in fairly close contact with one another after the split, occasionally playing together and even recording together again in both 1951 and 1953 (and also twice in 1949, when both were members of large bands assembled for recordings). There is certainly no evidence of animosity in Davis's recommending Dorham as his replacement, and even less in Parker's accepting the recommendation.

Parker's continuing regard for Davis's trumpet style and the contribution it made to the group sound is not shown so clearly in his selection of Dorham, whose style is closer to Gillespie's, but it is reaffirmed in his selection of Red Rodney as Dorham's replacement in 1950. Rodney seemed a surprising choice to many commentators, but the choice is surely explained by Rodney's appreciation of the style of Miles Davis. "I loved Miles Davis, I thought he was most beautiful," Rodney says. "I thought he changed the sound of the trumpet. He made it much more lyrical. He was a great creative jazz artist." After Davis, Rodney was perhaps the most satisfactory trumpeter to work regularly beside Parker, because he came the closest to giving Parker what Davis had given him – warmth of tone and a cool contrast to Parker's fire.

In the weeks immediately following Davis's resignation, Davis and Parker remained at close quarters. Parker stayed at the Royal Roost with his quintet until the middle of March; for two weeks in February and one more in March, the group appearing opposite Parker's was Tadd Dameron's Big Ten, featuring Miles Davis. Later in March, Parker's quintet and the Miles Davis–Tadd Dameron Quintet traveled together to France, where they took their turns on the stage of the Paris Jazz Festival. If Parker and Davis were no longer partners in the music they made, their circle nevertheless remained unbroken.

The early association of Miles Davis and Charlie Parker is unique in jazz annals. In an art form that does not have its own academic tradition, it is not at all uncommon for one great player to learn at the elbow of another great player. One thinks of the boyish Louis Armstrong rising out of the band of King Oliver, his patriarch on the cornet, and of John Coltrane searching doggedly for the harmonies he could hear but not yet play in the bands of Miles Davis in the 1950s. These examples, along with the example of Parker and Davis, are only the best known in an art form that, of necessity, has had to improvise its own apprentice system. But Oliver sent for Armstrong to join him in Chicago because he had already heard the genius in his playing, as anyone could hear it, almost from the first note. And Davis kept rehiring Coltrane, against his better judgment and common sense, as we shall see, because he knew, as some others also knew, that Coltrane would eventually break through that harmonic barrier. What did Parker see in the young Davis that assured him of his talent? What could he possibly see in a young man afraid to join in the jam sessions, hanging back in the shadows? Whatever it was, Parker's instinct was unerring. Davis's climb into the front rank of jazz musicians took about three years – only slightly longer than it took Armstrong, and much quicker than Coltrane's sluggish rise would be. By the time Davis walked off the bandstand and left the Charlie Parker Quintet in December 1948, he had already laid the foundation that would make him Parker's peer in the development of jazz. It had happened at the Royal Roost, with an experimental nine-piece orchestra that played together in public for only two weeks. To piece together that part of Davis's story, we must go back again to the summer of 1948.

4

Move
1948–50

Jazz sort of needs movements. They always remind some people of some things they haven't been paying any attention to, or bring about something new that is real crazy.
  Thelonious Monk

Jazz music was not the only art form in ferment in the New York of the 1940s. The city had borne the brunt of the Great Depression in the previous decade, and then the war, believed almost unanimously to be a war worth shedding blood in, a "just" war, came along and dispelled the Depression like a foul odor. In the United States the war was viewed not as a concerted effort by the Allied Forces against the malevolent Axis so much as an exercise of American courage and ingenuity to head off powers opposed to freedom and democracy. During the Depression, President Roosevelt had proclaimed that his fellow citizens had "nothing to fear but fear itself," and now, less than a decade later, many of them journeyed to the Old World to defend their inalienable rights against the forces of evil. In preventing the fascists from conquering the world, the Americans believed – as their movies, their newspapers, and their politicians gave them every reason to – that they were inadvertently conquering the world themselves, if not exactly by and for democracy, then by Coca Cola and Chiclets and know-how. The mood, despite the blood being shed, was euphoric, and the arts, finding themselves surrounded by euphoria for the first time in ages, were thriving. Jackson Pollock painted canvases with tubes instead of brushes, and for the first time there was an internationally known entity called American art, with a host of rising stars such as Willem de Kooning, Clyfford Still, Franz Kline, Robert Motherwell, and Grace Hartigan. In American theater, Eugene O'Neill had loomed as a solitary giant before the war, but during and after it he was not merely joined but supplanted by such new playwrights as William Saroyan, Tennessee Williams, Arthur Miller, and William Inge. Fiction flourished, with

Hemingway reborn, it seemed, by the war, and a host of tough new writers: Ralph Ellison, James Jones, and Norman Mailer. And the brilliance of all of them was matched, in their different ways, by the leaders of the bebop revolution with their American – *distinctively* American – music. Out of Lester Young and Charlie Christian a brand-new sound had emerged, the work of many minds: Kenny Clarke, Thelonious Monk, Bud Powell, Oscar Pettiford, and, especially, Dizzy Gillespie and Charlie Parker.

But the war ended – not suddenly, on a given day when some politicians signed some treaty or other, but imperceptibly, the way really important things happen. The men returned from overseas, not all at once but one by one, and the women threw out their coveralls and their Red Cross uniforms, not all on the same day but sooner or later. Instead of lining up to punch in at the munitions factory or to pick up the weekly ration of bacon, people started lining up instead to put their names on the waiting list for Hoovers and Chevrolets and suburban bungalows. The boom was every bit as high as the bust of the 1930s had been low. By 1948, some people could put their feet up and say, hey, look at us, first a depression and then a world war – what next?

Some of them were artists. Andrew Wyeth looked out his window and saw not only his own reflection but also trees and fields *and* his own reflection, all at once. Carson McCullers and J.D. Salinger and Truman Capote discovered that they were not so tough, maybe, as Hemingway's batmen, and they worried about that for a while, and then they stopped worrying. In the theater, whose headquarters, Broadway, would soon be shared with improvising musicians, the change was not so much in what was being written as in how it was being declaimed: the young actors studied by day at Lee Strasberg's Actors Studio, where they learned that the business of acting lay not so much in delivering the sense of the play, as the Lunts and the Barrymores had done so nobly for so long, as it did in delivering the sensibility of its action. There would be an entity, undreamed of until now, called American acting, as soon as the actors could find the parts. And they would find the parts.

The young actors studied and worked on Broadway, when they could afford the lessons and find the work. The rest of the time, which was most of the time in the beginning, some of them hung out at the apartment of the actress Maureen Stapleton, in a crumbling brownstone on fading 52nd Street, beside Leon and Eddie's, the old show-biz hangout that had lost the celebrities and was surviving, barely, on strippers. On a hot summer night, the actors could sometimes hear the overtones from Oscar Pettiford's group across the street or the applause for Charlie Parker's quintet down the street. But they had to be listening for it, and most of the time when they were at Stapleton's place they were not listening; they were talking about how it *should* be in the theater or how it *would* be some day, and they were most of all acting, trying out gestures and postures and deliveries on one another. The young actors who drifted in and out of there, as unemployment permitted, included, among many others now forgotten, David Wayne, Tom Ewell, Julie Harris, Jerome Robbins, Kevin McCarthy, Kim Stanley, Montgomery Clift, and Marlon Brando. At Maureen Stapleton's place, they and their friends constituted what would have been called, in eighteenth-century Europe, a *salon*. Eventually they changed the art of acting in the United States, and soon after that they changed it throughout the world.

At the same time there was a jazz salon – too precious a word for it, and one that none of its members would use, but the only word the language has for what it was. It was three blocks north, on 55th Street, where the rents were lower, and it belonged, in the sense that he held the lease for it, to Gil Evans, an arranger for Claude Thornhill's dance band. The one-room basement apartment belonged to Evans in almost no other sense. "I just left the door open," Evans says, "and people came in and out all the time for the next couple of years." Dave Lambert, the jazz lyricist and singer, says, "It was shared by around nine people. There was Gil, myself, my wife and daughter, Specs Goldberg the drummer, and Gerry Mulligan." And they were only the regulars. Irregularly, there were many more. "Being right near 52nd Street which was swinging at the time," Lambert explains, "Max, Miles and Bird would fall by, and, as soon as someone would get up from a bed, another person would jump on it. The people would lie crosswise so they could fit more bodies. It was a struggle, but fun." It was a struggle, apparently, just to get to the place. Lambert says, "You had to go down a short flight of stairs, pass a Chinese laundry, through a boiler room, and there it was – home."

"I don't know how Gil ever got anything done, because there were people there twenty-four hours a day," says Blossom Dearie, who rehearsed and sang with Lambert at the time. "Charlie Parker lived there for a while, and you'd generally find Dizzy Gillespie and Miles Davis and Gerry Mulligan and John Lewis. Or George Handy would be there, or George Russell or Barry Galbraith or Lee Konitz." George Russell remembers the place as a haven and a direct reflection of Gil Evans's personality. "A very big bed took up a lot of the place; there was one big lamp, and a cat named Becky. The linoleum was battered, and there was a little court outside. Inside, it was always very dark. The feeling of the room was timelessness. Whenever you went there, you wouldn't care about conditions outside. You couldn't tell if it was day or night, summer or winter, and it didn't matter. At all hours, the place was loaded with people who came in and out. Mulligan, though, he was there all the time. He was very clever, witty and saucy, the way he is now." Mulligan's wit often depended upon sarcasm, and Russell recognizes that there were tensions not far from the surface in him and in all of them, except Evans. "Gerry had a chip on his shoulder," he says. "He had more or less the same difficulties that made all of us bitter and hostile. He was immensely talented, and he didn't have enough of an opportunity to exercise his talent. Gil's influence had a softening effect on him and on all of us. Gil, who loved musical companionship, was the mother hen – the haven in the storm. He was gentle, wise, profound, and extremely perceptive, and he always seemed to have a comforting answer for any kind of problem. He appeared to have no bitterness."

Gerry Mulligan, the arranger and baritone saxophonist, was a year younger than Miles Davis. He had arrived in New York as a member of the Gene Krupa orchestra in 1946, while Davis was in California. His major accomplishments consisted of two arrangements recorded by the Krupa orchestra, *How High the Moon* in May 1946 and *Disc Jockey Jump* in January 1947. The frustrations that Russell mentions seemed to dog the young Mulligan especially, and even though he found a few opportunities to display his precocious talent in notable settings, he had to wait four more years, until 1952, before he gained public and critical recognition. That recognition, when it came, was enthusiastic and persevering, but by the time it arrived, Mulligan might justifiably have given up on it. He had already had, besides the arrangements for Krupa, two very attractive arrangements recorded by the Elliot Lawrence band, *Between the Devil and the Deep Blue Sea* and *Elevation*, in 1949 (reissued, with the Krupa sides, on Columbia PC 34803). Between these, he wrote arrangements for Miles Davis's nine-piece band that grew out of the Evans salon, and with that band he also displayed a highly personal and swinging sound on the baritone saxophone. For some reason, all his talents went unnoticed by most listeners until he moved to California and broke through, and in 1948, when he was living in Evans's apartment, he was struggling. Dave Lambert remembers him leading open-air rehearsals at the time. "Mulligan was rehearsing a band in Central Park," Lambert says, "because he had no money to rent a rehearsal studio. They would play in the grass till the cops came and chased them." Acclaimed now as one of the crucial arrangers and composers of postwar jazz, his formative experience was in the salon. "We all gravitated around Evans," he says. Mulligan calls Gil Evans Svengali, an anagram of his name.

The man who hosted the salon was, on the surface, an unlikely Svengali. George Russell's metaphor, "haven in the storm," fits better, and if the salon bustled like a cyclone, Gil Evans was its eye, its calm and unruffled center. Born Ian Ernest Gilmore Green in Toronto on 13 May 1912, of Australian parents, he soon moved to the Pacific coast, where he spent his youth in British Columbia, Washington, and California. His surname, Evans, was conferred on him by his stepfather. He led his first band in Stockton, California, in 1933, and a few years later, in 1936–7, his band became the house band at the Rendezvous Ballroom in Balboa Beach. Evans has always been a reluctant leader, unwilling and perhaps temperamentally unable to put up with the extramusical grief of dealing with booking agents and club managers. His first band was taken over in 1937 by the band's singer, Skinnay Ennis, and Evans remained with it as its arranger and director, a role that suited him better even if, in the pop music scheme of things, it reduced to anonymity his crucial creative contribution to the sound and the style of the band. As the band became more successful under Ennis, playing regular radio spots with Bob Hope as well as the Rendezvous dances, Evans was joined by a second arranger, Claude Thornhill, who stayed until 1939 and then left to form his own band in New York. In 1941, Thornhill sent for Evans to write arrangements for his new band. They were just becoming established when Thornhill enlisted in the army, where he stayed from 1942 until 1945; Evans enlisted soon after and stayed from 1943 until 1946, rejoining Thornhill when he was discharged.

In the new band, they experimented with combinations of instruments, adding french horns and a tuba to the stock sections of dance bands, and filled its ranks with several jazz soloists, including alto saxophonist Lee Konitz, clarinetist Danny Polo, guitarist Barry Galbraith, and trumpeter Red Rodney. Besides the obligatory dance band fare, Evans prepared meticulous arrangements of some of the current compositions being played on 52nd Street, including Sir Charles Thompson and Illinois Jacquet's *Robbin's Nest*, Gillespie and Parker's *Anthropology*, Parker's *Yardbird Suite*, and Davis's *Donna Lee*. Although the band's style did little to win over the jitterbuggers, relying instead on subtlety and understatement to a degree unheard of in the field, musicians and other discerning listeners soon realized what was happening. "Thornhill had the greatest band, the one with Lee Konitz, during these modern times," Miles Davis said in 1950, adding, "The one exception was the Billy Eckstine band with Bird." Evans was credited by the insiders for the band's essential musicality. He was earning the private praise of musicians eight or ten or – in Davis's case – fourteen years younger than himself. Reedy and pale and pensive, Evans thus discovered his musical fraternity not only among such arrangers as Mulligan, Johnny Carisi, and George Russell, but also among the volatile young blacks of the bebop revolution.

The respect that he earned was stranger still because, unlike most of the other great arrangers of jazz, Evans was not an instrumentalist. Although he played piano with bands he sporadically led during the 1960s and 1970s, he had almost never played publicly before that. He showed no interest in working to attain performing skills on the piano until around 1952, when he was already forty, and even then he hardly attacked the task; fifteen years later he told Leonard Feather, "Miles has asked me to play at different times, but I never had the nerve to do it." His arranging skills are, incredibly, self-taught, and so is his piano technique. "I never played scales and exercises, never in my life," he says. "I can sit down at the piano and just look at it for hours, maybe hit a note here and there. I can't just sit down and play." His lack of formal training may be a key to his originality, for he can arrange harmonies that no one else has ever arranged and cluster instrumental groups that no one has ever sectioned before. "He knows what can be done, what the possibilities are," Davis says. An orthodox academic background might only have limited those possibilities for him. Indeed, with an academic background, Evans would almost certainly never have hosted the 55th Street group at all, for the salon was partly his own graduate school. "I was always interested in other musicians," Evans told Nat Hentoff. "I was hungry for musical companionship, because I hadn't had much of it before. Like bull sessions in musical theory. Since I hadn't gone to school, I hadn't had that before."

If Evans is a reluctant leader and player, he is no less reluctant as a composer. It is all part of the essential anarchism of his character. He has never regimented himself to compose or arrange on any schedule, and he is not disturbed by writer's block any more than he is by writer's cramp. He simply does not conceive of himself as a producer of any kind. "If I feel the need for some emotional development, well, I think about music and play and even write," he says. "But as far as the product is concerned, there is no product." As for meeting deadlines, he says, "If it's the right time to do it, it works out fine." The wonder is that Evans, with his approach, should have produced any lasting work at all.

Evans's recorded materials are remarkably sparse and tend to cluster around certain productive moments of his career – 1957–9, 1963–4, and perhaps a couple of others – but some of the little work he has produced ranks with the very finest orchestrations in jazz, perhaps even placing him alongside Duke Ellington among the great arrangers. But any mention of Ellington in the same breath simply underscores again the anomaly of Evans's position. Not only was Ellington enormously prolific as an arranger, but he was an arranger only because he was first a composer; he was an arranger of his own compositions. Evans, in a professional career which – incredibly – spans as many years as Ellington's did, has managed only a handful of original compositions, and his greatest achievement is in arranging other people's. In this respect, he differs not only from Ellington but from almost every other major composer-arranger in jazz as well. Leonard Feather says, "He is perhaps the only great writer in jazz history who has always tended to work as an arranger of the works of others and rarely as a composer of his own material."

The list of Evans's original compositions can easily be listed (with the dates when they were recorded): *Blues for Pablo* and *Jambangle* (1957); *Gone* (1958); *La Nevada, Sunken Treasure, The Pan Piper, Saeta, Solea,* and *Song of Our Country* (1960); *The Flute Song* and *El Toreador* (1963); *Barracuda* and *Isabel* (1963 or 1964); *Las Vegas Tango* (1964); *Spaced, Proclamation* and *Variation on* the Misery (1969); Zee Zee (1973); and perhaps a few others in less accessible places. If the list is supplemented by the compositions written by Evans in collaboration with Miles Davis, his only collaborator and probably the only person capable of motivating Evans to compose at all, it is increased by these: Boplicity (1949); Miles Ahead (1957), an arrangement of Davis's 1953 composition; Song #1 and Song #2 (1962); Hotel Me (1964); Petits Machins (1968) or Eleven (1973) – two titles for the same composition; General Assembly (1969); and perhaps a few others. Nevertheless, what the list lacks in quantity it partly compensates for in quality, because many of these works are sumptuous and memorable compositions. One thinks of Boplicity, Miles Ahead, Blues for Pablo, Gone, La Nevada, Saeta, and Barracuda among the finest moments of recorded jazz.

Evans's originality does not require original compositions for its demonstration. His arrangements of other people's compositions simply sparkle with his individualism; they overflow with invention. Even such old chestnuts as St. Louis Blues and It Ain't Necessarily So, so well known that they might seem to have lost all charm, and such jewels of the jazz literature as Lester Leaps In and Manteca, so familiar in their original, classic arrangements, have been resuscitated by Evans so that listeners might think they had never heard them before. Among the composers Evans has arranged, he has certain favorites. Most surprising, and an indication of Evans's catholic taste, is Kurt Weill, from whom Evans has made brilliant use of the melodies of My Ship (1957), Bilbao Song (1960), and a weirdly funereal The Barbara Song (1964). In the late 1970s and after, Evans has shown a predilection for arranging the rock themes of guitarist Jimi Hendrix, and he has liberally selected works by composers between the two distant poles represented by Weill and Hendrix. He has often chosen to arrange works by the men who made up the salon on 55th Street in 1948, to their considerable advantage: Miles Davis, of course, most of all, but also Johnny Carisi (Springsville), J.J. Johnson (Lament), John Lewis (Concorde and Django), and George Russell (Blues in Orbit and Stratusphunk). Beyond these rather scattered relations, one searches in vain for any telling thread that determines Evans's selection of material. He has obviously ranged throughout the world of music with something close to absolute freedom, from the most tawdry pop tunes (Under the Willow Tree for Thornhill and I Don't Wanna Be Kissed for Davis) to themes from minor classics (Moussorgsky's Pictures at an Exhibition as The Troubador for Thornhill, and the second movement of Rodrigo's Concierto de Aranjuez for Davis). His tastes have been unencumbered by convention or bias, and his career has been almost untouched by self-promotion or self-aggrandizement. And he has managed, on his own terms and at his own pace, to produce a body of work that holds its own proud place in jazz.

That accomplishment might have been out of the question if he had never met Miles Davis. Just as Davis could stir up Evans's will to compose, so he has also been able to stir him to produce most of the arrangements on which his reputation stands. No one else has been capable of doing it, at least not consistently. A lucrative contract from Verve Records in the 1960s calling for four albums of music from Evans terminated after one album and a few out-takes; by way of contrast, Evans has collaborated with Davis on five albums and several additional tracks of released material, and on at least that quantity of unreleased material.

Davis met Evans in 1947, sometime after Davis's *Donna Lee*, recorded in May of that year, was released by Savoy. Evans approached Davis to ask him for the lead sheet of *Donna Lee*, so that he could make an arrangement of it for the Thornhill band. Davis agreed, on condition that Evans get him a copy of his arrangement of *Robbin's Nest*, recorded by Thornhill on 17 October, so that he could study it. The two men thus discovered the basis of their mutual respect. As Davis puts it, simply, "He liked the way I played and I liked the way he wrote." Evans agrees, although he puts it less simply. "We had this thing – this sound – in common," he told Zan Stewart. "We heard the same sound in music. Not necessarily the details; the first thing you hear when somebody plays or writes things or even talks is the sound, the wave form, and having that in common made it possible for us to be good collaborators."

Still, it is hard to guess how Davis reacted to Evans's arrangement of *Donna Lee*, which was recorded by Thornhill on 6 November as a piano solo by Thornhill accompanied by the band's rhythm section – Barry Galbraith on guitar, Joe Shulman on bass, and Billy Exner on drums. In contrast to the pert rendition by the Parker quintet, Thornhill plays it at a very slow, dreamy tempo. Davis's melody is transformed almost beyond recognition. Thornhill's version is not entirely surprising: he cultivated the dreamy quality in the band's book. "At first, the sound of the band was almost a reduction to inactivity of music, to a stillness," Evans notes. "Everything – melody, harmony, and rhythm – was moving at a minimum speed. The melody was very slow, static; the rhythm was nothing much faster than quarter-notes and a minimum of syncopation. The sound hung like a cloud." As the style grew more mannered Evans became bored by it, and it is ironic that his arrangement of Davis's melody should come to stand as a prime example of Thornhill's mannerisms. Finally, as the cloudy style dominated the band's sound more and more, Evans decided to leave Thornhill. "The sound had become a little too sombre for my taste, generally speaking, a little too bleak in character," he said. "It began to have a hypnotic effect at times. The band could put you to sleep." He resigned in the summer of 1948. Although Evans says that his leaving was friendly, Thornhill immediately reorganized the band and gradually eradicated Evans's contribution to its book. By 1953, bassist Bill Crow told Ian Crosbie, "Some of the Evans charts were used only as punishment, when the band was getting sloppy or drunk." That same year, 1953, Thornhill, troubled by depression and alcoholism, disbanded for the last time.

Looking back on the Thornhill band, Bill Borden, another of its arrangers, remarked, "Gil Evans changed the face of the band but, I think, undermined Claude's confidence in himself." The attention that Evans was getting from the young musicians on 52nd Street and Broadway might have encouraged Thornhill to find an alternative direction for the band that would again stamp it as his own creation rather than Evans's. By the late summer of 1948, Evans was seeking a band to write for that would allow him to express himself more fully. At the same time, Miles Davis, increasingly disturbed by the tensions in the Parker quintet, was also looking for a band that would allow him to exploit his own strengths as a soloist. The discussions in the salon about experimenting with new voicings and discovering some new dynamics for improvised music suddenly took a more practical turn.

Evans originally hoped that Charlie Parker, who spent as much time at Evans's place as he did anywhere else and thus qualified as a resident, might be the one to lead the salon's theoreticians in their assault on the world outside, but he soon abandoned that hope. "Months after we had become friends and roommates, he had never heard my music, and it was a long time before he did," Evans told Nat Hentoff. "When Bird did hear my music he liked it very much. Unfortunately, by the time he was ready to use me, I wasn't ready to write for him. I was going through another period of learning by then. As it turned out, Miles, who was playing with Bird then, was attracted to me and my music. He did what Charlie might have done if at that time Charlie had been ready to use himself as a voice, as part of an overall picture, instead of a straight soloist." Davis, of course, was ready.

The members of the salon all agreed that the perfect band for what they wanted to accomplish would need to have nine players, with the standard bop quintet of trumpet, saxophone, and rhythm supplemented by a second reed instrument and three more brass. The added instruments were all to be in the lower ranges – trombone, french horn, tuba, and baritone saxophone – which pretty well dictated that the other reed instrument would have to be an alto saxophone, which has a lighter sound and a higher register than the tenor. That choice of instruments was determined before Davis entered the discussions. "Gil Evans and I spent the better part of one winter hashing out the instrumentation for that nine-piece band," Gerry Mulligan says, adding, "but Miles dominated the band completely; the whole nature of the interpretation was his." It was a subset of the instrumentation of the Thornhill orchestra, which normally had eighteen or more pieces in it. Davis considered Thornhill's full band to be merely cumbersome rather than functional, especially because Evans was capable of grouping the voicings to get as much sound from fewer instruments. "Gil can use four instruments where other arrangers need eight," he says, and that was the proportion – half the instruments that Thornhill used – that was decided on. The only hope that the band had of playing in public lay in limiting the number of players as far as possible. Even nine men would seem extravagant to club owners used to paying trios, quartets, and quintets. However, "this was the smallest number of instruments that could get the sound and still express all the harmonies the Thornhill band used," Evans says. "Miles wanted to play his idiom with that kind of sound."

Without Davis, all the talk about the band would almost certainly have remained just that. He brought a new element into the salon, an ambition to translate the discussions into practice. "He took the initiative and put the theories to work," Mulligan says. "He called the rehearsals, hired the halls, called the players, and generally cracked the whip." Because he was better known among the managers of jazz clubs after working beside Charlie Parker for so long, he eventually got the band some public exposure beyond the rehearsal studio.

Gil Evans calls him "the complete leader" of the band, because "he organized the band, sold it for a record contract, and for the Royal Roost where we played." The record contract was with Capitol, one of the handful of large companies that dominated the record industry at the time, along with Columbia, Decca, Victor, and Mercury. As soon as the recording ban ended, Davis signed a contract to record twelve compositions for Capitol with the nonet. By the time the recording sessions started, the nonet had long since disbanded, having played their two weeks at the Royal Roost in September and finding no more opportunities for club dates. Fulfilling the contract proved to be a problem, as it became impossible to reassemble the original members for the three sessions required, and both the new members and the original members required rehearsals prior to each session because learning the complex charts amounted to much more than just reviving faded memories.

The first session did not take place until 21 January 1949, four months after disbanding, and the others were on 22 April 1949 and 9 March 1950. As a result, the impact of the nonet on critics and other musicians was dissipated. Only the few hundred who saw them live at the Royal Roost were fully aware of what they were attempting, and even for them their style was so innovative that their real accomplishment could hardly be appreciated. For most of the jazz world – musicians, critics, and listeners alike – their influence was not an impact at all but an insinuation; the recordings appeared at wide intervals and were not put together in a collection until May 1954, when Capitol released a ten-inch album containing eight of the compositions. The band were ahead of their time when they were first assembled, but by the time the recordings had eased their style into the jazz consciousness, their time was ripe.

Miles Davis forged ahead on the nonet project in the summer and fall of 1948, fighting the practical and commercial outlook of the day, urging Evans and the other arrangers to prepare their charts, and becoming the organizer and task-master for eight other musicians who were mostly, like him, employed in other bands. He was fully aware that he had discovered his own métier. In Gil Evans and the other members of the salon, he found the individuals gifted in theory and harmony who could continue his own education beyond what he had learned from Gillespie, Monk, Webster, and the others, including, of course, Juilliard and William Vachiano. He also discovered a musical setting that suited him better than the hard-core bebop he played nightly with the Parker quintet. Bob Wein-stock, who started Prestige Records soon after this time, says, "Gil Evans had a tremendous influence on Miles' musical thinking. Miles always spoke of Gil Evans, and he kept telling me, 'Get Gil Evans, get him to do an album. He's beautiful.' I think that Miles found his true element there, at *that* time. Here was a chance for all his sensitivity, compared to Bird's savageness and deep fire and emotion, which was overpowering Miles every time they played on the same stand; here was an outlet for Miles Davis to let out the sensitivity that he had as a musician."

The nonet also provided a chance for him to discover his abilities as a composer. "I didn't start writing until I met Gil Evans," he says, apparently overlooking *Donna Lee*, which provided the occasion for their first meeting. "He told me to write something and send it to him," Davis recalls. "I did. It was what I played on the piano. Later I found out I could do better without the piano. I took some piano lessons at Juilliard, but not enough. If you don't play it good enough, you'll be there for hours and hours." The first effects of Evans's interest in Davis's composing can be heard, at least faintly, in the four original compositions Davis recorded in August 1947 – *Milestones*, *Little Willie Leaps*, *Half Nelson*, and *Sippin' at Bells* – which are arranged for the instrumentation of a bop quintet but show hints of the salon style in their moods and tempos. Over the years, Davis has proven to be an important and interesting composer, with several jazz standards to his credit. He has nevertheless made his priorities clear. "There's a certain feeling you can get from playing that you can't get from composing," he says. "And when you play, it's like composition anyway. You make the outline." In the nonet, the control and clarity of his improvising often match the careful arrangements.

Some of the thornier problems in recruiting musicians for the nonet were solved simply by recruiting players from the Thornhill band. Bill Barber, a gradu-ate of Juilliard and the Manhattan School of Music, had been playing the tuba in

Thornhill's band for more than a year by the late summer of 1948, and he came highly recommended by Evans and the others who knew him. Mulligan says, "He used to transcribe Lester Young tenor choruses and play them on tuba." Sandy Siegelstein, one of Thornhill's french hornists, played at the first rehearsals with the band at Nola Studios, although he was not with the band when it played at the Royal Roost. By then he had been replaced by Junior Collins, about whom the only ready information comes from Mulligan's assertion that he "could play some good blues."

The members of the salon naturally became players in the nonet. John Lewis, one of the arrangers, was the piano player, and Gerry Mulligan, another of the arrangers, played baritone saxophone, as he occasionally had in the Gene Krupa orchestra and other big bands. In the smaller band, Mulligan had a chance to expose for the first time his ability as a soloist, revealing the personal sound and light touch that would mark him as one of the most interesting soloists ever to play that cumbersome horn.

Membership in the salon was not enough in itself to guarantee membership, any more than was membership in Thornhill's band. Lee Konitz, an alto saxophonist with an almost fragile sound compared to the bold sound of Parker and his followers, was one of Thornhill's best soloists, especially on Evans's arrangements of *Anthropology* and *Yardbird Suite*, and he was also entrenched in the jazz avant-garde of the day, not only participating in the discussions of the salon but also working and studying with pianist Lennie Tristano. Still, Davis's first choice for the alto saxophonist in the nonet was not Konitz but Sonny Stitt, whose style was very much in the mold of Parker. Stitt, had he been included, might have made an enormous difference to the band's sound, not only because of his individual contribution but also because his presence alongside Davis, Lewis, bassist Al McKibbon, and drummer Max Roach, all of whom were involved nightly in playing bebop, might well have tipped the balance and made their sound much more bop-oriented and bop-derived than it ended up being. Fortunately, Davis listened to Mulligan's advice and ended up asking Konitz instead of Stitt. "Gerry said to get Lee Konitz on alto because he had that light sound too," Davis says. Davis's hiring of Konitz meant that he had to absorb some criticism when he was away from the salon. "When I hired Lee Konitz, some colored cats bitched a lot about me hiring an ofay in my band when Negroes didn't have work," he says. "I said if a cat could play like Lee, I would hire him, I didn't give a damn if he was green and had red breath." Davis's attitude about following a color line in hiring players for his bands has consistently been the one he expresses here: the first consideration is talent, not color. Even during the 1960s and 1970s, when his public pronouncements on racial matters were zealous, his musical priorities often led him to hire white players.

Al McKibbon, the bassist, had replaced Ray Brown in the Gillespie orchestra in 1947, where he formed close ties with John Lewis, his partner in the band's rhythm section. Max Roach not only was a member of the Parker quintet with Davis but also shared his enthusiasm for what the salon was working toward. He was part of that circle, and his interest in composing probably dates from this period, although he did not record any original works until a few years after he had played with the group. Kenny (Pancho) Hagood was the tenth man in the nine-piece band; he was Gillespie's band singer, and he was added for some vocal choruses.

The remaining instrumental chair was the trombonist's, and filling it proved, surprisingly, to be a problem. J.J. Johnson, a member of the salon, would seem to have been an obvious choice, and later on he recorded with the nonet in their two later sessions. In the summer and fall of 1948, however, he was a member of the Illinois Jacquet band, and he was apparently either traveling with it or playing full-time at a New York club when the nonet were rehearsing. For a couple of decades the trombonist who worked with the nonet at the Royal Roost was incorrectly listed as Ted Kelly, a member of Gillespie's orchestra. Kelly may have been Davis's choice for a while, but he did not play with the band and seems not to have made any of the rehearsals with them either, at least none of those directly connected to the two-week engagement at the Royal Roost. Improbably, the trombonist in the working nonet was an eighteen-year-old college freshman who was home on vacation in the summer of 1948 when he was recruited by Davis. His name was Michael Zwerin, and he later wrote some interesting jazz journalism, including this account of his own recruitment into the celebrated nonet: "I was sitting in at Minton's Playhouse one night when I saw Miles standing, listening, in the back. When I was packing up my trombone, he asked me if I could make a rehearsal the next day at Nola's Studios." As simply and unexpectedly as that, Zwerin found himself in the nonet. (Later, Davis made similar unexpected approaches to several other musicians, some of whom went on to become key members of his bands.) The hiring of such an unknown and untried trombonist as Zwerin probably resulted from the unexpectedness of the public debut of the band.

"That whole thing started out just as an experiment," Davis recalls. "Then Monte Kay booked us into the Royal Roost on Broadway for two weeks." The band assembled for the first time at Nola Studios above Lindy's restaurant on Broadway, where some of the Savoy recordings were made, including the clandestine ones with Parker the next month, September, during the recording ban. Zwerin remembers that "Miles was pleasant and relaxed but seemed unsure how to be a boss. It was his first time as a leader. He relied quite a bit on Evans to give musical instructions to the players." Zwerin's impression of Davis's uncertainty may indicate only that at the time Zwerin did not realize the extent to which the whole project was a collaboration between Davis and the arrangers rather than simply Davis's project. Zwerin adds, "Miles must have picked up his famous salty act sometime after that, because I don't remember his being excessively sarcastic that summer."

By the time the band opened at the Roost, Zwerin and everyone else should have been fully aware of their collaborative nature, if only because of the billing they were given on the sidewalk sign outside the club. "There was a sign outside – 'Arrangements by Gerry Mulligan, Gil Evans, and John Lewis,'" Evans recalls. "Miles had it put in front; no one before had ever done that, given credit that way to arrangers."

The sign on the sidewalk was a concession that Davis got from Monte Kay and the Roost's owner, Ralph Watkins, from whom he could hardly expect many more favors. Booking the nonet had been a kind of concession, not only because of the size of the band, which increased its payroll, but also because the managers had no reason to expect any commercial payback from its engagement. "At the time the Royal Roost was probably the only nightclub in the country that would have taken a chance with this new and forbidding type of jazz," Nat Hentoff points out. That Kay and Watkins took the chance is a credit to their commitment to the music and also probably a sign of the goodwill Davis had earned while working there as a member of the Parker quintet, which played there in alternate weeks with the nonet and was scheduled to return there in December. The nonet took second billing to the Count Basie orchestra and probably helped initially to draw some of the bop fans who might otherwise have avoided showing up to hear Basie's Kansas City swing style. Whether the nonet could keep those fans coming after they had a taste of their subtle style is another matter.

The dates of the Royal Roost engagement were discontinuous. The radio broadcasts, now issued on record, are dated 4 September and 18 September, both Saturdays, with an intervening Saturday, the 11th, taken up by the Charlie Parker quintet with Tadd Dameron on piano. (A third broadcast, made on Saturday the 25th, also features Davis but with neither Parker nor the nonet; he is heard with Lee Konitz and a rhythm section, suggesting that a sub-group of the nonet were rehired for the following week. Some commentators, including Hentoff, have claimed that the nonet played at the Royal Roost for three weeks, against all the assertions of the men who were in the band, probably on the assumption that the last aircheck was also a nonet date.) If the dating of the broadcasts is correct, then the nonet played the first of their two weeks from 30 August until 4 September, and the second 13–18 September, with the Parker quintet filling the hiatus, 6–11 September; otherwise, the dates of the broadcasts may need correcting, with 11 September being the right date for one of them. Apart from this uncertainty, the details are as follows:

Miles Davis Nonet
Miles Davis, tpt; Michael Zwerin, tbn; Junior Collins, frh; Bill Barber, tba; Lee Konitz,
as; Gerry Mulligan, bs; John Lewis, pno; Al McKibbon, b; Max Roach, dms; Kenny
Hagood, vcl (on *Why Do I Love You?* and *Darn That Dream*). Royal Roost, New York,
4 September 1948
Why Do I Love You?; *Godchild*; *S'il vous plait*; *Moon Dreams*; *Hallucinations* [Budo]
(incomplete)
(all on Ozone 2 and on Durium-Cicala BLJ 8003)

Same personnel and place, 18 September 1948
Darn That Dream; *Move*; *Moon Dreams*; *Hallucinations* [Budo]
(all on Alto AL-701 and on Durium-Cicala BLJ 8003)
Hallucinations is Bud Powell's original title for this theme, and it is apparently identified
by that title in the announcements from the Royal Roost (not included on these recordings); when it was recorded by the nonet for Capitol on 21 January 1949, it was titled
Budo, and Miles Davis was credited as its co-composer along with Powell.

All but two of the arrangements played on the broadcasts from the Royal Roost
were later among the twelve sides recorded for Capitol Records. The exceptions
are *Why Do I Love You?* and *S'il vous plait*. This additional material on the radio
broadcasts, which only became generally available in the 1970s, thus provides the
first clue about the band's repertoire beyond the material on the Capitol recordings. *Why Do I Love You?*, with a vocal chorus by Kenny Hagood, contains a
highly forgettable lyric, but Gil Evans's arrangement does a good job of de-empha-
sizing it. The opening chorus, strictly instrumental, features harmonic layers by
the horns under Davis's lead, which gives way to a trombone lead for a few bars at
the bridge (the only bars in which the trombone is featured in any composition).
Evans's touch is obvious in the shifting textures behind the trumpet lead and also,
after Davis's solo and Hagood's vocal chorus, in an elaborately arranged ending
using stop-time. (The audience begins to applaud after the vocal chorus, where
vocal arrangements normally end, but stops short when the band keeps playing.)
For better or worse, Evans seems to have drawn the arranging chores for only the
slow dance tempos; while neither Mulligan nor Lewis could have handled them
as well, it might have been interesting to hear Evans's work at faster tempos too.
The only other vocal arrangement for the nonet that has survived, *Darn That
Dream* (on both the broadcasts and the recording) is by Mulligan; it is a more
straightforward arrangement for a vocalist, subjugating the band to Hagood's lead,
and is much less interesting instrumentally than *Why Do I Love You?*

The other arrangement that never made it into the recording studio, *S'il vous
plait*, is a fine example of the nonet's style. An uptempo instrumental, it sections

the horns into the brass and the reeds, and the melody is stated in counterpoint by the brass playing a motif in half-time while the reeds weave a lively second motif around it. (Jepsen's discography identifies this as *Chasin' the Bird*, Parker's composition using counterpoint, but there is no melodic similarity.) The arranger has been identified as Miles Davis (by Chris Sheridan, in *Jazz Journal*) but on the basis of aural evidence alone, one might guess that it is Mulligan, since he used counterpoint extensively, almost as a trademark. Whether the arranger is Davis or Mulligan, the arrangement makes an excellent frame for solos by Konitz, Davis, and Mulligan, the latter two playing over an arranged background of riffs. The reason for its not making the transition to studio recording might be its length, since the version played at the Roost lasts well over four minutes, but other compositions last almost as long in the broadcast version and were successfully pared down for the recorded versions. One is grateful, naturally, to have it preserved in any version at all, but it is hard not to mourn its omission from the Capitol sessions. Luckily, the home-made tapes of the Royal Roost broadcasts are nowhere near the worst examples of their genre and are quite listenable. On the 4 September broadcast, the piano is drastically underrecorded, and the tuba and the bass go almost unnoticed on both broadcasts. However, the broadcasts have a kind of spontaneity altogether missing from the recordings, which are polished to a point just short of distracting, and, of course, the broadcast versions feature longer and more varied improvisations.

Formally, the music played by the nonet departs sharply from the conventions for bebop performances of the day, and the difference was fully intended. After several years, the bebop format had become static, revolving primarily around twelve- or thirty-two-bar theme statements followed by a round of solos by all hands. The tempos were limited more and more to medium and uptempos, and the solos at any tempos included phrases of eighth- and sixteenth-note runs, very often recognizable in the work of lesser players as originating in the recorded solos of Gillespie and Parker. In every respect, Davis's nonet proclaimed a revaluation of bebop standards. Tempos ranged from fast on *Budo* and *Move*, both arranged by Lewis, to very slow – unusually slow for the jazz of the day – on *Moon Dreams*, arranged by Evans. The theme statements often took up several choruses, thus drawing attention to the arranged material rather than hurrying past it, and many of the solos were wholly or partly contextualized by arranged material in the background. And in Davis and Konitz, and only slightly less noticeably in Lewis and Mulligan, the band featured soloists who played quarter-notes most of the time and frequently incorporated rests as stylistic devices. "The group's musical approach has been subject to repeated analysis because it represented the first viable alternative to bop," says Max Harrison. "Several of the pieces – *Move*, *Budo*, *Venus de Milo* – were mainly vehicles for improvisation, yet it was more significant that the sounds of all instruments were fused in a texture whose parts moved with a supple fluidity that contrasted with the hard, bright, darting lines of bop."

Curiosity was piqued by the unorthodox band, and Barry Ulanov of *Metronome* magazine, who was more receptive to the newer music of the day than most other writers in the periodicals, asked Lee Konitz for an explanation of the nonet's style. Konitz's answer seems much more abstruse than does the music it was intended to explain: "Let's say we change the punctuation of a 32 bar structure, like carrying the second eight bars over into the bridge, making our breaks somewhere within the second eight and in the middle of the bridge instead of at the conventional points. Or better, since we have already altered the construction of the line, we re-paragraph a paraphrase. And that leads to the next logical point, to continuity and development. Because you've got to think in terms of both, so that everything holds together, so that you get not four choruses, but a four chorus statement." Is that clear? Not really.

Much clearer is the reaction of Count Basie, who listened to the nonet night after night for two weeks as he waited to take the stand with his orchestra after it finished. "Those slow things sounded strange and good," Basie remembers. "I didn't always know what they were doing, but I listened, and I liked it." So did several others in the audience during those two weeks, especially other musicians.

Probably the most important listener was Pete Rugolo of Capitol Records, whose company was then anticipating the end of the recording ban. Capitol, with the other large firms, had ignored bebop so far, while such small labels as Dial and Savoy, directed by men who were music fans as well as businessmen, took the initiative and recorded it. For the corporations, that situation was tolerable as long as the music had only a cult following, but since bop recordings had taken a commercial upturn the corporations had to begin competing. Rugolo spoke to Davis at the Royal Roost and, as soon as the ban ended, signed him to the contract for twelve sides. Although completing the contract took almost a year and a half, without it the influence of the nonet would have been peripheral and indirect; instead, their influence was central and direct, even though it was slow in making itself felt.

In the meantime, Davis carried on with other projects. He had recorded with the Charlie Parker Quintet for Savoy on 18 and 24 September, the first of those dates being the last Saturday of his nonet's engagement at the Roost. He was also leading a band at the Roost when the second Savoy session with Parker took place, and he is heard again on the remote broadcast from there for Saturday 25 September, with an all-star quintet drawn from the ranks of the nonet. The details are as follows:

Miles Davis All Star Quintet
Miles Davis, tpt; Lee Konitz as; John Lewis, pno; Al McKibbon, b; Max Roach dms;
Kenny Hagood, vcl (on *You Go to My Head*). Royal Roost, New York, 25 September 1948
Broadway Theme [*52nd Street Theme*]; *Half Nelson*; *You Go to My Head*; *Chasin' the
Bird*
(all on Session 101)
The broadcast opened and closed with incomplete versions of *Jumpin' with Symphony Sid*,
played as the theme, which are not included on the recording.

This aircheck is exceptionally well recorded, and the music is outstanding. The
piano and the bass are, for once, clearly audible throughout. Lewis plays a very
boppish accompaniment on *Broadway Theme*, which is the tune usually entitled
52nd Street Theme and credited to Thelonious Monk, although it was used by
dozens of bands as a closer when they played in clubs on 52nd Street and later on
Broadway (where it apparently underwent a change of title to accommodate the
change of venue). It was treated very much as communal property by the bop
musicians, useful especially at jam sessions because everybody knew it and could
play its conventional harmonies before launching into the string of solos. Davis's
bands used its familiar strains as a set closer until 1964. It is used here as an
opener, suggesting that this band was a pick-up group, relying on the communal
repertoire of bop rather than their own book.

The rest of the material is the familiar fare of the Parker quintet. On *Chasin'
the Bird*, Lewis displays a deft touch, leaving lots of space but toying ingeniously
with the melody. Konitz plays his contrapuntal line tentatively, as he does the
arpeggios around Kenny Hagood's vocal on *You Go to My Head*. Hagood's swag-
gering baritone, in the manner of Eckstine but without Eckstine's mannerisms, is
recorded so well that his lisp is noticeable. By contrast with the nonet broadcasts
of the preceding Saturdays, all the material except the ballad is uptempo, and the
arranged sections are minimal. The emphasis is on the solos, with Max Roach
taking a solo turn on all three bop standards, trading four bars or eight with Davis
and Konitz in turn. If there was any remorse about disbanding the nonet a week
before, it certainly does not show up in the playing of this band, which is ebullient
and inventive.

In December, Davis was back at the Royal Roost with the Parker quintet.
Parker's engagement there was long, lasting well into 1949, but Davis, as we have
seen, cut it short for himself by walking off the stand on 23 December, leaving
the quintet, with which he had played for twenty months, for good.

Davis immediately went back to the Three Deuces, where he joined Oscar
Pettiford's band, which also included trombonist Kai Winding, with whom he

would play several recording dates during the next year. He then moved with Pettiford's band to Broadway, where they opened a new jazz club called the Clique. It was owned by the owners of the Three Deuces, Sammy Kay and Irving Alexander, who were hoping to make the transition from 52nd Street to Broadway. Pettiford's band for the occasion were exceptional, including Davis, Fats Navarro, Dexter Gordon, Lucky Thompson, and Bud Powell, but the musicians made discordant music together, according to the historian Marshall Stearns; he remembers this engagement as a display of the worst excesses of the bop movement. The forty-five-minute sets were taken up mainly by one or two interminable solos while the other horn players disappeared from the stand. "Everybody was carving everybody and taking thirty minute solos to prove it," Lucky Thompson told Stearns, and Oscar Pettiford just said, "Nobody bothered about the audience." The owners were apparently as unlucky with their other featured bands as well, because they were forced to shut down the Clique after six months, in July 1949. Certainly it was not the Clique's location that caused its failure, because it was taken over by new management that summer and reopened as Birdland, perhaps the best-known jazz club of all time.

Less than two weeks after leaving Parker's group at the Royal Roost, Davis was back in the recording studio with Parker, but under unusual circumstances. The editors of *Metronome* assembled an all-star band almost as soon as the recording ban ended, on Monday 3 January, the first working day of the new year. The selection of players was remarkable, bringing together several men who, although they were not yet widely known, would exert a tremendous influence in jazz throughout the next decade. Davis was one of these, of course, and with him were J.J. Johnson and Kai Winding, the trombonists, and the drummer Shelly Manne. Winding and Manne and the bassist for the date, Eddie Safranski, had been featured with the Stan Kenton orchestra, which had made a popular impression with a voluble, brass-dominated style. Pete Rugolo, Kenton's chief arranger before he joined Capitol as producer, was appointed as the arranger and leader of the Metronome All Stars. Other players included the leaders of the current music – Parker, Gillespie, and the leader of his own highly individualistic branch of jazz, Lennie Tristano:

Metronome All Stars
Miles Davis, Dizzy Gillespie, Fats Navarro, tpt; J.J. Johnson, Kai Winding, tbn; Buddy DeFranco, clnt; Charlie Parker, as; Ernie Caceres, bs; Lennie Tristano, pno; Billy Bauer, gtr; Eddie Safranski, b; Shelly Manne, dms; Pete Rugolo, cond. New York, 3 January 1949
Overtime (two takes); *Victory Ball* (three takes)

(The first takes were both released on RCA Victor 20-3361, the alternate takes on RCA Victor LPT 3046.)
Davis, Navarro, Johnson and Caceres do not play on the first two takes of *Victory Ball*.
Rugolo arranged *Overtime*, and Tristano arranged *Victory Ball*.

With so many soloists working within the confines of the three-minute limit of these 78 rpm recordings, the musical interest of this session is predictably limited. Probably in an attempt to solve this problem, the first two takes of *Victory Ball* were made without Davis, Navarro, Johnson, and Caceres, which may also give a rough indication of the pecking order of the horn players. *Overtime* is reputedly so named because Parker pretended that he was unable to master the arrangement, causing numerous false starts that eventually put the session two and a half hours over the three-hour time limit imposed by the union and dramatically increasing the musicians' cheques by the new pay scale won by the recording ban of the American Federation of Musicians. Unfortunately, the complete session, if it was preserved, has never been collated. Perhaps the main interest of this music comes from the trumpet section, which brings together all three leaders of the younger generation of trumpet players for the only time. In their consecutive choruses on *Overtime*, Gillespie, Navarro, and Davis all play similar passages on open horns, so that it is not easy to tell where one of them ends and the other begins. This point was not lost on Gillespie, who cites this recording as evidence that the styles of Davis and Navarro derive from his own. "I know that each of them sounded like me because we played on a record together, the three of us, and I didn't know which one was playing when I listened – the Metronome All Stars date," Gillespie said. "I didn't know which of us played what solo because the three of us sounded so much alike." Davis, who later played with Navarro at Birdland, also noted that he and Navarro tended to alter their styles in each other's company. "He and I used to play together and we'd sound alike," Davis says, "but when we played separately, we didn't sound alike." The similarity among musicians with such highly personal approaches to their instruments in other contexts probably attests to the strength of their musical roots on 52nd Street, and the Metronome All Star session provides, if nothing else, a permanent record of it.

Later in January, Davis was back in the recording studio for the first of his sessions with the nonet for Capitol. Four months had elapsed since the nonet had disbanded, and assembling the players was a problem. Kai Winding replaced young Michael Zwerin, who had gone back to college, and Parker's piano player, Al Haig, and the bassist Joe Shulman from the Thornhill band came in as replacements for John Lewis and Al McKibbon, who were touring with the Gillespie orchestra. The recording session was called for a Friday afternoon:

Miles Davis Nonet
Miles Davis, tpt; Kai Winding, tbn; Junior Collins, frh; Bill Barber, tba; Lee Konitz, as;
Gerry Mulligan, bs; Al Haig, pno; Joe Shulman, b; Max Roach, dms. New York, 21
January 1949
Jeru; Move; Godchild; Budo
(all on Capitol M-11026)

It seems unusual, to say the least, that no arrangements by Gil Evans were
recorded at this first session, considering his importance in the development of
this music. *Jeru* and *Godchild* are Mulligan's arrangements (the former titled by
Davis, who called Mulligan "Jeru"), and *Move* and *Budo* are Lewis's. Perhaps the
decision about what to record was made by the producer, Pete Rugolo. Certainly
the medium tempos (both of Mulligan's) and the faster tempos (Lewis's) stood a
better chance of commercial success than Evans's slower arrangements.

No matter who made the decision, it cannot be faulted by its results. All four
compositions are perfectly played – and impeccably recorded, as they had to be if
all the nuances were to be preserved. The arranged sections are typically lengthy,
both in the introductions and conclusions and also as frames for the solos. While
the arrangements dominate, the solos are equally flawless, and they are so beautifully integrated into the arrangements that they have often been overlooked by
commentators, or at least undervalued. There is no lack of what is sometimes
called jazz feeling, and the band, especially its soloists – Davis on all four compositions, Mulligan on all but *Move*, Konitz and Roach on *Move* and *Budo*,
Winding on *Godchild* and *Budo* – are not unduly restrained, although they are
certainly disciplined. Perhaps the most striking example is Max Roach on *Move*,
who plays with enormous drive throughout but also manages a paradoxical delicacy. In that, he epitomizes the achievement of the nonet, and he is only one of
nine players who accomplish it on these recordings. The arrangements should
probably be credited with setting the tone, because they oblige the players to work
within a well-defined context, but no one had any reason to expect that the
players would meet the challenge so forcefully. Gil Evans has said, "These
records by Miles indicate what voicing can do, how it can give intensity and
relaxation." With the problems of shifting personnel and a drawn-out schedule,
Davis required consistency and concentration from all his sidemen, and they
responded. Mulligan said, much later, "I count myself fortunate to be there and
I thank whatever lucky stars were responsible for placing me there. There's a
kind of perfection about those recordings." Apparently Rugolo and the Capitol
executives recognized it as well, because they rushed them into print. *Move* and
Budo, John Lewis's uptempo arrangements, were released within a month (as

Capitol 78 rpm 15404); *Jeru* and *Godchild* came out in April (as Capitol 60005). Those buyers who listened carefully heard a new spirit in American improvised music.

In February, Davis was back at the Royal Roost, playing opposite the Parker quintet as a member of Tadd Dameron's Big Ten. Dameron was a gifted arranger and composer, among the best that bop had, and playing in his band allowed Davis to function in a musical context that was similar to the nonet in its attention to arranged materials as well as in its size. The circumstances surrounding Davis's joining Dameron's house band, a plum job because it was steady and at the heart of the musical activity, were not so happy. Dameron's regular trumpeter was Fats Navarro, but Navarro was heavily addicted to heroin and often suffered from assorted other ailments as well, especially heavy colds, which left him weakened. Navarro, born in Florida in 1923, had spent his youth there playing in regional bands and soon earned a reputation as a facile soloist among visiting musicians. He arrived in New York with Andy Kirk's orchestra in 1943. In 1945, he was chosen by Billy Eckstine as Gillespie's replacement in his big band, at Gillespie's urging, and the ease with which he stepped into that key role was the talk of all the musicians in the band.

His addiction soon made reliability a problem and also kept him chained to the New York area, where he could find his supplies. As a result, Davis replaced him in the Eckstine orchestra for their California tour. Now he was replacing him again, although Navarro still played for Dameron whenever he could. Davis stood in for him in Dameron's band for most of the winter of 1949 and is heard on two Saturday broadcasts from the Royal Roost in February and one in early March, as well as on an April recording session. Much of Dameron's writing for the Roost band revolved around Navarro's trumpet lead and his soloing strength, making Davis's task as his replacement far from easy; but Davis's playing on the broadcasts is confident and competent:

Tadd Dameron Big Ten
Miles Davis, tpt; Kai Winding, tbn; Sahib Shihab (Ed Gregory), as; Benjamin Lundy, ts; Cecil Payne, bs; Tadd Dameron, pno; John Collins, gtr; Curly Russell, b; Kenny Clarke, dms; Carlos Vidal, bongo. Royal Roost, New York, 19 February 1949
Focus; April in Paris; Good Bait; Sid's Delight [*Webb's Delight*]
(all on Beppo BEP 503)

Same personnel and place, 26 February 1949
Miles; Casbah
(both on Beppo BEP 503)

Probably the same personnel, same place, 5 March 1949
Good Bait; The Squirrel
(both unissued)

The broadcast repertoire consists of Dameron originals recorded for Capitol around this time. Dameron had recorded *Sid's Delight*, announced here as *Webb's Delight*, and *Casbah* in January with Navarro in the band, just three days before Davis's nonet session. The recordings with Navarro and the aircheck with Davis, although the arrangements are the same, have a very different sound, as Navarro dominates the ensembles in a way that Davis never does. Although the versions with Davis feature a better blend in the ensembles, they also fail to subdue the vibrato of altoist Sahib Shihab as thoroughly as the versions with Navarro did, and the band sounds, for brief moments, as if a refugee from a sweet band, perhaps Carmen Lombardo himself, had sneaked into it. Davis solos on all the numbers except *April in Paris*, a feature for guitarist John Collins, and he is showcased by Dameron's arrangements of the infectious *Good Bait*, which became a standard bop tune, and the ballad called *Miles*.

Davis was still playing in place of Navarro when Dameron's band was called for its second Capitol recording session, in April. The band is the one that played at the Roost except that J.J. Johnson, back in New York after touring with Illinois Jacquet, replaces Winding, and a vocalist, Kay Penton, is added for two titles, no doubt as part of Capitol's scheme to commercialize bebop:

Tadd Dameron and His Orchestra
Miles Davis, tpt; J.J. Johnson, tbn; Sahib Shihab, as; Benjamin Lundy, ts; Cecil Payne, bs; Tadd Dameron, pno; John Collins, gtr; Curly Russell, b; Kenny Clarke, dms; Kay Penton, vcl (on *What's New* and *Heaven's Doors Are Open Wide*). New York, 21 April 1949
John's Delight; What's New; Heaven's Doors Are Open Wide; Focus
(all on Capitol CAP M-11059)

Kay Penton was a clear-voiced but undistinguished band singer, with no affinity for bebop. Dameron's arrangement of *What's New*, with its attractive pop lyric, is mundane, and so is his arrangement of *Heaven's Doors Are Open Wide*, for which he wrote both the words and music. Dameron's Tin Pan Alley clichés in his lyric for *Heaven's Door Are Open Wide* thinly disguise some vaginal imagery:

Heaven's doors are open wide ...
There's love inside;

... You know I'm here
So wake up, dear,
Make my dream come true,
Heaven's doors are open wide, to you.

Surprisingly, Davis does not solo on any of the titles. *John's Delight* showcases John Collins, and *Focus*, an intriguing thirty-eight-bar melody that resolves into standard thirty-two-bar solos in 4/4 time, also has Collins soloing where Davis soloed on the Royal Roost version. The only indication of Davis's presence comes from the ensembles, especially in the trumpet lead on the out-chorus of *John's Delight* (where Davis is heard hitting a clinker once) and throughout *Heaven's Doors*. Otherwise, he is silent.

The next day, Davis returned to the Capitol studio with his nonet. J.J. Johnson returned with him, replacing Winding who had originally replaced Zwerin. Sandy Siegelstein from Thornhill's band replaced Junior Collins on french horn. The Gillespie band were back in New York, so John Lewis could take his place at the piano, but Al McKibbon had been replaced in Gillespie's band by Nelson Boyd, who now replaced him in the nonet as well. Kenny Clarke also returned to the Capitol studio for the second straight day, replacing Max Roach, who had returned to the Parker quintet in late January. Of all the changes, the loss of Roach might appear to be the most crucial, though no more so than the loss of John Lewis on the first date, and on that occasion the music did not suffer noticeably. Clarke is as adept as Roach technically, and more experienced, and the two men shared many stylistic traits as a result of Clarke being Roach's tutor in the beginning:

Miles Davis Nonet
Miles Davis, tpt; J.J. Johnson, tbn; Sandy Siegelstein, frh; Bill Barber, tba; Lee Konitz, as; Gerry Mulligan, bs; John Lewis, pno; Nelson Boyd, b; Kenny Clarke, dms. New York, 22 April 1949
Venus de Milo; Rouge; Boplicity; Israel
(all on Capitol M-11026)

Four different arrangers are featured on this date; *Venus de Milo* is Mulligan's, *Rouge* Lewis's, *Boplicity* Evans's, and *Israel* Johnny Carisi's. *Venus de Milo* is a relatively straightforward showcase for Davis's trumpet, as the title punningly suggests. The memorable little melody is stated by a trumpet lead, followed by Davis's solo, and then Mulligan spells him for a couple of choruses before he leads the ensemble out. Davis's tone is full and bold, recalling the early takes of *Billie's Bounce*, which he said sounded like Freddie Webster.

Rouge was never released on 78 rpm by Capitol, waiting around in their vaults until the first microgroove release in 1954. Certainly it would have done the nonet no harm had it appeared immediately. The arrangement is tight and apparently difficult, and there is a suggestion of tentativeness in the concluding section, especially by Clarke and perhaps also by Mulligan, who suddenly seems to break ranks for one bar in the ensemble before being absorbed into it again. But there is some fine playing. Its strengths are in Lewis's use of a peculiar little fanfare that opens the recording decorously and then recurs at unexpected moments throughout it, and in the solos by Lewis, Konitz, and Davis, which are polished variations on the theme.

Boplicity was written by Davis and Evans, but on its original release was attributed to Cleo Henry, Davis's mother. It moves along through numerous shifts of texture as the various horns are rearranged into new alliances, in what can only be described as a *tour de force* by Evans. Asked in 1950 to name his favorite example of his own work, Davis answered, without hesitating, *"Boplicity*, because of Gil's arrangement." André Hodeir says, *"Boplicity* alone is enough to make Gil Evans qualify as one of jazz's greatest arranger-composers."

For all its brilliance, *Boplicity* was overshadowed by *Israel* at the time of their release in October, and not altogether unjustly. Carisi's composition sounds impossibly complex, with the melodic line played first by a section made up of Davis, Konitz, Johnson, and Siegelstein, and then repeated while a second section led by Mulligan and an amazingly supple Barber introduces a counter-melody. Eventually, several melodies weave into one another. Davis's solo ranks as one of his very best on record to this time. Martin Williams has singled it out along with his solo on *Move* from the first date for special praise: "If [these recordings] proved nothing else, they would prove that Miles Davis, already an interesting and personal soloist, could produce two great improvisations, each one great in a different way. His blues solo on *Israel* is a beautiful example of classic simplicity of melody and a personal reassessment of the mood of the blues. His chorus on *Move* is a striking episode of meaningful asymmetry, and it has some phrasing that is so original that one can only say that, rhythmically, it seems to turn back on itself while moving steadily forward."

The pairing of *Israel* and *Boplicity* in an October release by Capitol seems almost an embarrassment of riches for jazz fans. The other pieces recorded with them, however, were not released at the time; *Rouge*, as already mentioned, was withheld for five years, and *Venus de Milo* was put out only a year and a half later, weakly backed by Kenny Hagood's vocal on *Darn That Dream*.

Tadd Dameron, an outstanding composer-arranger in his own right, was moved by what he heard from the nonet. "Davis is the farthest advanced musician of his day, and *Boplicity* is one of the best small group sounds I've heard," he said. As the two men continued to work together, Dameron's regard for Davis's contribution to his band led him to share the leader's duties, and eventually the joint leadership was acknowledged in the name of their band. It was called the Miles Davis–Tadd Dameron Quintet, and it was organized for a festival in Europe. Charles Delaunay, the principal organizer of Le Festival de Jazz 1949, to take place in Paris in the week of 8–15 May, had arranged for the Charlie Parker Quintet to headline the festival along with Sidney Bechet's band. Tadd Dameron and Miles Davis were invited to share the billing, and they put together a quintet that was a cross between a pick-up group and a set band. Davis and Dameron chose Kenny Clarke from Dameron's Big Ten, giving the group a core of players whose names were known to European jazz buffs. They added James Moody, the tenor saxophonist formerly with the Gillespie band who was then living in Europe, and a bassist selected by Delaunay. The bassist's name was Barney Spieler, an American expatriate studying at the Conservatoire national de musique de Paris but also an experienced player with visiting American jazz groups, including Benny Goodman's. With the Charlie Parker Quintet, which now included Kinney Dorham, Al Haig, Tommy Potter, and Max Roach, and the Miles Davis–Tadd Dameron Quintet, the festival already had some of the very best modern players, and to them were added Don Byas, who had stayed behind in Europe after touring there with Don Redman's band in 1946, and the best European piano player, Bernard Peiffer. Bechet's band included trombonist Russell (Big Chief) Moore, and the traditional styles were also represented by the boogie-woogie piano player Pete Johnson and cornetist Jimmy McPartland. Swing was represented by Oran (Hot Lips) Page, trumpeter-singer, supplemented by European swing musicians such as England's Carlo Krahmer and Belgium's Toots Thielemans. It promised to be a gala occasion.

The American contingent arrived by air only the day before the opening. The Davis-Dameron quintet played in the opening concert on Sunday, 8 May and again the next night, the 9th, taking two days off and returning for matinée and evening performances on Thursday, 12 May; after another day off, they returned Saturday evening, the 14th, and again played both a matinée and evening performance on the final day of the festival, Sunday 15 May. In what has become a venerable tradition at European jazz concerts, most if not all the performances were recorded privately. Some twenty-eight years later, the best of the private recordings of the quintet were selected and issued by Columbia Records:

Miles Davis–Tadd Dameron Quintet
Miles Davis, tpt; James Moody, ts; Tadd Dameron, pno; Barney Spieler, b; Kenny Clarke, dms. Salle Pleyel, Paris, 8 May 1949
Rifftide; Good Bait; Don't Blame Me (omit Moody); *Lady Bird*
(all on Columbia 34804)

Same personnel and place, 9, 12, 14, or 15 May 1949
Wah Hoo; Allen's Alley; Embraceable You (Moody on coda only); *Ornithology; All the Things You Are*
(all on Columbia 34804)
Performances of *The Squirrel, Crazy Rhythm,* and *Perdido* (probably *Wah Hoo,* which is based on *Perdido*'s changes) and a second version of *All the Things You Are* have not yet been issued.

Davis and Moody's problem of playing ensembles together with virtually no rehearsal was solved mainly by avoiding it altogether. On *Good Bait,* Moody plays the melody alone and Davis plays the bridge alone; on the ballads, *Don't Blame Me* and *Embraceable You,* Moody sits out altogether. When they do play together, it is on bop standards such as *Rifftide, Wah Hoo,* and *Allen's Alley,* but even that precaution does not help on *Lady Bird,* which features a ragged ensemble. The French critic Henri Renaud says, "James [Moody] was an unassuming, even shy man and the prospect of playing with such a figure as Miles nearly scared him to death." Moody is definitely subdued, and his only striking turn is on *All the Things You Are,* recorded late in the festival; the quintet uses an arrangement based on John Lewis's arrangement for Gillespie's band, where Moody must have played it several times.

Dameron is equally subdued on these recordings, and Davis dominates the band in every sense, even to the extent of his announcing the titles for the audience, a practice he gave up completely after he developed what Zwerin calls "his famous salty dog act." He plays an aggressive bebop style, not at all characteristic of his work in New York with the nonet and Dameron's Big Ten; his solos are marked by eighth- and sixteenth-note runs into the upper register, almost as if he set out to prove something to someone – perhaps to Parker. The striking difference in his approach became the main topic of reviewer's comments when these performances were issued years later. "Playing with a fiery attack that is closer to Fats Navarro than anyone else, his solos represent probably the best bebop he ever played," Michael Shera wrote in *Jazz Journal.* Scott Yanow, writing in *Record Review,* said, "His multi-note runs on uptempo numbers resemble the style of Gillespie ... It is on the ballads that Davis sounds most individualistic, coming close to the style he would perfect in the Fifties." The same reviewer calls the Paris Jazz Festival recording "the best pre-1954 Miles Davis album." That judgment seems remarkably short-sighted, considering the recorded work with Parker and especially with the nonet, but it does point out the excellence of his playing here, which should finally lay to rest the claim that he developed the warm, controlled style of his mature playing because he could not cope with the pyrotechnical Gillespie style. Here he not only copes with it, but he shows considerable mastery of it. Like all great artists, he knew exactly what he was doing when he set aside the stylistic elements in vogue in his formative years.

Apart from these tracks with the Miles Davis–Tadd Dameron Quintet, Davis also participated in the jam session that brought the festival to a close. It is as much a traffic jam as a music jam and does not reveal anything of his playing (or much of anyone else's):

Festival Jam Session
Aime Barelli, Bill Coleman, Miles Davis, probably Kinney Dorham, Oran (Hot Lips) Page, tpt; Russell (Big Chief) Moore, tbn; Hubert Rostaing, clnt; Sidney Bechet, Pierre Braslav-sky, ss; Charlie Parker, as; Don Byas, James Moody, ts; Al Haig, pno; Hazy Osterwald, vib; Jean (Toots) Thielemans, gtr; Tommy Potter, b; Max Roach, dms. Salle Pleyel, Paris, 15 May 1949
untitled blues
(on Durium-Cicala BLJ 8024 and on Spotlite 118)

Le Festival de Jazz 1949 certainly succeeded in disseminating the newer currents of American music to Europe, along with some traditional elements, which were already well entrenched there. Parker and Davis became European celebrities and were received with considerable pomp in Europe ever after. They might well have been received that way anyway, because of their status in the development of jazz music. A few of the other musicians, including Kinney Dorham and Al Haig, hardly went on to achieve what Parker and Davis did but they too remained favorites in Europe, and Haig owed his second career in jazz, beginning in 1973, after more than fifteen years of obscurity, to the enthusiasm of European fans, who sought him out and encouraged him to play bebop professionally again. Tadd Dameron went from the Paris festival to London, where he spent some weeks working with the Ted Heath orchestra, writing some charts for them and improv-ing the charts they were already using. The festival also instigated a number of more or less permanent exchanges. Toots Thielemans emigrated to the United States in 1951, and Bernard Peiffer in 1954. Sidney Bechet settled in Paris in 1951. Kenny Clarke, who had lived in Paris for several months in 1946, staying behind when his colleagues in the Gillespie band returned after their tour, settled there permanently in 1956, joining Bechet and Don Byas, among others, and eventually becoming an elder statesman in the growing community of jazz expatriates.

When the festival ended, Davis returned to New York with Kenny Clarke, Charlie Parker, and the rest of the American contingent. The time away and the easy camaraderie with musicians as diverse as Bechet and Hot Lips Page must have made it doubly difficult for them to settle back in at home, where there was a growing hysteria about the direction that jazz was taking.

Reviewers and fans were split decisively into two camps. One camp advocated traditional jazz as the only "real" jazz music, and the other acclaimed bebop as the culmination of decades of "progress" in American music. Almost everyone who had more than a casual interest was aligned on one side or the other, usually vociferously so. Most of the journalists who covered jazz in America, or in Europe, were traditionalists, except for the few who had formed their tastes during the era of the big dance bands, and thus stood a bit apart from the warring camps, as did many of the musicians who had emerged from the big bands – the so-called swing, or mainstream musicians. Band leaders such as Earl Hines, Cootie Williams, and Jay McShann employed boppers in the beginning and sometimes played arrangements of bop compositions, and men such as Coleman Hawkins, Roy Eldridge, and Ben Webster played alongside the younger musicians without qualms.

The mainstream players suffered most from the controversy. As the public and the press became polarized, the very malleability of the mainstream players left them without an audience that could identify with them. The traditionalists, known as moldy figs among the modernists, discovered the trumpeter Bunk Johnson and later the clarinetist George Lewis on the backstreets of New Orleans and lauded their technically limited playing as evidence of the authentic roots of jazz. Their advocacy of two-beat music over all other jazz created in turn an audience for the Chicagoans whose style was based on traditional New Orleans playing – men who gathered around Eddie Condon – and also for younger men who embraced the New Orleans players as their direct influence, among them Turk Murphy, Wally Rose, and Bob Wilber. The modernists looked, of course, to Charlie Parker and Dizzy Gillespie as the fount of jazz music, conveniently ignoring Parker's occasional nod toward Lester Young and Gillespie's frequent praise for Roy Eldridge. As the bickering heated up, it became more and more difficult to convince anyone that there were virtues on both sides, much less that both were authentic jazz.

In this irrational climate, the recordings of the Miles Davis nonet eventually exerted a steadying influence, winning over even some critics who had previously been opposed to the new music, such as John S. Wilson of the *New York Times*, as well as hundreds of fans who were similarly, although more quietly, opposed. Davis was himself a surprisingly open commentator on the controversy, considering the depth of his involvement in the bop movement. "I don't like to hear someone put down Dixieland," he told Wilson. "Those people who say there's no music but bop are just stupid. It just shows how much they don't know. I never played Dixieland myself. When I was growing up I played like Roy Eldridge, Harry James, Freddie Webster and anyone else I admired. You've got to start way back before you can play bop. You've got to have a foundation."

Davis found himself in a privileged position among some of the anti-boppers, who began to cite him as an exception to all the things they found wrong on the other side. John Hammond, the discoverer of Count Basie and Billie Holiday in the 1930s and many other great jazz players, got caught up in the debate and threw his not inconsiderable weight onto the side of the traditionalists. Looking back on it about three decades later, in his memoirs entitled *On Record*, he offered this reason for his stance: "Bop lacked the swing I believe essential to great jazz playing, lacked the humor, and the free-flowing invention of the best jazz creators. In their place it offered a new self-consciousness, an excessive emphasis on harmonic and rhythmic revolt, a concentration on technique at the expense of musical emotion. Instead of expanding the form, they contracted it, made it their private language. I extend this judgement even to such giants as Bird Parker, Monk, and Coltrane." And then Hammond added, "The superlative Miles Davis is exempted."

In the midst of all the hullabaloo, Davis unfortunately did not immediately resume the recording project with the nonet. Although he returned from Europe to find that club engagements were hard to come by, he devoted his time instead to getting together a large band, co-led by Dameron, and organizing their book and personnel. Little is known about the band because they never got past the rehearsal phase, but there were reportedly eighteen pieces. The personnel included trumpeters Red Rodney and Bernie Glow; trombonists Matthew Gee, Kai Winding, and Johnny Mandel; reedmen Allen Eager, Charlie Kennedy, Zoot Sims, and Cecil Payne; and a rhythm section with John Collins, Nelson Boyd, and Rossiere (Shadow) Wilson. With Tadd Dameron's ability as a composer and arranger and Miles Davis's strength as a leader as well as a soloist added to that list of players, the band looked very promising. The fact that they disappeared without a trace, never getting a booking or being recorded even on home equipment, is cause for regret. Perhaps they would have charted new directions for jazz as had the nonet, which also came perilously close to existing only as a rehearsal band.

Certainly the project was badly timed. All around there were signs that the age of big bands was ending. Concert dates for larger groups were scarce, and payrolls were becoming impossible to meet. Within a year, Count Basie would be forced to disband his orchestra, which he had led continuously since 1935, and reduce his working unit to a septet. The most modern of all the bands, Dizzy Gillespie's, would also disband, thus robbing Gillespie of the musical context that best suited his playing. "Everybody was sorry about that, man; cats were crying, not making any money. So was I," Gillespie says; and then he shrugs, "The fad was finished." For the Davis-Dameron big band, the fad never even began.

The winds of change were moving too strongly in the other direction and were being felt from other experimental quarters besides Davis's nonet. Lennie Tristano, a Chicago-born pianist, settled in New York after the war and began playing in the clubs on 52nd Street and elsewhere. Because he was blind, white, academically trained, and a natural teacher, he could hardly escape the notice of young and curious musicians, and before long he had his own coterie of pupils and disciples, including Lee Konitz, tenor saxophonist Warne Marsh, guitarist Billy Bauer, and drummer Denzil Best, the composer of the nonet's *Move*. Like Davis and Dameron and several others, Tristano was signed by Capitol Records when the recording ban ended. On 16 May, at Tristano's third recording session of the spring, his sextet, including all the musicians named above and bassist Arnold Fishkin, recorded two free-form tracks called *Intuition* and *Digression*. They had neither a set of chord changes nor a fixed tempo, but the sextet had been working for some time at discovering form and developing coherence extemporaneously, and Tristano reckoned that they were now ready to record their experiments. The producers at Capitol apparently thought otherwise upon hearing the result, which they felt had no commerical possibilities, and they refused to pay Tristano's men for the recordings or to release them. The recordings then became something of a cause when Symphony Sid Torin got hold of the masters and began to play them on his radio show. Finally Capitol was forced to make them available (and, of course, to pay Tristano for them). When they were reissued on microgroove in the early 1970s (on Capitol M-11060), Tristano commented: "These two sides were completely spontaneously improvised. A lot of people who heard them thought they were compositions. To my knowledge Miles Davis is the only noted musician who acknowledged in print the real nature of the music on these sides." Davis's response is an early indication of his awareness throughout his career of new directions in the music.

Though jobs were scarce throughout the rest of 1949, Davis worked, with or without Dameron, in several limited engagements in clubs. One of these is probably the source of an unidentified recording featuring Davis playing *Embraceable You*, which he had also used as a ballad showcase in Paris. The few available details are these:

Miles Davis Band
Miles Davis, tpt; unidentified trombone, tenor saxophone, piano, bass, drums. Unknown place and date
Embraceable You (Session LP 101)

The recording was made in a very noisy setting. Before the ballad begins, a tenor saxophone is heard noodling idly, and then the piano introduction begins and the saxophone player stops. Someone, apparently Davis, calls an instruction to the pianist – "Break it up, break it up" – who then introduces block chords. The track is an extended trumpet solo; only in the final statement of the melody are the tenor and (probably) trombone heard, playing harmony.

On Christmas night, Davis played in a concert at Carnegie Hall called the Stars of Modern Jazz Concert, promoted by Leonard Feather – his third Christmas jazz concert at Carnegie Hall, and the last. The main attractions were Sarah Vaughan and the Charlie Parker Quintet, with some new faces: Red Rodney for Dorham, and Roy Haynes for Roach; Roach played instead with one of the pick-up bands assembled for the concert. Lennie Tristano and his coterie were also there, including Konitz, Marsh, and Bauer, with Joe Shulman on bass and Jeff Morton on drums. One makeshift group put tenor saxophonist Stan Getz and trombonist Kai Winding in front of Parker's rhythm section, and the other one, with Miles Davis, was a septet:

Stars of Modern Jazz Jam Session
Miles Davis, tpt; Benny Green, tbn; Sonny Stitt, as; Serge Chaloff, bs; Bud Powell, pno; Curly Russell, b; Max Roach, dms. Carnegie Hall, New York, 25 December 1949
Move; Hot House; Ornithology (incomplete)
(all on IAJRC 20)

The concert was taped by Voice of America, the United States radio network in Europe, and parts of it were broadcast the next year. The recording of the concert issued by IAJRC in 1976 was reconstructed from the files of Voice of America and assorted home-made tapes from European collectors. The band with Davis plays at the beginning and the end of the concert, with the rhythm section alone starting off (with *All God's Children Got Rhythm*) and then being joined by the horns for *Move*, the uptempo number from the nonet's repertoire that became Davis's most recorded tune for the next few years. At the end of the proceedings, the seven pick-up players return to play two bop standards, *Hot House* and *Ornithology*, but the recording of the latter ends during the third solo, when the Voice of America tape ran out. The music by the group that includes Davis is standard fare, with perfunctory recitations of the melody by apparently unrehearsed ensembles and then the queue for solo turns. Jam sessions like this one became a fixture at concerts because they were part of the successful formula used by Granz's Jazz at the Philharmonic; fortunately the Stars of Modern Jazz Concert did not go so far as to emulate the JATP's excesses by bringing in honkers and gut-bucket specialists to excite the crowd, a function then being filled for JATP by Illinois Jacquet and Tommy Turk.

Leonard Feather, the English jazz writer who emigrated to New York in 1939, now marvels at his youthful nerve in promoting the concert. "Now that I look back on it, I wonder why I had the courage to do it, because it was a risky thing to do at the time," he says. "And I put my own money into it. I don't know what it came to, maybe a couple thousand dollars, which at that time was a lot to put into a concert." He adds, "But I had some other people involved, Monte Kay and Symphony Sid; we became involved together in putting these concerts on." The fact that the third Christmas concert was the last further underlines the state of recession into which jazz was slipping. However, all three concerts turned profits. "They did very well, surprisingly well, surprising in view of the fact that there was so much active, really nasty opposition to the music, particularly in the media," Feather says. "The daily press was just death on it; they didn't even acknowledge its existence." Indeed, the concert was mentioned neither in New York's major daily newspapers nor in the jazz magazines. Feather adds, "With the exception of *Metronome* and an occasional write-up in *Down Beat*, most of the musical press were violently opposed to it. Some very small magazines which wielded some power in jazz circles used to run whole articles attacking me and attacking bebop in general and attacking anything which was not New Orleans – Bunk Johnson and them. That's what was called the 'War of the Moldy Figs.'"

By early 1950, Miles Davis began mixing with the up-and-coming young players in jazz. He had almost always played with men older than he, apart from isolated exceptions such as bassist Nelson Boyd, who was even more precocious. Now, increasingly, there were younger men around the clubs, men such as Sonny Rollins, a tenor saxophonist from Harlem who was three years younger than he. Rollins had made his recording debut early in 1949 as part of the bebop round-up conducted by Capitol Records. He turned up, unheralded, in the band of bop singer Babs Gonzales on 20 January, along with J.J. Johnson and Benny Green, and burned a chorus on both of the tunes Gonzales's band recorded that day, *Capitolizing* and *Professor Bop*. Rollins's choruses are easily the most interesting music on either piece, but he moved to Chicago soon after and stayed there for the rest of the year, returning to New York early in 1950, where he played in the house band at a Harlem club. It was there that Davis first met him. "Miles already had a considerable reputation by that time," Rollins says. "He'd heard a few of my records and of course I'd heard him, so you could really say that we already knew each other." Davis was very impressed and invited Rollins to join his band for an engagement at the Audubon Ballroom later in the month. That band also featured Art Blakey, who had just left the Lucky Millinder band and was back in town.

Davis's interest started Rollins on the course that would soon lead to wider recognition, even rivaling Davis's stature for a short period late in the decade, but it was probably not difficult for Davis to pick him out as a musician of great potential. As a high school student in the Sugar Hill district of Harlem, Rollins already exuded the charisma that marked his personal and musical style as a

professional. Tall and imposing, his presence seems automatically to attract attention both on the bandstand and off it, although Rollins has never learned to feel
comfortable with the attention. For all the admiration given him, he suffers bouts
of self-doubt, but his admirers see only the power and the presence. Jackie
McLean, who was a high school freshman when Rollins was a senior, says, "He
influenced everybody uptown, playing every instrument."

Sugar Hill, when Rollins and McLean were growing up, was just beginning to
fade as Harlem's hub of affluence and culture. Coleman Hawkins lived there, and
so did Bud Powell, Teddy Wilson, and a covey of Ellingtonians including Duke
and his sister Ruth, Billy Strayhorn, and Mercer Ellington. Their neighbors
included the two finest poets of the Harlem Renaissance, Langston Hughes and
Countee Cullen, the novelist Ralph Ellison, and Roy Wilkins and Walter White,
executives of the National Association for the Advancement of Colored People.
In his program notes for the 'Sugar Hill Penthouse' movement of the suite *Black,
Brown and Beige*, Duke Ellington crowed, "If you ever sat on a beautiful magenta
cloud overlooking New York City, you were on Sugar Hill." Bounded by 145th
and 155th streets, with the Polo Grounds, home of the New York Giants baseball
team, on its periphery, Sugar Hill became populated by black families only in the
1920s, years after the rest of Harlem was solidly black. It flourished in the 1930s,
but by the end of the 1940s many middle-class blacks were no longer settling in
Sugar Hill or any other part of Harlem, choosing instead the borough of Queens
and the further suburbs. The last significant group of artists nurtured in Sugar
Hill were the young jazz musicians who emerged in the wake of the bebop revolution, and among them Sonny Rollins was the lodestar.

Jackie McLean remembers, "There were a lot of musicians in our neighborhood like [drummer] Arthur Taylor, [pianist] Kenny Drew, Connie Henry, who
played bass for a while, Arthur Phipps, who also played bass, and [alto saxopho-
nist] Ernie Henry, and there were guys who used to come from out of the neighborhood to see what was happening, like Walter Bishop [later Parker's pianist].
Sonny was the leader of all of them." They were all close to Miles Davis in age, if
not in experience, and soon after he met Rollins, Davis began spending his spare
hours with them. "When Miles came to town," McLean says, "he began to hang
out up there on the Hill with us." Most of the young musicians Davis befriended
there, including Rollins and McLean, used heroin and other narcotics, which
became readily available on the Harlem streets after the war.

Another relative newcomer whom Davis met at this time was John Coltrane, a
Philadelphian who joined the Dizzy Gillespie orchestra in its final year as an alto
saxophonist, even though his preference was clearly for the tenor saxophone.
Coltrane and Rollins, destined to be touted as rivals by the jazz press because they
were both gifted players on the same instrument, first played together with Miles

Davis, probably at the Audubon Ballroom early in 1950, with Art Blakey on drums. Rollins says, "Coltrane and I first met in 1950 in New York, where we worked together for a few memorable gigs with Miles Davis. I really had to listen carefully to him. I often wondered what he was doing, where he was going." Coltrane was already engaged in the painstaking search for musical form that would eventually elevate him to the ranks of the greatest improvisers jazz has had. As for the rivalry with Rollins, it seems always to have been trumped up for press copy, as might be expected from the personalities of the two men. Rollins says, "Later we became good friends. Good enough friends for me to borrow money from him, and Coltrane and Monk were the only two people I would ever ask for a loan." For more than a decade, Rollins and Coltrane were Davis's top choices to join him as the leading horns in his small bands, whenever he was in control of the hiring for the engagements he played.

Although many of the clubs that had recently supported jazz were shifting their entertainment policies, making the short-term prospects for jazz musicians bleak, the news was not all bad. In particular, Broadway continued to open up as the central location for jazz activity in New York, following the success, commercial as well as musical, of the Royal Roost. One new club, Bop City, opened at Broadway and 49th Street, billing itself in neon lights as "the jazz center of the world," and Birdland, in the same block, opened as almost a carbon copy of the Royal Roost, featuring a bullpen for listeners who did not want to drink and a weekly remote broadcast of live music. Birdland, named of course for Charlie Parker, would prove to be a force in jazz presentation, surviving until 1965, an amazing length of time as jazz clubs go; by the time it finally closed, both the Royal Roost and Bop City would be distant memories.

Davis played at Birdland in February, in an all-star band whose nominal leader was Stan Getz, a tenor saxophonist with a casual, lyrical style derived from Lester Young. Getz had become well known in Woody Herman's orchestra, especially for his playing on *Early Autumn*, a hit in 1948. Around this time, Getz recalls, "J.J. Johnson and I had a cooperative band together with Miles Davis, Bud Powell, Max Roach and Curly Russell." The band that broadcast from Birdland on Saturday 10 February substitutes Tadd Dameron for Powell and Gene Ramey for Russell. The details are as follows:

Stan Getz-Miles Davis Sextet
Miles Davis, tpt; J.J. Johnson, tbn; Stan Getz, ts; Tadd Dameron, pno; Gene Ramey, b; Max Roach, dms. Birdland, New York, 10 February 1950
Conception; Ray's Idea; Max Is Making Wax; Woody'n You
(all on Ozone 1)
On the remaining title from this date, *That Old Black Magic*, Getz is featured with the rhythm section; Davis and Johnson are not heard.

The aural evidence proves that this band was not simply a pick-up group. On all the pieces except Getz's ballad showcase, *That Old Black Magic*, where he is the only horn, the sextet execute relatively long and detailed arranged sections, including background riffs behind the soloists in several places. The spirit of Davis's nonet is evident in the band's musical priorities. The compositions played mark the first appearance in Davis's repertoire of three compositions destined to show up in later recordings as well. None is an original by Davis, but all come with pedigrees. Two belong to the Gillespie big band book, *Woody'n You* and *Ray's Idea*, and *Conception* is George Shearing's, recorded by him in July 1949. *Woody'n You* was actually somewhat older than is suggested by its fairly recent prominence in Gillespie's repertoire (recorded by his orchestra in December 1947), having been written and arranged by Gillespie for the Woody Herman orchestra – as its title rather awkwardly indicates – a few years earlier. *Ray's Idea* is a collaboration by bassist Ray Brown and Gil Fuller. Of all the compositions played here by the sextet, Shearing's *Conception* receives the most interesting arrangement, involving shifting leads between the trumpet and saxophone and sequences of altered time. The arrangement freely borrows Gil Evans's devices and is entirely worthy of Evans himself, but the credit for the arrangement belongs to Davis, a fact that emerged three weeks later, when this arrangement was recorded by the nonet on the final Capitol session. Directly or indirectly, Evans's craftsmanship reverberates throughout Davis's arrangement.

This Birdland aircheck represents the only surviving document of the collaboration between Getz and Davis, although the collaboration apparently lasted several weeks. Regrettably, it does not include a recorded instance of their playing a ballad together. Both men are recognized as masters at interpreting ballads, although the recognition of Davis was less secure than it would later become. Getz was already acclaimed for his ballad playing, and for that reason he took the leader's privileges by playing the ballad alone. Giving Getz those privileges might seem to be an unusually generous gesture, especially in a cooperative group that accords both Davis and Getz a single vote in such matters. The prospect of Davis and Getz working cooperatively in a band might fire the imagination of any jazz historian, because both men are notoriously prickly personalities, accepting no nonsense, real or imagined, from any quarter. That alone would seem to guarantee a difficult relationship, but they seem always to have held one another in the highest regard, perhaps because they share a melodic gift that leaves them with very few rivals. Davis says, "I like Stan because he has so much patience, the way he plays those melodies – other people can't get nothing out of a song, but he can. It takes a lot of imagination, that he has, that so many other people don't have." Their mutual respect comes through clearly in the few recorded minutes that have survived from the hours they spent working together in 1950.

Finally, on 9 March, a Thursday, a version of the Davis nonet convened in the Capitol recording studios to fulfill the third and final session that had been contracted almost sixteen months earlier. Surprisingly, the changes in personnel were not even as extensive as they had been for the second date. The only entirely new face was Gunther Schuller, the french hornist, who replaced Sandy Siegelstein (who had originally replaced Junior Collins). Schuller, less than a year older than Davis, had had a strict conservatory background and was a member of the orchestra at the Metropolitan Opera when he recorded with the nonet. He was nevertheless deeply interested in jazz and he went on to make several ambitious attempts at fusing jazz and symphonic music. He eventually became, along with John Lewis, one of the key figures in third stream music, an interesting hybrid that attracted less interest than it deserved from both jazz and symphonic music fans. In 1950, Schuller was just preparing to earn the credential that would give him some credibility among jazz listeners when he surfaced with his proposals for fusion, by playing with the nonet.

Apart from Schuller, the only changes were to bring back the two rhythm players who had worked with the nonet at the Royal Roost, Max Roach and Al McKibbon, and to add Kenny Hagood for a vocal arrangement:

Miles Davis Nonet
Miles Davis, tpt; J.J. Johnson, tbn; Gunther Schuller, frh; Bill Barber, tba; Lee Konitz, as; Gerry Mulligan, bs; John Lewis, pno; Al McKibbon, b; Max Roach, dms; Kenny Hagood, vcl (on *Darn That Dream*). New York, 9 March 1950
Deception; Rocker; Moon Dreams; Darn That Dream
(all on Capitol M-11026)

The four compositions were, not surprisingly after so long a hiatus, less interesting than the preceding ones. Some of the edge had undeniably been lost since the original Royal Roost engagement. At the previous recording sessions, it must have seemed a possibility that success in the recording studios could lead to the reactivation of the nonet on a permanent basis. Some records had been released, eliciting great interest in some circles and producing a modest commercial success, but too much had happened in the meantime to hold out any hope for the nonet, which by now would require revival, not merely survival.

Yet the recordings were as impeccably rehearsed and as carefully arranged. One might question Davis's choice of *Darn That Dream*, with Hagood's vocal and an arrangement by Gerry Mulligan, instead of *Why Do I Love You?*, if a vocal track had to be recorded. The version of *Why Do I Love You?* that survives from the Royal Roost broadcast has a more intricate, almost arabesque, arrangement by Gil Evans, which makes it more interesting musically, but perhaps its intricacy was the very reason that it was overlooked in favor of the straightforward *Darn That Dream*. At least Capitol seemed pleased with *Darn That Dream*; it was released in November, coupled with *Venus de Milo* from the April recording session. A reviewer in *Down Beat* considered Kenny Hagood to be "too tense" but lauded the arranger, whom he took to be Gil Evans: "Here is an arranger who has learned the individual instruments and their sound possibilities." Well and good, but the nonet's book also included *S'il vous plait* and perhaps other compositions that might have represented so much better what the nonet had accomplished.

Deception was arranged by Davis and credited to him as composer, although, as its title obliquely confesses, it is really George Shearing's *Conception*; *Rocker* is Gerry Mulligan's, and *Moon Dreams*, also played on both of the Roost remotes, is Gil Evans's. The recording of *Deception/Conception* points up the fact that the intervening months had somewhat altered the intentions of these recording sessions. Instead of providing a permanent document of the music of the nonet, *Deception* introduces brand-new material, since it could not have been part of the original repertoire, having been recorded by Shearing some nine months after the nonet's public appearances. In its style, the arrangement is worthy of the nonet, showing how thoroughly ingrained in Davis's music that brief phase of his career had become. The emphasis is upon the arranged sections to an unusual degree, with the band playing the arranged introduction twice in its entirety, leaving room only for Davis and a very cautious J.J. Johnson to solo.

Mulligan's *Rocker* became a post-bop favorite, showing up later in the year in an arrangement for Charlie Parker with strings – Norman Granz's latest attempt to enshrine Parker – and in various arrangements by Mulligan for his own groups, as well as in the repertoires of many house bands. Its bouncy, good-natured swing typifies Mulligan's best music, and in the next decade or so he would provide an abundance of that.

Moon Dreams, Gil Evans's retooling of a schmaltzy ballad by Chummy MacGregor, the pianist for Glen Miller and other sweet bands, sounds like an academic exercise in writing for the instruments of the nonet. Its thick, deliberate blend of the six horns inches along romantically. Occasionally one of the horns moves out of the blend to establish a lead for four bars or eight bars and then recedes back into it again – first Davis, and then Konitz, and then Mulligan – but there are no solos. It is a *tour de force* for the arranger, a brilliant display of inimitable talents. *Moon Dreams*, a kind of musical still life, is easy to admire but impossible to love.

The legacy of the Davis nonet was now, finally, complete. On the surface, the nonet had accomplished very little: a two-week engagement at the Royal Roost, and twelve recorded titles lasting about three minutes each. To accomplish even that, a total of no fewer than twenty musicians, counting Hagood, had played in the band, and two more, Johnny Carisi and of course Gil Evans, had also contributed to the writing. In the two weeks at the Roost, probably fewer than a thousand heard the group in person, and perhaps a few thousand more heard the remote broadcasts. Many of them must have just scratched their heads on hearing the nonet's sounds, and perhaps some others, mostly musicians, nodded theirs.

As the 78 rpm records came out, one by one, spread over a year and a half until there were finally eight sides available – four releases – a few fans probably watched eagerly for the next one, but with so few releases most people just heard the latest one somewhere and picked it up or simply missed it altogether. The nonet certainly did not blitz their audience. And yet, in the unaccountable way that quality sometimes perseveres, the nonet changed the face of jazz, and not especially slowly. Of course it was not *only* the nonet that forged the change, by any means. At the Stars of Modern Jazz Concert on Christmas day, while Davis was putting in the night with a pick-up group playing bebop, both the Lennie Tristano Quintet with Lee Konitz and the Stan Getz–Kai Winding Quintet were displaying a brand of careful, thoughtful chamber jazz that would very soon be known far and wide as cool jazz, which the nonet had pioneered. Their influence was felt directly by members of both those groups, since Winding and Konitz had both played in the nonet, but the style of music they played was partly their own creation too. And by the time Gerry Mulligan moved to California in 1952, he found dozens of musicians playing that same cool style, and most of them knew all about his role in that nonet and could hum every bar of *Israel* and *Boplicity* and *Venus de Milo*. Jimmy Giuffre and Sonny Criss and lots of other musicians on the west coast felt that the nonet had helped them to see more clearly the direction they had been moving in, without actually showing them that direction. The style of the nonet trickled into the jazz mainstream from so many sources that it soon formed one of its currents. By the time eight of the Capitol recordings were collected for release on a ten-inch LP in May 1954, under the title *Birth of the Cool*, they were already justly celebrated.

The rumor nevertheless persists that the nonet went unheralded and unheard, which is not true even of the live performances by the group and is much less true of the recordings. Thus Max Harrison has written: "Even if the music's commercial failure was unavoidable ... it still might have been expected, in view of the wealth of new resources, to affect other jazzmen. This it scarcely did at all ... The jazz community, in fact, turned aside, as so often, from an area of potentially major growth, and the error was confirmed by the jazz press of that time, which disliked the Capitol titles because of their refusal to sink into some convenient pigeonhole. Altogether, people began to forget about Gil Evans: his brilliance had been made obvious, but several years passed before anyone was reminded of that fact." Contrary to all of Harrison's claims, the recordings sold well enough to merit their quick release and continual reissue, their influence on other musicians was subtle, largely because of the distended recording schedule, but very significant, and the jazz press, not especially receptive to newer styles, gave more space to the nonet than might have been expected. *Down Beat*, for instance, published analyses of Davis's solos on *Godchild*, *Israel*, and *Move* and of Lee Konitz's solo on *Move*, by Bill Russo and Lloyd Lifton in four columns of its series "Jazz on Record." It also printed a letter from the pianist Herbie Nichols that said, "Miles proves melody and harmony in sufficient amounts will win out in the end."

A more accurate appraisal of the influence of the nonet comes from another English reviewer, Mike Butcher, who said in 1957: "Without exaggeration, it can be said that ninety per cent of the world's small, avant garde jazz groups – and many of the big bands, too – have been influenced by the Davis combo scores ever since, right up to this day." Nat Hentoff says, "These records were comparable in their impact on a new generation of jazz musicians to the Louis Armstrong Hot Five and Hot Seven records of the 1920s, some of the Duke Ellington and Basie records of the Thirties, and the records made by Parker and his associates in the early and middle Forties."

That impact, it must be admitted, was not entirely positive. The nonet's style also had a negative effect, and bebop, at least in the short term, suffered for it. André Hodeir, probably the first critic to assess the historical significance of the nonet's recordings, explained some of the positive effects and implied the major negative effect on bebop: "Quite apart from their value as pure jazz, sides like *Boplicity* and *Godchild* direct jazz toward a language that seems to hold great potential riches; *Israel* shows a fertile determination to investigate polyphonic writings; *Jeru* boldly calls for a re-examination of form, construction, and meter ... There may well result from all this, sooner or later, a completely renewed jazz that, without renouncing its tradition, would find its justification in a new classicism, which bop seems no longer capable of bringing about." For the time being, bop suffered by comparison to the cool chamber jazz of the nonet, and bop already had more enemies than it needed. The bop players, as musical revolutionaries affirming values such as intensity and virtuosity, had let the antipathy toward their music fall where it may among the established jazz clientele of the day. The latter were made up of a majority raised on the offerings of the big dance bands, a jazz style often on the fringes of vaudeville and pop music and sometimes wholly engulfed by them. Bebop came along and made its brash assertions in a tone and temper alien to that style – brazen, energetic, unsolicitous, unyielding, unbowing. It was a musical world as alien to most dance band fans as were the backstreets of Harlem where it had been nurtured.

Now, the nonet found a ready audience not only among the musicians, who appreciated their musical values, but also among the old fans, who found them comparatively accessible, orderly, and melodic. Nat Hentoff said: "The counter-revolutionary aspect of the Davis discs was that they again put the stress on ensemble playing. The soloist was still permitted to improvise, but he did so within a cohesive framework of relatively complex, freshly written ensemble material. The rhythmic and harmonic innovations of Parker, Gillespie and the rest were retained by the new men, but they aimed for a lighter and more flowing rhythmic pulse than had emerged from the guerrilla warfare that had sometimes existed in the early modern-jazz rhythm sections, and a considerably more sensitive and varied dynamic range. Some of the leaping cry and slashing spontaneity of the beginnings of modern jazz were lost, but the records established a standard for coping once again with the problem – solved by the early New Orleans bands for the first time, and by Ellington and Basie for theirs – of maintaining each player's individuality and at the same time emphasizing the organized expression of the group. The Davis records were an arranger's triumph." This interpretation puts the most optimistic face forward in assessing the achievement of the nonet.

But there is another side. Many of the bop values that were being supplanted by the cool music seem quite undeniably to be values that belong to the essence of jazz. One is improvisation, which is essential in the root sense of the term – a defining property of jazz – and while improvisation is retained, of course, in the cool paradigm, its role is greatly diminished, perhaps to the point that in the hands of some musicians it is no longer as highly valued as arranged music. Another is rhythm, which has undergone many changes in the history of jazz and has been the harbinger of further change on several occasions, but in cool music there is the beginning, at least, of a tendency to smooth out the rhythm and flatten its accents.

Neither rhythm nor improvisation is devalued to the extent that it flaws the work of the nonet, unless it is in *Moon Dreams*, which has no improvisation and virtually no pulse, but the tendency was there, and subsequently, in the hands of less gifted players and especially less talented arrangers, both elements would be disastrously devalued. The two sides of the cool movement were perceived by Hodeir, when he not only saw the possibility of "a completely renewed jazz" in the nonet's experiments but saw that "it is also possible to believe that music so essentially intimate and excessively polished may lose some of jazz's essential characteristics and cease to be anything but a devitalized successor. Only time will tell which of these two hypotheses corresponds to what the future actually holds."

Exactly the same peril lurks in the shift in emphasis on individual styles that the members of the nonet brought to the fore. The pyrotechnical displays of the boppers were supplanted by the highly personal musings of the cool musicians, a decidedly positive effect when undertaken by musicians of the caliber of Davis and Konitz. The danger arises when it is undertaken by lesser musicians. As Mike Butcher puts it, "The copyists who had emulated Diz and Bird now, in many cases, began to idolize Miles and Lee." Among lesser musicians, that idolatry sometimes led to something akin to a rejection of technique, and some musicians playing cool jazz felt no need to strive technically or emotionally for improvisational effects.

All the deleterious effects lay in the future. The nonet recordings embody the essential values of jazz music and give them a remarkably full and creative expression. There is about them, as Gerry Mulligan said, "a kind of perfection," comparable, as perhaps a dozen critics and historians have pointed out, even to Armstrong's Hot Fives and Hot Sevens. They are, of course, in no way blameworthy for the weaker elements of the tradition that they fostered. Remarkably – almost incredibly – when those weaker elements threatened to predominate, some four years later, it would be Davis who would, once again, supply the antidote.

For Davis, the nonet recordings stand as the first of his consummate achievements in a career that includes several. It was 1950, and he was only twenty-four years old. Accolades were already commonplace. In California, an entire school of musicians looked to him as the source of their music. Shelly Manne, who was prominent among them, recalls that time. "I think the main influence on West Coast Jazz, if one record could be an influence, was the album Miles Davis made called *Birth of the Cool*," Manne says. "That *kind* of writing and playing was closer to what we were trying to do, closer to the way a lot of us felt, out on the west coast. What we wanted to do was represented by that album. It had a lot to do not only with just improvisation and swing. It was the main character of the music we liked – the chance for the composer to be challenged too. To write some new kind of material for jazz musicians where the solos and the improvisation became part of the whole and you couldn't tell where the writing ended and the improvisation began. The spaces were right, it was lighter, maybe a little more 'laid back' kind of music. Maybe a little cooler, but still swinging. I felt that it was a good period, a creative period at that time."

Davis was suddenly being compared to Dizzy Gillespie, so recently his mentor, to Gillespie's disadvantage. "Years ago speed was everything," says Barret Deems, the traditional drummer. "The faster you were, the better you were. Not much else counted as far as the public was concerned. Technique was very important in the Thirties. Everybody tried to be a virtuoso. The drummer who played the fastest, the trumpeter who blew the highest – they were the best. Now it's the ideas that are important. It's what you do with the technique you have that counts. That's why Miles could be as big an influence as Diz, even though Diz has ten times the chops. It was the ideas, the stories they were telling." For Deems the difference was in ideas, but for Gil Fuller it was the tone. "As a musician, Dizzy didn't have the tone that everybody else had," he says. "He concentrated more on technique than he concentrated on tone and the kind of sound he had. His sound and tone wasn't as big as, say, Freddie Webster's. Or you could say that his tone wasn't like Miles's, because Miles tried to sound like Freddie Webster when he started out. And Miles had a softer tone. When you look at Miles as a whole, Miles didn't have the technical facility for getting over the horn like Dizzy had. So, I mean, like you develop in one area and you don't develop in the other. It's like specializing in something. Dizzy specialized in technique. Other fellas specialized in tones." For James Lincoln Collier, the difference is in Davis's use of rests as a stylistic device. "Where Gillespie, and the beboppers in general, exposed long, rolling lines sometimes lasting ten or eleven bars, Davis played in fragments, dropping short phrases in here and there over the ground beat, sketching rather than making complete pictures." And he adds, perhaps too grandly, "The development of this spare style was Davis's major contribution to jazz." Whatever the objective value of such comparisons, at least they show the shift in taste triggered by the style of the nonet. Davis emerged as the leading trumpeter in jazz, and one of its major figures.

Davis's rise to prominence would affect more than his music. As a young man, introverted and shy, Davis found himself respected by musicians both older and younger than he and courted by fans and the jazz press. Several people who knew him at the time say that cataclysmic personality changes resulted. Ross Russell's critical appraisal of Davis's music in 1948, when Davis was appearing as a sideman with Parker on Russell's Dial issues, had been both generous and clairvoyant. Russell, who was not much liked by Davis and thus hardly a sympathetic observer, offers this portrait of the new leader in Bird Lives!: "The one-time 'junior' of the first Charlie Parker Quintet and the leader's unwilling errand boy, Miles was now artfully turned out in tailored British tweeds. Miles made Playboy's list of best-dressed men, and drove an imported sports car. As a member of the Parker Quintet, he had found ample opportunity to study the art of the put-on from one of its masters. Miles now reshaped this experience to create the new image of the combo leader, aloof and disengagé. Miles did nothing so crude as to mistake a telephone booth for a men's room. He simply turned his back on the audience at the finish of his solos and walked off the bandstand to sit alone at a back table, indolently smoking a cigarette and staring with stony contempt at the customers. Outwardly, he seemed unemotional, unconcerned, and indifferent. Inside, he seethed with hostility. He worked out with boxers so that he could take care of himself in a brawl, forgetting, until an agent put him wise, that one good belt in the mouth could end his career ... One of his favorite ploys was to shake hands with an old colleague, apply an excruciating jiujitsu grip, and, as the other writhed in his grasp, hiss, 'I never liked you.' Or comment, in his snaky voice,

'Man, you're getting old.' The new Mr. Cool was small, tweeded, and nasty, the new culture hero, driving a sports car with a trunkful of custom-fitted golf sticks." Russell's description telescopes the trappings of Davis's private life so that they seem to have arrived at once, along with success. The best-dressed award, the sports car, the boxing workouts, even the "snaky voice" are all in the future and in themselves quite innocuous. What is missing entirely from Russell's account is any indication of or appreciation for the talent that supported such a lifestyle – Davis's music. For that, one might turn to André Hodeir again, in a remark that presages the brilliant continuation of Davis's career. "In the intelligent and allusive style of many of his solos, the young trumpeter shows a concern for alternation and contrast that augurs well for what he may create in the future," Hodeir says, referring specifically to his solos with the nonet. "Davis's phrasing has a variety that must be called rare."

That rare talent had barely begun to reveal itself in the nonet recordings. It would reveal itself, in a seemingly unending flow of creativity and explorations, for more than two decades. Such a long period of creative growth is unusual in any art form, but perhaps more unusual in jazz than in most others, where the conditions of employment take an excruciating toll on the artist's energy and resources. Jazz is a young person's art, by and large. If Davis had retired or simply coasted throughout the remainder of his career, his place in its history would have been secure. As the trumpeter beside Charlie Parker at the very height of Parker's enormous powers, and as the leader and featured soloist of his own nonet, Davis had already made an indelible mark.

For a while, it appeared that those achievements would stand as the apex of his achievement. Soon after the final recording session by the nonet, Davis's behavior became noticeably erratic, he frequently showed up unprepared and fumbling at engagements, including recording sessions, he disappeared and could not be found for weeks at a time, and he soon found himself struggling for any employment at all. Like Sonny Rollins, Jackie McLean, Gerry Mulligan, Stan Getz, and dozens of other jazz musicians, Davis was hooked on heroin. The story of how he fought off his addiction and eventually returned to his music not only recovered but reborn, to achieve new heights, is the subject of the next part.

PART TWO
MILES AHEAD

The music
From the trumpet at his lips
Is honey
Mixed with liquid fire.
  Langston Hughes

Miles Davis with Charles Mingus's Jazz Workshop; from left, Mingus, Ernie Henry, Teo Macero, and Davis (Robert Parent, courtesy of *Down Beat*)

5

Down
1950–4

The only jazz has come out of oppression and drug addiction and so on, although there have been individuals who weren't particularly poor: Ellington and Miles Davis, for example. When Miles was impoverished it was rather by choice than necessity, but in spite of his troubles he has consistently made excellent music throughout the years. So I don't feel that the lilies necessarily have to grow in a stinking swamp.   Archie Shepp

"I got hooked after I came back from the Paris Jazz Festival in 1949," Davis says. "I got bored and was around cats that were hung. So I wound up with a habit that took me over four years to break."

He makes becoming addicted to heroin sound easy, and it certainly was. Almost everyone associated with the bebop revolution used narcotics, so that needle tracks along one's arm became a member's insignia. One of the few who kept clean was Dizzy Gillespie, who thus became a spectator to the self-destruction around him. "Dope, heroin abuse, really got to be a major problem during the bebop era, especially in the late forties, and a lotta guys died from it," he says, and then he remembers the black humor that made the scene a little more bearable: "Cats were always getting busted with drugs by the police, and they had a saying, 'To get the best band, go to Kentucky.' That meant that the 'best band' was in Lexington, Kentucky, at the federal narcotics hospital." Another trumpeter, Benny Bailey, says, "Getting high, and so on, that was always the danger. A lot of cats were trying to be like Charlie Parker, including myself, to see how high they could get. That was a pretty dangerous period."

Looking back, the wonder is not that Davis became addicted to heroin but that he did not become addicted until the late spring of 1949, soon after his twenty-third birthday. He had been closely allied with Charlie Parker as a nineteen-year-old, and Parker was, by all accounts, the leader of the drug cult, by example if not by design. He had been using heroin and other narcotics since he was fifteen, before he left Kansas City, and by the time Davis met him, he was using enormous quantities. Even so, Parker was by no means an isolated figure among the musicians, even at the beginning. Gene Ramey, the bassist who played with Parker in Kansas City and left there for New York with him in Jay McShann's band, believes that Parker kept a degree of control over his habit until he made contact with the New York musicians. "In the McShann years, Bird was generally in control of his habit," Ramey recalls. "He wasn't scratching his face, which was always an obvious sign. It was very rarely you would see him nodding and that sort of thing, but you could tell. The other guys who were trying to be like him by using it were the ones who showed it worse ... But when Bird got to New York and was hanging out with Tadd Dameron, they were experimenting with everything. He was even soaking the reed in his mouthpiece in Benzedrine water. That was a waker-upper. The drug was a go-to-sleeper." Parker's partner in drug experiment, by Ramey's recollection, Tadd Dameron, was of course Davis's closest musical associate immediately after he left Parker's quintet.

It was apparently not the direct influence of either Dameron or Parker that led to Davis's addiction. Somehow he resisted that. Instead, it was the younger musicians he worked with after returning from Paris. They included Sonny Rollins and the circle of his Harlem friends; Max Roach and another pace-setting drummer, Art Blakey; Stan Getz, who would be arrested attempting to rob a drugstore in 1954; Gerry Mulligan, who was arrested for possession in Los Angeles in 1952 – to name a few who survived and are consequently remembered. Davis's partner when he started using heroin, he told Cheryl McCall in 1981, was Gene Ammons, the Chicago-born tenor saxophonist who was the star soloist in Billy Eckstine's band when Davis was in it. "Gene Ammons and I done that, we just started doin' it," Davis said. "First we started snorting it, then we started shooting it, and I didn't even know what was happening." Ammons was only a year older than Davis but he had made a brilliant start with Eckstine. Because of his addiction, he spent most of his career close to home in Chicago. In 1962 he was arrested on a narcotics charge and sentenced to fifteen years in prison. He served seven of those years before he was released, but he had less than five years left after that to resume his career before he died of cancer in 1974.

For Davis, the addiction seems bitterly ironic. Ever since he arrived in New York he seemed to be destined to be a leader, not a follower. But now, after sharing the front line with the likes of Parker and Dameron on the bandstand, he appeared ready to trade his hard-earned equality by joining Parker's sycophants in the search for a chemical high. Heroin was, of course, readily available among the night people who inhabit jazz clubs, and had been for years, and some jazz musicians would inevitably have been among its users under any circumstances. But in the late 1940s in New York and Los Angeles, far more modern jazz musicians

Sonny Rollins (courtesy of *Down Beat*)

Sonny Rollins and Thelonious Monk at the Five Spot (Marvin Oppenberg, courtesy of *Down Beat*)

Gene Ammons (Don Schlitten, courtesy of *Down Beat*)

used it than did not. Beyond any reasonable doubt, one of the reasons for the drastic increase in heroin use and addiction was the idolatry of Charlie Parker.

The effect that Parker had on his young admirers was something that he almost certainly could not comprehend in the beginning, and something that he seems to have sincerely regretted later on. Hampton Hawes, the Los Angeles pianist who spent several years in prison on narcotics convictions before he died at the age of forty-eight in 1977, was an aspiring young musician of seventeen when he was first allowed into his hero's inner sanctum. During Parker's first, ill-fated sojourn in Los Angeles, the young Hawes used to drive Parker to the club where he was playing. "When I came early one night he motioned me to follow him up to his room," Hawes recalled in his autobiography, *Raise Up Off Me*. "I waded through piles of sandwich wrappers, beer cans and liquor bottles. Watched him line up and take down eleven shots of whiskey, pop a handful of bennies, then tie up, smoking a joint at the same time. He sweated like a horse for five minutes, got up, put on his suit and a half hour later was on the stand playing strong and beautiful." The lesson, to the awestruck young piano player, was clear: "Those of us who were affected the strongest felt we'd be willing to do anything to warm ourselves by that fire, get some of that grease pumping through our veins. He fucked up all our minds. It was where the ultimate truth was." He was not the only one to draw that conclusion. Hawes recalls that the addicts on the West Coast had a secret code that they used to identify one another: they whistled the opening three notes of *Parker's Mood*.

The effect was the same in New York. Sonny Rollins, a year younger than Hawes, recalls: "I had gotten into hard drugs at the time, just like everyone else did in the community after the war. Heroin just flooded the community. We all knew Bird used drugs, and it made me feel that it can't be that bad if Bird is doing it. I wanted to be like Bird in every way I could. Later, after I'd been into it a while and I was going through a lot of hassles, I realized that Bird didn't really want people to get involved in that kind of life. By certain looks he would give me, I knew he didn't dig what I was doing. I realized he didn't think it was the hippest thing to do, be a little junkie following him around trying to be like him. He treated me like his son in a way, and I could see that he felt bad about what I was doing." Jackie McLean, the youngest of Rollins's high school friends, got the same message from Parker: "He said that using narcotics would be the one thing that could ruin us, the new group of guys coming up. One night, he even asked me to kick him in front of a club in the Village – he bent over and said, 'Come on, kick me in the ass! All these young guys are messed up 'cause of me, go on, kick me.' It was very embarrassing to me." It also proved to be ineffective as a lesson; McLean was imprisoned on narcotics charges while he was in his twenties.

Heroin abuse became a symbol, one of the trappings affected by the boppers just as dark glasses and pegged cuffs were, except that the heroin was potentially lethal. Probably the only musician ever to deny that it was part of the lifestyle is Miles Davis, an individualist if ever there was one. "You do drugs 'cause you like to," he told Julie Coryell in 1978, "not 'cause it's a lifestyle." However, many other statements indicate that he, no less than every other addict, had to keep on using heroin long after any pleasures it may have held for him were lost. One's choice of intoxicants became a symbol of where one stood in the jazz strata. Many of the swing musicians, the men whose styles were challenged and subverted by the boppers, were heavy users of alcohol, and many of the best of them, including Ben Webster, Lester (Prez) Young, and Coleman Hawkins, suffered bouts of alcoholism.

In the musical fervor of the day, alcohol and drug abuse developed into aspects of the contending ideologies. "The guys who drank whiskey were condemned by the guys on the other side of the street who used dope," Gene Ramey says. "They'd see Ben or Prez or Hawk half-way drunk and say, 'Man, you a drag. You a damned drunkard.' You couldn't turn around and tell a guy who was high and bent all out that he was a dope addict, because that would be squealing! Drinkers like Ben and Roy used to talk about this. 'Man, this guy's hitting me,' they'd say, 'and I can't fight back.'" Heroin became part of the bop style, and even Ramey seems to confuse the music and the drug. "With heroin came the idea that guys had to play with a straight sound, a symphonic sound," he says. "They put everybody down who was playing the other way."

For Davis, heroin addiction happened in the wake of his first creative peak, when his achievements in Parker's greatest quintet and his own nonet were still fresh. Buoyed by that peak, he managed to sustain a high level of creativity for a time, but perceptibly over the next three years he went through a descent that left him technically impoverished. By the time he cured himself, his talent had been dismissed by all but a handful of musicians and fans, and even those who remembered his potential of a few years earlier had long since given up hoping for the return of his powers.

A grim premonition of the course that Davis had started on was ominously close at hand in May 1950, when he led an all-star group at Birdland. Most of the players were drawn from his close associates of the time: J.J. Johnson, Tadd Dameron, Curly Russell, and Art Blakey. The tenor saxophonist was Milton (Brew) Moore, a native of Mississippi with a style derived from Lester Young, who had been on the fringe of The Street scene for several years. And there was also, unexpectedly, a second trumpeter, Fats Navarro.

Theodore Navarro was only twenty-six at the time of Davis's Birdland engagement, but he was making one of his last appearances on that stage or any other.

Seven weeks later he would die, the official cause of death listed as tuberculosis. Throughout the previous year, he had made only sporadic appearances in the jazz clubs, but he apparently felt well enough to play in public for at least part of this week in May, and he certainly needed whatever pay it would bring. Probably Davis took the suggestion to include him to the Birdland managers, who worked out an arrangement for expanding the group to a septet. Such an accommodation was not all that unusual when Navarro was the musician in question, because he seems to have been universally liked, even loved. "He was very sweet," Dizzy Gillespie remembers. "He was like a little baby."

Navarro was also, until a year or so before his death, a very creative trumpeter. Until he lost control of his heroin addiction, Navarro played the trumpet with great strength, detailing facile solos in a clear, full tone. He was expected, along with Davis, to take his place in the line of succession of great trumpeters. Under the circumstances, it might have been natural for Navarro and Davis to have emerged as competitors. Both were highly regarded on The Street a few years earlier, and listeners inevitably debated their relative merits; both were young, Navarro being only two and a half years older than Davis, and both started out as disciples of Gillespie. But Navarro seems to have had no competitive instinct, even before his addiction drained away all his worldly ambition, and his benign personality seems to have defused any competitive instinct in those around him. He and Davis learned from one another directly as well as indirectly. "He's one of the greatest players I ever heard," Davis told Julie Coryell. "I used to show him some things. He couldn't play a ballad. He would always play the same things, so I loosened him up. I told him what it was he was trying to play and couldn't. I showed him: I said, 'It's this chord right up here. You don't have to play the same thing every time you play this part; play something different right here – invert the chord.' That's the way I used to talk to him. He used to call me 'Millie'; he'd say, 'Millie, why can't I play something different on *I Can't Get Started?*' I said, 'Because you don't know what you're doing. You know in the end of the part that turns around – the first eight bars – you have to go back.' He didn't know how to do that, so I showed him what it was. 'All you have to do is run these two chords differently and you can go back.' He said, 'Oh.' Then he said, 'Thanks.' Fats and I would jam all night. It's nice to do something you like."

To all appearances, the two men were opposites. In spite of the similarity of their styles when they recorded together for the Metronome All Stars in January 1949, which caused Dizzy Gillespie to remark that he could not tell his own solo from either of theirs, their mature playing developed quickly, and they soon came to sound unlike Gillespie and one another. Davis's introspective, spare lines contrast with Navarro's powerful, long statements, at least when he was relatively healthy. The ebullience of Navarro's style suited his personality perfectly. "He was a fat, lovable character, playing the most beautiful horn," singer Carmen McRae remembers. "He was jovial and always laughing; he was typical of his size. He was really big before he got on the stuff. You should have seem him. They called him 'Fat Girl' because he was sort of a cherub, big fat jaws and a fat stomach." By the time he appeared alongside Davis at Birdland, any resemblance to the cherub of a few months earlier was gone. He weighed about 100 pounds, where formerly he had carried 175 pounds on his short frame, and his hacking cough seemed to rattle his bones. The fact that he could summon the energy to play at all surprised most of his friends, but the fact that he could occasionally still rip off some passable solos, with at least some of the old spirit, amazed them.

What remains of Fats Navarro's performance at Birdland has to be reconstructed in part from the incomplete transcripts made on Wednesday 17 May. The details are as follows:

Birdland All Stars
Miles Davis, Fats Navarro, tpt; J.J. Johnson, tbn; Brew Moore, ts; Tadd Dameron, pno; Curly Russell, b; Art Blakey, dms. Birdland, New York, 17 May 1950
Wee [*Rambunctious Rambling*] and *Deception* [*Poohbah*] (Alto 701); *Hot House* [*Miles' Midnight Breakaway*] (Session 101); *Eronel* [*Overturia*] and *Slow Broadway Theme* (Session 102)
The titles in brackets identify the titles on the Alto and Session releases, which came out in 1974; soon after, all or most of these tracks were also released together as one side of an album on the Beppo label. On *Deception*, Johnson and Moore do not solo, but the saxophone can be heard in the background on the out-chorus.

The transcripts of these performances are particularly disjointed, and many of the details have been subject to debate. *Hot House* is missing the opening theme; it begins with Davis's solo. *Slow Broadway Theme* is tagged onto the end of *Eronel*, probably signaling the end of the broadcast, but it is cut off abruptly. The original tapes presumably include an announcer's remarks at the beginning and the end of the broadcast, the former superimposed on *Hot House* and the latter on *Slow Broadway Theme*. The identification of these transcriptions as a single broadcast and the date of the broadcast itself are not completely certain. One of the mysteries of these transcripts arises on *Deception*, where only the trumpets and the piano solo; Davis leads off, followed immediately by a second trumpeter, apparently Navarro, but he in turn is followed by what sounds like a third trumpeter, whose presence has so far been unacknowledged. If *Deception* includes one trumpeter too many, *Hot House* closes with one too few. It features good bop solos by both Davis and Navarro separated by solos from Moore and Johnson, but on the closing choruses only Johnson, Moore, and Davis return to trade bars with Art Blakey; Navarro has vanished.

These discographical puzzles should not, however, overshadow the fact that beneath the din of the home-made recording some spirited bebop reverberated through Birdland that night. Especially on *Eronel*, an extended version of a theme composed by Sadik Hakim but invariably credited to Thelonious Monk, the players show their form in leisurely solos. Navarro sounds out of breath when his turn begins but he gathers strength as he goes along and in the end he manages to capture some of the boyish exuberance that marked his best playing. The solo was probably the last one that he ever recorded.

If the date of Davis's Birdland engagement with Navarro is correct, then it coincides with his first work ever in the recording studios of Columbia Records, the corporate giant with which he would be associated for all his later career. The occasion was a series of ballad recordings by Sarah Vaughan, and the results indicate that Columbia's producers recognized the commercial potential in Vaughan's flashy vocal style. Vaughan's accompanist, Jimmy Jones, assembled a good band to play his arrangements on these recordings but kept the band in tight check behind her. The recordings make a superb showcase for Vaughan:

Sarah Vaughan with Jimmy Jones's Band
Miles Davis, tpt; Benny Green, tbn; Tony Scott, clnt; Budd Johnson, ts; Jimmy Jones, pno; Freddie Green, gtr; Billy Taylor, b; J.C. Heard, dms. New York, 18 May 1950
Ain't Misbehavin'; Goodnight My Love; It Might As Well Be Spring
(all on Columbia CL 745)

Same personnel, except Mundell Lowe, gtr, replaces Green. 19 May 1950
Mean to Me; Come Rain Or Come Shine; Nice Work If You Can Get It
(all issued as above)

Sarah Vaughan and Jimmy Jones had been featured in the Stars of Modern Jazz concert at Carnegie Hall on Christmas day, 1949, where Davis and Benny Green were also on the bill, and Jones probably invited them then to rehearse for these recording sessions. The band were used very cleverly to Vaughan's advantage, making these ballads among her finest recordings. For the musicians, the hours in the Columbia studios no doubt helped to keep the pot boiling, but gave them little opportunity to show off *their* talents for the larger audiences. All four horns take eight-bar solos between the vocal choruses on *Ain't Misbehavin'*, which is the closest that any of the recordings comes to using the jazz format. Davis is heard most prominently on *It Might As Well Be Spring*, where he plays an effective obbligato behind the first twenty-four bars of Vaughan's vocal, and on *Nice Work If You Can Get It*, where he plays the solo interlude between the vocal choruses in a nicely controlled, full tone. These tracks offer proof, if further proof is needed, of his growing mastery of the ballad form, and especially his ability to project a sensitive and thoughtful interpretation in only a few notes.

For the country at large, 1950 was a kind of turning point. The exhilaration of the post-war years was abating. Economically, supply was finally catching up to demand, and there were automobiles, refrigerators, washing machines, and bungalows in the suburbs for everyone who wanted them, and that meant practically everyone. Where Manhattan had been invaded nightly by servicemen in uniforms just a few years before, it was now occupied daily by men in grey flannel suits, many of them ex-servicemen, who commuted to Long Island or Connecticut or New Jersey as soon as the office closed. The nightclub audience dwindled, and the audience for live jazz dwindled even further. The Street was already a fading memory, something that the younger musicians only heard about; its clubs changed owners and changed names frequently, but their bill of fare remained essentially the same – comedy and striptease.

Sometime in 1950, Davis led the last bop band on 52nd Street. The finality of the occasion made it almost a symbolic act, what Ira Gitler called "a last gasp for the modern" on The Street. The host club was the old Onyx, now known as the Orchid or Black Orchid. For the valedictorians, Davis chose another habitué of The Street, Bud Powell, and a couple of relative newcomers, Wardell Gray on tenor saxophone and Sonny Stitt on alto and tenor saxophones. When they finished their last set on whatever Saturday night in 1950, The Street's long association with jazz closed with them. Beginning soon after that, the brownstones that had housed the basement jazz clubs since 1934 were torn down, to be replaced by lofty office buildings providing daytime spaces for even more commuters.

The big bands also continued to fail. Count Basie was forced to disband in 1950, reducing his working unit to a septet with some bop-oriented players including Clark Terry and Wardell Gray. One of the casualties was guitarist Freddie Green, the rhythmic soul of the Basie bands from the beginning; he would be invited to rejoin Basie in 1951, when Basie expanded to an octet, but for the time being, he scuffled for work like so many others of the swing generation, playing occasional recording dates (as he did for Sarah Vaughan's Columbia session with Davis) whenever he could get them.

Dizzy Gillespie's orchestra also disbanded in early 1950. The orchestra had made some memorable music, some of it on records but much of it unfortunately recorded only in the memories of the musicians who played it and the listeners who happened to be there at the time. One performance involving Davis as a guest soloist is recalled by Cecil Payne, the baritone saxophonist with the orchestra since 1948. "The reason why I remember the concert with Dizzy and Miles," Payne says, "was because when Miles came up to the bandstand, we were playing a number that Miles didn't actually know. And when Miles started taking the solo, Dizzy was calling the chords off in his ear. And when he called the chords off, Miles was playing them and running them all through the thing. They really knew what they were playing," he says, adding, "Yeah, it was remarkable."

In an attempt to fill the void after Gillespie's band were finished for good, the managers of Birdland tried out an all-star big band for one week, probably in the spring or early summer of 1950. Billy Taylor, the pianist in the band, remembers: "Everyone was in it – the personnel consisted almost entirely of sidemen who wanted to be leaders, or had been leaders from time to time. I think the trumpet section consisted of Dizzy Gillespie, Miles Davis, Fats Navarro, Kenny Dorham and Red Rodney; the trombones were J.J. Johnson, Kai Winding and Benny Green, and the saxes included Gerry Mulligan and Lee Konitz; the rhythm section was Art Blakey and Al McKibbon and myself." This personnel overlaps at many points with Davis's recorded groups in the spring of 1950, including five members of the nonet that recorded for Capital on 9 March (Johnson, Mulligan, Konitz, McKibbon, and Davis) and four members of the Birdland septet in May (Navarro, Johnson, and Blakey, as well as Davis).

Birdland's managers undeniably gathered an aggregation deserving of the epithet all-star but, collectively, as Taylor also remembers, the music they made was a mixed blessing. "They were all marvelous musicians and the solos were the greatest," Taylor says. "The only trouble was that when they tried to play the arrangements (using Dizzy's big band book) they sounded awful." They sounded so awful that no one wanted to be named as the leader, leading to a chain of buck-passing that made the story worthy of a place in Leonard Feather and Jack Tracy's *Laughter from the Hip*. "Birdland wanted to bill it as 'Dizzy Gillespie's Dream Band,'" Taylor continues, "but Dizzy said, 'No, that's not my band, don't put it under my name.' So they decided to use the name of Symphony Sid, who ran the radio show out of Birdland, and call it Symphony Sid's Dream Band. And Sid said, 'No, don't put my name on it – I'm not responsible.' I guess none of the other musicians wanted their name on it either, so they just couldn't name a leader. They wound up calling it just 'The Birdland Dream Band.' That sure was a strange dream – I guess everybody was relieved when they woke up the following week." So far, perhaps mercifully, no transcriptions of the band have been issued, although some must certainly have been made.

While the opportunities for jazz musicians to make a living were drying up in New York, Davis's addiction to heroin was increasing. In the early fall, he left the city to tour with Billy Eckstine, whose stylized vocals were in vogue on the supper club circuit. The tour came to a disastrous climax for Davis when he and Art Blakey, the drummer in the band, were arrested in Los Angeles in September for possession of heroin. The jazz press had so far turned a blind eye to the growing problem of narcotics addiction in the ranks of the musicians, even though the reporters and columnists closest to the scene were well aware of it. Now the mood of the press was changing. The problem had grown alarmingly, with the pathetic wasting away of Navarro, who had died in July, and the conspicuous diminution of people such as Billie Holiday and Charlie Parker, among the greatest musicians jazz had known. The press could hardly ignore the problem any longer and remain responsible. *Down Beat*, then the most influential journal covering jazz, chose to break the silence with an editorial in its issue of 17 November. It began: "*Down Beat* has usually not given prominent display to news stories about musicians who run afoul of the law because of their habit. We did not wish to be accused of sensationalism. We knew, of course, that Miles Davis, the trumpet star, and drummer Art Blakey were picked up recently in Los Angeles on a heroin charge. We did not print it." The editorial then continued with a general indication of the rise in heroin abuse among musicians and an exhortation to musicians and club owners to bring the problem under control.

Necessary though the editorializing undoubtedly was, *Down Beat's* phrasing was certainly unfair to Davis and Blakey, singling them out, and, by doing so, seeming to lay the problem squarely on them, even though they had only been arrested, not convicted. Many club owners, possibly in response to the editorial as well as to the increased vigilance by the police in their clubs, assumed a tougher stance by refusing to hire known or suspected addicts. Because of the editorial, Davis and Blakey were suddenly among the most widely "known" users in the business. Neither man could command his fair share of the available jobs any longer. For Davis, the consequences were disastrous. According to Leonard Feather, "It is doubtful whether he worked more than six or seven weeks in 1951." His documented performances include five recording sessions and only a few more nightclub engagements, including two at Birdland for which broadcast transcriptions have survived. Even if this documentation is incomplete (as it almost certainly is), it still points to a year – and more – of relative inactivity, which in turn probably exacerbated the drug problems. Professionally and personally, Davis's fortunes took an abrupt turn downward.

During the Christmas holidays in 1950 and the first week of January 1951, Davis played at the Hi-Note in Chicago at Clark and Illinois streets, leading the band that accompanied Billie Holiday. Holiday arrived in Chicago from California, where she had probably hired Davis at the end of his Eckstine tour. By this stage of her career, Holiday was notoriously erratic, often failing to show up at all or, sometimes, showing up incapacitated by drugs and alcohol. It is hardly surprising that Davis could find employment at the Hi-Note so soon after the *Down Beat* editorial, since any manager willing to take a chance on Holiday would hardly need to screw up his courage to hire Davis. The engagement was a complete success, and Holiday and Davis played to capacity audiences for every set. The manager of the Hi-Note, Mart Denenburg, praised Holiday warmly. "She's a wonderful person, very easy to get along with, goes on stand on time," he said, refuting all the rumors of the day. "I couldn't ask for more."

For Davis, the stint not only afforded him some weeks of work but also placed him in Chicago for Christmas again. The booking was available only because Anita O'Day, a Chicagoan who was regularly featured as the singer at the Hi-Note, had accepted a booking in Milwaukee for the holidays. She was still in Chicago when Holiday and Davis opened at her home club, and she recalled Davis's visit there in her memoirs, *High Times Hard Times*. As she remembers it, she was sitting at the bar waiting for the musicians to arrive and idly scatting a tune she calls *Cent and a Half*: "After a bit, this good-looking black man got off one of the stools and came over to ask, 'Where'd you get that tune?' 'Oh, I don't know,' I said. 'It's in the air. Kind of a favorite of mine.' 'I wrote it,' he said, matter-of-factly." The man was Davis, although the tune he laid claim to is not one that is identified with him, at least not by that title. In the week before she left for Milwaukee, O'Day says, "we formed a mutual admiration society." O'Day was not so lucky in her relationship with Holiday. Although she idolized Holiday and acknowledged her debt to her as a jazz singer, Holiday seems always to have derided O'Day, treating her as just another second-rate white imitator who would cut her out of the bookings she deserved. O'Day does not mention Holiday's presence during Davis's stay at the Hi-Note.

Davis's professional association with Holiday seems to have begun and ended with the job at the Hi-Note, but he retained an indelible impression of her as a victim who was preyed on by unnamed exploiters. "She was the nicest woman in the world, you know," he said more than a quarter of a century after their booking in Chicago. "All she wanted to do was sing. They picked on her and picked on her to get money out of her." A few years later, when Davis had regained his health and Holiday's was declining rapidly, Davis used to visit her at her home on Long Island. "She was in love with one of my kids and his curly hair – he used to ride my bicycle and watch the horses at Aqueduct." In the years immediately before her death in 1959, Holiday was drinking gin by the quart and taking whatever narcotics she had access to. By all reports, she was not very good company, but for Davis, visiting her with his son in tow, the image that persists is different. "Her mouth was so sensuous," he recalls, "she was pretty and she would say certain words and her mouth would quiver, and she always had this white gardenia and long gloves." He was describing her as she must have appeared in the Hi-Note shows.

Soon after the Hi-Note engagement ended on 7 January Davis was acquitted on the heroin charge in Los Angeles. It was welcome news, of course, but did little to undo the publicity that had followed the charge.

Later that month, on 17 January, Davis put in a marathon session in the studios, recording four titles with Charlie Parker for Verve records, four more with his own pick-up sextet for Prestige, and a single title – as a pianist – in a quartet led by Sonny Rollins, also for Prestige. The frenzy of the day-long recording sessions makes an ironic contrast to the weeks of inactivity that lay ahead.

The reunion with Parker came a little more than a year after Davis had quit his quintet. Parker was now recording exclusively for Norman Granz's Clef and Verve labels, and this reunion session was produced by Granz for Verve. Under his new contract, Parker always recorded with various combinations rather than a set band. The familiar presence of Davis, as well as Max Roach, must have been a blessed relief after more than a year of coping with less familiar musicians in more elaborate productions. Six takes from their recording session, presumably all the complete takes, survive:

Charlie Parker and His Orchestra
Miles Davis, tpt; Charlie Parker, as; Walter Bishop, pno; Teddy Kotick, b; Max Roach, dms. New York, 17 January 1951
Au Privave (two takes); *She Rote* (two takes); *K.C. Blues*; *Star Eyes*
(all on Metro 2356 087)
The surviving takes are the second and third for *Au Privave*, the third and fifth for *She Rote*, the first for *K.C. Blues*, and the second for *Star Eyes*. All others are unissued.

These performance are typical of the Parker quintet's work in the studios for Dial and Savoy in years past. The first two titles are Parker originals that required some rehearsal, though apparently less than most listeners would expect. *Au Privave* opens and closes with unison passages at a medium tempo, executed flawlessly by Parker and Davis on the two surviving takes. The second available take has Davis playing a chorus in an uncharacteristic staccato, laying out a succession of careful notes directly on the beat. As usual, he plays much more interestingly on the early take. *She Rote* opens and closes with a perfunctory ensemble passage over stop time, little more than the minimum felt necessary for introducing the cycle of solos. The last two titles are fillers, invented on the spot, and are in many ways the most interesting. *K.C. Blues* is an improvisation on blues changes and a magnificent performance by Parker, who displays great feeling and intonation on some conventional figures learned undoubtedly in his Kansas City youth. His opening and closing solos are so powerful that the statements by Davis, muted, and Bishop that fill the interval pass by almost unnoticed. Parker's blues style on this track seems obviously to be the direct source for the style of Julian Adderley, who would emerge four and a half years later as one of Parker's most worthy successors on the alto saxophone. The ballad, *Star Eyes*, features an equally brilliant rendition by Parker of the attractive melody, cleverly framed by an introduction and coda played by muted trumpet over latin rhythms.

The pianist, Walter Bishop, remembers this recording date mainly because of the facile manner in which Parker put it all together. "With Bird," he says, "if you didn't know a tune, he would take the time to acquaint you with it. Sometimes we got to a record session without any rehearsal. Bird would have some little bits of marks on scraps of paper. 'Here, Miles, this is how it goes.' We did a number, *Star Eyes*. I didn't know how the tune went, but Bird knew I had big ears. He just ran it down once or twice and I got it." This casual approach is hardly evident in the music. Mark Gardner, the English specialist in Parker's music, was amazed by Bishop's revelation about the casual preparation leading to the recording of *Star Eyes*. "It sounds meticulously rehearsed – Miles's muted trumpet intro riding over Bishop's firm chords and then Bird's soaring melody statement," he says. "*Star Eyes* here becomes a miniature masterpiece."

For Davis, the day's work had barely begun by the time *Star Eyes* was in the can. On this cold and slushy Wednesday, he still had his own recording session for Prestige to look after. It was no ordinary session either, because it marked his first recording under the terms of an exclusive one-year recording contract he had signed with Prestige soon after returning to New York from Chicago. That contract, though it must have seemed like a windfall to Davis, had not been sought by him. Instead, he was pursued by Bob Weinstock of Prestige, who recalls: "Miles sort of disappeared from the scene, and I was on a business trip out to St. Louis, and I knew Miles lived around there. I made some calls, there were a few Davises in the phone book, and I reached his home. They told me he was in Chicago. I said, 'Please, if you should hear from Miles, ask him to call me in New York. I want to record him.' Finally he got in touch with me, and he came back east."

The recording personnel for the first of the three sessions he signed for was settled to Davis's satisfaction, although Weinstock had some reservations about his choice of saxophonist. "He liked Sonny Rollins, as crude as Sonny was at that time," says Weinstock, "and also John Lewis. On his first date, you can hear a very different Miles Davis than on the Capitols." True enough, although the extent of the difference may be greater than any of the musicians really intended, because Davis's best playing of the day was already behind him when he left the Verve studios. The Prestige recordings, although they have strengths of their own, show signs of fatigue, and worse, in his playing:

Miles Davis and His Band
Miles Davis, tpt; Benny Green, tbn; Sonny Rollins, ts; John Lewis, pno; Percy Heath, b; Roy Haynes, dms. New York, 17 January 1951

Morpheus; Down; Blue Room (two takes); *Whispering*
(all on Prestige 7674)
Green does not play on either take of *Blue Room*, and Rollins does not play on the second take. The first take is a composite of two takes spliced together; the masters are now lost, and the reissue of the first take is mastered from a well-used copy of the original release.

Davis's debut for Prestige began moderately well and deteriorated steadily as the evening wore on. *Morpheus*, a John Lewis original, attempts to recapture the nonet style. It features complex ensemble passages broken up only briefly by solo choruses for Davis, Rollins, and Lewis. The contrapuntal theme statement, based on drum figures at the opening and on shifting trumpet-trombone leads in the extended closing, sounds enormously complex and probably is, although the evidence of technical failures and carelessness later in this recording session suggests strongly that this band might have found *any* arrangement too complex on this day. Davis's original twenty-four-bar blues, *Down*, the first of several memorable original compositions he would record during this period, retains some interest mainly because Sonny Rollins strides through his solo turn in a manner that should have served notice that a major talent was emerging, but Davis's tone falters at least twice during his solo and he misses a couple of notes in the closing ensemble. On *Whispering*, a limp, romantic ballad notwithstanding its contribution of the chord sequences for Gillespie's *Groovin' High*, Davis states the melody alone and seems unsure of it throughout.

But the takes of *Blue Room* were technical disasters. Both takes are built around simple restatements of the doleful melody over the spare, tasteful accompaniment of John Lewis. Lewis plays beautifully on both takes. Davis, however, misses notes and fades away into uncomfortable silence; on the second take, he seems to lose his way several times until Lewis rights him by striking assertive chords. The occasional but persistent critical claims that Davis is a technically deficient trumpet player, which are amply refuted by dozens of hours of recorded evidence, may very well rest on these few minutes in the recording studio.

For all the problems, the session has received some generous notices. Barry McRae, reviewing the reissue of these sides in 1975, says, "It hardly seems to matter that Davis was well below form, Rollins was still immature, or that on tracks like *Down* Haynes plods dreadfully." The saving grace, if there is one, is expressed in Michael James's assessment: "Despite obvious technical shortcomings on Davis's part, there is no mistaking the very personal air of sour nostalgia that pervades this performance." Certainly *Blue Room* (take 2), Davis's worst performance technically, is suffused by the anguish of an artist losing control. A few years after this session, in late 1956, the critic Alun Morgan met Davis in

Paris and asked him what had happened on the recording of *Blue Room*. "Hell, man, I was playing badly on that date," Davis replied. "I was – you know."

The remaining record date of the day was a continuation of the one before, with a nominal change in leaders from Davis to Rollins, and a change of piano players. Davis insisted that Weinstock give Rollins a chance to make a recording as leader, and he remained undeterred even when his own recording session ran late and John Lewis had to leave. He simply took over the keyboard himself:

Sonny Rollins Quartet
Sonny Rollins, ts; Miles Davis, pno; Percy Heath, b; Roy Haynes, dms. New York,
17 January 1951
I Know (Prestige 7856)

The single track, lasting about two and a half minutes, is essentially Parker's tune *Confirmation* (as Davis's title *I Know* slyly suggests) without the melody, here credited to Davis as composer. Davis is not at all tentative in the role of piano accompanist, and Rollins bristles through his extended solo, making a good start, however briefly, in his debut as a leader.

Davis's own debut for Prestige did not show nearly as much promise, and no one would have blamed the Prestige company if they had questioned their commitment to record Davis twice more in 1951. Under the peculiar circumstances of the jazz recording industry then, they probably did not entertain such doubts even for a moment. On the contrary, they entered the agreement knowing very well that they would have to put up with certain vagaries in Davis's behavior and inconsistencies in his playing. They knew when they signed him that he was a heroin addict. The apparent paradox of Davis being actively pursued by Prestige and offered a contract for three recording sessions at the very moment when his personal problems were growing and his self-control was diminishing is not a paradox at all. Several recording producers knew that the surest way to turn a profit on jazz recordings, with their limited short-term sales prospects, was to record musicians who would accept a ridiculously small fee as an advance against royalties. If the cash on the line was paltry enough, the companies faced almost no financial risk in producing the records because almost any release by a relatively well-known jazzman would recoup their small investment. Needless to say, musicians suffering from drug addiction were exactly the ones most likely to enter into this kind of one-sided agreement, if their need for cash was great enough, as it usually was. The companies were dealing with artists who, in effect, had no bargaining power at all.

Just six days later, Davis was back in the recording studio, this time for Capitol, with the 1951 edition of the Metronome All Stars. The format was much the same as it was on Davis's first outing with the All Stars two years earlier, with too many good players wedged into too few minutes of playing time. The two tracks that resulted are interesting mainly as an index of the shifting tastes in jazz. Where the 1949 All Stars had played big band bop, the 1951 All Stars pick their way through two carefully arranged pieces:

Metronome All Stars
Miles Davis, tpt; Kai Winding, tbn; John LaPorta, clnt; Lee Konitz, as; Stan Getz, ts; Serge Chaloff, bs; Terry Gibbs, vib; George Shearing, pno; Billy Bauer, gtr; Eddie Safran-ski, b; Max Roach, dms. New York, 23 January 1951
Early Spring (comp, arr Ralph Burns); *Local 802 Blues* (comp, arr George Shearing) (both on Capitol M-11031)

Early Spring, composed and arranged by Ralph Burns, who had scored a jazz hit with *Early Autumn* for the Woody Herman orchestra and made Stan Getz, its soloist, an 'all star,' is patently modeled on the style of the Davis nonet, featuring ensemble passages with subtly shifting leads and short solos (of eight, twelve, or sixteen bars). *Local 802 Blues* exploits the other main commercial thrust of the previous year, the sound of the George Shearing Quintet; the ensemble is played by the piano and the vibes in unison, the same pretty voicing that the blind English pianist would exploit for the next twenty-five years. The most effective solos are simultaneous improvisations by two of the players, matching Konitz and Davis, and Winding and Roach, among others. The experimental atmosphere in the use of simultaneous improvisation reflects the mood of Lennie Tristano as well, and some of the players – Konitz, LaPorta, and Bauer – were from Tristano's coterie. Considering that both the tracks by the Metronome All Stars add up to only a few seconds more than five minutes of music, the All Stars session makes a surprisingly comprehensive statement about the shift of emphasis in jazz, giving them a historical status that overshadows any intrinsic interest in the music itself.

The next month, Davis led a band at Birdland stocked by his friends from Sugar Hill, including Sonny Rollins and Kenny Drew. They broadcast on Saturday 17 February, but the recordings remain unissued, and further details are unknown. This is probably the Birdland engagement at which Davis introduced the young alto saxophonist Jackie McLean to downtown jazz audiences. In any event, sometime before McLean's twentieth birthday in May, Davis included him in a band he led at Birdland. McLean had made impressive progress on his horn but the prospect of playing at the most famous jazz club of the day definitely unnerved him. On the first night of the engagement, with Dexter Gordon and other jazzmen sitting in the audience, he bolted from the bandstand toward the washroom but was sick to his stomach halfway there. But his playing made an impression on the audiences, and he was soon being hailed as a rising young talent. His rapid development over the next year was a direct result of Davis's exposing him to audiences, and at least indirectly to the lessons he learned playing beside him. "Miles influenced me with his choice of notes and the way he played, even though I couldn't copy anything directly from his concept," McLean says.

In March, Davis recorded for Prestige again, but as a sideman. It is a surprising session because of his thorough relegation to a supporting role behind the leader, Lee Konitz. In a sense, the real leader for the first half of the session is George Russell, the composer and arranger of the first two titles, who was making a return to music after suffering a relapse of the tuberculosis that had dogged his health since he was a teenager. For the Konitz session, Russell prepared two charts of considerable complexity, and Konitz assembled a sextet made up of four Tristano students, counting Konitz himself, plus Davis and Max Roach, thus providing Russell with players literate enough to negotiate his charts:

Lee Konitz Sextet
Miles Davis, tpt; Lee Konitz, as; Sal Mosca, pno; Billy Bauer, gtr; Arnold Fishkin, b; Max Roach, dms; George Russell, comp, arr (on *Odjenar* and *Ezz-thetic*). New York, 8 March 1951
Odjenar; Ezz-thetic; Hi Beck; Yesterdays (omit Roach)
(all on Prestige 7827)

Odjenar, named for Russell's wife, the painter Juanita Odjenar, features weaving counter-melodies by saxophone, trumpet, and guitar, with no fixed time, creating a solemn mood; Konitz steps out from the interplay to solo over a slow 4/4 rhythm. *Ezz-thetic*, a title alluding to the heavyweight boxing champion of the day, Ezzard Charles, is appropriately tougher, and a *tour de force* for both Russell and Konitz. The composition and the solos are superimposed on rapid, solid brushwork by Max Roach; over it, Davis plays two slim melodic figures repeatedly while Konitz plays what might be called an obbligato except that it is in the foreground. The set piece gives way to a burning Konitz solo for several choruses, surely one of the most impressive turns he has ever recorded, while Davis reappears at intervals playing the melodic figures behind him and then has sixteen bars to himself before the close. These pieces are miniature masterpieces in the corpus of George Russell, whose presence as an active contributor in jazz has been much too infrequent.

The remaining two titles are much less ambitious, and less interesting. *Hi Beck*, credited to Konitz, is really an improvisation on *Pennies from Heaven*; Davis is allowed a full chorus following Konitz, his longest solo during this session. On *Yesterdays*, Davis plays the introduction before Konitz comes in to state the attractive melody and play variations on it; Davis returns only to play four bars leading up to the closing chord.

While the music is undeniably interesting, its strengths are very closely circumscribed. For Russell, it is a show of strength after a period of inactivity, and a new revelation of arranging skills to rival those of Gil Evans, without calling forth in any way the elements of Evans's style. For Konitz, it is an incisive display not only of skill but also of feeling, from an improviser whose inclination throughout a long and well-documented career has been to favor skill. For the others, it seems to have been an exercise in self-effacement. They function adequately in the background of the two Russell compositions, although Bauer plays his countermelody on *Odjenar* stiffly and Davis fluffs some notes playing behind Konitz's solo on *Ezz-thetic*. Otherwise, they do not get heard much and for Davis, if not for the others, that is uncommon. Under the circumstances, however, it was probably not unwelcome.

Davis's recording session with Konitz was a relief from the periods of inactivity that were beginning to crop up more frequently and to last longer. Birdland also provided him with a few more weeks of work in 1951, in early June and again in late September. For the first engagement, he surrounded himself with some familiar faces. Some of the music they made has been preserved, albeit in low fidelity, from the regular Saturday radio broadcast:

Miles Davis All Stars
Miles Davis, tpt; J.J. Johnson, tbn; Sonny Rollins, ts; Kenny Drew, pno; Tommy Potter, b; Art Blakey, dms. Birdland, New York, 2 June 1951
Move [Moo]; *Half Nelson* [Two]; *Down* [*The Blues, Mick's Blues*]
(all on Session 102, Ozone 7, and Beppo 501)
The titles in brackets identify these tracks on some of the microgroove issues. On the Session 102 issue, but not on Ozone 7, a few bars of the closing theme are heard after *Down*.

The sound on all issues is flat and indistinct, with obtrusive drums throughout (surely only partly the fault of the unbalanced taping). The most notable feature is the strained attempt at providing arranged sections as an adjunct to the usual sequence of solos. The repertoire is otherwise very familiar, with *Half Nelson* brought forward from 1947 and *Move* from 1948 as well as Davis's good blues, *Down*, recorded five months earlier. All the players handle the familiar fare readily enough except for the new ensemble sections, probably introduced to give a semblance of the nonet's music. On *Move*, the horns play a ragged riff between drum breaks toward the end, and the ensemble eventually breaks down completely when Davis enters ahead of the others; he saves face by persisting with a statement of the melody, calling the others in to close the tune. On *Half Nelson*, the short ensemble following Kenny Drew's recitation of some patented Bud Powell phrases features Davis squeaking some attempts at high notes. On *Down*, the horn soloists double the tempo after an initial chorus, but only Rollins succeeds in sustaining the increased tempo on his last chorus, in spite of Blakey's insistent cues. The performances are not just unpolished; they are barely controlled.

For the September engagement at Birdland, after a lapse of almost four months, Davis must have had much less say in the conditions. While Blakey was also hired and the bassist was Charles Mingus, recently arrived from California, probably both Davis's choices, the rest of the band appear to be somebody else's choice. Possibly Davis was not the leader but just a featured performer in the band assembled by the Birdland management, although he assumes the leader's privileges by taking the first solos on the transcriptions preserved from the Saturday broadcast and he clearly had a say in the choice of repertoire:

Miles Davis and Eddie 'Lockjaw' Davis All Stars
Miles Davis, tpt; Eddie (Lockjaw) Davis, ts; George (Big Nick) Nicholas, ts; Billy Taylor, pno; Charles Mingus, b; Art Blakey, dms. Birdland, New York, 29 September 1951
Move [Mod]; *The Squirrel*; *Lady Bird*
(all on Ozone 7 and on Beppo 501)

This band seem strange company for Davis, and yet the music they made is far more rewarding than that of the more compatible band he had taken into Birdland a few months before.

Billy Taylor, a literate player just gaining stature then as an accompanist, had established himself as the regular pianist in Birdland house bands; he strengthens the ensembles by embellishing the melodies with neat phrases and abets the soloists with tasteful chords, but his own solos, for which he has seldom been praised, are equally interesting here, featuring long bop statements with the right hand and a severely economical left hand, which chips in with a chord or two occasionally, sometimes letting a whole chorus pass between chords. Taylor's frugal use of the bass clef anticipates the style that Horace Silver and others would bring to the fore a few years later.

Davis's co-leader, Eddie Davis, had been a regular sideman and frequent leader for a decade in Harlem clubs, including Monroe's Uptown House and Minton's when they were the cradles of bebop, but it would take a stint in Count Basie's reconstituted big band, starting in 1952, to bring him international recognition. His brawling tone on the tenor saxophone, featuring the unashamed use of vibrato, could hardly be more different from the approach of Davis, but the two make an amicable enough pairing. Best of all, Eddie Davis's gusto seems to rub off on all the others, including the trumpeter, inspiring him even to make a challenge out of *Move*, by now a tired old commonplace. On *Move* and Tadd Dameron's *Lady Bird*, Eddie Davis plays extended chase sequences, alternating four-bar phrases with the other saxophonist, Big Nick Nicholas; the chase device, a kind of mock cutting session for the saxophonists, pits the two players against one another directly, and most listeners will probably be surprised to hear Davis pressed hard by Nicholas, a player who never made his mark with a sizeable audience. Among the New York musicians, however, Nicholas was as well respected as any member of the band, having played in several big bands, including Gillespie's band of 1948, and having led the house band in a Harlem club called The Paradise, where he was in a position to hire musicians such as Parker and Monk and to be heard playing beside them.

Easily the most obscure musician was Charles Mingus, who first played beside Miles Davis in Los Angeles five years earlier. Mingus left California in 1950 as the bassist with the Red Norvo Trio, a successful group completed by Tal Farlow on guitar. He quit the trio in New York, partly because of the indignity of being unbilled when the group was advertised as "The Red Norvo Trio featuring Tal Farlow," and he was struggling to find work in New York. It was Davis who arranged the first breaks for Mingus, getting him into the band at Birdland and later making room for him in a recording studio, but apparently Davis was helpful without being particularly friendly. Mingus, in *Beneath the Underdog*, reconstructs a conversation he had with Fats Navarro just before Navarro's death, soon after Mingus arrived in New York. The dialogue at one point turns on Davis's penchant for keeping his feelings to himself. Navarro, in the course of introducing himself to Mingus, says: "You play with Diz and Bird when they was in California? See, I knowed of you before you knowed of me ... You ain't so undiscovered. Miles played once with you. He used to tell about the band you guys had." At this piece of information, Mingus, incredulous, exclaims, "He did? He hardly said a word except with his horn. How cool can you get when you don't even say hello."

Davis's second recording date for Prestige as a leader, in October, became the occasion for Jackie McLean's recording debut. It was also one of the first recording sessions that set out to exploit the possibilities of the new microgroove technology, which finally freed the musicians of the strictures imposed by the three-minute limit of 78 rpm records. Microgroove technology had been available for more than a year, but studio sessions had never altered their time-honored format to accommodate it and the new 33⅓ rpm recordings, pressed onto ten-inch vinyl discs, the same diameter as the 78s, had been used almost exclusively for pressings of live performances. Now producer Ira Gitler brought Davis and his band into the studio to record compositions at whatever length the musicians chose, and the result was enough music to fill two ten-inch long play (LP) records.

In his liner note for the first release from this session (Prestige LP 124), Gitler extols the technological advance for his customers, saying: "This album gives Miles more freedom than he has ever had on records for time limits were not strictly enforced. There is an opportunity to build ideas into a definite cumulative effect."

Gitler's comments apparently attempt to break down whatever consumer resistance might be lurking, a vague fear shared by the rest of the recording industry, which sat back waiting for someone to try the new wares. But the resistance did not materialize, notwithstanding the increase in prices – ten-inch LPs cost about three times the price of ten-inch 78s – and even the most hidebound record buyers needed no persuading. The record-buying public was so receptive that ten-inch LPs gave way almost immediately to twelve-inch LPs, which not only increased the price to almost four times the cost of 78s but also altered the very dimensions that records had typically had since Edison's old cylinders became relics.

Microgroove technology established itself so rapidly that its revolutionary effect on musical forms has gone unnoticed. In jazz, its obvious impact was in destroying once and for all the artifical distinctions between recorded performances and live performances, by permitting, even encouraging, expanded formal frameworks and fully developed improvisations on record. The superficial similarity between jazz and American popular song had been promoted inadvertently by the limits of 78 rpm recording technology from the beginning. Popular song forms fit very comfortably into those limits, probably too comfortably for the fit to be purely accidental, since the song forms themselves became fixed at the same time as sound recording was developing. The succinct form of American song was established by Jerome Kern, Irving Berlin, and other songwriters in the early decades of this century. The lyric was set in only thirty-two bars segmented into four equal movements, probably as much because of the strictures of the early recording technology as because of any intrinsic, structural considerations. Popular song forms that developed *prior* to the recording industry tend to be structurally more complex; operatic and operettic arias, *Lieder*, and narrative folk songs always fit uneasily onto 78 rpm pressings. So, really, did jazz, in the forms it usually took at performances.

For decades, jazz musicians adjusted to the recording strictures by adopting American popular songs as their vehicles for improvisation, and by composing originals with the same structure. Throughout the 1930s and 1940s, when sound recording became a big business, nearly all recorded jazz took that form, so much so that musicians schooled in those years assumed that the thirty-two-bar format belonged to jazz no less than to popular song. Probably because of the musicians' predilection, it continued to dominate in jazz compositions throughout the 1950s, but its grip loosened in the 1960s, and in the 1970s the younger jazz musicians, to whom 78 rpm records were just museum pieces or old junk, seldom used the form at all. (Over the same period, American popular songs also began to depart from the conventional thirty-two-bar form, and any list of the best songs of the 1960s and 1970s will inevitably include several – Don McLean's *American Pie*, Joni Mitchell's *The Circle Game*, Paul Simon's *Dangling Conversation*, Lennon and McCartney's *Eleanor Rigby* – with unconventional forms; the only realm where the thirty-two-bar form retains its currency is in theater music, presumably because Kern, Berlin, and their successors such as Gershwin, Rodgers, and Porter used the form too impeccably for their precedent to be ignored.)

In jazz history, Davis's microgroove recording for Prestige in October 1951 stands as a milestone in introducing the new technology both to musicians and to fans. The session retains a reasonable share of intrinsic interest as well:

Miles Davis All Stars
Miles Davis, tpt; Jackie McLean, as; Sonny Rollins, ts; Walter Bishop, pno; Tommy Potter, b; Art Blakey, dms. New York, 5 October 1951
Conception; Out of the Blue; Denial; Bluing; Dig; My Old Flame; It's Only a Paper Moon
(all on Prestige 7744)
Jackie McLean does not play on *Conception*, *My Old Flame*, and *Paper Moon*. The first ten-inch LP issued from this session (Prestige LP 124) included *Conception*, *Dig*, *My Old Flame*, and *Paper Moon*; the other compositions were issued later on a second ten-inch LP (Prestige LP 140).

This session turned up an ambiguous result, with some excellent work on some titles and some very ragged performances on others. *Dig* made considerable impact upon its release, providing Rollins with an opportunity to record a powerful solo, his best to that date by far; giving McLean a chance to display his distinctive solo style, which juxtaposes short bop phrases in a choppy but coherent sequence; and exposing Davis's best bop style not once but twice, because the new LP format allows him to play at length both before and after McLean. This track again, incidentally, shows how unconcerned the jazz musicians of the day were about composer credits: *Dig*, credited here to Davis, was recorded seven months later as *Donna* and credited to McLean; by either title and author, it is a bebop line superimposed on the chord sequence of *Sweet Georgia Brown*. *Conception*, George Shearing's fine tune already better known as *Deception* from the nonet version of March 1950, where it was credited to Davis, restores not only Shearing's title but also Shearing's name to the piece, although it is played here in the nonet's arrangement. *Denial* is an improvisation on Parker's *Confirmation*, exactly the same gambit used earlier by Davis and Rollins for Rollins's debut as leader, when it was entitled *I Know*.

The recording session began with the well-rehearsed version of *Conception* and then descended perceptibly through various degrees of poorer preparation on the other titles, ending with the standard ballads *My Old Flame* and *It's Only a Paper Moon*. On *Bluing*, a blues improvisation that stretches out to almost ten minutes, Blakey apparently became distracted from his time-keeping chores; he keeps on drumming after everyone else has stopped playing, prompting Davis to turn to him and bark, "Play the endin', man. You know the arrangement." Rollins, on *Bluing* and elsewhere, was bothered by a squeaky reed. Fortunately he continues playing in spite of it on most tracks, including *Dig*, but on *Denial* he drops out after one wooden chorus. According to Ira Gitler, he had at this point given up on his own horn and was trying out J.R. Montrose's, who happened to be in the studio watching. Montrose was not the only spectator; Jackie McLean recalls that "Mingus had come to the studio with Miles that day, carrying his bass on his back, and stood at the piano, running over the tunes." There is no indication that Mingus got to use his bass during the session, but the bassist figures prominently in the background of *Conception*, playing a stop-time figure at the bridge of each chorus behind all the soloists, and it would not be at all surprising to discover that it was Mingus rather than Tommy Potter playing it.

Davis's best work came quite late in the day, long after the rest of the players had given their own best efforts. On *Paper Moon*, the closer, he fails to reach some high notes during his solo, but on *My Old Flame*, the sentimental old ballad that Parker had featured when Davis was a member of his quintet, he is less ambitious technically and more successful melodically. His performance is not up to the standards he set a few years later, or even a few years earlier, but it is good enough compared to his playing elsewhere in this period to be noteworthy, especially coming so near the end of a long recording session that had a party atmosphere from the beginning, and at a time in his life when his self-discipline had deserted him almost completely.

By the fall of 1951 Davis's addiction to heroin dominated his life. It was not only sapping his strength but also costing a great deal of money, much more money than he could hope to make playing music sporadically in clubs and studios. Twenty-three years later he told Gregg Hall, "When I was using dope it was costing me a couple of grand a day and I used to take bitches' money." Max Roach remembered those days too. "Miles was a heroin addict with a stable," he said, and then went on to explain: "I don't know the details, but I know he used drugs and he had to do everything he could to take care of his habit because you couldn't support it by just playing music." "I was a pimp, I had a lot of girls, I was doin' this, doin' that," Davis told Cheryl McCall. "I had more money then than I have now." His stable included about seven prostitutes, but his business arrangement with them, as he described it for McCall, fell far short of the malevolence described by crime novelists and moviemakers. "They didn't give all their money to me," he said; "they just said, 'Miles, take me out. I don't like people I don't like, I like you, take me out.' That's like a family they like to be in." In turning to pimping, Davis is not alone among jazzmen. Numerous others also found pimping one of the more profitable sidelines of the subculture in which they lived and worked. Jelly Roll Morton and Charles Mingus both talked openly about their adventures in the skin trade half a century apart, and the number of others who did not talk about their adventures cannot even be guessed. Certainly the opportunity was always there for the right man. When trumpeter Freddie Hubbard arrived in New York in 1959 from Indianapolis – "a real country boy," by his own admission – he was amazed, and more than a bit flattered, by the attention he received from the prostitutes in the nightclubs where he found work. "I could have become a successful pimp," he told Leonard Feather; "prostitutes just used to beg me." It was an opportunity that many jazzmen who needed cash to support their habits could not pass up.

Even pimping could not always sustain Davis, and he found himself bereft on several occasions. Clark Terry tried to help on one occasion but found it a doubly thankless task. "I remember one day on Broadway I found him sitting in front of one of those ham-and-egg places," Terry told Leonard Feather. "He was wasted, actually sitting in the gutter. I asked him what was wrong and he said, 'I don't feel well.' After buying him some ham and eggs I took him around to my hotel, the America on West 47th Street. I was getting ready to leave on the bus with Basie's band, and I told him, 'You just stay here, get some rest, and when you leave, just close the door.' The bus waited longer than I'd expected, so I went back to the room. Miles had disappeared, the door was open, and all my things were missing." Terry had been duped in a way that was known and expected by people who knew junkies, but coming from Davis he was not willing to sit back and accept it. "I called home, St. Louis, and told my wife to call Doc Davis to see if he could get Miles, because he was obviously in bad shape and had become the victim of those cats who were twisting him the wrong way. And you know what? Doc Davis was very indignant. He told her, 'The only thing that's wrong with Miles now is because of those damn musicians like your husband that he's hanging around with.' He was the type of guy who believed his son could do no wrong. So he didn't come to get him."

Although Doc Davis could rise to his son's defense, he was by no means untouched by his plight. Davis's sister Dorothy says that his addiction sent shock waves through the family. "Up to this very day," she told George Goodman in 1981, "none of us discuss it publicly."

For the next two and a half years, Davis's movements became far-flung and sudden. Sometimes he left New York to front a local band for a week or so in another city, but more often he just disappeared from the city for parts unknown. Bob Weinstock, whose job at Prestige involved trying to get a quorum of addicts into the recording studios at the right time, says, "In those days a lot of guys used to disappear from the scene for months at a time." The musicians' disappearances were sometimes forced by pressure from narcotics investigators and sometimes by the need to find a new source of narcotics when a man had used up all his credit with the local suppliers or to avoid violence from the people he had duped. For Davis, there was also another, more positive motive, at least later on, for he has said that when he hit bottom he began searching for a place where he could straighten himself out. Eventually he succeeded, but for the time being his ramblings merely added more uncertainty to what was already a chaotic existence. By 1952, Davis's movements had become so unpredictable that apparently even Weinstock could not keep track of him, and his recording contract with Prestige was not renewed.

In the spring, he surfaced in his hometown, where he was taped playing as a guest soloist with a local group:

Miles Davis with Jimmy Forrest
Miles Davis, tpt; Jimmy Forrest, ts, vcl (on *Ow!*); Charles Fox, pno; John Hixon, b; Oscar Oldham, dms; unidentified bongo player (on *Our Delight* and *Lady Bird*). Barrelhouse Club, St. Louis, spring of 1952
All the Things You Are; Wahoo; Our Delight; Ow!; Lady Bird
(all on Jazz Showcase 5004)

This home-made taping, an unexpected document, is more interesting as an example of the company he kept on his catch-as-catch-can tours than for the playing itself, which is a standard rundown of some bop themes. Inevitably it is poor technically, with saxophonist Forrest more favorably picked up on the tape than any of the others and the bass player hardly noticeable at all. The beginning of *Ow!*, including Davis's solo (if there was one), is cut off entirely, leaving Forrest's scat vocal with its commercial references ("Super suds, super suds ...," he sings at the beginning) the center of attention.

Jimmy Forrest, though he was based in his hometown, was by no means unknown beyond its borders. Born in St. Louis in 1920, six years before Davis, he had worked all over the United States during the 1940s as a sideman in the bands of Jay McShann, Andy Kirk, and Duke Ellington before returning to his birthplace. Soon after returning, he recorded a rhythm-and-blues instrumental called *Night Train*, based on Ellington's *Happy-Go-Lucky Local*, which became a popular hit and then went on to occupy a prominent place in the repertoire of bands accompanying striptease acts. Soon after, he settled in Los Angeles and, much later, beginning in 1973, he joined Count Basie as the featured tenor soloist, bringing him a measure of international acclaim before his death in 1980. In many ways, Forrest gets the best of his stint with Davis in St. Louis, and it is not solely because he is better recorded. His solos, in a big bluesy tone but without the bawling mannerisms of rhythm-and-blues players, are bright and witty, full of oblique references to dozens of obscure songs, just as his brief vocal, which he apologetically prefaces by announcing that it is "for kicks only," interlards the nonsense syllables with jingles and blues references. The audience clearly belongs to him, even with one of the best musicians ever to come out of the St. Louis area sharing the stage with him.

The other musicians in the group, when they get a hearing, which is seldom, do not rate at all. They were probably strictly local musicians (although a pianist named Charles Fox had recorded with Dexter Gordon on Dial in 1947) and seemed destined to remain just that. The unidentified bongo player on *Our Delight* and *Lady Bird* may have been an old acquaintance of Davis's who was enjoined to sit in. Drummer Oldham unlooses some hefty bass drum accents on *Ow!*, making his most conspicuous move of the evening a display of a drum style that the New York bop drummers had abandoned years before. Pianist Fox, who gets a solo turn on every track, sticks close to the melody and often uses a stride left hand. For all that, the music is spirited, especially when Davis and Forrest trade four-bar phrases on Benny Harris's *Wahoo* and Tadd Dameron's *Our Delight*. In finding a musician of Jimmy Forrest's caliber in the Barrelhouse Club band, Davis was probably much luckier than he usually was when he played in clubs outside New York.

Sometime in early 1952 Davis toured with a concert package known as Jazz Inc, put together by Symphony Sid Torin. The itinerary is now forgotten, but also on the tour were Milt Jackson, Zoot Sims, and, later, replacing Sims, Jimmy Heath.

Davis's closest associate in New York remained Jackie McLean. The two shared an apartment on 21st Street between 6th and 7th Avenue, and Davis spent some of his time tutoring McLean and promoting his career in his curiously nonverbal manner. Both of them were heroin addicts, but the stronger bond between them was the music they played. When Davis was scheduled to open at Birdland just two days after he returned to New York, probably from the Jazz Inc tour, he gave McLean the responsibility of putting together a band for him. McLean called up two of his Sugar Hill neighbors, pianist Gil Coggins and bassist Connie Henry, to form the rhythm section along with drummer Connie Kay. Alongside Davis and himself in the front line, McLean added Don Elliott, a multi-instrumentalist with a Juilliard background whose main experience was in lounge bands. The group were heard on broadcasts from Birdland on both the Friday and Saturday nights of their engagement, and the transcription was released on record several years later:

Miles Davis All Stars
Miles Davis, tpt; Don Elliott, mellophone (on *Confirmation* and *Weedot*), vib (except on *Confirmation*); Jackie McLean, as (except on *It Could Happen to You*); Gil Coggins, pno; Connie Henry, b; Connie Kay, dms. Birdland, New York, 2 May 1952
Conception [*Evans*]; *Confirmation*
(both on Ozone 8)

Same personnel and place, 3 May 1952
Weedot; *The Chase*; *It Could Happen to You*; *Conception* [*Opmet*]
(all on Ozone 8)
The tracks identified as *Evans* and *Opmet* ('tempo' spelled backwards) are based loosely on George Shearing's *Conception*, yet another *Conception* deception.

Surprisingly, there is no attempt at ensemble playing, even on *Confirmation* and *Conception*, regularly featured in standard arrangements. Instead, Davis states the melody accompanied only by the rhythm section, usually including Elliott's vibraphone. The group approach is thus about as rudimentary as it can be in jazz music, with Davis playing a loose variation of the melody and then striking out in the first of the sequence of improvisations; the other soloists always follow in the same sequence, with McLean after Davis, then Elliott on one or the other of his instruments, and back to Davis again, who either trades four-bar phrases with Connie Kay (on *Confirmation* and *Weedot*) or returns directly to the closing statement of the melody. The absence of ensemble playing and the strict sequence of solos indicate the lack of rehearsal time, and the music is interesting mainly because it documents the growing confidence of Jackie McLean.

For McLean, this Birdland engagement brought recognition that the twenty-year-old alto saxophonist could hardly even imagine just six months earlier. "In 1952 I had a gig with Miles at Birdland, and Bird came on the stand," McLean remembers. "It was the first time I played with him. He was always kind and appreciative of my musical efforts. One evening he kept applauding my solos loudly. I know, because there wasn't much other applause. When I was through with the set, he rushed over and gave me a kiss on the neck." Miles Davis, needless to say, was not so effusive. His relationship with McLean, as close as it was, never really became a friendship in the sense of a meeting of equals. "I looked up to Miles, and he helped me in a lot of ways," McLean says. "He was the same way he is now. People say that Miles has gotten arrogant since he became successful, but Miles was arrogant when his heels didn't point in the same direction. I learned a lot from him, both on and off the bandstand. You might say that I was in the University of Miles Davis. I remember once when he got after me about a tune that I didn't know; the tune was *Yesterdays*, and I passed it off by saying that I was young, like, I'll learn it before I die. Miles cursed me out so bad, and he could really curse, that I never used that excuse again." In the years that followed, numerous musicians passed through the University of Miles Davis, and very few of them seem to have gotten any closer to the dean than McLean was able to. For the others, as for McLean, the tuition was too valuable and the lessons were too important to bother much about the distance that he always seemed to put between himself and the people he worked with most closely.

Davis's fury at McLean over *Yesterdays* took place at a recording session in the Blue Note studios less than a week after the Birdland engagement ended. Gil Coggins as well as McLean was retained from the Birdland band for what would prove to be Davis's only studio date of the year:

Miles Davis All Stars
Miles Davis, tpt; J.J. Johnson, tbn; Jackie McLean, as; Gil Coggins, pno; Oscar Pettiford, b; Kenny Clarke, dms. New York, 9 May 1952
Dear Old Stockholm; Chance It [Max Is Making Wax]; Donna [Dig] (two takes);
Woody'n You (two takes); *Yesterdays; How Deep Is the Ocean*
(all on United Artists UAS 9952 [in North America], Blue Note BST 81501/2 [in Europe])
Johnson and McLean do not play on *Yesterdays* and *How Deep Is the Ocean*.

The music recorded on this day, a Monday, is interesting, as is shown by the somewhat surprised tones of its reviewers when it was reissued twenty years later, in 1972. Mark Gardner, reviewing it for *Jazz Journal*, says, "This is durable music which has survived the passing of two decades and the introduction of many subsequent styles without losing any of its brightness and impact"; and then he adds, with the ominous tone of the bebop fan who by 1972 knew he had been deserted by Davis, "I wonder if we will be able to say the same of Miles Davis's current output in 1992." The reviewer for *Down Beat* said: "By 1952, [Davis] could encompass the warmth of *Dear Old Stockholm*, the dancing mood of *Donna*, and the bitter lyricism of *Yesterdays*. The last is a statement which ranks only a little behind Billie Holiday's interpretation of this challenging Kern song, and which has all the tonal (and emotional) edginess that would characterize his ballad playing, masterful, good, and just routine, over the next decade."

As good as the music is, it suffers by comparisons with both earlier and later work by Davis. *Donna* is a peculiarly methodical reading of the bouncy tune recorded under the title *Dig* for Prestige just seven months earlier, and the same deliberate, cautious ensemble playing mars this version of *Woody'n You*, Dizzy Gillespie's swinging composition. The two ballads, tacked on at the end of the recording session in the by-now familiar routine, have a faint pulse, and the emotionalism seems more than a little labored. They nevertheless provide very impressive displays for Gil Coggins as an accompanist, as he improvises harmonies and picks up short phrases from Davis's line for fills. A.B. Spellman called Coggins "one of the greatest piano accompanists of the era," but Coggins left music two years later to sell real estate and returned only sporadically, probably leaving behind too little evidence to justify such an accolade.

The high point of the session is *Dear Old Stockholm*, a beautiful ballad recorded by Stan Getz in Sweden the year before. Davis's arrangement sets off the delicate melody on the trumpet by superimposing it on dramatic ensemble passages. So effective is the arrangement that Davis would resuscitate it four years later in his first recording session for Columbia Records, when his trumpet-playing had the gentle assertiveness that would turn the whole performance into a brilliant recording.

But something was missing. Whatever the physical toll his addiction was taking, its psychological toll was much more obvious. Although he had so recently been acclaimed the top man on his instrument, his ability to retain that stature deserted him, and if jazz listeners in Madison and Montreal and Manchester were unaware of his failing powers, happily misled by the inevitable lag between recording sessions and record releases, there was still no hiding the fact of his failing powers from himself or from the musicians and managers and other insiders. Bad news travels fast, and by the middle of 1952 there were people watching Davis with furrowed brows wherever he played. He soon began to doubt himself.

To make things worse, the rumor mills were working as always in the jazz business, and people were returning to New York full of news about young trumpeters coming along for whom Davis, they implied, was no match. One name beginning to be heard was Chet Baker's. Charlie Parker had hired him for a quintet he formed in Los Angeles between tours with Jazz at the Philharmonic, and they had played together at Billy Berg's in Los Angeles and in some concerts in Vancouver. Baker says, "When Bird went east he told Dizzy and Miles, 'You better look out, there's a little white cat out on the West Coast who's gonna eat you up.'" As soon as Parker returned to the east coast, Baker joined the newly formed Gerry Mulligan Quartet and began playing ingenious counterpoint alongside Mulligan's baritone saxophone and spinning fragile, memorable melodies that made the quartet, and Baker, enormously popular in California. Within a year, the Mulligan quartet's records brought them much the same success in New

York and everywhere else. Although Baker's approach to the trumpet derived directly from Davis's work in the nonet and proved to be strictly limited to that delicate style, his reputation grew formidably, and he soon enjoyed most of the acclaim that had so recently been reserved for Davis.

Another young trumpeter with a growing reputation among musicians was Clifford Brown, then playing in bar bands around Philadelphia. Brown had been encouraged by Fats Navarro when he was a high school novice on his instrument in 1948, and by the time he had completed his apprenticeship playing rhythm and blues he seemed to have no technical limitations at all. He could play the fastest tempos in all registers with little loss of tone, and he could also play attractive ballads – and he was still learning. To further his learning, he intended to move to New York in 1953.

Another highly touted trumpeter was Joe Gordon. Musicians returning to New York from Boston, Gordon's hometown, brought back story after story of Gordon's prowess, especially of his aggressive playing in jam sessions. Gordon arrived in New York in 1952, and one of his first moves, long anticipated by musicians, was to sit in with Davis one evening at Birdland. The result, as told several years later by Cecil Taylor – a fellow Bostonian who admired Gordon and has no love at all for Davis, later a caustic critic of Taylor's avant-garde piano style – may be somewhat embroidered, but it indicates as well as any instance preserved from this period the debilitation of Davis. "Miles heard Joe play," Taylor says, "and then walked off the stand. And Bird ran up to Miles and grabbed him by the arms and said, 'Man, you're Miles Davis.' And Miles sort of came back and stood around shuffling his feet." The incident is all the more revealing with the advantage of hindsight, for Gordon, a trumpeter who made a few good recordings, notably one with Thelonious Monk (Riverside RLP 12-323), before his death in a fire in 1963, was never a serious rival for Davis in either ability or style. He only appeared that way to Davis from his distorted perspective in 1952.

Superficially, 1953 opened with much better prospects. Davis had a new recording deal with Prestige, and that would at least guarantee him some exposure and a little income. He wasted almost no time in starting to fulfill his commitment. Near the end of January he took an all-star band into the Prestige studios for his first session, which was marked by good intentions that, perhaps predictably, got buried in the execution. The sextet assembled by Davis included two tenor saxophonists, one of whom was Sonny Rollins. The other one was identified as Charlie Chan when these sides were finally released almost four years later, but the notes accompanying them made it clear to anyone who could not guess that the man behind the pseudonym was Charlie Parker. Parker was under some pressure, not only because he had an exclusive contract with Mercury, but also because the trumpeter in his regular band, Red Rodney, had been arrested and committed to the federal prison in Lexington. Parker believed that he was being watched by narcotics agents, according to Ross Russell, and he had given up narcotics for the time being and was consuming large quantities of alcohol instead. During the rehearsal period, when he was supposed to be getting used to the new King tenor saxophone that he brought with him to the studio, he drank a quart of vodka. As the confusion in the studio increased throughout the afternoon, the engineer became fed up and announced that he was leaving at 5:30. He told the musicians that the studio would close at 6:00 and that his assistant would look after any recording that might get done in the last half-hour. The musicians had managed to play only two titles, with a grand total of only three complete takes. In the remaining half-hour, they tried Monk's *Well You Needn't* a few times but could not get through it, and finally, with fifteen minutes to go and no chance for straightening out the problems on *Well You Needn't*, managed to make a complete take of another Monk composition, *Round about Midnight*:

Miles Davis All Stars
Miles Davis, tpt; Charlie Parker, Sonny Rollins, ts; Walter Bishop, pno; Percy Heath, b; Philly Joe Jones, dms. New York, 30 January 1953
Compulsion; *The Serpent's Tooth* (two takes); *Well You Needn't* (unissued); *Round about Midnight*
(all but *Well You Needn't* on Prestige LP 7044; reissued on Prestige 7822)
According to Ira Gitler's notes on the original release, Rollins does not play on *Round about Midnight*; however, on aural evidence, the tenor saxophone chorus following Davis's solo is probably Rollins rather than Parker, who solos before Davis; a second saxophone can also be heard playing a few notes in the background on the out-chorus.

The confusion in the recording studio is reflected in the music, although, as always when Parker was a participant, the irregularities had a less disastrous effect on the music than one might expect. In opening the recording session with his original composition *Compulsion*, Davis almost seems to be laying bare the potential problems on the date. Parker is expected to wrestle with his unfamiliar instrument on the fastest tempo that Davis will call all day, and he is also asked to solo immediately ahead of Rollins. Rollins turns out to be enormously more fluent than Parker on this title. On the two takes of *The Serpent's Tooth*, another Davis original, Parker improves noticeably and seems more in control even on the brighter tempo of the second take than on the medium tempo of the first. By the time the band gets around to playing *Round about Midnight*, Parker is capable of treating the tune as a feature, playing the first solo with obvious feeling and a measure of grace that bely his technical limitations on the unfamiliar horn.

Indeed, on *Round about Midnight* the technical limitations belong much more prominently to Davis, who hits half a dozen sour notes playing the melody at the beginning and end.

This chaotic session marked the first appearance of Davis's new favorite among drummers, Philly Joe Jones. Three years older than Davis, Jones attached the name of his hometown to his own given name in hopes of avoiding confusion between himself and Jo Jones, Basie's longtime drummer – though Philly Joe was almost completely unknown. Although he seemed rather old to have made no mark among jazz drummers, he was far from untalented. The best indications of his strengths at his debut session with Davis come on the first take of *The Serpent's Tooth*, where the bop melody played over a medium tempo offers lots of opportunity for assertive drumming. Jones punctuates the phrases of the melody and of the solos with resounding accents and yet somehow manages to remain integral and unobtrusive as well. He shows a rare combination of aggression and sensitivity, a preview of the gifts that he developed magnificently during the next five years behind the leadership of Davis. In 1953, he was as involved in other aspects of night life as in music, and many musicians knew him better as a streetwise hipster than as a drummer.

Three weeks later, Davis was back again in the Prestige studios with an entirely different band. After the fiasco with 'Charlie Chan' and the others, Weinstock took no chances and chose Davis's sidemen himself. The band are an interesting mix of some solid musicians. Only John Lewis and Kenny Clarke had been associated with Davis before this. The two tenor saxophonists, Al Cohn and John (Zoot) Sims, had been together in Woody Herman's Second Herd in 1948–9 as members of the famous Four Brothers saxophone section and both approached their horns in a style derived from Lester Young, as did almost all white tenor players of the day. Cohn was a literate soloist and a fine arranger, and Sims an ebullient, inventive swinger, one of the most consistently pleasing soloists on the instrument all through his long, uninterrupted career. So well did their talents mesh that they were often matched in later recording sessions and led a quintet of their own in the late 1950s. Putting them together for the Prestige session pretty well ensured a listenable result, no matter how uneasy their presence made the leader:

Miles Davis with Al Cohn and Zoot Sims
Miles Davis, tpt; Sonny Truitt, tbn (on *Floppy*); Al Cohn, Zoot Sims, ts; John Lewis, pno; Leonard Gaskin, b; Kenny Clarke, dms. New York, 19 February 1953
Tasty Pudding; Willie the Wailer; Floppy; For Adults Only
(all on Prestige 7674; originally on Prestige LP 154)

All the music is composed and arranged by Al Cohn, and it is unabashedly bright, friendly, and extroverted – a bit of an oddity for Davis. It is also meticulously arranged, requiring some concentration by the players. *Willie the Wailer* is over-arranged, resulting in a cluttered ensemble with the horns crowding the drum breaks. The rest of the music is intricate but not precious. *Tasty Pudding* features Davis, in the only solo apart from a short turn by John Lewis, and it rides over a cushion of harmony provided by the saxophones. It is the one sure sign that Davis is the leader of this session, because elsewhere he shares the solos equally with Sims and Cohn, even alloting them the first solos on *For Adults Only*, where he follows their neo-swing styles with a strangely cautious solo in which he seems to place each note deliberately before going on to the next. On *Floppy*, an uptempo number where the melody is little more than an excuse to get into the round of solos, Cohn and Sims follow their individual turns by alternating part-choruses, a version of the tenor chase used in jam sessions. Though Davis played better than he had for more than a year, the exuberance of Sims and Cohn on that chase sequence consummates the session.

Davis's flurry of recording activity for Prestige preceded another session for Blue Note, in what appears to be a companion session to the one he recorded for that label almost a year earlier. J.J. Johnson returned as trombonist and Gil Coggins returned as pianist, but Jimmy Heath is the reed player in place of Jackie McLean, with Jimmy's brother Percy, who had played with Davis on the Charlie Chan date, and Art Blakey filling out the sextet:

Miles Davis All Stars
Miles Davis, tpt; J.J. Johnson, tbn (except *I Waited for You*); Jimmy Heath, ts (except *I Waited for You*); Gil Coggins, pno; Percy Heath, b; Art Blakey, dms. New York 20 April 1953
Tempus fugit (two takes); *Enigma*; *Ray's Idea* (two takes); *I Waited for You*; *Kelo*; *C.T.A.* (two takes)
(all on United Artists UAS 9952)

These recordings took Davis back into the familiar confines of bebop, featuring reckless tempos on the three titles that required second takes: Bud Powell's *Tempus fugit*, *Ray's Idea* by Ray Brown and Walter Gil Fuller, and Jimmy Heath's *C.T.A.* J.J. Johnson contributed a couple of medium-tempo tunes, *Kelo* and *Enigma*, the latter built on the chord changes of *Conception/Deception*. The only ballad, Fuller's *I Waited for You*, played by Davis and the rhythm trio, was borrowed from the old Gillespie band book. (With *Woody'n You* recorded by Davis for Blue Note in May 1952 and the two Fuller tunes at this session, Davis shows an unexplained predilection for Fuller's music in these Blue Note record-ings.) The session was not especially distinguished except for the quantity of music recorded – nine complete takes of six different titles, more than thirty min-utes of music. But a listener can hardly fail to pick out the frailty of Gil Coggins's solos on both takes of *Ray's Idea*, the only tracks where he is given solo space, and, more positively, Davis's flowing bebop solo on the alternate take of *Ray's Idea* and Blakey's thunderous drumming on the master take of *Tempus fugit*, a bright spot more easily appreciated by contrast to his relative restraint on the alternate take. Yet a malaise hangs over the session, suggesting that it meant little more to the players than a few hours of work.

So far, 1953 had found Davis amid some very unlikely company, beginning with the tenor-toting Charlie Chan and continuing with the Al Cohn–Zoot Sims pairing. He next turned up at Birdland in a band accompanying a hip vaudevil-lian, Joe (Bebop) Carroll, a comedy singer garbed in loud-checked suits, a beret, and dark glasses. Carroll had been a member of Dizzy Gillespie's big band in their final years, 1949–51, an adjunct blatantly designed to increase the size of the audience. Most jazz fans tolerated Carroll's presence in the Gillespie band as a necessary evil for keeping the band together in the economic climate of the day. But Gillespie thrived on Carroll's nonsense onstage, willingly playing second banana. After the big band folded, he hired Carroll for his small bands, which hardly needed a burlesque component, and kept right on playing the fool along-side him.

Years after Carroll's role was forgotten, Gillespie kept the jive monologues and the nonsense vocals in his 'act,' often diluting his wizardry as a trumpeter in a way that caused the purists and sometimes the not-so-purists in his audience to shake their heads. In the beginning, the jargon and the costumes caricatured the bebop revolution, taking the trappings of that movement to such extremes that it became laughable. Although the joke did not remain truly funny for more than a fraction of the time that Gillespie has kept on telling it, it is so much a part of Gillespie's *schtick* that his performances are unimaginable without it. If pressed, Gillespie would almost certainly try to vindicate his use of low comedy by saying that jazzmen of his generation were expected to be entertainers, as Louis Arm-strong was before them.

The idea of a jazzman surviving by music alone came later, and one of the people responsible for the change was Miles Davis. "He was the first one," accord-ing to Gillespie, "that came along in our business and figured he didn't have to smile at everyone, didn't have to tell no jokes or make no announcements, didn't have to say thank you or even bow. He figured he could just let the music speak for him, and for itself." No stage manners could be more diametrically opposed than Davis's and Gillespie's, since Gillespie has spent decades projecting an

Joe (Bebop) Carroll and Dizzy Gillespie (Arthur Zinn, courtesy of *Down Beat*)

Ahmad Jamal (courtesy of *Down Beat*)

onstage character that seems to be a composite of a musician and a clown. The clownish part of that character originated in Joe Carroll. Davis's shared billing with Carroll at Birdland could hardly have been more out of character, but it was arranged by Gillespie and no doubt agreed to by Davis because of his financial needs.

For reasons now forgotten, Gillespie found himself unable to front his band for part of its engagement at Birdland in May, and Davis stood in for him. On the broadcast of Saturday 16 May, Davis is the only trumpeter; on a later broadcast, probably the following Saturday, Gillespie rejoins the band and Davis appears as a guest along with Charlie Parker. So far only one title from these two broadcasts (*I Got Rhythm*, from the first broadcast) is available on record. The details are as follows:

Miles Davis with Dizzy Gillespie's Band
Miles Davis, tpt; Sahib Shihab, bs; Wade Legge, pno; Lou Hackney, b; Al Jones, dms; Candido, conga; Joe Carroll, vcl (on *I Got Rhythm*). Birdland, New York, 16 May 1953
I Got Rhythm; *Move*; *Tenderly*; *Night in Tunisia*; *Dig*; *Lullaby of Birdland* (theme)
(*I Got Rhythm* on Chakra CH 100; all other titles unissued)

Miles Davis, Dizzy Gillespie, tpt; Charlie Parker, as; Sahib Shihab, bs; Wade Legge, pno; Lou Hackney, b; Al Jones, dms; Joe Carroll, vcl. Birdland, New York, possibly 23 May 1953
The Bluest Blues; *On the Sunny Side of the Street*
(both unissued)

On *I Got Rhythm*, Carroll sings a tangential version of the Gershwin tune and then launches into a chorus that includes scat syllables and pop allusions, including the line "How much is that doggie in the window?" from the tawdry novelty song that was earning a fortune for Patti Page on the pop charts. Davis's solo, which follows, repeats single notes and short phrases, along the way tossing in a reference to the theme from *Dragnet*, a radio detective series then popular. Only on his last chorus does Davis sound at all like himself.

Between the two Birdland broadcasts, Davis was making more significant music with a quartet in his third recording session of the year for Prestige:

Miles Davis Quartet
Miles Davis, tpt; John Lewis, pno (except *Smooch*); Charles Mingus, pno (on *Smooch*); Percy Heath, b; Max Roach, dms. New York, 19 May 1953
When Lights Are Low; *Tune Up*; *Miles Ahead*; *Smooch*
(all on Prestige LP 7054; reissued on Prestige 7822)

This session offers little that is novel in Davis's work. He plays lyrically through-out, in good command technically, and he is well supported by the rhythm players; John Lewis and Percy Heath were now regular partners in the newly formed Modern Jazz Quartet, a cooperative unit that originated the year before (as the Milt Jackson Quartet) and would continue under the new cooperative arrangement for more than two decades.

In the perspective of Davis's career, the session takes on more interest. More than any other individual session of the period, it shows him building up the resources he would refine throughout the later part of the decade. Two of the compositions Davis recorded here for the first time, Benny Carter's *When Lights Are Low* and the original *Tune up*, credited to Davis, would remain in his reper-toire for several years; he recorded them again in definitive performances for Prestige in October 1956. Davis's other original, *Miles Ahead*, did not remain in his active repertoire, although it deserved a place. It reveals a great deal of Davis's musical development during his first twelve years in New York, because it rein-vents his composition *Milestones*, recorded for Savoy in August 1947. As *Miles Ahead*, the original melody has been pared down and clarified (although Davis meanders and misses some notes in the final chorus, apparently searching for the melody he opened with). It will be reinvented yet again by Davis and Gil Evans in 1957, in a big band showcase. *Smooch* is a nonce effort credited to Davis and Charles Mingus, who takes over from Lewis as the piano player. It is a moody, pulseless piece with Davis as the only soloist.

Following this brief flurry of activity in New York early in 1953, Davis again left the city, for an even longer time than usual. His next documented appearance there was not for some ten months, when he would record again for Blue Note. In the interim he seems to have spent some time at home in East St. Louis, and he probably played in clubs in the Midwest as a guest soloist with local rhythm sections, as he had during his previous travels during this period. He spent a large part of the fall and winter in and around Los Angeles. The arrangements for his California sojourn were probably made during his May recordings for Prestige, because two of his sidemen then, Max Roach and Charles Mingus, were already planning moves to California. Mingus still considered Los Angeles home, although he had been away for a couple of years. Roach, who was as dissatisfied with the jazzman's lifestyle in New York as Davis was, decided to make a break by accept-ing a steady job in the house band at a club called The Lighthouse in Hermosa Beach, California.

Modern jazz in the Los Angeles area was suddenly attracting a large following after years of languishing in the shadow of more traditional styles. Popular maga-zines such as *Life* and *Newsweek* ran features on its popularity, branding it West

Coast jazz and extolling its virtues as clean-cut, tightly organized, lightly swinging music. It had become the musical counterpart of the Ivy League fashions then sweeping into vogue, featuring narrow lapels, thin ties, and close-cropped hairdos; like the Ivy League accoutrements, the jazz coming from the opposite coast presented the appearance of immaculate neatness. West Coast jazz had given rise to a whole roster of musicians whose names were becoming internationally known. Along with Gerry Mulligan and Chet Baker, whose pianoless quartet had broken up because of Mulligan's imprisonment on a narcotics charge before its records caught on beyond California, the leaders of the style, at least in the beginning, were men who had left the bands of Woody Herman and Stan Kenton to settle in the Los Angeles area. The leading exponents, trumpeter-arranger Shorty Rogers and drummer Shelly Manne, arrived in California by this route and supplemented their jazz jobs with lucrative day jobs in the Hollywood studios. So did many of the others who came out of the big road bands – trumpeters Pete and Conte Candoli, trombonist Milt Bernhart, and saxophonists Jimmy Giuffre, Bob Cooper, Bill Holman, and Bud Shank.

Mixed in with them were a number of musicians raised in the area, especially pianists, including Hampton Hawes, Russ Freeman, and Claude Williamson, whose debts to a younger, healthier Bud Powell were evident in everything they played, and the jarring individualist Dave Brubeck. Art Pepper, the alto saxophonist, was raised in Los Angeles and was also a veteran of the Kenton band; Paul Desmond, a San Franciscan, starred as the altoist in Brubeck's quartet; and multi-reed player Buddy Colette was a childhood friend of Mingus's who stayed at home and for a short time met with better success than the big bassist. Besides Manne, the drummer most closely associated with the style was Chico Hamilton, first noticed in the Mulligan-Baker quartet and then as the leader of his own quintet with Colette. As the cult of West Coast jazz gained breadth and popularity, so did the list of its proponents, until it included classicists such as pianist André Previn and guitarist Laurindo Almeida, who joined the ranks as soon as they could master the rudiments of swing. Along with the pool of capable musicians, West Coast jazz quickly developed its own record producers, among which the most abiding were the labels Pacific Jazz, Fantasy, and Contemporary Records.

Jazz clubs sprang up, many of them short-lived, such as the Haig, where Mulligan's quartet got its start. The longest-lived and probably the most important club was The Lighthouse. Its jazz policy was overseen by Howard Rumsey, a former bassist with Kenton, and he installed Shorty Rogers and Shelly Manne in the house band. Rumsey also inaugurated a record label called Lighthouse when he saw the commercial potential of his house band, pressing an all-star session onto discs of red transparent vinyl to sell to the aficionados who turned up for "our most popular feature of the week – a continuous concert from 2 p.m. to 2 a.m. every Sunday throughout the year." By the middle of 1953, everyone knew that California was a great place to play jazz, and Max Roach, one of the leading lights of the bebop revolution a few years earlier, was joining The Lighthouse band, replacing Shelly Manne.

Roach did not travel west alone. Howard Rumsey told Leonard Feather: "When Max Roach came in from New York to take over Shelly Manne's chair, he drove up with Charles Mingus and Miles Davis in the car with him. Miles was just starting to play again after a long sabbatical back home in St. Louis. He hung around for a while, stayed at my home for a week, and did a couple of guest shots at the club. One of them was recorded, but the stuff was never released; I just heard Contemporary is finally going to put it out." The session with Davis remains unreleased in spite of frequent rumors, dating back to 1953, that it will finally see the light of day. Eventually it will be issued, and only then will another rumor, one of the most persistent in jazz, finally be squelched. For The Lighthouse recording has been eagerly anticipated not only because it contains material from one of Davis's silent periods but also because Davis is believed to share the leadership on the recording with Chet Baker, whose star seemed to be ascending just as Davis's seemed to be flickering. The rumors of a recorded meeting of Davis and Baker, fueled most recently by the listing in a 1980 discography (included in Baker's *Once Upon a Summertime* LP, Artists House 9411) of unissued material from September 1953 by Baker, Davis, and The Lighthouse All Stars, are, sadly, untrue. The two did not meet for another year, when Baker arrived in New York for the first time and looked up Davis, and then the meeting was brief and unmusical. Davis's recording at The Lighthouse probably includes Max Roach and some prominent West Coast players, but Baker is not among them.

Davis did not find many other opportunities to work in California but he stayed, living with Max Roach and hanging around The Lighthouse bar. After a few weeks he had certainly worn out his welcome at The Lighthouse and probably at Roach's apartment as well. The tensions came to a head on Roach's birthday, when Davis staged an impromptu celebration at the bar for which he could not pay. Davis told the story to Julie Coryell: "The cat at the bar says, 'Max says you have to pay the bill.' I said, 'Shit, Max, it's your birthday, you pay the bill.' The bartender said, 'I'm gonna kick your ass 'cause you're a black motherfucker.' It's a funny thing, 'cause I had a knife on me, in my pocket; I had just taken it away from Max, who I was living with. So Max says, 'I'll leave this [situation] with you,' and goes on the bandstand. The bartender says, 'When I get off, I'm gonna kick your ass.' So I said, 'If you're gonna kick my ass, you don't have to wait until you get off – you might as well get off right now!'" The end of the story remains untold.

Some changes seemed inevitable. Davis's decline – his long absences from play-ing, his technical failings when he did find an opportunity to play, and his pre-occupation with extra-musical problems – had been going on unabated for some four years. By now the decline had become obvious even to listeners far removed from Davis's live performances. André Hodeir detected Davis's lack of control from recordings released in France, even though the recorded evidence was spo-radic and selective. "The extreme unevenness of Miles Davis's recordings, which seem to give a faithful picture of the great trumpeter's current work, makes it impossible to consider him any longer as a leader," Hodeir wrote. "It is hard to define the reasons for this decline beyond pointing out that they are instrumental in nature, but in any case, far from being affected by it, his historical position is stronger than ever. Trumpeters as different from each other as Chet Baker and Clifford Brown have in common a certain way of proceeding, a certain idea of sonority, that is in a sense their share of the heritage left by Davis's discoveries."

Davis was only twenty-seven, and already his career was being assessed by one of his most astute critics in terms of its historical contribution. Hodeir's assump-tion that Davis's best work was behind him was shared by many others, and if most listeners could not have reached Hodeir's conclusion with the same clarity, any study of the works of these years, especially compared to the works imme-diately preceding, could only lead to the same conclusion. Thus Martin Williams, looking back, says: "By the early fifties, it may have seemed that the productive career of trumpeter and flugelhornist Miles Davis was just about over. Between 1950 and 1954 his work had become uneven. Obvious aspects of his style had already been siphoned off and popularized by several trumpeters, particularly on the West Coast." Davis's decline seemed to fit the well-known pattern for a jazz career; jazz artists who do not die young are likely to relax into complacency. He seemed to be a prime prospect for one or the other of those fates.

The listening public was nearly ready to write him off: in the *Down Beat* reader's poll for 1954, Davis barely made the list of top trumpeters, showing up ninth. It was no disgrace to find himself behind such perennial stars as Dizzy Gillespie (second), Roy Eldridge (fourth), and Louis Armstrong (sixth), or even the swing trumpeter Harry James (third), but the other front-runners were about the same age as Davis and had been learning their scales or sitting anonymously in band sections when he was already making innovations. All of them were asso-ciated with the West Coast. Maynard Ferguson (seventh) was featured promi-nently as Stan Kenton's high-note man, and the others, Conte Candoli (eighth), Shorty Rogers (fifth), and the surprising first-place choice, Chet Baker, displayed in their different ways the West Coast sound that was derived from Davis's inno-vations. Following Davis were Bobby Hackett and Clifford Brown; Brown also won the New Star award among trumpeters.

Whatever anyone else may have thought about Chet Baker taking first place, Baker did not think much of it. "I played some nice things on the first Gerry Mulligan album," Baker concedes. "It was a different style – soft, melodic. I think people were wanting and needing something like that and it just happened that at the time I came along with it and it caught on. But I don't think I was half the trumpeter that Dizzy was, or Kenny Dorham. Clifford was around then, Jesus Christ! So it just didn't make sense to me that I should have won the poll. It was a kind of a temporary fad kind of thing that was bound to work itself out." For Davis, Baker's ascendancy and his own loss of stature were further blows to what was left of his pride. They might have sounded his death knell, and no one would have been very surprised; but they seemed instead to reactivate that slumbering pride. Davis may have been down but he suddenly knew that he could stay down no longer. He was determined to put his heroin addiction behind him once and for all. And in the end it was not a rival trumpeter with a good press agent or a record producer with a handful of nickels and dimes or even a ham-fisted thug with his I.O.U. in his pocket who made him keep his promise to himself when he had failed to keep it so many times before. Instead, it was an athlete with a winning smile and a winning right hook.

Like every boxing fan of the day, Davis particularly admired Sugar Ray Robinson, the longtime welterweight champion who was called the best boxer, pound for pound, of all time. Sugar Ray was a celebrity, a strikingly handsome champion known as a ladies' man. Between fights, he appeared in New York society, photographed by the *Herald Tribune* or the *Times* stepping out of a limousine in a velvet cape and wide-brimmed hat. But when he went to Madison Square Garden to defend his title, any resemblance to that smiling socialite disappeared. He appeared instead as a trim, grim athlete, superbly conditioned and prepared. In the two sides of Robinson, Davis saw everything admirable, and somehow he projected his own dilemma onto the situation that Robinson mastered so gracefully. The main difference, in Davis's mind, was that he had become incapable of defending himself. That much he would learn from the boxer. "Sugar Ray Robinson inspired me and made me kick a habit," Davis said twenty years later. "I said, 'If that mother can win all those fights, I can sure break this motherfuckin' habit.' I went home, man, and sat up for two weeks and I sweated it out." Of Robinson's example he says, "Man, he didn't know it [that he inspired the cure, but] when he started training, he wouldn't make it with chicks. He disciplined himself and all that." He was exactly the model that Davis needed.

If it took Robinson's example to show him the self-discipline he needed, it was Max Roach who goaded him into using it. In the aftermath of his argument with the bartender at The Lighthouse, Davis berated Roach bitterly, and Roach, who had already put up with him at close quarters for a long time, tried his best to placate him. "Max Roach gave me $200 and put it in my pocket, say I looked good," Davis told Cheryl McCall. The money and flattery did not placate him at all; they just made him angrier. "I said that motherfucker gave me $200, told me I looked good, and I'm fucked up and he knows it. And he's my best friend, right? It just *embarrassed* me to death. I looked in the mirror and I said, Goddam it, Miles, come on." Davis left California immediately and headed for his father's farm near East St. Louis. Doc Davis was waiting for him when he arrived. "We walked out in the pasture," Davis recalls, "and he said, 'If you were with a woman and the woman left you, I would know what to tell you; you could get another woman. But this you have to do by yourself, you know that, 'cause you have been around drugs all your life. You know what you have to do.'"

Davis knew very well. He cured himself with the most primitive, and most successful, therapy of all, by locking himself in his bedroom at the farmhouse and suffering while the demons of his addiction contended inside him. For almost two weeks he lay in the darkened room. Once in a while the maid would ask him if he wanted some food sent in and he would shout back, "*Get* outta here," but the rest of the time he lay there in silence, because, he told McCall, "my father was next door and I was sure not gonna let him hear me holler and scream." He described the cure for Marc Crawford in *Ebony:* "I made up my mind I was getting off dope. I was sick and tired of it. You know you can get tired of anything. You can even get tired of being scared. I laid down and stared at the ceiling for twelve days and cursed everybody I didn't like. I was kicking it the hard way. It was like a bad case of flu, only worse. I lay in a cold sweat. My nose and eyes ran. I threw up everything I tried to eat. My pores opened up and I smelled like chicken soup. Then it was over."

He needed a period of recuperation after that, a time for working at his music and staying away from his old connections. New York was no good, and Los Angeles was no better. He liked Chicago, of course, and Sonny Rollins had already disappeared into the bowels of America's second city more than once in his attempts to rehabilitate himself, but the temptations in Chicago rivaled those in New York and Los Angeles. Davis chose Detroit, a city with a huge working-class population serving the automobile industry and, not incidentally, with a vital local jazz scene still largely undiscovered beyond the city limits. In the next few years it would not escape discovery, as it turned out such progeny as pianists Hank Jones, Tommy Flanagan, and Barry Harris, brass players Thad Jones, Donald Byrd, and Curtis Fuller, saxophonists Billy Mitchell and Yusef Lateef, bassist Paul Chambers, drummers Oliver Jackson and Elvin Jones, singer Betty Carter, and many others. The local musicians were good, but they were better than they knew. Detroit still had no reputation as a center for jazz, and Davis's residency impressed the locals. He moved into the Bluebird Inn as the guest artist with Billy Mitchell's house band, which also included Tommy Flanagan and Elvin Jones. Guest soloists normally played at the Bluebird for a month at a time, but Davis stayed for several months. Lonnie Hillyer, the trumpeter, was only fourteen, a student of Barry Harris's, as were many of the Detroit musicians, when he first caught sight of Davis in his hometown. "It was an experience for me – impact," Hillyer recalls. "He lived there for a while in Detroit. I was impressed with all the things kids are usually impressed with – personality as well as the playing, the whole thing, you know, the manner, know what I mean? Appearances – all the glamorous things. Jazz people are the smartest people in the community. They always seem to be a little ahead of everybody else. You have to be *equipped*." Whether or not Davis was equipped when he arrived in Detroit, he certainly was after a few months there. His playing became confident again, he worked out several new compositions, and he lost the desire for drugs as well as the dependence on them. As soon as spring arrived, he felt the need to move back to New York where he could renew the career he had walked out on.

For Davis the years of heroin addiction were over, and only the scars remained. The needle tracks on his arm faded soon enough, but perhaps there were deeper scars, left over from wounds that were never so visible. To someone such as Babs Gonzales, who has watched the healing process more times than he can count, those scars seem obvious. "Miles came from a prosperous upper middle-class home and was even spoiled a little as a boy," Gonzales reasons. "Therefore there doesn't seem to be any reason for the suspicion he has toward people, right? But he knew some grim times before all this success. For one thing, when he was strung out on heroin – and he's one of the very few who broke the habit all by himself, completely without treatment – Miles was desperate enough to fall in with some pitiless people. Some of them exploited him musically, made him play for very little bread, but he badly needed that little bread. Also, the hoods who ran the jazz clubs in New York used to beat up on Miles and Bud Powell and other musicians who were strung out and in hock to them. Miles has always been a proud man, and while they didn't break him, they hurt him for a long time. Ever since then he's been leery about everybody. With exceptions – and they never know who they'll be."

But if Davis's suspicious, sometimes erratic behavior dates from his addiction, to him it must seem a small price to pay. "I ought to be dead from just what I went through when I was on dope," he says. Before, during, and after his days as an addict, he has often found himself surrounded by musicians who are killing themselves by degrees with narcotics. Only a few of them have been more than nodding acquaintances of his once they leave the bandstand for the evening.

With narcotics no longer occupying most of his waking hours or sapping his strength, Davis found himself on a creative peak that he would sustain unbroken for six years. Jazz, or any other art form, has seldom known anything comparable to such sustained invention over such a long period, but Davis himself sees it as nothing more than substituting a real narcotic for a more ephemeral one. "Music," he said, years later, "is an addiction."

6

Walkin'
1954–5

Miles Davis has reached back two generations and brought a seminal style up to date. More than any other player, Miles Davis echoes Louis Armstrong; one can hear it, I think, in his reading of almost any standard theme. And behind his jaded stance, beneath the complaints, and beneath the sometimes blasé sophistication, Miles Davis's horn also echoes something of Armstrong's exuberantly humorous, forcefully committed, and self-determined joy.   Martin Williams

It was a strangely formless musical scene that Miles Davis moved back into in New York in the spring of 1954. It had been a few years, of course, since he had participated fully in that scene, and in those few years several tendencies had taken a decisive turn. The longtime leaders were no longer leading. Charlie Parker was suffering musically as well as physically; his erratic behavior caused him to miss almost as many engagements as he showed up for and often to play terribly when he did show up. The managers of Birdland, the club that had been named for him, would finally ban him after an onstage shouting match with the ailing Bud Powell, and many of his most fervent followers of a few years before had begun drifting away. Dizzy Gillespie, although as healthy and technically proficient as ever, was playing many of the same tunes in the same arrangements he had played ten years earlier, and while no one else played them as well, listeners were looking elsewhere. The West Coast school, with its roots in the Davis nonet and the post-swing bands, attracted the jazz as well as the popular press, and its proponents moved in to take more than an even share of the jobs from the old pros in New York. The same currents that fostered the West Coast school's popularity were also at work in the rest of the country. In New York, people were beginning to notice the band that billed itself as the Modern Jazz Quartet, a cooperative unit made up of John Lewis, Milt Jackson, Percy Heath, and Kenny

Clarke (who would be replaced the next year by Connie Kay). Under Lewis's direction, the MJQ played fastidiously arranged chamber jazz. Their glossy facade allowed the admirers of West Coast jazz to identify with them, but behind the facade, and almost unnoticed in the first waves of enthusiasm they felt, lurked more substantial roots in the blues that made their music more durable than most. The academic strain of Lennie Tristano and his student-followers continued to draw attention, as did the George Shearing Quintet, which spawned more than a few combos riding the crest of popularity on pretty, quasi-jazz ensemble sounds, including such groups as the Australian Jazz Quartet, the Calvin Jackson Quartet, and many others now forgotten.

While no one would deny that some good musicians were involved in the new developments, many musicians complained that the music had become *too* cool – too effete and emotionless. "Musically speaking, the cool period always reminded me of white people's music," Dizzy Gillespie said, decades later. "There was no guts in that music, not much rhythm either. They never sweated on the stand, Lee Konitz, Lennie Tristano, and those guys. This music, jazz, is guts. You're supposed to sweat in your balls in this music. I guess the idea was not to get 'savage' with it, biting, like we were. But that's jazz to me. Jazz to me is dynamic, a blockbuster. They sorta softened it up a bit, but the depth of the music didn't change. Because we had the depth already. You couldn't get too much deeper than Charlie Parker." As for Davis's role as the patriarch of cool music, Gillespie recognized that Davis was no longer truly represented by the music that went by that name. "Miles wasn't cool like that, anyway," he said. "Miles is from that part of St. Louis where the blues come from. Just part of his music is played like that, cool. They copped that part – the cool – but let the rest, the blues, go, or they missed it."

No one knew that better, of course, than Davis himself. Returning to New York full of creative energy, having been humbled in so many ways by club owners and audiences and reader's polls in the past few years, he was ready to declare emphatically that the bebop revolution was not finished, that emotion or guts or whatever one cared to call it belonged in the music no matter how literate its players might have become, and that the music of the present needed to draw on, not turn away from, the great music of the recent past. As usual, he was not inclined to discuss such matters, but his music of the period leaves no doubt about his convictions. Whether or not he believed he would find an audience is impossible to guess. After being practically written off for the previous few years, he must have known that he would have to struggle to regain his audience. He was certainly prepared. With his confidence intact, he played with a new intensity and produced a string of recordings in 1954–5 with moments of great brilliance.

They were only the buildup for what he would accomplish in the second half of the decade, but they crystallized his own mature style and convincingly subverted the more effete aspects of the cool style.

His first recordings back in New York were for Blue Note, early in March. Davis approached Alfred Lion, Blue Note's owner, soon after he resettled and made arrangements for a recording date with a rhythm trio. The details are as follows:

Miles Davis Quartet
Miles Davis, tpt; Horace Silver, pno; Percy Heath, b; Art Blakey, dms. New York, 6 March 1954
Well You Needn't; Lazy Susan; Weirdo [Sid's Ahead]; The Leap; Take off; It Never Entered My Mind
(all on United Artists UAS 9952)

In Percy Heath and Art Blakey, Davis chose rhythm players with whom he had often been associated before, but in Horace Silver he found an important new piano stylist. Silver, who was twenty-three, had been around New York for almost four years, playing in bands lead by Stan Getz and Lester Young, among others, but he remained virtually unknown because he had not found enough opportunities to record. He and Blakey knew one another well, and their musical partnership remained close for a few more years after these recordings, notably in the first edition of Blakey's successful band called the Jazz Messengers, formed about a year later with Silver as the piano player. Silver's presence on Davis's Blue Note date and also on his next three recording sessions during this prolific spring gave him exactly the kind of exposure he needed. His immediate blossoming as a major young talent further enhanced Davis's reputation as a jazz mentor, although more than a little luck was involved in bringing the two men together.

When Davis moved back to New York he lived at first in a hotel on 25th Street, and Silver happened to be living in the same hotel. They got to know one another because Silver had a piano and Davis needed to use it. "I had a little upright piano in my room and Miles used to come in all the time and play it," Silver remembers. It was inevitable that they would talk about music and natural that Silver would become Davis's student. "I learned a lot of things from him about music," Silver says. "He's a hell of a teacher." Silver was obviously an able student, because he became Davis's regular piano player for the time being. By the end of the year, partly as a result of Silver's playing on these recordings, he would be named the New Star on piano in *Down Beat's* international poll of critics.

On the Blue Note session, Silver is clearly under the influence of Davis, especially when he submerges his already considerable individuality to play in Thelonious Monk's style on *Well You Needn't* and to play conventional ballad accompaniment on *It Never Entered My Mind*. (Conventional though it was, the latter ballad was effectively incorporated into Ralph Burns's soundtrack for the 1974 movie *Lennie*, starring Dustin Hoffman, a melodrama about the ill-starred monologist Lennie Bruce; Burns also used *Well You Needn't* from this session and *Tempus fugit*, the 1953 recording by Miles Davis for Blue Note, in his soundtrack.) Silver's style shows up better on the other four tracks, as he strings together blues-tinged phrases with a facile right hand while the left hand ventures neat, occasional chords almost imperceptibly. The essentials of that style would soon be adopted by dozens of other piano players.

Davis's selection of *Well You Needn't*, one of a dozen or more Monk themes that are among the treasures of post-war jazz, seems almost calculated to redress some of the problems that Davis had so recently put behind him, for this was the tune that Davis and the tenor duo of Sonny Rollins and Charlie (Chan) Parker had failed to make into a presentable version for Prestige a little more than a year earlier. This time, it is more than simply presentable, as a restrained romp sustained by Silver's oblique, splayed imitation of Monk's pianistics. *Lazy Susan*, *The Leap*, and *Take off*, all written by Davis, have their moments too, notably Heath's and Silver's repeated figure in stop time on *Take off* and Davis's decidedly un-cool staccato bursts on *The Leap*. But it is the other Davis composition, *Weirdo*, that stands out. Recorded again in 1958 by his sextet under the title *Sid's Ahead*, *Weirdo* consists of a single declamatory phrase with harmonic variants. As a compositional technique, the phrase and variants soon become characteristic of Davis's best work, showing up time and again in his original compositions. Simple though it is, it provides a versatile framework for what is essentially an improvised art form, the declamatory statement functioning as a kind of proclamation that opens and closes the improvised core and at the same time establishes the mood or context of the improvisations. *Weirdo/Sid's Ahead* is also interesting as a compositional sketch based on the more elaborate *Walkin'*, a composition originally credited to Davis but later correctly credited to Richard Carpenter, which would be given its first and definitive recorded statement by Davis just a few weeks later. The comparative simplicity of *Weirdo* may have been dictated by the limits of the quartet format, but it is nonetheless a virtuous simplicity, as Martin Williams has observed: "In this piece, Davis has abstracted his theme of *Walkin'* and reduced it to an essence of three notes, and he has done it so brilliantly as to make the delightfully original *Walkin'* seem overdecorative." The virtue of musical simplicity has been one of Davis's main themes, both in theory and practice, throughout his career.

Just four days after the Blue Note recordings, Davis returned to the studios, this time for Prestige, with exactly the same rhythm trio, to record two more original compositions and a ballad. This session was his first installment on a new three-year recording contract he had signed with Prestige, a long-term commitment he would come to regret, and the previous Blue Note session had been hastily arranged in order to squeeze in an extra payday before the new contract took effect. Although the sponsoring labels are different, this session is a continuation of the one before it. The details are as follows:

Miles Davis Quartet
Miles Davis, tpt; Horace Silver, pno; Percy Heath, b; Art Blakey, dms. New York,
10 March 1954
Four; That Old Devil Moon; Blue Haze
(all on Prestige LP 7054; reissued on Prestige 7822)

Davis's only concession to his new employers was in saving *Four* for them instead of recording it for Blue Note. A jazz classic, *Four* remained in Davis's repertoire for twelve years and received several other renditions from his own later quintets (*Four* played by five, as it were) as well as by other musicians, including one notable version by Sonny Rollins backed only by bass and drums (*Four* by three, reissued on Quintessence QJ-25241). One of the compositions most closely associated with Davis's name, *Four* has recently been claimed by Eddie (Cleanhead) Vinson, who says that he gave Davis permission to record both it and another of his themes, *Tune up* (first recorded by Davis in May 1953), and then stood silently for more than two decades as both tunes appeared and reappeared in new versions and reissues crediting Davis as the composer. Vinson, now known as a good blues saxophone player, was then more highly regarded as a blues singer and could not use *Four* and *Tune up* in his own recording sessions. Davis remains their credited composer, and both bear his imprint, fairly or not, in the jazz canon. On the original recording, the tune is taken at a slightly slower tempo than it was usually given later, and it has a mellow feel.

Little else of real consequence came out of the Prestige session, probably because Davis had used up so many of his resources so recently for Blue Note. His arrangement of *That Old Devil Moon* tinkers with its song form, imposing stop time on its three A sections and breaking into 4/4 swing only for the B section. The device encodes the melody attractively enough, but it is also sustained throughout the improvisations as well, and the playing seems to get bogged down in the artifice of the form. *Blue Haze* is a standard blues, introduced by Percy Heath's walking bass line for two choruses. Its title comes from the fact that it was recorded with the studio lights turned off as the players improvised in the reflected light from the control booth.

Only a little more than three weeks later, Davis was back again recording for Prestige, this time with Kenny Clarke replacing Blakey, and with an alto saxophonist named Dave Schildkraut added to make the group a quintet:

Miles Davis All Stars
Miles Davis, tpt; Dave Schildkraut, as (except on *You Don't Know What Love Is*); Horace Silver, pno; Percy Heath, b; Kenny Clarke, dms. New York, 3 April 1954
Solar; You Don't Know What Love Is; Love Me Or Leave Me; I'll Remember April
(first three titles on Prestige 7608; the fourth on Prestige 7054)

The aural evidence suggests that Schildkraut's presence was not particularly welcomed by Davis or the others. He is treated as an appendage to the proceedings, given little contact with the rest of the ensemble on any of the three titles on which he plays. His role in the arranged parts is restricted to playing a simple riff on *Love Me Or Leave Me* and *I'll Remember April*, and even that he plays very tentatively. As a veteran of several big bands including those of Buddy Rich, Stan Kenton, and Pete Rugolo, Schildkraut was certainly a more proficient player than he appears to be on this session, which might otherwise have given his career a boost. He was known at the time only as an imitator of Charlie Parker; in the original notes accompanying these records, Ira Gitler refers to him as "an ornithologist." The music shows that Schildkraut's rote recitation of set phrases, even if the phrases did originate with Parker, cannot add up to an effective solo. Dick Katz, the pianist and critic whose commentary on Davis's work of this period for the *Jazz Review* remains among the most perceptive critiques on any jazzman, notes that Schildkraut, whom he calls "a very gifted but erratic player," "sounds ill at ease, and there is a lack of rapport between the two horns." As a result, Katz concludes, "The session is notable mainly as a superb example of Kenny Clarke's brushwork." It is certainly that, but it is also a superb example of Davis's use of the muted trumpet. Curiously, Clarke stays with brushes and Davis with the mute throughout the entire session, even on the uptempo pieces, *Love Me Or Leave Me* and *I'll Remember April*. Neither of them suffers noticeably for the self-imposed restriction, although it must have made the tunes harder to manage for both of them. Even more striking than anything in the musicians' performances at this session, the most positive result was the exposition of the moody *Solar*, yet another stunning original composition by Davis, with a beautiful melody based on the chord structure of *How High the Moon*. Although Davis seems to have neglected *Solar* as soon as it was satisfactorily recorded, other musicians have rediscovered it over the years and given it the airing it deserves.

All of Davis's hours of recording activity in the spring of 1954 seem like little more than a warm-up for the session he produced in the Prestige studios later in April. He returned this time with a sextet, including the same rhythm team of Silver, Heath, and Clarke, by now a cohesive unit accustomed to the way Davis worked in the studio. To them he added his occasional front-line partner for many years, J.J. Johnson, and the tenor saxophonist Lucky Thompson, with whom he had recorded on Charlie Parker's first Dial session, in California in 1946. The ideas for this remarkable session were worked out in advance on Silver's upright piano in the hotel. (Silver adds that Davis did not own a trumpet and had to borrow one for the recording date; the borrowed trumpet belonged to Jules Colomby, and it leaked, but it certainly did not hinder him at all.) In some intangible way, the mix of musicians and music for this session worked perfectly, and the result, amounting to twenty-one and a half minutes on two titles, is a classic jazz performance. Dick Katz called it "artistic and of lasting value," and Whitney Balliett, reviewing the first appearance of this music on a twelve-inch disc in 1957, noted that it includes "some of the best jazz improvisations set down in the past decade."

There is, however, even more to this music than just the sum of its excellent solos, as numerous critics have pointed out. Martin Williams remarked that "in these excellent performances, so immediately effective even at a casual listening, there is going on a reassessment of the materials, the devices, and the aims of jazz." Ralph J. Gleason agreed, and added that the reassessment was overdue: "As part of the reaction in the years following World War II, jazz seemed lost in the ethereal clouds of intellectualism, its roots no longer in the blues, shaped instead by the specter of European orthodoxy. With one record, *Walkin'*, Miles Davis changed all that and brought back lyricism and melody (and the blues) to jazz. In the same motion he reaffirmed that one could play pretty and still play jazz. It seems unlikely that jazz will ever forget the lessons it has learned from Miles Davis." Frank Kofsky hears *Walkin'* as "the clarion call of the hard bop movement," referring to the revitalization and broadening of the style inaugurated by Parker, Gillespie, Powell, and the other leaders of the bebop revolution that came in the wake of these recordings. "As cool grew increasingly inbred and passionless, its inability to fashion a music of any emotional substance emerged with greater and greater clarity, especially when juxtaposed against the infinitely more demonstrative and muscular hard bop styles," Kofsky wrote. "The massive shift in taste that was heralded by Miles Davis's *Walkin'* in 1954 soon made it clear that all but a few cool stylists had fallen permanently from public favor." Kofsky probably overstates the destructive effect of the revaluation on cool jazz, but not the positive effect of this session on jazz in general. It had, as James Lincoln Collier put it, "a measurable effect on both musicians and the jazz public." The details are as follows:

Miles Davis All Star Sextet
Miles Davis, tpt; J.J. Johnson, tbn; Lucky Thompson, ts; Horace Silver, pno; Percy Heath, b; Kenny Clarke, dms. New York, 29 April 1954
Blue 'n' Boogie; Walkin'
(both on Prestige 7608)

Davis's revival of *Blue 'n' Boogie*, a piece written by Dizzy Gillespie in 1945 and perhaps not played by Davis since he worked with Charlie Parker in Los Angeles in 1946, suggests that his reappraisal of the recent past in these recordings was entirely deliberate, because the theme is itself a bebopper's abstraction of an old barroom swing style. To listeners aware of the recent history of jazz, Davis's new version reverberates with multiple reflections, his 1954 sextet adapting Gillespie's 1945 adaptation of, say, a 1936 Kansas City blowing session. Davis quite literally filters the blues through bebop into a new style, to be called hard bop or neo-bop in the years to come. Dick Katz described the session as a seminar: "*Walkin'* and its companion *Blue 'n' Boogie* are acknowledged to be classics. To me they represent a sort of summing up of much of what happened musically to the players involved during the preceding ten years (1944–54). It's as if all agreed to get together and discuss on their instruments what they had learned and unlearned, what elements of bop they had retained or discarded. An amazing seminar took place."

The use of Lucky Thompson also underlines Davis's purpose, because Thompson, although only two years older than Davis, had modeled his tone and his approach on pre-bop saxophonists. His opening chorus on *Walkin'* reminds the listener, probably deliberately, of Ben Webster, even to the breathy vibrato. Yet Thompson is completely comfortable playing bebop, and he spent most of his career doing just that. His presence here is another multiple reflection.

The reflections do not end there. Katz discerns another ghostly undertone in Davis's voice on *Blue 'n' Boogie*. "Miles's spelling out of triads and general diatonic approach is reminiscent of early and middle Armstrong," he says. "Further, his precise, split-second sense of timing and swing are not unlike those of the early master. Each is a master of economy – few, if any, of their notes are superfluous. Of course, there the comparison stops. The feelings and conception each projects couldn't be more different – for obvious reasons – age being one and Miles's much larger musical vocabulary being another."

Comments such as these risk emphasizing the historical significance and neglecting the music itself, but no commentator is likely to ignore it for long. Especially in *Walkin'*, it is memorable, swinging, free; it is, as Martin Williams says, "immediately effective even at a casual listening," and its effect does not depend on knowledge about the state of the art in jazz on the day it was recorded. Amid a wealth of superior performances, Davis's blues on *Walkin'* is singled out for special plaudits. "Davis's solo work exhibits all the earmarks of his style: it is hesitant, tentative, spare," James Lincoln Collier says; "Davis's style was now mature, the influences melded into a single, unified and unique conception. Both musicians and audiences responded to it immediately." Katz says: "Miles's solo is as good as any he has recorded, before or since. His sound ideas and execution, and the feelings he projects are prime examples of his art. Every idea that Miles states here is clearly formed and will stay with the listener afterwards." For Davis, *Walkin'* and *Blue 'n' Boogie* proclaimed emphatically that he had returned to the forefront of jazz.

In May, still months before *Walkin'* would be heard by the public, Davis's status received another boost with the release of the first significant collection of the nonet sides. Capitol finally put eight of the twelve recordings on a single ten-inch LP called *Birth of the Cool* (Capitol 459), a title that has been attached to all later releases and that immediately became the jazz fans' catchword for all the nonet's studio recordings. *Jeru*, *Godchild*, *Israel*, and *Venus de Milo*, until then available only as 78 rpm records, were included in the collection, along with *Rouge*, *Moon Dreams*, *Rocker*, and *Deception*, released for the first time. Three of the uncollected titles, *Budo*, *Move*, and *Boplicity*, had been released in separate anthologies by Capitol in 1952 and 1953 and were left out because they were still available. Their omission was unfortunate, since they are, with *Israel*, the very best of the nonet's recordings. They were not collected alongside the other eight titles for three more years, when *Birth of the Cool* (Capitol 762) was issued as a twelve-inch LP. The complete set of twelve titles, including Kenny Hagood's vocal on Gil Evans's arrangement of *Darn That Dream*, was collected on a single LP only in 1971, by Capitol's Dutch subsidiary (*The Complete Birth of the Cool*, Capitol M-11026). This piecemeal and disorganized release schedule was caused partly by the low artistic esteem in which jazz has generally been held, which makes the notion of an artist's oeuvre almost laughable to many American recording executives, and partly by the peripheral involvement of Capitol Records in jazz, which has meant that its managers, even more ignorant about jazz than most, did not understand the value of what they were burying in their vaults. But it was also caused partly by the confusing and rapid technological advances in the recording industry at the very moment when the nonet recordings were mastered. In little more than a decade, beginning in the late 1940s, the recording industry moved from wax masters of three-minute performances to acetate (tape) masters of longer performances pressed on microgroove vinyl, and from single (monaural) microphone placement to mike separation (high fidelity) and finally to multi-tracking (stereophonic). The variety of forms that the various titles of the nonet's recordings went through reflects some of the confusion in the industry, and especially at Capitol, during that decade. Still, the collection of eight titles in May 1954, even without the strengths of *Boplicity*, *Move*, and *Budo*, made available the evidence of Davis's considerable accomplishment in the recent past. *Birth of the Cool* helped to fix the attention of jazz listeners on him at a time when he was poised to reveal a great deal more to them.

Davis had put together the rhythm section that he felt could carry his revitalized music to new heights. Horace Silver and Percy Heath had been his constant accompanists since he returned to New York, and, after he tried Art Blakey on a couple of sessions, Kenny Clarke was established as his drummer. They comprised an excellent unit, and even though good bookings were still hard to come by for Davis, he began thinking about putting together his own band. Just as he had no doubt about whom he wanted in his rhythm section, so he knew whom he wanted to share the front line with him. Sonny Rollins, whose commanding stature was matched by a commanding tone, the perfect foil for Davis's delicate sound, had been his first choice for years and would continue so long after it became clear that he would never accept a permanent commitment to Davis's band. In mid-1954, Davis still hoped that Rollins would join his band, when he was in a position to put a band together. A preview of what that band might accomplish came when Davis led this quintet into the recording studio two months after the *Walkin'* session. The results were excellent:

Miles Davis Quintet
Miles Davis, tpt; Sonny Rollins, ts; Horace Silver, pno; Percy Heath, b; Kenny Clarke, dms. New York, 29 June 1954
Airegin; *Oleo*; *But Not for Me* (two takes); *Doxy*
(all on Prestige LP 7109; reissued [1970] on Prestige 7847)

This time, none of the compositions was Davis's own. The three originals, *Airegin* (Nigeria spelled backwards), *Oleo*, and *Doxy*, are all by Sonny Rollins. *Airegin*'s infectious bop melody is introduced by Rollins playing a vamp, reminiscent of some of Dizzy Gillespie's pieces. *Oleo*, also bop-oriented, is based on the chord changes of *I Got Rhythm*. (Its title comes from the name of the butter substitute, oleo margarine, which was then being marketed in the United States for the first time.) The arrangement modifies the piano's role by having Silver play only on the bridge all through the piece; in the statement of the melody, the unison line, played by muted trumpet and tenor saxophone, stops while Silver enters to play eight bars with the rhythm; throughout the piece Silver returns to accompany Davis and Rollins only during the bridge of their solos. In constraining the piano player in this way, Davis gives an early example of a device he would later use occasionally with Red Garland and Herbie Hancock. One advantage of having the piano player lay out on *Oleo* is that Percy Heath takes the responsibility for comping (that is, playing accompaniment) throughout, thus making a brilliant exposition of his abilities even on a session where he does not solo at all. The general advantage of having the piano player lay out is that the pianoless accompaniment loosens the ensembles and permits the soloist a broader range of choices than he has when the pianist feeds him harmonies.

Doxy is a sixteen-bar melody with a basic blues feeling, the kind of uncomplicated jazz melody then beginning to be described as funky. The term seemed especially apt for the style of Horace Silver, and Silver's playing on *Doxy* and similar pieces soon made him a favorite among both musicians and fans.

George Gershwin's *But Not for Me* – at first glance just a good pop song chosen to fill out the session – attracted Davis's attention because it was featured in the repertoire of a pianist named Ahmad Jamal, whose trio was beginning to be heard in supper clubs in Chicago and New York. While Jamal never seemed to win the approval of jazz reviewers, his particular genius was soon recognized by many musicians, and by none more forcibly than Davis. In short order, Jamal would become Davis's final formative influence in the line from Elwood Buchanan through Freddie Webster and Dizzy Gillespie to Gil Evans and the other members of his 55th Street salon. In 1954, Jamal's influence on Davis was still nascent, but Davis's selection of his signature ballad is meaningful. The first take, at a sprightly tempo close to the one at which Jamal plays it, seems somehow rushed when played by Davis's quintet, and the second take, at a slower tempo, succeeds much better, in spite of Rollins's squeaking reed. The issue of both takes led Dick Katz to comment, "I don't see the point in releasing both takes of *But Not For Me*. For celebrated performances the documentary value of such releases is real, but in this case, neither take is up to the standard of the rest of the date." Nevertheless, the two takes are different and add to the scant documentation on what might have been intended as Davis's first working quintet.

If Davis did hope to make a permanent band of these men, he was destined to be disappointed. Heath and Clarke were committed to the Modern Jazz Quartet. When Clarke gave up his commitment to the MJQ, it was because he was disillusioned with the situation of the jazz musician in America, and in 1956, a year after leaving the MJQ, he departed for France, where he has lived and worked ever since. Heath never left the MJQ, staying with it until it disbanded in 1974. Silver, the youngest man in the rhythm section, joined Art Blakey's new band, the Jazz Messengers, when it was formed in 1955; his growing reputation, based partly on his work with Davis in 1954, later made it possible for him to lead his own band.

The quintet that Davis led into the Prestige studios in June could have been a scintillating jazz band if they had become a working unit. Judging by their one recording session, they might eventually have become as good as the quintet that Davis finally formed as his working group a year later, in 1955.

Davis was still in no position to support a working band. Notwithstanding his recovery of technique after the years of faltering and the superb taste with which he was now playing, he still had some dues to pay for the neglect of his art. He was temperamentally incapable of helping his cause either by promoting his music in any conventional way or by making a public display of his renewed dedication to it. Long gone were the days when he would introduce titles or sidemen on stage as he had, for instance, at the Paris Jazz Festival in 1949, before his addiction. To some members of the audiences who turned out to hear him as he traveled around playing guest spots, he appeared hostile. To club owners and managers, he appeared disdainful.

Even when his musical reputation was fully restored, his aloofness and his candor brought sharp criticism, although by then it was inevitably mixed with grudging respect. In the mid-1950s, when he needed and deserved a few breaks, the criticism was not tempered with respect. Around this time, a booking agent told Nat Hentoff: "He's basically not a nice guy. His conversation, when he bothers to talk to you at all, is made up mainly of insults. That sonofabitch is bad for jazz. He doesn't give a damn for audiences, and he lets them know it by paying no attention to them. I mean you don't have to wave a handkerchief or show your teeth like Louis Armstrong to let the audience feel you care what they think about your music. But not him." In refusing to make any concessions, he was serving notice that his success would be on his own terms. The front that he showed to audiences and managers was often belied by the music he made for them, with its growing sensitivity and undeniable grace. The critic Dan Morgenstern has said: "Those who know him at all well have found him a generous, kind man whose true self is not revealed by his flamboyant, provocative behavior, but rather by the introspective, complex, often shifting style of his music." But very few people were allowed to see the man behind the music. Davis has been, as Babs Gonzales said, "leery about everybody. With exceptions – and they never know who they'll be."

Even Thelonious Monk proved to be no exception. During a remarkable recording session led by Davis late in the year the two men clashed with such bitterness that the session has become almost as famous as the brilliant music that it produced. The occasion was Christmas eve, and the place was, as usual, Rudy Van Gelder's recording studio in Hackensack, New Jersey. Davis had lined up an all-star band that was billed in all the releases as the Modern Jazz Giants. Percy Heath and Kenny Clarke were among them, along with a third member of the

MJQ, Milt Jackson, and Monk. The session started between 2 and 3 p.m., but by the time Ira Gitler, Prestige's consultant for the session, left for dinner, "not much had been accomplished." Gitler had persuaded the producer, Bob Weinstock, to allow Davis to include Monk's composition *Bemsha Swing* in the day's repertoire. Davis wanted to include it to placate Monk, who was disgruntled because Davis was insisting that Monk should not play behind Davis's solos on the other titles.

Monk brooded throughout the afternoon, which was spent on rehearsals, and when the recording began he became more uncooperative. He found the idea of laying out during Davis's solos humiliating, and as he grew more disruptive he prompted some unfriendly exchanges with the others, especially Davis. At the beginning of the first take of *The Man I Love*, during Milt Jackson's introductory bars, Monk suddenly interjects, "When'm I supposed to come in, man?" The music stops abruptly and the others groan ("Ohhh!"; "Oh no!" and other assorted noises are heard), and one of them says, "Man, the cat's cutting hisself." Monk, in a kind of a whine, says, "I don't know when to come in, man. Can't I start too? Everybody else – ." But Davis cuts him off and calls to Van Gelder in the control booth, "Hey, Rudy, put this on the record – *all* of it." It is on the record, and so is a brief, indecipherable exchange of unpleasantries between Monk and Davis during Monk's solo on the second take of *The Man I Love*. It was rumored that Davis ended up punching Monk, but he did not. When Gitler asked Monk about it later, Monk said, "Miles'd got killed if he hit me." In spite of the discord, or perhaps because of it, some magnificent music was made, by Monk no less than by the others.

The musicians knew that their work that day was superior and that the tension contributed to the result. When Gitler met Kenny Clarke at Minton's later that evening and asked how the session had gone after he left, Clarke said, simply, "Miles sure is a beautiful cat." The British critic Raymond Horricks, writing in the late 1950s, calls these "four of the most inspired jazz performances of the decade." The passage of time has hardly dulled them, especially *Bags' Groove* and *The Man I Love*, both of which survive in two complete takes and both of which remain outstanding examples of the improvisers' art.

That such results could be attained by five musicians who did not come out of a stable, working band seems paradoxical, but these circumstances were so regularly part of the professional jazzman's life that the musicians had to devise ways of coping with it. One way is what André Hodeir calls a "prepared jam session": "One can imagine a good many intermediate stages between the small improvising group whose members are closely united by long experience playing together, and the true jam session in which the participants hardly know one another. There is, for example, the 'prepared jam session,' so called because the musicians involved form a well-defined group and because the music displays structural qualities usually lacking in a true jam session. Here the musicians use introductions and codas that have become traditional with them. Most of the so-called blowing sessions ('just come and blow') recorded during the past few years belong to this category, which has produced some of the greatest masterpieces of jazz, like Miles Davis's famous *Bags' Groove*, with Thelonious Monk, Milt Jackson, Percy Heath and Kenny Clarke." The details of this famous session are as follows:

Miles Davis and the Modern Jazz Giants
Miles Davis, tpt; Milt Jackson, vib; Thelonious Monk, pno; Percy Heath, b; Kenny Clarke, dms. New York, 24 December 1954
Bags' Groove (two takes); *Bemsha Swing*; *Swing Spring*; *The Man I Love* (two takes)
(*Bags' Groove* [both takes] on Prestige 7109; all others on Prestige 7150; the complete session available on Prestige PR 7650 [1969])

Bags' Groove, Milt Jackson's celebratory blues (Jackson's nickname is Bags), went through two complete takes, with the first one usually considered slightly superior. Of Davis's solo on the first take, Dick Katz wrote: "Miles's solo is near perfect – a beautiful, unfolding set of memorable ideas, each a springboard for the next. His sound or tone has a real vocal-like quality,of expression. His interpretation of the blues here is deeply convincing, and it is without exaggerated 'funk'. He establishes a mood and sustains it." Whitney Balliett notes that it is on medium-tempo blues such as *Bags' Groove* that "Davis is capable of creating a pushing, middle-of-the-road lyricism that is a remarkable distillation, rather than a one-two-three outlining of the melodic possibilities; indeed, what comes out of his horn miraculously seems the result of the instantaneous editing of a far more diffuse melodic line being carried on in his head." As for Davis's making Monk sit silently throughout his solo, Katz says, "His purported rejection of Monk's services as an accompanist is irrelevant. The end result is superb. And when Jackson enters with Monk behind him, the contrast is strikingly effective." Whatever feelings Monk may have been harboring certainly did not affect his own solo adversely. "Monk's solo is one of his best on record," Katz maintains. "By an ingenious use of space and rhythm, and by carefully controlling a single melodic idea, he builds a tension that is not released until the end of his solo." Balliett agrees that "Monk is superb. In the first version his solo is broken by such long pauses that it appears he has left the studio; then he suddenly resumes, with clumps of clattering, off-beat dissonances. In the second version, his pressure up, he engages in a dizzy series of jagged runs." Of the second take, Katz says, "Davis's solo contains several 'pops' which sound like saliva in the horn, which mar an otherwise fine solo. Also, this version is not as concentrated as take 1, but Jackson's solo maintains the high level of the first – take your pick. Monk surprises with a completely different solo – different in approach and feeling. Here he is more concerned with playing the *piano*, less with developing a motif, and is much more extravagant with his ideas. A fine solo, but take 1 was exceptional." Most listeners would be hard pressed to choose between the two takes, and fortunately there is no need to choose, because Prestige has always included both in all releases. "In both versions, Davis's solos, which are played on open horn, have an oblique relentlessness and are full of neat, perfectly executed variations," Balliett says, adding, "This is an indispensable record."

On *Bemsha Swing*, the only title on which Monk was permitted to accompany Davis, a stunning exchange takes place at the transition from Davis's solo to Monk's. Davis closes his solo with some patently Monkesque phrases, which are then picked up by Monk and incorporated into his solo. The exchange is open to a number of interpretations, and the reviewers have offered a couple of possibilities. Dick Katz sees it this way: "Miles seems quite distracted by Monk, and it breaks the continuity of his solo. His discomfort is finally expressed by his quoting a couple of well-known Monk phrases. Monk in turn acknowledges Miles's sarcasm (or compliment?) and lo and behold, they end up playing a duet." Stanley Crouch hears it quite differently; according to him, "In order to tell Monk that he loved him even though he wouldn't allow him to play while he was soloing, Davis quotes some Monk licks in the trumpet section that precedes the piano solo. The rankled giant responds by taking the lick and building an incredible solo of virtuosic colors, turns, harmonies and rhythms that seem to say, 'Excuse me, young man, but if you intend to piddle around with my shit, see if you can ever get to *this!*' By no means was Monk to be undone or outdone. He was ready and had been ready for a long, long time." Whether the exchange signaled détente or war, Monk takes a glorious turn. Few of his many excellent recorded solos match this one in its eccentricity. Whitney Balliett, in an entirely unrelated context, remarked that Monk "approaches a keyboard as if it had teeth and he were a dentist." On *Bemsha Swing*, he makes the keyboard sparkle.

Swing Spring, a stately melody by Davis, was prepared for this session and then promptly forgotten by him, if not by his listeners. Four years later, Nat Hentoff played Davis a version of *Swing Spring* recorded in France by Kenny Clarke and a French band with an arrangement by André Hodeir, and Davis felt the shock of recognition. "That's my tune, isn't it?" he exclaimed. "I forgot all about that tune. God damn! Damn! You know, I forgot I wrote that." After hearing the French version, Davis added, "I think I'll make another record of this tune. It was meant to be just like an exercise almost." He then went to the piano and picked out a scale for Hentoff, explaining, "It was based on that scale there and when you blow, you play in that scale and you get an altogether different sound. I got that from Bud Powell; he used to play it all the time." Davis's description reveals

Swing Spring as one of his earliest compositions based on a scale – that is, a modal composition of the type that George Russell had been investigating – rather than on chord changes. The innovation toward modal organization, allowing more freedom of choice for the improvisers than a progression of chord changes, was an inevitable development in jazz history, because the best players had always strained against the strictures of the chordal form. "Virtually all the superior players are never *chained* by the chordal structure of their material," Dick Katz explains. "The chords are merely signposts. The sophistication in Monk, Rollins and Davis lies in the fact that after years of 'making the changes' they now often only imply them, leaving them free to concentrate on other aspects of improvisation, such as expression, rhythm, etc."

From a system where the chords are only implied, it is a short leap to a system where they are ignored altogether, although it took jazz several decades to make that short leap. The leadership in restructuring the formal basis of jazz naturally fell to performing musicians who had gained the sophistication in running changes of which Katz speaks. While George Russell explored the idea of modal composition in jazz academically, it would be Davis who eventually brought it forcefully into the studios and onto the stages. His most influential modal works were still a few years away when *Swing Spring* was recorded, but when Hentoff played Kenny Clarke's version of it for him in 1958, he was already busy writing and recording the modal works that would influence the next generations of jazz musicians. *Swing Spring* played no part in that movement; Davis seems to have forgotten it again soon after Hentoff's reminder, and he never did re-record it.

On *The Man I Love*, a beautiful Gershwin melody, the first take serves as a kind of model for what the second take is expected to be but is not. The first take opens with a ringing introduction by Jackson which provides an entrance for Davis to state the melody; Jackson then doubles the tempo for his own flowing solo, and Monk follows at the same tempo with a staccato solo, based on the stunning device of spreading the melody over twice the number of bars; Davis re-enters and after a chorus halves the tempo again and plays a haunting variation of the melody. By any standard, take 1 is a marvelous ballad performance, mixing moods and atmospheres and individuals but making a single, consistent entity. It seems nearly perfect, but it has been completely overshadowed – in everyone's account – by the second take, in which things go wrong. (I find myself struggling against great odds to maintain a semblance of objectivity about the second take, because it was the first music by Davis that I ever heard. The record belonged to a high school friend, and when we got it home from the record store and put it on the turntable, we were – I can think of no other word that is nearly adequate – transfixed. For weeks afterward we could hardly wait for the final bell at school – there were days when we didn't bother waiting for it – so we could get back to his place and listen to it half a dozen more times before supper. By now I know very well that is not Davis's 'best' record, much less his most significant, most interesting, or most revealing, but to me it remains, after literally hundreds of listenings, every bit as powerful as the first time I heard it.) The basic elements of the second take are the same as those of the first take, but the nuances of their execution add a powerful new element. Dick Katz describes the development: "After a lovely Jackson introduction, Miles unfolds an exceedingly lyrical introduction of the melody. His use of rhythm and his completely original manner of phrasing here should continue to enrich a listener for years. Jackson doubles the tempo with a four-bar break and takes a fine solo which does not quite sustain interest all the way, probably because of its length. Monk follows with the *pièce de résistance* by getting carried away with his own self-made obstacle course. He tries to rearrange the melody rhythmically by extending the sequence over a number of bars. However, he gets lost (or so it seems to me), and comes to an abrupt halt about the 28th bar or so (long meter). What follows is a model duet between Clarke and Heath which could serve as a lesson in graceful walking for anyone. Along about the 14th bar of the bridge, Miles leads Monk back on the track, and he comes roaring in in his best 1947 style. Miles comes in on his heels with a delightful bit and then surprises by quickly jamming a mute into his horn and continuing – an electrifying effect. A return to the original tempo at the bridge halts the discussion between Monk and Miles and the piece ends on a note of agreement."

What happens at the point where Monk suddenly stops playing is not clear. Katz assumes that he "gets lost," and Alun Morgan concurs: "The pianist tried a bold experiment which, seemingly, was doomed to failure. He attempted to spread the original melody over twice the number of bars, and actually succeeds in doing so until he reaches the middle eight ... In the process of collecting his thoughts, Monk allows two or three bars to slip by and Davis, doubtless under the impression that the pianist's departure from convention has caused him to lose his place in the chorus, enters abruptly with an angry-sounding paraphrase of the melody." But both Katz's and Morgan's accounts overlook the fact that Monk had successfully brought off exactly the same rhythmic device just minutes earlier, on the first take. Monk's losing his way on the second take after finding it on the first seems unlikely, and it seems much more probable that he was willing to stop his solo there out of sheer bloody-mindedness. Raymond Horricks apparently hears it that way too. In his description, "Monk unaccountably ended his solo after only half a chorus, leaving Percy Heath to take up the tune in his stead. Miles didn't feel it that way, and at the far end of the studio picked up his horn and blew it irritably for the pianist to come in again. Monk answered the call and the music righted itself." Whatever the cause, the interlude between Monk and Davis sublimates the tension between the two men into musical terms that cannot fail to be felt by any listener.

On Christmas eve in the Van Gelder studios, Miles Davis and the Modern Jazz Giants created music of unusual power, which was partly a sublimation of the tensions among the musicians, especially between Monk and Davis. "Aware that they were on trial before each other musically, both men approached their solos with anxious intent," Horricks says, "and, in effect, unconsciously, they encouraged each other towards greatness as they played. Miles himself blew with the soul, the sensitivity and something of the lyric vision of a poet." Dick Katz puts it much more simply. "This performance would be absolutely impossible to repeat," he says. "God bless Thomas Edison."

A few years after the clash, Nat Hentoff asked Davis about his feelings toward Monk. "Monk has really helped me," Davis said. "When I came to New York, he taught me chords and his tunes. A main influence he has been through the years has to do with giving musicians more freedom. They feel that if Monk can do what he does, they can. Monk has been using space for a long time." About his decision to make Monk lay out when he was soloing, Davis remained unrepentant. "I love the way Monk plays and writes, but I can't stand him behind me. He doesn't give you any support," Davis claims, adding, "Monk writes such pretty melodies and then screws them up." At the time of that interview, in 1958, Davis was at the peak of the line of development that began in the period covered here, and Monk was at the peak of his own commercial success, finally receiving the critical and popular acclaim that he had long deserved, and appearing regularly in New York at the Five Spot. "You have to go down to hear him to really appreciate what he's doing," said Davis, who was a frequent member of the audience at the Five Spot. Davis's great sextet also regularly featured Monk's compositions *Round about Midnight* and *Straight No Chaser*, and Davis told Hentoff that he was interested in adding more Monk compositions to his repertoire. "I'd like to make an album of his tunes if I can ever get him up here," he said. But the two men, the most formidable jazz artists of the 1950s, never recorded together again after the second take of *The Man I Love*.

As the decade reached its mid-point, jazz activity remained diffuse. There was a potential audience for jazz that was growing by leaps and bounds, made up of young, middle-class whites all over North America and Europe. They had been attracted to jazz initially by the West Coast movement, which was nothing if not accessible music. They had sought it out in the first place as an alternative to pop music, which was dominated by talentless chattels like Tommy Sands and Fabian singing three-chord banalities over a chorus of doo-wahs. At the same time, West Coast jazz was wearing a little thin, apart from Dave Brubeck's Quartet with Paul Desmond and Gerry Mulligan's Quartet with valve trombonist Bobby Brookmeyer, neither of which had ever been part of the core of Hollywood studio musicians who played jazz on weekends.

The spirit of the bebop revolution, which had carried along most of the rising young musicians for more than a decade, was finally spent. Its symbol was Charlie Parker, and his capacity for intoxicants and other forms of self-abuse seemed at last to be reached. No longer the messiah capable of preaching his creative message while nodding out, he often appeared as a stumblebum, hardly capable of forming a sentence. Frank Sanderford, Parker's frequent companion for years whenever he played in Chicago, witnessed the decline. "The last time I saw him was at the Beehive in Chicago," Sanderford remembers. "The owner had asked me to get Charlie to go on. He was in a little room where they stored beer. I went back there; Charlie met me at the door and threw his arms around me as if I were the only person in the world. He couldn't go on the stand, he said; he was in no condition. He looked bad. The house was jammed. I asked him to take a look and see how many people had come just to hear him play, and I opened the door a little. He glared out. 'They just want to see the world's most famous junkie,' he growled. I will always be guilty, because I did get him to go on the stand. He made a few, awful bleating sounds. He couldn't play. He was disgusted, afraid, and frustrated somehow. He was a beaten man."

Charlie Parker died in New York on 12 March 1955, at the age of thirty-five. His death was not wholly unexpected, but it was sudden. He was supposed to be on his way to Boston for a weekend date as a guest soloist but he stopped off instead at the Manhattan apartment of the Baroness Pannonica de Koenigswarter, the jazz patroness, complaining of stomach pains. The baroness summoned her doctor, and when they could not persuade Parker to enter a hospital, they ministered to him in her living room. The news of his death three days later sent shock waves throughout the jazz world, and beyond it. In New York, Babs Gonzales and four of his friends took the subway lines in different directions and left a trail of graffiti proclaiming "Bird lives!" In Paris, David Amram, the composer, conductor, and musicologist who was then best known as a jazz french hornist, was playing a concert with Raymond Fol, Bobby Jaspar, Lars Gullin, and other European jazzmen when he heard the news. "I went backstage," Amram recalls, "and as the other band was finishing their number, someone came running up and said to Raymond, 'Man, did you hear the news?' 'What's that?' Raymond said. 'Charlie Parker is dead.' We all suddenly seemed to shrink. Everyone backstage quieted down. All the heroin and other drugs were quietly put away. People just stood there in silence while the band onstage, oblivious of this terrible news, kept on wailing." When a reporter got in touch with Miles Davis, all he could think to say was, "New York will never be the same without Charlie Parker."

Inexplicably, many people thought about Davis after they had absorbed the news of Parker's death. Perhaps the reason for it was simply that they were dusting off their old Parker records and inevitably replaying the old Dials and Savoys with Davis on them and remembering the excellence of that band. Parker had done the same just before his death, according to Robert Reisner: "Not long before his death, he was standing on a corner, reminiscing and optimistically planning, 'I'll get my old group together, Max and Miles, Duke and Tommy.' And then he, who created so much of the music, said with a laugh, 'If I don't know the tunes, I can learn them.'" It seemed somehow like a natural progression for the leadership to pass from Charlie Parker to Miles Davis.

"I'm sure that Miles considered himself a leader in the new movement, within our movement, because he wasn't that far away from us to be considered 'away,'" Dizzy Gillespie says. "There was a change in the administration of the music, I guess you would call it, a change in the phrasing. The phrasing went a little differently. Phrasing changes every so often, and you can tell what age the music comes from by the way it's played. But Miles only knew what to play from what had gone on before, then he began to find his own identity." It was not only that he knew what went on immediately before. Approaching the full development of his powers, Davis was making a highly personal amalgam of jazz styles both before and after bebop. Whitney Balliett says, "His playing sounds predominantly sweet and restrained, yet it conceals, much of the time, the basic hotness of men like Louis Armstrong and Roy Eldridge."

The essential jazz 'feel' of his predecessors, which Davis retained, was the very element that seemed to be threatened in the cool popularizations going on around him, but there was also something entirely new in his playing, and much harder to define. Gil Evans put it this way: "Miles changed the tone of the trumpet for the first time after Louis – the basic tone. Everybody up to him had come through Louis Armstrong, though they might not have sounded exactly like him, as with Roy Eldridge. But then all of a sudden Miles created his own wave form. It became another sound. Miles didn't even realize this, he just knew he had to have a certain sound. I mean you can describe it any way you like, but it's a different sound and the whole world took it over." Listeners who were willing to pay attention could hear the sound in Davis's music for a year before Parker's death; after his death, many more listeners seemed willing to pay attention. The first palpable result was that Davis tied Gillespie in *Down Beat's* international jazz critics poll as top trumpeter for 1955; an editorial comment maintained that Davis had surfaced in the poll "practically ... from out of nowhere."

In June, Davis again recorded for Prestige, his first recordings since Christmas eve. This time he fronted a quartet, and some significant new faces replaced the rhythm team he had used throughout 1954. Equally significant, though invisible, was the presence in spirit of Ahmad Jamal. The details are as follows:

Miles Davis Quartet
Miles Davis, tpt; Red Garland, pno; Oscar Pettiford, b; Philly Joe Jones, dms. New York, 7 June 1955
I Didn't; Will You Still Be Mine; Green Haze; I See Your Face before Me; A Night in Tunisia; A Gal in Calico
(all on Prestige LP 7007; reissued on Prestige 7221)

A Night in Tunisia might have been intended as homage to the memory of Parker, with whom Davis had recorded this Gillespie composition in 1946, but, if so, it is certainly an oblique gesture, because Davis plays the bop anthem as a wry abstraction, almost a parody of bebop. Another oblique reference occurs on *I Didn't*, a Davis original based on Thelonious Monk's *Well You Needn't*, to which its title forms a reply.

Green Haze contains a reminder in its title of *Blue Haze*, which Davis recorded with another quartet a year earlier, and like it, *Green Haze* is an extended, extemporaneous blues. Whereas the earlier *Haze* with Horace Silver and company was a basic, funky blues, simple and countrified, the new one is sophisticated and urbane. The essential difference seems to emanate from the presence on this one of William (Red) Garland, on piano. Garland, a Texan, had been around New York and Philadelphia for a few years working as a piano player in pick-up bands, often with Philly Joe Jones. He has a light keyboard touch that does not lend itself to percussive playing, even at quick tempos, which led Whitney Balliett to label him "a bright, dandyish pianist," and it was no doubt that touch that first attracted Davis's attention. The two men met through Philly Joe Jones, who recorded with Davis on the unhappy 1953 session that included Charlie Parker as a tenor player. Garland may also have impressed Davis for entirely extramusical reasons, because he once, according to a rumor that has since grown into a legend, made his living as a boxer. Davis discovered also that Garland was not only a very capable piano player but that he was malleable, in contrast to Horace Silver and Monk. Davis now had a very specific notion of how his piano player should sound – like Ahmad Jamal. "Red Garland knew I liked Ahmad and at times I used to ask him to play like that," Davis has said. "Red was at his best when he did."

Jamal's enormous influence on Davis gets its first significant airing at this session, and it will persist until it becomes an inseparable element of Davis's style. Here, it is most obvious in the choice of tunes. Both *A Gal in Calico* and *Will You Still Be Mine* were part of Jamal's repertoire, and the bright, almost bouncy tempo at which Davis plays them is borrowed directly from Jamal's treatment of them. He had included *But Not for Me* in a recording session a year earlier, and this Gershwin melody would become known as Jamal's song with the commercial success of his 1958 recording of it. Soon to come were several other Davis recordings of titles borrowed from Jamal's repertoire, including *Surrey with a Fringe on Top*, *Just Squeeze Me*, *My Funny Valentine*, *I Don't Wanna Be Kissed*, *Billy Boy*, and the Jamal originals *Ahmad's Blues* and *New Rhumba*. No other individual had exercised so decisive an effect on what Davis played since his early explorations of the Gillespie-Parker bebop repertoire.

Jamal's influence went much deeper than just the selection of titles. Melodic understatement, harmonic inventiveness, and rhythmic lightness were part and parcel of Jamal's style and became central to Davis's style and the style of his finest bands. Davis's debt to Jamal can never be calculated precisely, of course, because Davis possessed all of these traits to some degree long before he heard of Jamal's trio. In Jamal, he recognized a kindred spirit, and he freely used whatever he could from him. Most of the borrowings, apart from the repertoire and large swatches of Red Garland's phraseology, are quite subtle. Martin Williams associates the Davis bands' playing "in two," that is, "accenting the second and fourth beats, once the weak beats, in a kind of upside-down Dixieland," with Jamal's influence, although it is usually credited to Philly Joe Jones, who would be Davis's drummer more often than not for the next three years.

Jamal's impact on Davis's musical thinking was pervasive, and Davis made no effort to conceal his debt. "Ahmad is one of my favorites," Davis said; "I live until he makes another record. I gave Gil Evans a couple of his albums, and he didn't give them back." To Nat Hentoff, who had the temerity to tell Davis that he considered Jamal "mainly a cocktail pianist," Davis simply said, "That's the way to play the piano." He then began playing Jamal's records for Hentoff and pointing out Jamal's strengths: "Listen to how he slips into the other key. You can hardly tell it's happening. He doesn't throw his technique around like Oscar Peterson. Things flow into and out of each other." Julian Adderley later became an advocate of Jamal under Davis's influence and he made the same point: "He has a potful of technique, but he has learned restraint." Davis says, "Listen to the way Jamal uses space. He lets it go so that you can feel the rhythm section and the rhythm section can feel you. It's not crowded." For Davis, Jamal's appeal was unqualified. "All my inspiration today," he said in the late 1950s, "comes from the Chicago pianist Ahmad Jamal."

Jamal was born and raised not in Chicago but in Pittsburgh, in 1930. He began playing the piano at the age of three, and he studied classical piano soon after that and through his teenage years. It was not until he was a student at Westinghouse High School that he decided to concentrate on becoming a jazz player, but by the age of fourteen he was already a member of the musicians' union and a featured local player. While still in his early teens, he is said to have been heard by Art Tatum, who called him a "coming great." His first successes came in Chicago. After touring the Midwest as a member of George Hudson's big band and as the accompanist for a song-and-dance act called the Caldwells, he formed his own trio in 1951 and began working in Chicago nightclubs. Around the same time he converted to Islam and assumed his new name, dropping his christened name, Fritz Jones.

Jamal's trio, comprised of piano, guitar, and bass for the first four years, drew favorable notices playing at a club called the Blue Note and moved into the Lounge of the Pershing Hotel in 1952, where Jamal played regularly for years, with occasional engagements at the Embers in New York and other piano bars and supper clubs throughout the country. The trio also made their first recordings in 1952 (later collected on Epic LN 3631, but now long out of print); among the first titles Jamal recorded were *A Gal in Calico* and *Will You Still Be Mine*. Many of Jamal's musical hallmarks can be picked out on these first recordings, but any listener familiar with his recordings from a few years later will certainly miss the cohesion of the later Jamal Trio, which became an almost uncanny meeting of minds when Jamal altered the instrumentation and began working with Israel Crosby on bass and Vernell Fournier on drums. John Hammond, who touted Jamal's work from the beginning, said, "Ahmad's trio is not just Ahmad, not all piano like Errol Garner. It's a *trio*."

The trio were never better than in 1956–9, the years with Crosby and Fournier. Israel Crosby started with Jamal in his original trio in 1951 but left in 1953 to tour with Benny Goodman and then returned to the trio in 1956. A native Chicagoan, he had a rich history as a jazz bassist before Jamal came along, beginning with the boogie-woogie piano player Albert Ammons in 1935 when Crosby was only sixteen and recording what might be the first jazz showcase ever for the string bass, a composition called *Blues For Israel*, with Gene Krupa's Chicagoans that same year. Vernell Fournier, originally from New Orleans, gained a local reputation in Chicago as the drummer in the house band at the Beehive, where he worked for almost three years before joining Jamal's trio. Despite his exposure in the trio, Fournier never received full credit and remains relatively unknown, but he is a percussionist of extraordinary delicacy. Jack DeJohnette, a much younger Chicago drummer, says, "One day I heard Ahmad Jamal at the Pershing, and I heard Vernell Fournier on drums. His brush work was so incredible – I mean just impeccable."

DeJohnette adds, "Ahmad's always been his own man – way ahead of his time in terms of using space and chord voicings, which is one of the reasons Miles liked him so much. Ahmad knew how to get the most out of his instrument, so that a piano trio sounded like a symphony orchestra. He's a great organizer, and his concept is so sophisticated and intelligent, yet so loose and funky." Jamal's best qualities were all caught in a live recording his trio made at the Pershing Lounge on 16 January 1958, which became one of the best-selling jazz LPs of all time (Argo LP 628; reissued as part of Chess 2ACMJ-407). *Ahmad Jamal at the Pershing* remained on the national top ten list of best-selling albums for 108 weeks.

The popularity of Jamal's record did nothing to mollify his critics, who maintain that he is not a jazz player at all, but it has obviously delighted thousands of listeners, and it certainly had some influence at the height of its popularity. Anthony Braxton, a Chicago teenager at the time, says, "I was into rock and roll – the Flamingos, Frankie Lyman and the Teenagers, that record still arouses memories – that was the music happening in the '50s, and I was a real rock and roll fan. And later I heard an Ahmad Jamal record, *At the Pershing*, and it kind of changed my whole scene." One wonders how many thousands of other listeners first came around to jazz through Jamal.

Notwithstanding the accolades Jamal has received from musicians and fans, most jazz critics have been less than kind to him. Martin Williams led off his review of *Ahmad Jamal at the Pershing* in *Down Beat* by saying, "Apparently this is being marketed as a jazz record"; he concluded that it was not jazz at all but "innocuous ... cocktail piano." Several critics compared Jamal unfavorably to Errol Garner, Jamal's older contemporary from Pittsburgh who also attended Westinghouse High School. Dom Cerulli, also writing in *Down Beat*, said, "Jamal is working an area which Errol Garner works, but without Garner's wit and drive," and Ralph J. Gleason called him "a sort of refined, effete Errol Garner." To his persistent critics, Jamal replies, "Sometimes people don't identify with purity – that's what my music was then and that's what it is now. I've endured some of the harsh statements, but for every harsh statement there have been 99 complimentary ones. What I've done and am still doing is a product of years of blood, sweat and tears, and as long as I am completely secure in the knowledge that what I am doing is valid, then eventually even the most stupid critic has to acknowledge the validity of my work."

Part of the problem critics have with his music, according to Jamal, is that it is understated. "Anybody can play loudly," he says. "It is more difficult to play softly while swinging at that same level of intensity you can get playing fortissimo. To swing hard while playing quietly is one of the signs of the true artist." Almost completely overlooked by the most negative critics is Jamal's flawless technique. It is a virtue that other musicians, especially piano players, talk about with reverence. Cedar Walton says, "I never heard Ahmad even come close to playing anything without a great deal of technique, taste and timing. When he goes across the piano, he just doesn't ever miss a note – there's never any question. For me, that's still a great thrill, just to hear somebody do that."

One of the most bewildering facts of all for Jamal's critics is his influence on Davis. "Miles Davis was clearly influenced by the trio of pianist Ahmad Jamal," Martin Williams concedes. "One can readily understand why, since Jamal is a sophisticated harmonicist and, like Davis, uses space and openness in his music. Despite the impeccable swing of Jamal's group, however, his music seems chic and shallow – all of which is another way of saying that good art, and particularly good popular art, can be strongly influenced by bad." On another occasion, Williams contrasted Davis's musical integrity with what he saw as Jamal's show-biz pyrotechnics. The result is one of the most caustic condemnations that Jamal ever received. "Jamal has the same interest in openness of melody, space and fleeting silence that Davis does," Williams began. "But for the trumpeter these qualities can be aspects of haunting lyric economy. For Jamal they seem a kind of crowd-titillating stunt-work ... Jamal's real instrument is not the piano at all, but his audience. On some numbers, he will sit things out for a chorus, with only some carefully worked out rhapsodic harmonies by his left hand or coy tinklings by his right. After that, a few bombastic block chords by both hands, delivered *forte*, will absolutely lay them in the aisles. And unless you have heard Ahmad Jamal blatantly telegraph the climax of a piece, or beg applause en route with an obvious arpeggio run which he drops insinuatingly on the crowd after he has been coasting along on the graceful momentum of Crosby and Fournier, then you have missed a nearly definitive musical bombast." Faced with this kind of critical reception, Jamal maintained the outward calm of an ascetic, and his music remained as unruffled and good-natured as ever. His consolation came unfailingly from the audiences during his peak years. If that were not enough, he might have recalled Davis's greatest wish: "I'd love to have a little boy someday," he told Nat Hentoff, "with red hair, green eyes and a black face – who plays piano like Ahmad Jamal."

Whatever the critical consensus on Jamal's music, his influence is undeniable. For Miles Davis, who had learned his art at the side of the demonic genius who did more than anyone else to forge the bebop revolution's charter, Charlie Parker, the influence of Jamal expanded that art in an unexpectedly civil direction. Where popular songs had formerly existed in Davis's lexicon primarily for their chord sequences, they now began to function as winsome melodies to be given depth and meaning by an improviser's variations. Where tempos had once raced along recklessly as if to discourage outsiders and second-raters, they now began to be manipulated and disassembled, even admitting sprightly, finger-popping figures that had to be incorporated into the fabric of the new melodies. This direction posed considerable risks, for it gave the music a facile veneer and seemed to invite the improviser to embellish the veneer rather than to probe it. If Jamal sometimes did just that, as so many of his critics claimed, Davis never did. He had learned far too much from Parker and Freddie Webster and Gillespie and Monk in the decade since he arrived in New York to settle now for superficiality. Those early lessons could never be unlearned. Instead, they were integrated into a new conception, and by 1955 Davis's music was as unlike Jamal's as it was unlike Parker's, but it included elements of both. And for the time being, it was largely undiscovered.

The public image of Miles Davis was refracted, like an object catching the sun in a clouded pool. He was regarded as inconsistent and undependable, but the addiction that had made him that way was now cured. His records showed him struggling technically and playing indifferently, but he had recently recorded music that was both technically proficient and passionately stated. He was considered by even the well-informed fans as a figure from jazz's recent past, but he was actively working at a new aesthetic and surrounding himself with important new sidemen. The gap between the public image and the reality narrowed almost overnight.

The setting, improbable though it must have seemed, was Newport, Rhode Island, a small New England city that John Hammond, himself a Vanderbilt, calls "one of the snob communities of this fair land." The occasion was the first annual Newport Jazz Festival, which was inaugurated there in the first week of July 1955. (There had been a two-day trial run the previous summer that never gets counted in the official history of the event.) The impetus for bringing jazz musicians to fashionable Newport for a week-long series of matinée and evening concerts came from Elaine and Louis Lorillard, patrons of the arts who had been involved for years with a summer program of concerts by the New York Philharmonic in Newport. They were interested in extending the community's involvement by adding a series of jazz concerts. As their producer for the jazz festival they chose George Wein, a piano player from Boston who showed unmistakeable entrepreneurial instincts in mounting concerts in Boston, managing and eventually buying jazz clubs there, and producing records for his own small label, called Storyville, which was also the name of his best-known club. Wein organized the Newport Jazz Festival in the first years simply by presenting the best known big and small jazz bands as headliners and filling in the gaps with either lesser-known bands or with all-star groups playing jam sessions.

In 1955, the headliners included the big bands of Count Basie and Woody Herman and the small bands of Dave Brubeck and Louis Armstrong. The all-star group lined up to play at the closing concert, between Basie and Brubeck, were made up of Zoot Sims, Gerry Mulligan, Thelonious Monk, Percy Heath, and Connie Kay. Shortly before the festival began, too late to list him in the program for the closing concert, Miles Davis was added. Perhaps someone noticed that the group for that evening lacked a brass instrument; perhaps Davis, who needed both the work and the exposure, appealed to Wein or one of his acquaintances on the festival board to include him; or perhaps someone who knew about the clash between Monk and Davis the previous Christmas eve thought that their presence together might create a newsworthy situation. Davis arrived to take his turn with the all stars and when he was finished he was suddenly one of the most talked-about and sought-out jazz musicians in the country.

The protocol for the jam session that evening followed the familiar format. The rhythm section started off, and then the horns were added to the rhythm players one by one, until all of them were on the stage. Monk opened with Heath and Kay supporting him on *Hackensack*, and then Mulligan joined them, and then Sims, and finally Davis. "Within the ranks of the professional critics, there was not too much notice taken when he joined the group on stage," Bill Coss, the editor of *Metronome* magazine, remembers. "Professional listeners are blasé, especially when an artist is as unpredictable as Miles; unpredictable, that is, in terms of the relationship between what he can do and what he will do." The group continued with *Now's the Time*, dedicated to Parker's memory, but it was Davis's muted solo on *Round about Midnight* that brought the audience to its feet. "On this night at Newport," Coss continues, "Miles was superb, brilliantly absorbing, as if he were both the moth and the probing, savage light on which an immolation was to take place. Perhaps that's making it too dramatic, but it's my purely subjective *feeling* about the few minutes during which he played. And over-dramatic or not, whatever Miles did was provoking enough to send one major record label executive scurrying about in search of him after the performance was over. And dramatic enough to include Miles in all the columns written about the Festival, as one of the few soloists who lived up to critical expectations." Those expectations had been deflated by the discrepancy between his recent work and the level at which he was working when the critics last took notice. As André Hodeir put it: "Miles Davis's 'comeback' at the 1955 Newport Jazz Festival was hailed as a major event precisely because the halo of glory attached to his name a few years earlier had managed to survive a period of temporary neglect." Davis felt the same about it, but he put it more succinctly. "What's all the fuss?" he asked. "I always play that way."

Davis's career began to blossom again after Newport. Not all of his sudden activity resulted from his Newport coup. He was already scheduled to record with Charles Mingus soon after Newport. He was also busy organizing his own quintet for a debut engagement at the Café Bohemia in Greenwich Village; the Bohemia date was being treated as a trial run, and if the audiences turned out in large enough numbers Davis was ready to book the quintet into jazz clubs in other cities in the fall. All the Newport publicity did was sharpen the public's respect for Davis's current music, practically guaranteeing the turnout of press and fans for at least his opening night at the Bohemia. After that, it would be up to him to keep them coming back.

But there was more, and it came as a direct result of the Newport appearance. George Avakian, the jazz producer at Columbia Records, was the executive whom Bill Coss and the others had seen scurrying around as soon as Davis left the stage at Newport. He contacted Davis and began talking to him about signing an exclusive contract with Columbia. At the moment, Columbia's jazz department was a bit thin: Davis had recorded for the label a few years earlier in the backing band for Sarah Vaughan, but Vaughan had moved on; Duke Ellington had recently left Columbia for Bethlehem Records, a jazz specialty label, but he seemed to be struggling anyway, as did their other stalwart in the jazz department, Louis Armstrong, especially when compared to younger men such as Dave Brubeck, whom they had recently signed. Columbia was definitely interested in updating its jazz representation. In the next few months, Ellington would return, and Art Blakey's Jazz Messengers and Errol Garner would be added to its list. Columbia offered a good opportunity for a jazz musician, because it had lots of working capital brought in by strong popular and classical divisions, and a broad and growing international distribution. Avakian wanted Davis, and Davis let him know that he wanted to join Columbia. Only later did Avakian discover that Davis was still carrying a long-term contractual obligation to Prestige, but by then Avakian had convinced himself that he needed Davis at Columbia and, instead of being deterred, he set out to negotiate a settlement with Prestige for the rest of the contract. Bob Weinstock at Prestige knew as much about Davis's potential as Avakian did, and he made it clear that any settlement would have to be attractive. The negotiations began, but they were not likely to be settled very quickly.

Davis was scheduled to record within a week of his Newport appearance, but he was recording neither for Columbia nor for Prestige. Instead, he was going into the studios for Debut Records, a label owned by Charles Mingus. Mingus had started up Debut in 1952, partly as an outlet for his own music, which was considered too adventuresome to attract an established company. But there was more to Debut than that. Mingus always aspired to manage his own affairs, and he was never reluctant to manage other people's affairs either, given half a chance. His willingness to manage either himself or others, however, was never matched by a commensurate capability for it. The manager's role sat uneasily on Mingus's broad shoulders, which surprised no one who was familiar with his emotional, not to say brawling, response to the world around him. Nevertheless, he had produced his first records as a young man in Los Angeles, including the long-lost sides with Davis in 1946 in the band he called Baron Mingus and His Symphonic Airs, and he would keep on trying right into the 1960s with a label called Charles Mingus Records.

Debut was in many ways the most successful of all of Mingus's record ventures, its status firmly established with the release of a classic recording made at Toronto's Massey Hall in 1953, when Dizzy Gillespie, Charlie Parker, Bud Powell, and Max Roach were reunited for one night only and played magnificently. Mingus was their bassist that night only because Oscar Pettiford, who had played the bass with them on 52nd Street and was originally lined up to play in the reunion band by the Toronto promoters, broke his arm and had to drop out. Mingus planted a tape recorder on the stage and thus preserved an irreplaceable moment in jazz history. It proved to be his greatest accomplishment as a record producer, and it also illustrates his managerial shortcomings as well, for Mingus, who was willing and able to lecture the world endlessly on its abuse of artists such as him, never got around to paying royalties or any fee at all to the other men on the record. It is hard to believe that his failure to pay them was motivated by anything more malicious than sheer mismanagement. Nevertheless, he never really gave up on his managerial ambitions, no matter how successful he became as a performing jazzman, and in that role he was soon to realize many of his ambitions.

By the mid-1950s Mingus was acclaimed as one of the finest bass players around, and by the late 1950s he was equally acclaimed as a significant composer and a superb bandleader. Not that success made life much easier for him; with Mingus, nothing seemed easy. As both musician and manager, his successes no less than his failures proceeded from a personal intensity so fierce that it sometimes erupted into mania. Nat Hentoff described Mingus hovering over his sidemen on the bandstand "like a brooding Zeus making up the scorecard for eternity." Among the more notorious incidents in a career filled with them were Mingus's knife fight with trombonist Juan Tizol while they were playing in Duke Ellington's orchestra, and a few years later, in his own band, Mingus's clobbering Jimmy Knepper onstage because he purportedly misplayed his part.

Charles McPherson, the alto saxophonist who played in Mingus's bands off and on for twelve years beginning in 1960, described what it was like. "Working for Mingus was a challenging situation because he was a very complex personality type – one way one day, another way another day, very intense, very honest – painfully honest," McPherson said. "Sometimes it was frightening: my first night on the gig, because he didn't get all his money from the club owner, he proceeded to take apart a Steinway grand piano with his hands – the insides, the guts, he commenced to plucking steel strings out." For Mingus, it was a recurring pattern. Sensitivity vented itself in brutality, and it was all, to Mingus's mind, in defense of his rights. "Sometimes I think if all black people were like me there wouldn't have been any slaves," he said in his autobiography; "they'd of had to kill us all!"

Few jazzmen have been as willing to take on all comers over such a profusion of principles. One other who has, of course, is Miles Davis. They very idea of Mingus trying to produce a record by Davis summons up a situation for jazz historians to conjure with. In the end, however, Mingus and Davis ignored one another almost completely during the recording session, and the session, like the recording it gave birth to, was about as uneventful as it could possibly be.

Bill Coss, who attended the recording session in order to gather material for the album's liner notes, met Davis at his hotel that Saturday morning at the appointed hour when they were supposed to be picked up by a taxi and taken to the studio. Davis "waited one hour in front of his hotel, leaning detachedly against a fire plug, apparently never doubting that he would be driven to the recording studio, which was only two blocks away, as he had been promised," Coss remembers. Finally the taxi arrived, and Davis settled back for the five-minute ride through traffic. "Then, on the way to the studio, his one major comment: 'I hope I don't have to hit Mingus in the mouth.'" Coss adds: "This, of course, despite the fact that Mingus could carry two of Miles around the block in a half-gallop." When they arrived at the studio they found vibist Teddy Charles still working on the arrangements they were going to record. "Miles moved into a corner and waited," Coss says, while Mingus, who had been haranguing drummer Elvin Jones when they arrived, "alternately fussed and fumed like a great rooster in attendance to a hatching." Somehow, Mingus and Davis kept out of one another's way until the arrangements were finally ready and the recording could begin. The details are as follows:

Miles Davis All Stars with Charles Mingus
Miles Davis, tpt; Britt Woodman, tbn; Teddy Charles, vib; Charles Mingus, b; Elvin Jones, dms. New York, 9 July 1955
Nature Boy; Alone Together; There's No You; Easy Living
(all on Debut DEB 120; reissued [1972] in Europe on America 30 AM 6051, in the United States on Fantasy M6001)
Alone Together is arranged by Charles Mingus; the other three titles, by Teddy Charles.

If most listeners had not been keeping track of the recent developments in Davis's style, Mingus was one who obviously had. The session was clearly calculated to exploit Davis's wistful, romantic ballad playing – too calculated. The tempos are uniformly ponderous, and only *There's No You*, which is a little more spirited than the others, sustains any rhythmic interest at all. To make up for the lack of pace, the rhythm is carried along most of the time by arranged ostinato figures played by Mingus on bass and Britt Woodman on trombone. Elvin Jones, who would soon be earning plaudits for his aggressive polyrhythmic drumming, goes almost unnoticed throughout.

The arrangements seem cluttered and often stilted. In Teddy Charles, Mingus had lined up an arranger with an academic background whose wont was to interpolate European musical devices in jazz contexts, exactly the thrust that Mingus himself, who was always involved in some form or other of musical experiment, favored at the time. Mingus's arrangement of *Alone Together* is hardly less formalistic than any of Charles's. Mingus was starting to counter his infatuation with European forms with devices from American music, especially from Ellington and gospel music, but had not yet discovered how to incorporate them into his arranging, although they were always abundantly evident in his playing. Over these contrived backgrounds, Davis picks his way cautiously, sticking close to the melody most of the time in an aloof, emotionless manner.

When this recording was reissued in Europe in 1972, reviewer Ron Brown called it "an unbelievably lacklustre session." The noncommital attitude of Davis is summed up in an occurrence that Coss noted at the time: "On one take Miles wandered so far afield that he was completely lost. But he made no mention of it, not even a request for another take, although, fortunately, another was made, almost as if he didn't really care, was above caring, whether anyone had discovered the error." (The first take was apparently destroyed, since it has never been released; the entire session produced only twenty-seven minutes of music, barely enough to fill an LP.) Davis, however, is by no means the least satisfactory player on the date. Brown comments also that "Britt Woodman and Teddy Charles play their front-line roles on these slow ballads as if exhausted." "Although Mingus is on form," Brown says, "he's actually responsible for a degree of imbalance, for his forceful soloing exposes his soporific colleagues even more than if the bass player was asleep too."

The recording, though, is not uninteresting. Mingus managed to orchestrate – both literally and figuratively – a context that would expose one aspect of Davis's playing, that of the self-indulgent, bemused lyricist; the tougher, blues-oriented bopper is completely eradicated. The record thus became a kind of starting-point for a peculiar breed of Davis fans, who read into his detached musings not a lack of feeling but some higher order of feeling, perhaps the apotheosis of feeling. They came to share Bill Coss's opinion of this record, that "through it all, none of the musicians show Miles' finality of mood, but they do perfectly match him as if they shared the same secret." (My own copy of the original release, scarred and worn from the countless listenings of a high school clan hoping to tap that elusive secret, has seldom commanded playing time since those days.) The music itself, stacked up against its promise, simply seems anticlimactic.

If Davis seemed uninvolved, he probably had good reason. He was preoccupied with assembling a new band of his own for the engagement at the Café Bohemia, and for the first time since he assembled the short-lived nonet in 1948 he had some realistic hopes of keeping this band together as a working unit. Of course he knew exactly who he wanted for most of the positions, and the main problem was making sure that they were available for the date. Sonny Rollins, naturally, was his choice to share the front line with him, and Red Garland and Philly Joe Jones would form two-thirds of the rhythm section. On the quartet recordings in June, he used Oscar Pettiford on bass with Garland and Jones, and he had used Percy Heath regularly before that, but there was no hope of getting a bassist of that stature. Jackie McLean, however, raved about a young bassist from Detroit with whom he had been working in the George Wallington Quintet. The bassist, whose name was Paul Chambers, had arrived in New York only a few months earlier and had already been seen working with the promising new quintet of J.J. Johnson and Kai Winding before he landed with Wallington. Davis decided to give him a try.

After a couple of informal rehearsals, the new Miles Davis Quintet moved into the Bohemia. Two of the titles they played on the Wednesday of what was probably their first week there have been preserved:

Miles Davis Quintet
Miles Davis, tpt; Sonny Rollins, ts; Red Garland, pno; Paul Chambers, b; Philly Joe Jones, dms. Café Bohemia, New York, 13 July 1955
Bye Bye Blackbird; *Walkin'* [*Rollin' and Blowin'*]
(both on Chakra CH 100)

Bye Bye Blackbird, which became a perennial favorite in the book for Davis's bands for several years, gets a spare, Jamalesque statement from Davis on the muted horn, his solo dotted with quotations from Leonard Bernstein's ballad *Maria* from *West Side Story*, then the hit of Broadway. Rollins's two choruses are more expansive, even including some sixteenth-note runs. The lack of playing experience for this band as a unit shows up especially in *Walkin'*, another perennial in Davis's book, where the theme is stated only once at the beginning before giving way to the round of solos, which includes not only Davis, Rollins, and Garland, but also a bowed chorus by bassist Chambers, whose contribution throughout is simply outstanding.

Davis must have known from the beginning that he had put together a rhythm team of great potential. Chambers fitted in immediately with Garland and Jones, who were already comfortable with one another, and Chambers and Jones seem to rally in support of Garland's solos, which are usually attractive and always competent but almost never adventuresome, the bass and drums thus adding color and pace to them and saving them from becoming a letdown in the proceedings. Even in these relatively unpolished performances, Davis could hear all the essential elements he wanted in his band. He seems never to have doubted that Rollins's burly tone made the perfect complement for his own playing; and in the rhythm team he heard the kind of unabashed spirit that would set them both off.

It was already a good band at the Bohemia, and beyond any doubt it could become a great one. Best of all, the crowds were there to hear them, attracted at first perhaps by the good notices from Newport but hanging on throughout the entire engagement, even though it was July, the toughest month to draw an audience into a jazz club in any city. Davis went ahead and booked a tour of jazz clubs outside New York for the fall.

Apart from Davis's triumphal entrance at Newport, the jazz event that drew the most notice in the summer of 1955 was the first appearance in New York of a rotund saxophonist named Julian Adderley, better known as Cannonball, with the Oscar Pettiford Quartet at the Café Bohemia in the weeks immediately following Davis's engagement there. Adderley spun out paragraphs of blues-based improvisations on the alto, which looked like a toy up against his bulk, and he did it with such facility that his audiences at the Bohemia, including the reviewers, could hardly resist comparing him to Charlie Parker. Adderley, who was almost twenty-seven, was a high school music teacher in Fort Lauderdale, Florida, and the New York audiences, including most of the musicians in town, could hardly believe that such a talented player could exist outside the hub.

One musician who spent several hours at the Café Bohemia that summer was Davis, and he was impressed enough by what he heard that he took Adderley aside and offered him some advice. "Miles helped me when I first came to New York," Adderley says. "He told me whom to avoid among the record companies, but unfortunately I didn't take his advice." Adderley ended up signing a contract with Mercury-EmArcy that summer, and for the duration of the contract he was told by the label's producers what to record, who would arrange it, and who would publish it. Davis, under contract to Prestige and being courted by Columbia, recommended neither of them. "Al Lion of Blue Note was one man he recommended," Adderley recalls, "and Miles also told me about John Levy," the man who became Adderley's manager. Davis also tried to talk to him about his playing, but without much success. "Miles began telling me something musically about chords, but I sort of ignored him," says Adderley, remembering the glow of his summer as the toast of the New York jazz world. "I was a little arrogant in those days. Then, about three months later, I saw an interview in which Miles said I could swing but I didn't know much about chords. But by that time I'd begun to listen to Sonny Rollins and others, and I realized I knew very little about chords. You can play all the right changes and still not necessarily say anything. Finally, I learned how to use substitute chords and get the sound I wanted."

The attention that Davis paid to Adderley that summer was probably not gratuitous. Sonny Rollins was again grumbling about life in general and threatening to get out of music and out of New York for good. Even though Davis did not believe he would follow through, he was keeping an eye out for a possible replacement just in case, and Adderley must have looked like a good prospect. If so, Davis had a surprise coming, for Adderley was not available, at least not in the immediate future. He was obliged to return in September to his high school job in Fort Lauderdale. By the time he returned to New York to work as a professional musician the following spring, Davis already had a saxophonist and Adderley formed a quintet of his own with his brother Nat, a cornetist. He eventually joined Davis's band, but not until two years after his auspicious summer debut.

Davis's efforts at putting together a permanent band were interrupted one more time that summer by his obligations to Prestige, for which he was set to record another all-star date. Some of the players in the band were longtime studio associates, including Milt Jackson, who was listed as co-leader on the first release of this session, and Percy Heath. Jackie McLean was also along for two of the four tracks, which he composed, and he brought along the drummer from the George Wallington Quintet, Arthur Taylor, yet another of McLean's neighbors from Harlem. The piano player was Ray Bryant, who had played occasionally with Davis in Philadelphia at the Blue Note, where he had been the house pianist for several years before his recent move to New York. The details are as follows:

Miles Davis and Milt Jackson All Stars
Miles Davis, tpt; Jackie McLean, as (on *Dr. Jackle* and *Minor March*); Milt Jackson, vib; Ray Bryant, pno; Percy Heath, b; Arthur Taylor, dms. New York, 5 August 1955
Dr. Jackle; *Bitty Ditty*; *Minor March*; *Changes*
(all on Prestige LP 7034; reissued [1967] on Prestige 7540)

McLean's *Dr. Jackle* is a theme that Davis obviously relished, judging from his long skittish solo here, and he kept it in his repertoire for a few years. The other piece by McLean, *Minor March*, is basic bebop, all the more readily identifiable because of McLean's quotation of some Parker phrases in his solo. The session amounted to one more LP of competent post-bop playing. The most noticeable difference between this session and Davis's other recent recordings comes from the presence of pianist Ray Bryant, who works much more actively in the bass clef than most of the other young piano players of the time. His solo on his own *Changes*, a blues chord sequence with no set melody, is a carefully made, two-handed recital, which previews the best of his later work as a featured pianist.

The record date with a pick-up band again seems to have been little more than a distraction for Davis. His main interest was in lining up his own quintet for the round of club dates starting in September, but he was not making much headway. Sonny Rollins disappeared, as he had threatened to do, and when Davis tracked him down he told him that he was giving up music and moving to Chicago. He would not be dissuaded. Davis began searching for another tenor saxophonist for the quintet. First he tried a young Chicagoan named John Gilmore, a man who had listened carefully to Rollins and learned some of his style from him, although Gilmore was an adventurous player who would not confine himself to styles that were already worked out. He had grown up amid the first winds of an avant-garde movement in Chicago, had played there with a singular organization called the Arkestra led by a mysterious figure who called himself Sun Ra, and had made his first recordings with the Arkestra for Sun Ra's Saturn label earlier in the year. Davis tried Gilmore in a few rehearsals and then tried another tenor player, John Coltrane, on the recommendation of Philly Joe Jones, who had often played with Coltrane in Philadelphia.

Davis knew Coltrane slightly. He had been around New York a few years earlier, playing alto saxophone in Dizzy Gillespie's orchestra and tenor saxophone at some club dates, and their paths had crossed then and later, when Coltrane usually stayed close to home in Philadelphia. Coltrane proved to be a competent player and a very willing sideman, practicing almost constantly between rehearsals, but much of the time he was simply mystified by Davis. "After I joined Miles in 1955, I found that he didn't talk much and will rarely discuss his music," Coltrane said later. "He's completely unpredictable ... If I asked him something about his music, I never knew how he was going to take it." For Coltrane, a serious, almost solemn man, asking questions about the music they were rehearsing seemed as natural as breathing. For Davis, who expected his sidemen to answer their own questions in their own terms as they grew independently within the musical context he determined for them, Coltrane's quizzical attitude went against the grain. The personality differences between them did not make any long-term association look very promising. When Coltrane had to return to Philadelphia to fulfill a playing commitment after rehearsing with Davis for a few weeks, he was probably not surprised to read a newspaper item quoting Davis as saying that he expected Sonny Rollins, who was rumored to have started playing again in Chicago, to join his quintet in time for the fall tour.

Rollins did not return. In his place, Davis reinstated Coltrane at the last minute. Davis probably had little choice in the matter; apart from Rollins, no one but Coltrane knew the band's book. How much longer it took the taciturn Davis to discover that in Coltrane he had discovered an exquisite element for his music no one will ever know for certain. It would take a little while before he could bring himself to laud Coltrane's playing, but he must have known his value much sooner, probably within a few weeks, when the members of the quintet had begun to work as a unit. It did not take much longer than that for Davis's listeners to recognize the superb balance of the new Miles Davis Quintet, and many of them could discern Coltrane's crucial counterweight in that balance. They discovered that the little-known saxophonist had, in Whitney Balliett's phrase, "a dry, unplaned tone that sets Davis off, like a rough mounting for a fine stone."

7

Cookin'
1955–7

With the single exception of Louis Armstrong and the classic discs he made with his Hot Five and Hot Seven, there has been no series of recordings in jazz history that has had the impact of the Miles Davis Quintet and Sextet records, nor the later albums with Gil Evans and the large band ... Seen against the backdrop of all jazz, it is a great achievement; seen against the backdrop of contemporary music as a whole, it is even greater; and against the backdrop of all contemporary art, it is perhaps more significant than we yet realize.   Ralph J. Gleason

Jazz buffs learned that the new Miles Davis Quintet, with John Coltrane, Red Garland, Paul Chambers, and Philly Joe Jones, had something special for them to hear long before all but a handful of them actually heard it. The network that links the cognoscenti had begun its rumblings about Davis's intentions of forming a new 'boss' group soon after he had walked off the stage at Freebody Park in Newport in July. The rumble amplified when the quintet played their first notes in public, which happened shortly after 9 a.m. at a small club called Anchors Inn in Baltimore on Monday 28 September 1955. The quintet's first recordings were made for Columbia one month later, exactly the interval that Davis wanted in order to let the individuals in the band resolve into a working unit, but even these performances the public did not get to hear for a long time because of the contract dispute between Columbia and Prestige. The general public's first taste of the quintet's music came with the release in April 1956 of a November 1955 recording session for Prestige.

By that time, the quintet had played before only a few thousand listeners in several cities in the United States, and the men in the quintet already knew, as almost none of their listeners did, that no matter how successful they became – and they must have realized that they would become, in jazz terms, phenomenally successful – life as a member of the Miles Davis Quintet would never be easy. The tensions within the group, which surely worked to fuel its creative fires, were scarcely evident to outsiders, whether they were following the quintet's itinerary in the pages of *Down Beat* hoping they would come within range of their cities and towns, or riffling through the accumulation of LPs from these years. Davis's artistic course in the last half of the 1950s has the appearance of a steady upward spiral at the head of the cohesive quintet, spelled occasionally by special projects with Gil Evans, and onward into an expansion of the quintet into a sextet that was perhaps the greatest small band in jazz history. (The sextet years are the subject of the next chapter.) Looked at more closely, the progress is not nearly so smooth. In the twenty-seven months from its debut in Baltimore until it became a sextet, the great quintet was disbanded no less than four times when one or more of the sidemen, usually John Coltrane or Philly Joe Jones and sometimes both, fell out of grace with the leader. Davis would then re-form it eventually, sometimes after a period of months. The quintet was a working entity only a little more than half of the time that it held sway over the jazz world.

The quintet remained Davis's reference point through all this period and never failed to satisfy him musically no matter how disgruntled he might become with the members either personally or professionally. In spite of his various attempts to dismantle the quintet once and for all, he relented whenever he had an important performance to make and called the members back to the fold. And, of course, the men never failed to return to him, no matter what curse they had left under. What matters is what remains of the quintet – their music – and the vagaries of their daily existence only help to elucidate the circumstances in which some great music came into being. "This Quintet represented a high-water mark in post-war jazz," says Alun Morgan, an opinion that is virtually unanimous. These years in jazz belonged to the Miles Davis Quintet, even during the weeks when their leader thought that he had banished them from the scene.

After Newport it became a possibility that Davis would be in a position to establish his own band, and he turned immediately to the Shaw Artists Corporation, run by Milt and Billy Shaw, the veteran bookers and managers from the days of 52nd Street. All the jazz veterans knew the Shaws, and the Shaws knew the jazzmen. On the one hand, they knew that Davis had a lot of potential, and on the other hand they knew that he was not a particularly manageable man. In jazz, the managers were accustomed to exercising considerable control over their clients. Of course, the days were past – but just barely – when a successful jazz musician required a street-smart white manager to get any work at all, but the spectre of Irving Mills dictating to Duke Ellington and Joe Glaser piloting Louis Armstrong, which seem now to be chapters more appropriate in the annals of the American Civil War than of the Roaring Twenties, remained vivid in 1955. Davis allowed the Shaw Agency no illusions about the relationship he expected when he took on a manager. "It's all right to be in business with a white man," he said, "but for him to own everything and dictate to you is outdated, and it was outdated when I was born." The Shaws assigned Davis to the dossier of one of their junior partners, a man named Jack Whittemore, and the two struck up an enduring, if sometimes uneasy, partnership. "Jack and I are good friends," Davis says. "Jack asked me, 'Miles, what do you want me to do, which percentage do you want me to take – five, ten, or what?' If I don't feel like paying him shit, I ain't gonna say nothing, but I wouldn't take advantage of him, because of my attitude. And I don't want him to take advantage of me."

Whittemore set up the first itinerary for the new Miles Davis Quintet, putting them in Baltimore from 28 September to 3 October, in Detroit for 5–10 October, into Chicago's Sutherland Lounge starting 12 October, and into Peacock Alley in St. Louis after that. From St. Louis, they would return to New York, presumably having worked out most of their musical kinks. They were booked into the Café Bohemia, the jazz club on Barrow Street in Greenwich Village where Davis had tested the climate for his music in the summer with Sonny Rollins in the band. Davis hoped that they could make their first records during the Bohemia engagement.

The fuss over his tenor saxophonist when the tour was about to begin ruffled Davis a bit, at least momentarily. By the time Sonny Rollins finally begged off, John Coltrane was back in Philadelphia playing a club date with the organist Jimmy Smith. Things were looking up for Coltrane because Smith had asked him to join his band permanently. He was pondering the offer and talking it over with Naima Grubbs, the woman he lived with in Philadelphia, when Philly Joe Jones telephoned from New York to tell him that the tenor chair in Davis's band might still be available. Naima and he decided that, if the offer came, he would go with Davis rather than Smith, because it would give him a better chance to play his music than he was likely to get playing in the shadow of Smith's domineering organ. Philly Joe Jones finally called him again on 27 September and told Coltrane to join the band in Baltimore the next day. Coltrane hastily arranged for Odean Pope, a good local saxophonist, to fill in for him in the week remaining with Jimmy Smith. He left for Baltimore and joined the others in time for a late afternoon rehearsal before starting their first set. For all the haste, the first set went off smoothly enough, and so did the rest of the engagement. "It was just a natural thing," Red Garland said later.

The members of the quintet hit it off when they were not performing. At the end of their week in Baltimore, on 3 October, Naima arrived and she and Coltrane were married, with the others in attendance. As the tour moved into the Midwest they grew closer together. The week in Detroit was important to Davis, who still had close contacts among the local musicians, and it was equally important to Paul Chambers, who was returning home. "We'd hang out together during the day – the whole band," Garland says. "We'd go eat, stop off at a bar, walk around the streets and just have fun. We liked each other. Local musicians would organize a jam session and we'd go to those during the day." Chambers was no stranger to Chicago either, and when the band moved there, he shared an apartment in the Sutherland Hotel with Doris Sydnor, Charlie Parker's widow.

Musically, Coltrane still seemed to have some uneasy moments on the stand, probably because he had joined the group relatively cold. During the Sutherland engagement, a Selmer salesman came in to show Davis his line of trumpets and when he stayed over to hear the quintet he thought he detected that Coltrane was having some problems with his instrument. He arranged to take Coltrane the next day to the Selmer plant in Elkhart, Indiana. This incident was repeated almost ritually by Coltrane every time he visited Chicago thereafter, and then was carried out in almost every city in the world where saxophone manufacturers could be found, in what amounted to an obsessive search by Coltrane for the perfect instrument, the perfect mouthpiece, and the perfect reed. He had been working intensely on his music for years now, and the intensity would continue until the day he died.

That intensity was felt by some members of his audience even in his performances on this first tour, when Coltrane was almost completely unknown. "I saw Trane when everybody was expecting Sonny Rollins in St. Louis, Missouri," Leon Thomas, the improvising vocalist, told Arthur Taylor, recalling the quintet's last stop on their inaugural tour. "East St. Louis had turned out for Miles's gig at the Peacock Alley. Paul Chambers, Philly Joe, Red Garland, Miles and Trane showed up. The people were drug because they didn't know who Trane was. They had never heard of him, and he was a last-minute substitute for Sonny. They knew they wouldn't dig the way he was playing. I was sitting up front, and he just blew me out of the place. Wasn't nobody else after that, nobody!' But Thomas's reaction was not always shared by other members of the audience as their first impression of Coltrane.

For all his work so far, Coltrane still had made scant progress. Andrew White, the tenor saxophonist and 'Coltranologist,' points out that "he was pretty much playing in standard bebop style until he joined Miles Davis in 1955." The union with Davis, which came so close to not materializing, was crucial. "The time spent with Miles, who many musicians accurately called the 'star-maker,' was the starting-point of the Coltrane legacy," White says. "Miles had a way of putting bands together with musicians who were as diverse in their playing as they were in their personal lifestyles. But some sixth sense seemed to give him the ability to bring out the best of everybody ... Many years later, Coltrane recalled that he was pretty much content to sound like anybody else until he joined the Davis band, that Miles had the ability to relax you while keeping you professional at the same time." It was not necessarily Davis's presence that was the catalyst for Coltrane's development. White adds: "He could also have pointed out that when Miles left the bandstand Trane *had* to play – he was the only horn left." Whether or not Davis's absence would have worked so effectively for other players seems doubtful, but for Coltrane it worked perfectly. "It was the constant professional pressure to produce that sparked the level of ingenuity in Coltrane's playing that would soon set him apart from the rest of the tenor players and mark him as the foremost player of the Sixties, a crystallizer of the bebop era, and the so-called 'father of the avant garde,'" White says.

Coltrane's progress as a member of the quintet was by no means unique, although it was undoubtedly the most dramatic – possibly the most dramatic individual development in jazz history, since he was already twenty-nine, his birthday coming the week before he joined the quintet, well past the age when jazz musicians generally attain their mature styles. He was just four months younger than Davis, and Davis had established the main elements of *his* style more than five years earlier. If the other members of the quintet did not progress as dramatically as Coltrane, they nonetheless went through some considerable changes.

Red Garland, whose seemingly modest gifts were prodded purposefully by Davis as he encouraged him to incorporate the beauties he heard in Ahmad Jamal's playing, quickly emerged as one of the most influential piano players of the day. Garland's stature did not come solely from what he took from Jamal, as the French pianist and critic Henri Renaud points out. "Garland is a marvelous pianist in his own right," Renaud says, "an original artist with a very personal and creative approach to melody, rhythm, beat and sound. Yet there can be no denying that about 1955, when he made his first recorded appearance with Miles Davis, he was instrumental in most younger pianists the whole world over going in for both Ahmad Jamal's rhythmic conceptions (the 'Charleston' syncopation) and Errol Garner's harmonic ones ... The Garnerian influence is obviously at work in Garland's system of chord inversions: Garner never strikes the tonic with the left hand's little finger. Here indeed lies the essential differences between the pianistic sound that was prevalent during the Parker era and the one that was to supersede it in Coltrane's time."

Partitioning the joint influences of Garner and Jamal on Garland is not as straightforward as Renaud makes it sound. The harmonic innovation that he traces from Garner was also an important element in the fabric of Jamal's style, and Jamal may well have learned it from Garner, his older colleague from Pittsburgh. But it was Garland, more than either Garner or Jamal, who transmitted the innovation to the younger jazz players, because he had the best forum as a member of the Miles Davis Quintet. Garland "brought a new approach to keyboard voicing," according to Jerry Coker, the saxophonist and educator, who explains it this way: "He omitted the root from the bottom, if not altogether, placing instead a seventh or third (usually) on the bottom, and played the voicings more in the middle and upper rather than the lower portions of the keyboard. Within a very short time, virtually all jazz pianists made a similar change, sometimes modifying Garland's exact voicings. It was plain to see that we were not going to be hearing many root-oriented voicings again, except perhaps in ballads or at important cadence points in faster selections." Clearly, Garner, Jamal, and Garland and their immediate successors such as Bill Evans shared a light touch on the keyboard as compared to such contemporaries as Oscar Peterson, Ray Bryant, and Dave Brubeck. The impression of that light touch probably derives partly from eliminating the root of chords, though that was also part of the stock-in-trade of some older pianists too, especially Billy Taylor and John Lewis, long among Davis's favorite players. With Ahmad Jamal and Red Garland, the technique was used more frequently and became a predominant aspect of their styles.

Paul Chambers was only twenty when he joined the Miles Davis Quintet, but he made his mark within the first few months. In the ensembles, his presence is felt rather than heard, as a sturdy walking bass line that pins down the chordal foundation and frees the piano player's left hand. But it was as a soloist that Chambers drew most attention. "Paul Chambers concentrated all his career on solo work," says Percy Heath, one of the many older bassists who began listening carefully to what Chambers was doing. "I've always liked his solos better than his choice of notes as an accompanist. I have the feeling that his notes are more like tenor saxophone notes." From the start, Chambers took occasional solo turns arco rather than pizzicato, a technique that was rarely used by jazz bassists except for Slam Stewart, who for years had been bowing his solos and humming along in unison, giving him one of the most unique sounds, though hardly the most pleasant, in all of jazz. With Stewart, the use of the bow was considered to be a novelty (he was once part of a jazz vaudeville act – Slim and Slam – on 52nd Street with guitarist Slim Gaillard), but with Chambers it was considered a feat, and those bassists who had had any training in the use of the bow quickly set about sharpening their skills. Chambers was voted the new star on his instrument in *Down Beat*'s International Critics Poll for 1956.

Philly Joe Jones was already thirty-two when the quintet was formed, the same age as Red Garland and three years older than Davis, and he had been around the jazz scene on the east coast for several years without making any appreciable impression. Amazingly, his time with Davis would elevate him right to the top rank of modern jazz drummers, where Kenny Clarke, Max Roach, and Art Blakey had been unchallenged for years. A whole generation of rising drummers would emerge imprinted with Jones's style, among them Jack DeJohnette, who would become Davis's drummer in 1968. "I really got into Miles' music,"

DeJohnette remembers, "and Philly Joe was making it happen. Philly Joe was like the acrobatic dancer of the rudiments. He took rudiments and made them swing." The transformation of Jones's drumming came directly from Davis's conception, both for the band and for himself, which suited Jones's bright, pulsating ingenuity perfectly. Jones explains it this way: "Most bandleaders and drummers, they have a marriage. We feel each other and know each other. I know everything he's going to do – almost. After a few weeks it comes that he can't make a move without I know he's going to make it – and I anticipate it. A lot of times Miles would say, 'Don't do it *with* me, do it *after* me.'" The impact on jazz drumming was almost immediate. "During the time Philly was with Miles he started playing that rim shot on four," Horacee Arnold, another drummer, recalls. "You'd get a gig with somebody and they'd say, 'Play the Philly lick' ... You'd go to a record date and they wanted everybody to play what Philly did." Although Jones's technical gifts were considerable, his elevation depended upon their exposure in Davis's deliberately uncluttered ensemble, which left lots of spaces for the drummer to fill. After Jones, Davis would employ other drummers who would also rise from obscurity to the forefront for the same reason, most notably Tony Williams in the 1960s. But Williams, like every other drummer of *his* day, would arrive in the band with the technical arsenal derived directly or indirectly from Jones.

It was not only the drummer, of course, whose role was enhanced by Davis's conception of how a small band should sound. All the sidemen were assigned a function that both challenged the player and drew attention to his work. It has become a cliché to say that for a bandleader such as Duke Ellington the band is his instrument. The cliché works almost as well for Davis, although the dominance of a leader of a small band can be nowhere near as specific as it is for the leader of a large band, where sections must be coordinated internally as well as structurally in the band as a whole. By and large, Davis's success as a leader has the same source as Ellington's and consists essentially in discovering and exploiting the individual strengths of his sidemen. In this, Davis has become a model for a small band leader, a point that is emphasized by Herbie Hancock, who became a successful leader after spending four years with Davis's band in the 1960s. Hancock explains the key to leadership, which he calls "Miles' philosophy," this way: "A lot of bands go through musicians like drinking water, but what I try to do, rather than, for instance, always looking for another drummer to play a specific thing, is try to see what my drummer has to offer already, and function from that." As a basis for building a band, the strategy of exploiting individual talents is, of course, no more than sound common sense. It is not, for all that, easy, judging from the relative lack of brilliant, as opposed to merely adequate, leaders in jazz history. The mystery is how a leader implements the strategy. Davis seems to lead by indirection rather than by direction, seldom or never talking to his sidemen about his music. Even the musicians who have been through his bands have no clear idea about how he pulled the band together. When asked directly about it, Davis himself simply says, "I just bring out in people what's in them."

By the time the quintet returned to New York for their engagement at the Café Bohemia in late October, the five men already had a sense of their collective strength. One frequent visitor at the Bohemia was George Avakian, who was still intent on signing Davis to a Columbia contract. His most vivid memory of that Bohemia engagement was of John Coltrane, whom he had not heard in person before. Coltrane impressed him greatly, and Avakian later described him as a man who "seemed to grow taller in height and larger in size with each note that he played, each chord he seemed to be pushing to its outer limits." Avakian's strong impression of Coltrane was shared by a small but growing minority of listeners wherever the quintet played.

Avakian's negotiations on Davis's recording contract were running into some snags. In his view, Davis was too demanding and Prestige was uncooperative. His reaction was predictable, because Columbia was in a vulnerable position. Finally, he made a little headway by getting Davis to come to terms. Davis's agreement did not come cheaply: he received a $4,000 advance to join Columbia, then a sizeable fee for any recording artist and an unheard-of fee for a jazzman. (In 1981, the *New York Times* stated that the terms of Davis's original contract with Columbia also called for "a reported annual fee of $300,000," a large stipend for a jazz artist in 1980, let alone 1955; so far, the figure has not been corroborated.) Prestige proved to be more difficult. It had Davis under contract for another year, with four LPs stipulated as the year's production, and it would not consider releasing him outright, notwithstanding Davis's expressed wish that he be released. Terms of Davis's contract with Prestige were eventually fulfilled to the letter. During the next twelve months, Davis recorded music for Prestige that was eventually released on five and a half LPs with one title left over. Of these, five LPs and the extra title were by the regular quintet, and the other half-LP was by an all-star quintet. The half-LP was a leftover obligation from 1953, when the recording session with Charlie Parker on tenor had dissolved, leaving less music than was required. The extra title completed Davis's obligations to the company for 1954, when the total studio output had ended up a few minutes short of four full LPs. The first of the quintet sessions amounted to one LP, which completed his obligations for 1955, since two LPs had already been recorded. And the other four LPs, which would be recorded in two marathon sessions in 1956 (along with the extra title), then completed the final year of his contract. The oft-repeated, conventional account of these negotiations in the jazz literature (always unattributed) gives Prestige credit for some generosity, claiming that while it required its four LPs, it waived the year-long term of the contract and released Davis from it as soon as he recorded the required amount of music. It did no such thing. Davis's final recording date for the company, 26 October 1956, was exactly one year after the Café Bohemia engagement when the negotiations took place.

Nevertheless, Avakian won a small concession from Prestige. He was allowed, for inducements unknown, to begin recording Davis at Columbia in six months instead of waiting for the full year to expire. That agreement meant that Davis could start working in the Columbia studios around the end of May 1956; neither Davis nor Columbia, for whom he would record for decades, wasted any time in activating the contract, and he made his first official recordings for the company on 5 June.

These arrangements look fairly straightforward: essentially, Prestige would receive everything it had coming to it, and Columbia won the right to a concurrent agreement for part of the remaining contract year, at Davis's request. However, in the recording industry nothing is likely to be as it appears, and the agreement had been violated before the ink was dry on the contract. Davis and his quintet made their first recordings for Columbia on 27 October, while they were still playing at the Café Bohemia. The session was probably arranged by Avakian and Davis as soon as Davis settled his own negotiation with them, presumably on the assumption that Prestige would either negotiate a release with Columbia or give Davis his outright release. When Prestige refused to release him at all, the Columbia session had already taken place.

Columbia was then stuck with an LP's worth of the first recordings of the new Miles Davis Quintet to which it apparently had no legal rights. This suspicion is reinforced by Columbia's circuitous course in issuing the results of the session. The music consists of four bebop compositions played reasonably well, certainly well enough to merit its release in the usual manner under ordinary circumstances. However, the four titles have never been released together or even listed together. Instead, they have come out at odd intervals between 1956 and 1979. *Ah-Leu-Cha* was issued a little more than a year after it was made, along with titles from Davis's first official Columbia session, and with no indication that it did not date from the same session as the others. *Budo* first appeared in 1957 on an anthology that also included tracks by Louis Armstrong, Dave Brubeck, Eddie Condon, Duke Ellington, Errol Garner, Gigi Gryce and Donald Byrd, J.J. Johnson, Art Blakey's Jazz Messengers, and Turk Murphy – the palpable results of Avakian's recruiting program for Columbia's jazz department. *Budo* reappeared on a French CBS recording in the late 1960s. On an American release in 1973, it appeared along with *Little Melonae*, a previously unknown title from the same session (but incorrectly dated as 1958, although *Budo* was correctly dated); the two showed up together again (both correctly dated) in a 1977 release. *Two Bass Hit* remained unreleased – and unlisted – until 1979. It seems reasonable to guess that this schedule was determined by contractual problems at the time the music was recorded.

The Miles Davis Quintet made their recording debut, for Columbia, a few days less than a month after they had made their performing debut in the Baltimore nightclub:

Miles Davis Quintet
Miles Davis, tpt; John Coltrane, ts; Red Garland, pno; Paul Chambers, b; Philly Joe Jones, dms. New York, 27 October 1955
Ah-Leu-Cha (Columbia CL 949); *Two Bass Hit* (Columbia 36278 [1979]); *Little Melonae* (Columbia C32025 [1973]; JP 13811 [1977]); *Budo* (CBS [French] BPG 62637; also available on the issues listed for *Little Melonae*)

The repertoire is uncharacteristic of subsequent recording dates by the quintet and of Davis's recording dates for Prestige in the previous year, which usually mixed ballads and jazz compositions with an imbalance in favor of the ballads. Here, Davis calls three bebop classics and a new bebop title.

Ah-Leu-Cha is Parker's tune, recorded by Davis and Parker in the last days of the original Parker quintet, in 1948; it had hardly been played at all since then by anyone, and Davis seems to have removed it from his quintet's repertoire after the first few months. It deserved a better fate, probably, because it is an affecting uptempo melody based on a counterpoint chase by the two horns. On this version, Philly Joe Jones plays the melody at the bridge, and Davis solos coolly while the rhythm blasts around him.

Two Bass Hit, by John Lewis and Dizzy Gillespie, was recorded by Gillespie's orchestra in 1947, and the quintet pay homage to Lewis's original arrangement by preserving some of his arranged figures in their version. Here and for the rest of the decade, *Two Bass Hit* functions as Coltrane's showcase in the quintet; he is the only soloist apart from a drum break by Jones, and he charges through nine choruses, accompanied by Davis's obbligatos for the last one. Until this recording came to light in 1979, it was still possible for listeners to assume that Davis remained lukewarm about Coltrane's playing for the first months of the quintet's existence, but the fact that he gave Coltrane a showcase from the very beginning and also recorded it at the first opportunity disproves that assumption. In 1975, Davis told Jimmy Saunders, "When I first went into the studio with Coltrane, they asked me, 'What are you doing with a sad-ass saxophone player like him?' So I said, 'Just shut up and get behind the controls – before we leave.'" Davis's confidence in Coltrane is more than vindicated by his long solo on *Two Bass Hit*, which opens with a patented Coltrane charge that seems to carry him all the way through it.

Little Melonae, the only new title, was contributed by Jackie McLean, and it might have helped McLean gain some recognition as a composer if it had been released at the time, especially in conjunction with McLean's other contributions to Davis's repertoire, including *Dr. Jackle*, *Minor March*, and *Dig*. *Little Melonae* features long improvisations by Davis, Coltrane, and Garland (who plays an odd, exotic solo in the lower half of the keyboard) and gives Chambers a chance to be heard in the break at the bridge.

Budo, of course, is yet another version of Bud Powell's *Hallucinations*, as originally revamped for the nonet in 1949. It features Davis on muted trumpet, and an aggressive ride cymbal by Jones, which is either over-recorded or imbalanced in the mix. Although the selection of compositions is far from typical, it was apparently made to give reasonable exposure to each member of the quintet, and it should have assured Columbia that it had made the right move in pursuing Davis.

Davis's apparent haste in moving over to Columbia even before settling with Prestige might seem to be harsh treatment for the small, independent company that had employed him almost continually since 1951, giving him recording exposure when many other companies would not and providing him with some income when he had almost no other. For the time being, of course, he remained in their employ. Three weeks after recording for Columbia, he took the quintet into the Prestige studios to record the remaining LP of his commitment for the calendar year. The details are as follows:

Miles Davis Quintet
Miles Davis, tpt; John Coltrane, ts (except *There Is No Greater Love*); Red Garland, pno; Paul Chambers, b; Philly Joe Jones, dms. New York, 16 November 1955
Stablemates; *How Am I to Know*; *Just Squeeze Me*; *There Is No Greater Love*; *The Theme*; *S'posin'*
(all on Prestige LP 7014; reissued [1963] on Prestige 7254)

Ironically, the 1963 reissue of this recording session came out under the title *The Original Quintet (First Recordings)*; the original issue had been called simply *Miles*.

Most of the session is made up of standards that the quintet seem to have gone in and just played, without many preliminaries, so that in its design this session is a scale model for the remaining quintet recordings for Prestige that would take place the following year. There are no ensembles except on *Stablemates* and *The Theme*. On all the other titles, Garland plays a few bars by way of introduction, Davis enters to play the melody and variations of it, and then Coltrane steps in cold to play his solo. As perfunctory as that scheme seems, the result is more than just desultory. The quintet are already good enough, collectively and individually, that their playing consistently swings and their solos consistently work.

While their best work for both Prestige and Columbia was still to come, their efforts this day were in many ways more satisfying than what they had recorded for Columbia a few weeks earlier. The contrast between these two early sessions would recur throughout the months of concurrent obligations to the two companies: the Columbia recordings were made from staples of the active repertoire and the Prestige recordings more often from standards swotted up for the day; the former balanced improvisation and ensemble skills while the latter used head arrangements to get into the round of solos. Given these differences, Columbia's files of the quintet's recordings should have a clear advantage over Prestige's files from the same period, but jazz listeners would face a difficult task if they had to choose between them.

The quintet's first work for Prestige is best remembered for *Stablemates*, an attractive composition written as a song form by a twenty-six-year-old tenor saxophonist from Philadelphia named Benny Golson, a close friend of Coltrane. Golson was eking out a living playing his saxophone locally, but his main interest was in composing, and Coltrane asked Davis to include *Stablemates* in order to give his friend a boost. It opens and closes with a simple ensemble statement, suggesting at least some minimal rehearsal time on it, but it was apparently not added to Davis's active repertoire. Nevertheless, it gave the attractive melody enough exposure that it was picked up by other bands and recorded several times. The other title that includes an ensemble statement is *The Theme*, the old 52nd Street draft horse with which Davis's bands had long been ending every set. Instead of playing the Monk-like theme once and leaving the stand, they dust it off for an extended blowing session. Between theme statements, Chambers, Davis, and Coltrane each play two choruses, and Jones plays a chorus of his own before the end. Less satisfying are the two standards played as moderate uptempo swingers, *How Am I to Know* and *S'posin'*. Coltrane seems unfamiliar with the former and feels his way through his solo, but Davis, muted for both, and Garland run through the changes on both unreflectingly. *No Greater Love*, which leaves Coltrane out altogether, is played as a pulseless threnody by Davis, a good example of his lyric tone but little else. This song is lifted from Ahmad Jamal's book but Davis's arrangement does not resemble Jamal's, where it comes off as a slow but lilting *tour de force* for bassist Israel Crosby. Jamal's influence is much more clearly felt on *Just Squeeze Me*, Duke Ellington's novelty song from 1946, which is played puckishly by Davis on muted trumpet over Jones's dancing brushwork. Although Coltrane still sounds more than a little self-conscious in this light-hearted context, the song is as good as anything the quintet played at this session, and it points ahead to the good ballad performances with which the quintet would soon enrich Prestige so abundantly.

The recording that resulted from the afternoon's work was released the following April and became the harbinger of the quintet for those fans who were beyond its physical reach. Nat Hentoff reviewed the record in the pages of *Down Beat* (16 May 1956) and gave accolades to *almost* everyone in the band. Miles Davis is, he said, "in wonderfully cohesive form here, blowing with characteristically personal, eggshell tone, muted on the standards, open on the originals." Garland, he says, "plays some of his best choruses on record here" (which must have been a fairly easy judgment, since there were so few others), Chambers "lays down support that could carry an army band," and Jones is "pulsatingly crisp as usual." However, Hentoff gave the record four stars rather than five, in that strange, criticism-defeating polling system that *Down Beat* maintains to this day, and his reason for holding back the fifth star was Coltrane's playing: "Coltrane, as Ira Gitler notes accurately ... is a mixture of Dexter Gordon, Sonny Rollins and Sonny Stitt. But so far there's very little of Coltrane. His general lack of individuality lowers the rating." Hentoff is justified in assessing the album as less than excellent, and he is right in pointing out Coltrane as the individual who, on the day, had the most conspicuous problems (although one wonders about his lack of individuality being the key to them). For the next few years, Coltrane's playing would continue to pose a stumbling block for some listeners, but for others it would prove to be instantly and unstintingly enticing.

Coltrane was sensitive to the cool reception that sometimes greeted his work, whether it came from musicians or fans or reviewers. His response, so characteristic of the man, was to work harder at his music, to spend even more of his waking hours practicing, and to keep on searching for the perfect mouthpiece. "I began trying to add to what I was playing because of Miles' group," he says. "Being there, I just couldn't be satisfied any longer with what I was doing. The standards were so high, and I felt I wasn't really contributing like I should." Musicians started spreading the word about Coltrane in the form of a one-liner that simultaneously mocked him gently and shone with admiration for him. "If you go by Trane's house at any time of the day or night and you don't hear saxophone playing," the line goes, "then you know that John isn't home." He was constantly developing his technique, or his tone, or his approach, and listeners who were in a position to hear the quintet regularly began to notice the difference between his playing in person and on his most recent records.

Nesuhi Ertegun, the producer at Atlantic Records, first noticed Coltrane's development when he spent hours in the audience at the Café Bohemia during the quintet's engagement in the spring of 1956. "Coltrane was already way ahead of any records he'd previously made," Ertegun says. "His music seemed so different from what the rest of the band was playing. The construction of his solos, his advanced harmonics, the strange way the notes succeeded one another, and the speed with which they were played – I found all these things most intriguing, but not all that comprehensible at one sitting." David Amram had returned from Paris that spring and he too caught the quintet at the Bohemia. "When I first met John Coltrane he was standing in front of the Café Bohemia on Barrow Street," he told J.C. Thomas, one of Coltrane's biographers. "This was in the spring of 1956, when Miles Davis was playing there. I went outside during intermission and there was Coltrane eating a piece of pie. I remember his eyes, huge but not staring, friendly and almost bemused. We looked at each other for the longest time, until I said hello and told him how much I liked his music. I'd played with Charles Mingus, and I mentioned this to Coltrane, who said he was quite an admirer of Mingus' music. He also said that one of the things he was trying to do was to take music beyond the 32-bar song form, to constantly develop and improvise on an idea or a simple line, as Indian musicians do with raga. I think it was the most serious musical discussion during the shortest amount of time I've ever had in my life."

As spring turned to summer, the quintet had chalked up enough successes in their personal appearances and with their one record release that they seemed to be a fixture. The sidemen grew together even more. Coltrane, who had come into the group under the aegis of Jones and Garland, was closest to young Paul Chambers, with whom he usually roomed when they were on the road. Davis seemed pleased with what he had wrought – the group sound, the critical attention directed at all his sidemen, and the way they all reacted to his own playing. He found it even less necessary to say anything in particular to them now that they were working well together – or to anyone else. He subscribed to the essential lesson of the hipster about the world beyond the bandstand, that it is Us against Them. He had never questioned Charlie Parker's perspective on that, and he was unlikely to start now. The band was, in his view, self-contained. Even the noisiest of nightclub audiences could not penetrate the band's concentration. "I figure if they're missing what Philly Joe Jones is doing, it's their tough luck," he said. "I wouldn't like to sit up there and play without anyone liking it, but I just mainly enjoy playing with my own rhythm section and listening to them. The night clubs are all the same to me. All you do is go and play and go home. I never know what people mean when they talk about acoustics. All I try to do is get my sound – full and round. It's a challenge to play in different clubs, to learn how to regulate your blowing to the club." Yet he was not indifferent to the effect of his playing on the audience, and he was adept at bringing it around when he wanted to. "I know what the power of silence is," he told Julie Coryell. "When I used to play in clubs, everybody was loud; there was a lot of noise. So I would take my mute off the microphone and I would play something so soft that you could hardly hear it – and you talk about listening!" Sometimes, but not often, he slips up and shows that he is neither indifferent to nor unaware of the world beyond the bandstand. "You can sell anything," he once said. "If you want to sell a car, paint it red. It can be the raggedest car in the world, but somebody'll buy it."

The audience was turning out to be the least of his problems as leader of the quintet. He knew he could satisfy it. The gut issues, the contentions that really affected the quality of life on the bandstand, came from the club owners and managers. Matters had hardly changed since his days on 52nd Street, and Davis began challenging some of the assumptions that were still taken for granted. "Things were changing during the 1950s but you still had to fight almost every step of the way and teach people," Dizzy Gillespie says. "One good example of that is Miles. He found out that he was powerful enough to demand certain things, and he got them. Miles was the first one to refuse to play 'forty-twenty.' In the old days, you would come into a club and play from twenty minutes after the hour to the end of the hour, and then you would come on twenty minutes later and so on. Miles broke that up. He came to Philadelphia once and told the owner he was going to play three shows. The owner didn't want to go for it, and Miles told him, 'Well then, you ain't got no deal.' Now, musicians play only two shows a night in some places. Miles did a lot for musicians." In most clubs, jazz groups now play three sets a night, with at least an hour in between, certainly an improvement over the old system.

The security of the quintet's success gave Davis the leverage to challenge other antiquated conditions as well. Jack Whittemore, his agent, remembers Davis confronting another situation that he felt needed reforming. Whittemore says: "Back in the days when he was only getting a thousand dollars for a concert, Miles was booked into Town Hall. The tickets were selling very well, so the promoter suggested doing two shows instead of one. As was customary in such cases, Miles was to get half fee, $500, for the second concert, but when I approached him with this, he looked puzzled. 'You mean I go on stage,' he said, 'pick up my horn, play a concert, and get a thousand dollars. Then they empty the hall, fill it again, I pick up my horn, play the same thing and get only five hundred – I don't understand it.' I told him that this was how it was normally done, but he was not satisfied. Finally he turned to me and said he'd do it for $500 if they would rope off half the hall and only sell half the tickets. When the promoters heard this, they decided to give him another thousand for the second concert."

Davis's business prowess is for him a source of not inconsiderable pride. In the early 1970s, he helped the singer Roberta Flack in what he saw as a business coup. "I got Roberta Flack $25,000 instead of $5,000 for Atlanta," he boasted to Gregg Hall. "She called me up and she was so mad because her lawyer put her name down to appear for $5,000 on behalf of the Mayor. So I straightened her out ... I told her that when she refused a date she shouldn't say that she doesn't want to make it but instead make her price so high that they either say yes or they say no. She finally got $25,000 – and the place was sold out." Similar dealings by Davis on his own behalf in the second half of the 1950s quickly made him one of the highest-paid jazz musicians of all time.

His dealings with the business side of the jazz world could not often be carried out at a safe remove, as they were for Roberta Flack. Usually they required confrontation, which has ended up in a collision on more than a few occasions. It is the classic case of two unrelenting forces poised on opposite sides of an issue. On the one hand, the managers, owners, and entrepreneurs, especially in the 1950s, were accustomed to dictating the conditions under which jazzmen would work for them, and if any of those conditions were deemed to be negotiable they would certainly not be negotiated with a trumpet player, much less with a black one. On the other hand, Davis demanded all his rights and a few privileges too, and he considered them his due; he was not interested in bargaining for what was his due or in presenting his case tactfully, which was a waste of breath.

The potential for collision was obvious to Davis, and from the earliest days of the quintet he took a step that guaranteed that he would not be totally unprepared when difficulties occurred. He retained a lawyer named Harold Lovett to oversee his interests. Davis's relationship with Lovett became an alliance that is legendary among jazz musicians of Davis's generation. "It's a matter of business maneuver, so to speak," Duke Jordan says. "From what I understand, when Miles formed his new group, the first thing he did was contact a lawyer, a young lawyer who was interested in handling musicians. This particular guy Miles was up with helped him tremendously, so when Miles came up with an idea of – whatever it might be – he would say to his lawyer: 'Hey, look, man, this guy is giving me a hard time. I'm supposed to be here for four weeks but I'm going to be here for two weeks and then quit because I don't dig what's going on. What kind of trouble can I get into if I do this?' And the lawyer would straighten him out." Davis's association with Lovett went well beyond legal advice. "Lovett is probably Miles' best friend and most constant companion," Joe Goldberg wrote in *Jazz Masters of the Fifties*. "He is one of the few people who stuck by Miles during the bad years ... One person remarked of Lovett, 'he makes Miles look like a choirboy,' and another person says that he has heard Miles talk about Lovett admiringly on several occasions, as though Lovett's 'coolness' were the ultimate in behavior. Asked about this, one club owner said, 'I think Miles is much cooler than Harold. Harold tends to worry about Miles, but Miles never worries about Harold.'"

Lovett's work for Davis often involved a lot more than investments and contracts. At a concert in Chicago, where the quintet were appearing as part of a package tour (probably Jazz for Moderns, a touring concert in the late 1950s), Davis walked in one night after the opening curtain had gone up, which was the promoter's deadline, but well before he and the quintet were scheduled to go onstage. When the promoter, who was not on cordial terms with Davis, charged toward him backstage, announcing loudly that he was going to fine him $100 for being late, Davis flattened him with one punch and then walked to the phone to call Lovett in New York.

In the winter of 1956, Davis canceled a scheduled engagement at a jazz club in Toronto at the last minute. When he was asked why, he said, "Because that motherfucker who owns it told me to fire Philly Joe because he's too loud! Nobody can tell me what to do with my music." Naturally, some legal hassles followed. And by the time Davis canceled the engagement, Coltrane and Chambers had already left New York for Toronto, where they found they had no place to play.

Soon after the Toronto fiasco, Davis disbanded the quintet for the first time. The main reason was that he had to lay off for a while in order to undergo surgery that would remove a growth on his larynx. It had been bothering him for almost a year, affecting his speech and causing hoarseness. The quintet were scheduled to make a recording in May, so the disbanding was only temporary.

Davis's throat ailment had caused him to speak in a whisper since the previous summer, a marked change from the voice recorded in the angry exchanges with Monk in 1954. Well before the operation, Bill Coss wrote: "The bother and anxiety about a growth in his throat had made the cat-slight Miles speak and talk in such whispers that his always present, kind of nose-thumbing withdrawal seemed nearly complete." The whispers became Davis's permanent mode of speech because he got caught up in a shouting match too soon after the surgery and permanently damaged the larynx. His adversary was a promoter by one account and a co-owner of a record company by another. "I wasn't supposed to talk for ten days," Davis says. "The second day I was out of the hospital, I ran into him [the businessman] and he tried to convince me to go into a deal I didn't want." To make his point clear, Davis found it necessary to raise his voice, for what turned out to be the last time. Leonard Feather claims that his hoarse whisper is "a source of psychological and physical discomfort, and a subject he prefers to avoid" discussing, but in recent years Davis has pointed with quite undisguised pride to the fact that Cicely Tyson, the actress who became Davis's fourth wife in 1981, imitated his voice when she played the feisty 110-year-old lead character in the television drama The Autobiography of Miss Jane Pittman, which won her an Emmy award in 1974. Since the operation, Davis's voice has been as distinctive as his trumpet-playing, and it is very much part of his character. The English reporter Michael Watts describes it this way: "Miles' voice is a phenomenon. It's a hoarse whisper, strained through his larynx like a sieve. He dredges it up slowly through the whole of his body, but it barely leaves his lips. It just hangs, a vague sibilance in the air, like the effort of a dying man. At first, it's both incomprehensible and comic. Instinctively you cock your head to one side to catch what he's saying. But gradually, you adjust to its level, as you would twiddle the dials on a radio to get its tuning." The voice certainly makes people attentive to him when he does choose to speak, not unlike his gambit of opening a set in a noisy club with an off-mike muted ballad.

During his period of recuperation, Davis led a pick-up group into the Prestige studios to dispatch the half-LP he still owed the company from 1953. Only Paul Chambers was brought in from the quintet. Although these recordings were slated to be released along with the material recorded in 1953 by the sextet with Charlie Parker on tenor, only Sonny Rollins was brought back from that band. Rollins had finally regained his confidence during the winter in Chicago and had joined the Max Roach-Clifford Brown Quintet, replacing Harold Land, when they were playing at the Beehive there in late December, almost two months after he had turned down Davis's invitation to join his quintet. The Roach-Brown group were almost continuously travelling from city to city, but they were based in New York and Rollins was living there again. He was rounding into his peak individual form, and the group were formidable, playing brittle, aggressive neo-bop. Their constant traveling kept them from putting in as much time in the recording studios as they might have wished, but they had completed three recording sessions for EmArcy in January and February and had another session scheduled under Rollins's name for Prestige just six days after Rollins played there in Davis's group. Those four sessions would be the only studio recordings ever made by the Roach-Brown-Rollins alliance because Brown was killed in a car crash along with the group's piano player, Richie Powell, and Powell's wife, on 25 June. Brown was only twenty-six.

At the moment of Davis's recording, Sonny Rollins was at a pinnacle and he showed up ready to play. Philly Joe Jones had been the drummer on that abortive 1953 date, but he was not recalled for this complementary session. In his place, Davis called in Arthur Taylor. The piano player on that earlier date had been Walter Bishop, a graduate of Parker's bands, but Davis this time brought in Tommy Flanagan instead. The details are as follows:

Miles Davis All Stars
Miles Davis, tpt; Sonny Rollins, ts; Tommy Flanagan, pno; Paul Chambers, b; Arthur Taylor, dms. New York, 16 March 1956
In Your Own Sweet Way; No Line; Vierd Blues
(all on Prestige LP 7044; reissued [1970] on Prestige 7847)

No Line and *Vierd Blues* just happened in the recording studio, although both are credited as Davis's compositions. *No Line*, as its title indicates, has no beginning or end, just a middle. It opens with what might as easily be the fifth chorus of a cheerful uptempo solo by Davis on muted trumpet, and it peters out with Chambers and Taylor left suddenly on their own, and sounding stranded. In between, Rollins, Flanagan, and (again) Davis take their turns. *Vierd Blues* is a slow blues with a minimal head played by the two horns, and it features a notably calm solo by Rollins, as if he is trying to match Davis's calmness before him. *In Your Own Sweet Way* presents an entirely different feeling. This handsome melody by Dave Brubeck is treated with some reverence. Paul Chambers is at the heart of Davis's arrangement, reflecting the novel use of time that makes this melody work so well and interpolating stop-time intervals between the soloists. Davis's muted playing has some rough edges, and there is no doubt that the performance would have benefited from a second take, as would *No Line*, but there were no second takes at this recording session, which was set up to fulfill an old obligation. At the end of *In Your Own Sweet Way*, almost before the last throbbing note of the bass has been taped, Davis rasps, "Yeah, Rudy," to Rudy Van Gelder in the control booth.

Although this record date hardly seems memorable, Tommy Flanagan recalled it twenty-four years later. "It was my birthday, that's how I remember; my twenty-sixth birthday," he told Michael Ullman. "He had the date and I got the call." Most of all, he remembered the spontaneity of the session being broken by Davis's introducing *In Your Own Sweet Way*. "We just cooked," he says. "All except that one Brubeck tune. That came about strangely. Miles had that tune in his back pocket – a sketch of the chords. I remember him telling me how to voice the intro. He always knows exactly what he wants. It makes him easy to work with. If you don't play what he wants, he tells you like this [whispering hoarsely] – 'Play block chords, but not like Milt Buckner. In the style of Ahmad Jamal.' I didn't really get into it too much, but Red Garland really grasped that. I love Ahmad's playing, but I didn't want to play like him ... I know what Miles likes about it – he plays that way himself. With the spaces – it just gives you a lot of room to play inside of. Like Ahmad can repeat a phrase to death, but with taste. Not the kind of monotony that really wears on your nerves – he gets a lot of good out of it." On this occasion, Tommy Flanagan played his short session with Davis sounding not at all like Jamal and very much like himself.

Within two months, Davis was back in the Prestige studio to begin working off his contract obligations for 1956. This time he surrounded himself with the working quintet, and they completed the first of two incredible sessions that would yield enough music to fill all four LPs called for in his contract, with one track left over. The first session, in May, was the more prolific, producing fourteen complete takes in the space of one Friday afternoon and evening. Nevertheless, the music is varied in tempo and form, careful and sometimes brilliant in execution, and usually ingenious in invention:

Miles Davis Quintet
Miles Davis, tpt; John Coltrane, ts; Red Garland, pno; Paul Chambers, b; Philly Joe Jones, dms. New York, 11 May 1956
In Your Own Sweet Way (Prestige LP 7166); *Diane* (Prestige LP 7200); *Trane's Blues* [*The Theme*] (Prestige LP 7166); *Something I Dreamed Last Night* (Prestige LP 7200); *It Could Happen to You* and *Woody'n You* (Prestige LP 7129); *Ahmad's Blues* (Prestige LP 7166); *Surrey with a Fringe on Top* (Prestige LP 7200); *It Never Entered My Mind* (Prestige LP 7166); *When I Fall in Love* and *Salt Peanuts* (Prestige LP 7200); *Four, The Theme I*, and *The Theme II* (Prestige LP 7166)
Coltrane does not play on *Something I Dreamed Last Night*, *It Never Entered My Mind*, and *When I Fall in Love*; neither Davis nor Coltrane plays on *Ahmad's Blues*. *Trane's Blues* is a version of *The Theme*. The Prestige issues listed above refer to the first releases of this material, called *Workin'* (7166), *Steamin'* (7200), and *Relaxin'* (7129); the music has been reissued in North America with new catalog numbers at least twice, but the album titles as well as the selections have remained the same.

To record this material, the quintet assembled at Van Gelder's Hackensack studio and Davis called out the titles one after the other, as if they were playing an extended nightclub set. There were no second takes, and even the second recording of *The Theme* at the tail end of the day is not a second attempt at it but merely a brief coda to the whole set; the version that precedes it is a full-blown swinger. Something of the atmosphere was preserved in the recordings by including some of Davis's directions to the men in the control booth: at the start of the version of *The Theme* that was released as *Trane's Blues* he announces, "The blues"; after *It Could Happen to You*, he calls up to Bob Weinstock, "How was that, Bob?," and on being assured that it was fine, he announces, "OK, we're gonna do *Woody'n You*"; and after *Woody'n You*, he is heard asking "OK?," and when he is apparently told in jest to do it over, he says, plainly irritated, "Why?," but Coltrane, nonplussed, is heard saying, "Could I have the beer opener?"

The shifting instrumentation on several numbers is typical of their club performances at this time, with Coltrane usually sitting out on the slow ballads and the rhythm trio taking a feature on their own. Two of the ballads without Coltrane, *Something I Dreamed Last Night* and *When I Fall in Love*, are the least interesting pieces, although not directly because of his absence. Both are played as pulseless ballads in which Davis places his mute within a centimeter of the microphone, and though his ballads in this style were useful in attracting listeners who had previously listened only to ballad singers such as Frank Sinatra and Jo Stafford, they now seem sentimental and cloying. The other ballad without Coltrane, *It Never Entered My Mind*, is entirely different: an ornate arrangement polished by club performances, it features a repeated Chopinesque countermelody on the piano and a repeated stop-time figure on the bass. Davis fashions the melody on his muted trumpet in the space between the piano and bass, but he does not solo, leaving that to Garland, who plays a delicate, static, semi-classical set piece with all the accoutrements of Ahmad Jamal but none of his swing. The total effect is what one might expect if Jamal were to write an arrangement for the quintet, and the unassimilated, even undigested, foisting of Jamal's mannerisms onto the members of the quintet represents the apogee of Davis's fascination with Jamal. Even *Ahmad's Blues*, the rhythm trio's rendition of a tricky, trilled original recorded by Jamal in 1952, retains the individuality of the players better.

The other ballads show the unmistakeable touch of Jamal too, especially in their jaunty beat and their understated melodies. Brubeck's *In Your Own Sweet Way*, which Davis had introduced to the men in the control booth just a few weeks before, this time gets its due. *Surrey with a Fringe on Top*, a silly Rodgers and Hammerstein song from *Oklahoma!*, the charms of which were unearthed by Jamal, gets a surprisingly gritty ride by the quintet that lasts nine minutes and might be the one title from this session, if you could choose only one, you would most want to take with you to a desert isle. Among its glories is the first recorded instance of the arranged dynamism between Davis and Coltrane, as Davis's lacy, romantic exploration of the melody on muted trumpet gives way to a four-bar break in which Coltrane comes roaring in to take over in no uncertain terms. The device, based on a simple contrast that was always implied in the styles of the two men, is exploited consciously here, as it would be in all their finest work together.

In simply rattling off such a quantity of music, Davis was displaying either unbounded confidence – not to say chutzpah – or fathomless desperation. There can be no doubt that he wanted to rid himself of his Prestige contract, but if in doing so he had left behind a legacy of slipshod performances the damage to his reputation might have been irreparable. More likely, he knew the strengths of the quintet, and every nightclub performance with them was, in a sense, a rehearsal for the Prestige sessions, even if some of the titles were new. He was a veteran of the recording studios in a sense that very few performers of the day were. He had been in them often and long, and his approach to recording was formed to some extent by Charlie Parker, who disdained them thoroughly. He was also a pioneer in the microgroove technology. All these factors allowed Davis to become more and more cavalier about recording sessions after the carefully rehearsed nonet sessions of the early 1950s, to the point where he seldom called for retakes, even when they were needed, as in his recent date with Sonny Rollins and Tommy

Flanagan. From now on, his approach to the recording studio, probably buoyed by the success of the first Prestige marathon, would be quite consciously casual, a point that drew the attention of other musicians. J.J. Johnson says, "I've recorded with Miles and I know how he operates. Most of the time, he goes into the studio and one take is it! Goofs or not, there's no second or third take. That's his philosophy on the recording bit." He said so himself, a few years later, talking to Ralph J. Gleason. "When they make records with all the mistakes in, as well as the rest, then they'll really make jazz records," he said. "If the mistakes aren't there too, it ain't none of you."

As if to balance some psychological ledger, Davis and the quintet were in the recording studio for Columbia early the next month. After the outpouring for Prestige, this Columbia session has a frugal look, producing only three titles:

Miles Davis Quintet
Miles Davis, tpt; John Coltrane, ts; Red Garland, pno; Paul Chambers, b; Philly Joe Jones, dms. New York, 5 June 1956
Dear Old Stockholm; Bye Bye Blackbird; Tadd's Delight [Sid's Delight]
(all on Columbia CL 949)

This session contrasts with the previous one not only in quantity but also in attitude. Here the resources of the quintet are under tighter control, with solos framed neatly in arrangements and the exuberance of the group's bulls, Coltrane and Jones, reined in. They do not suffer noticeably for the control: Coltrane is set up for his solos on the two ballads so that he loses the awkwardness that is sometimes felt in the Prestige counterparts of these ginger ballads, and Jones sublimates his more raucous tendencies into nimble, showy drumming that never takes the center of the stage but is never far from it. The resuscitation of *Tadd's Delight* – Dameron's bebop theme broadcast as *Webb's Delight* by Dameron and Davis in 1949 and recorded for Capitol as *Sid's Delight* (on M-11059) by Dameron and Fats Navarro that same year – adds to the stockpile of bop tunes by the quintet at Columbia. It suggests again that Columbia was still looking to the Davis quintet as potential leaders in the hard bop movement, then enjoying considerable success in record releases by the Max Roach-Clifford Brown group and Art Blakey's Jazz Messengers. Columbia was about to discover, however, that Davis's real strength lay elsewhere and that its commercial success would dwarf that of the hard boppers. Davis probably knew already what was happening, judging from his treatment of *Tadd's Delight*, which was brief, straight, and only moderately upbeat, a far cry from what the Jazz Messengers might have done with it.

The ballads were a different matter. *Dear Old Stockholm*, played only slightly slower than *Tadd's Delight*, opens with a motif played by Garland and Coltrane and sustained by Garland throughout. Over it, Davis plays the haunting Swedish folk melody discovered by Stan Getz, and Paul Chambers takes the first solo; when Coltrane enters, the rhythm toughens perfectly, but it softens again when Davis returns for his muted solo. All the elements of Davis's beautiful arrangement of this song were already in place when he recorded it for Blue Note in 1952 – Getz's original version (long out of print, but last on Roost SLP 2249) had none of these elements – but by comparison there is a definite coarseness to the motif in Davis's earlier version, when it was played by J.J. Johnson and Jackie McLean, and to Davis's lead work too, played open rather than muted and sounding a little flat. Comparing the two versions, four years apart, shows clearly that Davis's progress lay not in his musical conception but in the refinement and discipline he could now exercise over it. The other ballad, *Bye Bye Blackbird*, an old song that a couple of generations of Americans grew up knowing although it was never a popular hit, is suffused by a blues feeling that popular songwriters often tried for but seldom found, except in the best work of Harold Arlen and perhaps some of Gershwin and Hoagy Carmichael. It also carries vague sociological implications: in the 1930s the few blacks who participated in white activities, such as the semi-professional National Football League, were serenaded with the song by the all-white spectators. Davis's tightly muted rendition seems to be a distillation of everything he ever learned from Billie Holiday: it is sorrowing, and it is pained, but it is not self-pitying. More than that, compared to the two pulseless ballads he had played for Prestige, this one swings.

This Columbia session continued, in effect, about three months later, producing even more magnificent music. This date also served the first public notice – though few people knew about it at the time or for several years after – of Davis's musical reunion with Gil Evans. To all appearances, the date was just another brilliantly successful day in the recording studios for the quintet, which was now beginning to get used to such days. The details are as follows:

Miles Davis Quintet
Miles Davis, tpt; John Coltrane, ts; Red Garland, pno; Paul Chambers, b; Philly Joe Jones, dms. New York, 10 September 1956
All of You (Columbia CL949); *Sweet Sue* (originally on Columbia CL919; reissued on CBS [Fr] 62 637 [1968], Columbia C 32025 [1973], and JP 13811 [1977]); *Round Midnight* [*Round about Midnight*] (Columbia CL949)
Sweet Sue is arranged by Teo Macero; *Round Midnight* is arranged by Gil Evans. The original issue of *Sweet Sue* includes a narration by Leonard Bernstein.

This recording session is partitioned into two parts, with the recording of *All of You* and *Round Midnight* standing in many ways as consummations of Davis's work with the quintet, and the recording of *Sweet Sue* a minor curiosity.

Sweet Sue came about because of Leonard Bernstein, then conductor of the New York Philharmonic and composer of an enormous range of music from the symphony *Jeremiah* to the music for *West Side Story* and the scores for the film *On the Waterfront*. Bernstein also acted during the 1950s as writer, narrator, and performer on the television program *Omnibus*, a Sunday afternoon lecture-entertainment on music which, ironically, was probably more responsible for his nationwide celebrity than his prodigious musical talent. Along with expositions of topics such as Bach, opera, and conducting, he included a program called "The World of Jazz", which was telecast on 16 October 1955.

The show had its inane moments: toward the end Bernstein says, "Jazz used to advertise itself as 'hot'; now the heat is off. The jazz player has become a highly serious person. He may even be an intellectual. He tends to wear Ivy League clothes, have a crew cut, or wear horn-rimmed glasses." It also had its moments of insight as Bernstein wended his articulate and highly accessible way from variations on a theme by Mozart through jazz instruments and period styles. The program had an inestimable effect, now forgotten and even then underappreciated, on broadening the audience for jazz, a part of the upward spiral that began with the white middle-class attraction to West Coast jazz and would continue with fashionable college concerts, festivals, and government-sponsored international goodwill tours.

At the end of the show, to illustrate some of the style shifts in the history of jazz, Bernstein played excerpts of *Sweet Sue* from recorded versions by Bix Beiderbecke and Benny Goodman and then introduced what he considered to be an up-to-the-minute updating – "an advanced sophisticated art mainly for listening, full of influences of Bartók and Stravinsky, and very, very serious," he called it in his introduction – by bringing on a band made up of clarinet, flute, english horn, bass saxophone, bass, and drums to play an arrangement of *Sweet Sue* by one Danny Hurd. It was, needless to say, anticlimactic.

A few months later, when Columbia Records approached Bernstein to make an LP on jazz along the same lines as his television program but using its resources, both past and present, for illustrative material, one of the pieces that most clearly required revision was the post-Goodman version of *Sweet Sue*. George Avakian contacted the tenor saxophonist Teo Macero, a Juilliard graduate active in jazz-classical fusion experiments, to prepare both a swing arrangement – the Goodman recording used on the original show belonged to RCA Victor – and a modern arrangement. Macero's swing arrangement was accepted and eventually appeared on Bernstein's LP *What Is Jazz?* (Columbia CL919), played by the Don Butterfield

Sextet, with a tenor solo by Macero. But when Macero showed Bernstein his modern arrangement of it, Bernstein declared it "too lugubrious."

Macero prepared a second introduction, and Avakian brought in Davis to decide how to play it for the recording. Whether Davis chose Macero's first or second attempt is uncertain, but in any case all that survives of Macero's arrangement is an introductory tag lasting only a few seconds. Even less survives of the original melody known as *Sweet Sue*, for at the point when Macero's tag ends and one expects Davis to state some semblance of the melody, he launches instead into an improvisation that at no point refers directly to the melody. Coltrane follows, and Garland follows that, and the hoary old melody is never heard from. There is no chance whatever of its arising in the simultaneous improvisation by Davis and Coltrane that caps off the performance – Coltrane sounding timid, Davis taking charge, and the listener, even the stodgiest, dreaming he hears Bernstein in the control booth exclaim, "Far out!" while Philly Joe and the others try to hide their smiles.

All of You, Cole Porter's Hollywood hit for Fred Astaire just the year before, and *Round Midnight* (Monk's *Round about Midnight* with its title streamlined due to the new currency of the sung version) are something else again. *All of You* gets Davis's masterly treatment of the Jamal ballad style, the kind of integration into the quintet's style that he had been working toward for some time. It is played in Jamal's gentle, swinging tempo, with full value given to the rhythm players behind the horns, but the performance is a triumph of individual skills used to collective advantage. Davis pays unusual homage to Porter's melody at both the open and the close over a bobbing bass line by Chambers that mixes eighth-notes and rests; Coltrane is heard for the first time after Davis's solo, and at his entrance a new force from the rhythm section takes over as Chambers walks and Jones hits rim shots to close each bar.

All of You is one of Davis's finest ballad performances, but it has received less attention than it deserves because it was superseded immediately by *Round Midnight*, one of the most striking ballad performances in all of jazz. One notices first the symmetry of the arrangement, which presents three movements, the first and the third featuring Davis on muted trumpet playing variations on Monk's melody accompanied by Coltrane's obbligatos, the middle movement featuring Coltrane, introduced by a trumpet-saxophone fanfare. The middle movement doubles the tempo of the others, and Coltrane invents a beautiful melody for two choruses. On either side of it stand Davis's cooler tone poems. The ensemble passages are brief but effective, consisting of a variation of the familiar introduction and a fanfare to introduce tempo changes. Within the frame of the arrangement, the individual players all shine; they seem free to play and not at all fettered by the weight of the arrangement, the balance between the individual and the group marvelously maintained. That balance had grown with familiarity, but it went beyond that and was put in motion by Gil Evans, the arranger. Evans's role was not credited publicly until this title was reissued in 1973. The acknowledgement came as a surprise mainly because it came so irresponsibly and irremedially late, but was no surprise musically.

Since the working days of the short-lived Miles Davis nonet in 1948, Evans had eked out a living as a freelance arranger around New York. He worked for some radio shows, but the demand for original music on radio was waning fast, and he picked up some jobs in television, which was just coming into its own, but mostly he took whatever jobs came to him. He contributed supper club arrangements for popular singers such as Pearl Bailey, Tony Bennett, the actress Polly Bergen when she tried her hand at torch singing, and Johnny Mathis. Some of the work he did edged closer to jazz, such as his scores for the trumpeter Billy Butterfield, himself a freelancer surviving on studio work and records that used his pure tone in the saccharine context of mood music, and his arrangements for singers Helen Merrill and Peggy Lee, who had come up through the ranks of band singers before making it on their own. There was also a bit of work in jazz, for conservatory-influenced jazzmen such as Teddy Charles and Hal McKusick, and also for Benny Goodman and Gerry Mulligan, and three arrangements for Charlie Parker on Norman Granz's Clef label with the Dave Lambert Singers on *If I Love Again*, *Old Folks*, and *In the Still of the Night*. He was not languishing, but his activity was too diffuse, even with the nonet records coming out at intervals, to keep his name before the jazz public. He also had some bad luck; the Parker-Lambert recordings turned out to be, according to the critic Charles Fox, "the least individual and least successful pieces of writing Evans has done."

Still, one might have expected that more opportunities would come to him, no matter how effacing he tended to be. "As for jazz dates," Evans said later, "one reason I didn't do much was that nobody asked me." "Eight years after *Boplicity*, seven years after *Moon Dreams* – these figures are a disgrace to the world of jazz – Evans was commissioned to do a series of arrangements for a Miles Davis album," André Hodeir says, referring to the 1957 LP that for many years was thought to mark Evans's reunion with Davis. He continues: "In the meantime, everyone had forgotten who he was; jazz people don't give much thought to anyone who doesn't sing, play the trumpet, or lead a band. Gil's friends were a bit uneasy."

The turning point in Evans's fortunes came indirectly through his work for Helen Merrill, a fine ballad singer who failed to attract the audience she deserved in North America, although she had more success in the 1960s in Europe and especially in Japan (where she lived for several years before returning to New York in 1973). In the 1950s Merrill was featured for a while in the Earl Hines band, in which her husband, Aaron Sachs, played reeds, and her considerable potential as a singer won her a record contract with EmArcy, for which she made some excellent records, although she had to battle the management to get to make them on her own terms. Her first record for them, in 1954, featured the new-comer Clifford Brown playing obbligatos behind her, and a later record, made in July 1956, featured Gil Evans's arrangements. "That was only because Helen insisted," Evans says. "The a & r man [EmArcy's producer] didn't want me. I had a lot of trouble with him." Merrill not only insisted on using him, she also insisted on telling other people about him. One of the people she told was Miles Davis, whose quintet was touring in a concert package that summer that also included Merrill. She told Davis: "'I just finished this album with Gil Evans and, boy, you've got to use him.' Miles said, 'Well, yeah, I forgot about Gil; and I think I'll give him a call.' That's all he said," Merrill remembers, "and the rest is jazz history." The first step in that piece of jazz history, although almost no one knew it at the time, was Evans's arrangement of *Round Midnight* for the quintet on 10 September.

That fact that Evans was already involved in Davis's work in the fall of 1956 gives a new perspective on Davis's next recordings, which were also for Columbia but involved neither Evans nor the quintet. Instead, they involved two old col-leagues from the nonet, John Lewis and J.J. Johnson. Both Lewis and Johnson harbored ambitions to expand the horizons of jazz toward a new legitimacy by composing extended forms within the jazz idiom. They were by no means alone. David Amram, who had long worked in both symphonic and jazz music, explained how he and many others were beginning to approach the fusion of the two streams: "After working in both for so long I no longer saw a distinction, except the distinction that existed in other people's minds. There may be differences in terms of idioms, in approach and performance techniques, but ultimately it's all part of a world that expresses itself through a beautiful series of sounds. There was no reason I could not combine these sounds in terms of my life experience to make my own kind of music." Amram, Lewis, and Johnson belonged to a loose alliance of musicians trying to do just that, and their movement was gaining momentum at the end of the 1950s. Gunther Schuller, who now made his living as the principal horn in the Metropolitan Opera Orchestra, was the leading spokesman. He defined the movement's musical objectives as no less than the fusing of "the improvisational spontaneity and rhythmic vitality of jazz with the compositional procedures and techniques acquired in Western music during seven hundred years of musical development," and he coined the term for the fusion, "third stream music," implying the confluence of European and Afro-American tributaries. Its votaries were to have their most significant successes in the last half of the 1950s. Teo Macero and the trombonist Bill Russo were commissioned to write works for the New York Philharmonic, and a little later David Amram became the Philharmonic's composer in residence, all under the influential tutelage of Leonard Bernstein. In 1957, Brandeis University commissioned Schuller, Charles Mingus, George Russell, and the saxophonist Jimmy Giuffre to compose third stream works for their Festival of Arts. John Lewis was introducing fugues, rondos, and other European forms in a jazz context nightly with his Modern Jazz Quartet. J.J. Johnson, who had joined Columbia's roster of jazz talent, took up conservatory-influenced composition during an enforced layoff from jazz in 1952–3, when he lost his cabaret card, a sort of license to perform in New York clubs administered by the police department, because of drug charges.

In late 1956, he and Lewis were scheduled to record extended third stream compositions for Columbia with a brass and rhythm ensemble. Miles Davis was chosen as the principal soloist on both works. The details are as follows:

The Brass Ensemble of the Jazz and Classical Music Society
John Lewis, comp, arr; Gunther Schuller, cond; Miles Davis, Bernie Glow, Arthur Strutter, Joe Wilder, tpt; Jim Buffington, frh; Urbie Green, J.J. Johnson, tbn; Milt Hinton, b; Osie Johnson, dms; Dick Horowitz, tympani, perc. New York, 20 October 1956
Three Little Feelings (Columbia CL941; reissued on CBS [Fr] 62 637)

Same personnel except J.J. Johnson, comp, arr; Miles Davis, flugelhorn; omit Horowitz. New York, 23 October 1956
Jazz Suite for Brass (issued as above)

This music is virtually unknown to North American listeners. The original issue seems to have been a closely guarded secret, at least among jazz buffs, and there are apparently no commentaries and no reviews from North America. In a way, such neglect is a shame, because the music is ambitious and generally interesting, and because Davis and Johnson solo particularly well. Lewis's *Three Little Feelings* is the more successful of the two pieces. *Jazz Suite for Brass* suffers from sequences that seem unrelated, perhaps even left over from something else, notably at the beginning of the second movement and through most of the third. In all fairness, however, it should be noted that the English reviewer Max Harrison does not hear it that way at all. He says, "While the main thread is undoubtedly held by the soloists, the writing is everywhere precise in its intention, a genuine, if oblique, extension of Johnson's remarkable trombone playing." Harrison is especially enthusiastic about the first movement, on which it might be easier for other listeners to agree with him: "The rapid pace of the movement proper comes as a surprise, and dark mixtures of open and muted sound lead quickly to Davis's first contribution. He is heard on flugelhorn, and, in combination with the swift tempo, his melancholy creates an ambiguous feeling that is resolved by the extroversion of the composer's solo, which follows. Each improvises on the theme, thereby strengthening the movement's unity, and the ensemble is pointedly active behind them, not just accompanying but adding further perspective to their discoveries." The second movement provides a curious point of interest; its only soloist is Bernie Glow, who plays in a straight tone with emphatic vibrato, and the contrast between his feeling in this context and Davis's in the first movement provides an object lesson in the chasm between classical and jazz styles.

Three Little Feelings features Davis's open trumpet on the first and second movements and Johnson's trombone on the third. Of the first movement, a swinger, Harrison writes: "In the beginning three motives are announced, then piled on top of each other. Davis, on trumpet this time, improvises around one of them, a chromatic four-note figure. He sounds even more forsaken than in Johnson's [*Jazz Suite*], but is, of course, responding to the more emotional nature of the musical material. It is noteworthy that his acutely subjective art can fit into so deliberately organized a setting, but perhaps that is a commentary on both desire for freedom and desire for discipline." The second movement brings Davis even further into the foreground by reducing the role of the ensemble merely to sustaining chords behind him, in a ballad format. Another English critic, Ronald Atkins, notes the similarity between this movement and the later work of Davis with a large orchestra directed by Gil Evans. He says: "The second movement is on par with the outstanding Miles Davis–Gil Evans collaborations ... even though the backing might seem monochromatic by comparison. In what essentially is a ballad context, Davis is driven to excel himself and we must assume Lewis bears some responsibility for this." Atkins's point about the similarity can easily be taken further. The voicings behind Davis are remarkably similar to the voicings that Gil Evans was working on, although not as full-sounding in Lewis's arrangement as in Evans's because Evans's orchestras will be considerably larger and have more varied instrumentation. This impression of similarity cannot be dismissed as a kind of aural illusion, the result, say, of hearing Davis's familiar sound in front of a large orchestra, because the similarity in voicing is every bit as obvious in the third movement as well, where Johnson, not Davis, is the soloist.

It is ironic that the American audience, which was so quick to recognize the brilliance of the Miles Davis–Gil Evans collaborations, has never paid much attention to John Lewis's *Three Little Feelings*, its single most influential precursor. The gap is a disservice to Lewis as well as a missed opportunity. It is probably a consequence of the fairly rapid eclipse of the third stream as a movement, for it petered out by the mid-1960s. Its spirit survives in occasional orchestral works by those who were there when it bloomed, some of whom are now associated with the New England Conservatory in Boston, and by younger musicians such as

Anthony Braxton, Michael Gibbs, Allyn Ferguson, and Patrick Williams. However, it no longer has a recognized spokesman or an identifiable audience, two factors that discourage the record companies from keeping these and other recordings from the time in print.

Three days after the recordings with the Brass Ensemble, Davis was poised for the second of his marathon sessions with the quintet in the Prestige studios. The details are as follows:

Miles Davis Quintet
Miles Davis, tpt; John Coltrane, ts (except *My Funny Valentine*); Red Garland, pno;
Paul Chambers, b; Philly Joe Jones, dms. New York, 26 October 1956
If I Were a Bell (Prestige LP 7129); *Well You Needn't* (Prestige LP 7200); *Round about Midnight* (Prestige LP 7150); *Half Nelson* (Prestige LP 7166); *You're My Everything, I Could Write a Book*, and *Oleo* (Prestige LP 7129); *Airegin, Tune up, When Lights Are Low, Blues by Five*, and *My Funny Valentine* (Prestige LP 7094)
Again, the issue numbers refer to the original issues titled *Relaxin'* (7129), *Cookin'* (7094), *Workin'* (7166), and *Steamin'* (7200), except for *Round about Midnight*, which first appeared on *Miles Davis and the Modern Jazz Giants* (7150), along with titles from the Christmas eve 1954 session.

In the five and a half months since the first Prestige marathon, the quintet have gone through some developments that become clear in the comparison. First, Coltrane is now generally included on the slow ballads. Earlier he had been asked to sit out; here he does so only on *My Funny Valentine*, a tune that came to bear Davis's signature from repeated playings over the years. "I played *My Funny Valentine* for a long time and didn't like it," he once said, "and all of a sudden it meant something." His audience certainly assumed it meant something to him when they heard this, his first, recording of it. On the other slow ballads, *Round about Midnight* (in Evans's arrangement again) and *You're My Everything*, the tempo doubles for Coltrane's turn, but he proves himself, as he had apparently proven himself to Davis's satisfaction in the intervening months, to be an effective ballad soloist.

Second, the rhythm section has become amazingly fluid, using all kinds of devices while in motion, regardless of tempo. They double tempos and halve them routinely on the ballads; Jones alone doubles his tempo behind Coltrane on *When Lights Are Low* while the others hold the original; Chambers walks throughout *Oleo* while the other rhythm players enter only for the bridge; and they play the gamut of tempos from the breakneck *Airegin* to the slow *My Funny Valentine* with no diminution of strength. Chambers is especially effective on his two solo turns, playing a showy arco solo on *Well You Needn't* and a pizzicato solo on *Blues by Five*, a head arrangement, that rivals Mingus's clarity and sounds more than a little like his choice of notes. By the fall of 1956, the prowess of this rhythm trio was widely recognized. They had recorded as a trio for Prestige, making an LP on which Garland introduced *If I Were a Bell* so effectively that Davis immediately added it to the quintet's repertoire, and musicians everywhere were buzzing about them. During a desultory set by the quintet at the Café Bohemia around this time, someone remarked that little seemed to be happening and Teddy Charles replied, "Watch the rhythm section. This is the best rhythm section in jazz, the hardest swinging rhythm section. Watch out when they loosen up."

In order to produce the quantity of music that Prestige needed from him, Davis was obviously digging deeply into his memory to come up with enough titles. The tunes he called at the two Prestige marathons make a kind of loose index of the music that he had worked on since arriving in New York. *Half Nelson* is one of the most venerable, dating from his first record date as a leader, in 1947, but Dizzy Gillespie's tunes, *Salt Peanuts* and *Woody'n You*, played at the first session, go back even farther, being among the most widely heard themes on 52nd Street when Davis arrived there. *Woody'n You* was added to Davis's recorded stock in 1952, the same year that he first recorded *Dear Old Stockholm*. *Tune up* first shows up in 1953, and so does Benny Carter's *When Lights Are low* (misidentified in Ira Gitler's notes for this session as *Just Squeeze Me*). *Four* was first recorded in 1954, and so were Sonny Rollins's contributions to his book, *Oleo* and *Airegin*. *In Your Own Sweet Way* and *Round Midnight* had entered his favor so forcibly that they were also recorded just weeks before their re-recording at the marathons. A few compositions destined to recur, notably *My Funny Valentine* and *If I Were a Bell*, get their first airing, and the sessions are rounded out by a list of pop songs apparently intended as fillers.

At least as interesting as what he dragged forward to play is what he left behind untouched. Whatever happened to the 1947 *Milestones*, recorded with *Half Nelson* and apparently forgotten along with his other originals of that day? What about the large repertoire he had played nightly with the Parker quintet: the Parker originals *Now's the Time*, *Ornithology*, *Chasin' the Bird*, *Scrapple from the Apple*, and so on, or the favored standards of the day, such as *My Old Flame* and *Embraceable You*? What of *Boplicity* and *Israel*, and the Dameron originals *Good Bait* and *Lady Bird*? Perhaps most surprising of all the omissions is Davis's fine blues *Down*, first recorded in 1951 and kept in the repertoire for a while but obviously forgotten when it might have been used to fill one of the blues slots at these sessions; instead they were filled by the head arrangements for *Blues by Five* and three renditions of *The Theme*. *Down* is not the only good original that might have made a reappearance; that list includes *Solar*, *Miles Ahead*, *Swing*

Spring, and lots of other titles. Davis's repertoire is always in flux, with favored entries eventually losing their place to newer ones. There seems to be no special structure to it, no pattern for what will be included and what will be omitted, and no highly conscious tinkering with it. Titles get added almost by chance, as *My Funny Valentine* suddenly took on meaning for Davis, and they get left off by chance too, as *Swing Spring* just never entered Davis's mind after it was recorded.

The rationale for Prestige's packaging of all these hours of music is a bizarre combination of business sense and discographical nonsense. *Cookin'* (LP 7094) came first, and promptly. It included a single slice of the last session, the last five titles in the order in which they were recorded except that the last two titles were reversed. It reached the market, perhaps as part of the contract terms, prior to Columbia's first album by the Davis quintet (although *Sweet Sue*, on Bernstein's *What Is Jazz?* LP, appeared before both of them). Since Davis tended to call the uptempo tunes toward the end of the marathon sessions, *Cookin'* is made up predominantly of hard swinging music played on the open trumpet, with a leaven of *My Funny Valentine* and the medium ballad *When Lights Are Low*. In selecting a predominance of fast, boppish tracks, Prestige was clearly aiming at the current market for neo-bop.

Columbia, which had proportionately much more neo-bop by the Davis quintet and much less ballad work, apparently had learned something about the métier of the quintet, and especially of Davis, because its first release, called *Round about Midnight* (CL949), made a judicious selection of the materials it was holding and came out with a predominantly lyrical program with each side ordered symmetrically as ballad-swinger-ballad (*Round Midnight*, *Ah-Leu-Cha*, and *All of You* on side 1, and *Bye Bye Blackbird*, *Tadd's Delight*, and *Dear Old Stockholm* on side 2).

Prestige probably learned from that selection, because its second selection from the marathons, *Relaxin'* (LP 7129), released the next year, presented a highly successful imbalance of two swingers (*Oleo*, *Woody'n You*) and four of the most attractive ballads (*If I Were a Bell*, *You're My Everything*, *I Could Write a Book*, and *It Could Happen to You*). That was followed only a few months later by *Workin'* (LP 7166), a selection of titles so strange that it suggests Prestige knew very well by then that Davis's records would sell adequately even without thoughtful programming; *Workin'* included all three versions of *The Theme*, counting the one called *Trane's Blues*, and the trio showcase *Ahmad's Blues*, with *Four* and *Half Nelson* and two good ballads (the ornate *It Never Entered My Mind*, and *In Your Own Sweet Way*). By the time it got around to packaging what was left over on *Steamin'* (LP 7200), in July 1961, Prestige had the dregs of the ballads (*Something I Dreamed Last Night* and *When I Fall In Love*), a frail waltz (*Diane*), and two reckless swingers (*Salt Peanuts* and *Well You Needn't*), with only *Surrey with a Fringe on Top*, a performance easy to underestimate because of the tune's dubious genealogy, drawn from the better half of the quintet's efforts.

Successive reissues have maintained the order and the mix of selections intact, and *Round about Midnight* has never been collected with the others. Almost everyone who listens to jazz has some or all of the Prestige packages in one or another of their releases, and one can only hope that the company will come to realize that to sell these performances again it must repackage and even do some selecting as well.

Davis's triumphs were not confined to the recording studio. Playing at the Café Bohemia when he was in New York, he nightly faced a huge poster of himself on the opposite wall, one of the gallery of jazz portraits that included Parker, Gillespie, Powell, and Roach and was the main attempt at decoration. He faced also a challenging contingent of musicians in the audience on most nights, including Mingus and the members of his first Jazz Workshop, who also worked at the club, Roach and Rollins from the Roach-Brown band, and Thelonious Monk. The shift of the jazz clubs away from Broadway and into Greenwich Village, where the Village Vanguard was also located, set the jazz musicians among some of the most creative young artists in all fields, for whom the Village was the hub of activity.

The garrets and studios of the Village were under unusual scrutiny at the time because the *New York Times* and other journals were touting a new wave in the arts in America, which they labeled the Beat Generation. Jack Kerouac, the novelist who surfaced as the new wave's leading spokesman, explained the label this way: "Beat means beatitude, not beat up. You *feel* this. You feel it in a beat, in jazz – real cool jazz or a good gutty rock number." Like all such labels, this one played down the individualism of the poets, novelists, and painters who were saddled with it and created a convenient fiction of uniform activity that was easier for outsiders to grasp. The Beats, according to their journalistic image, were amoral, apolitical bohemians who celebrated their freedom in quick sexual liaisons and spontaneous art works. Whatever the complex reality of creating art, the beatnik image fired the popular imagination. Jazz was part of it, and the Village was its setting. "Suddenly there were millions more people on earth, and they all seemed to be coming to Greenwich Village," said one habituée. Kerouac's novel *On the Road* was published by Viking Press in September 1957, crystallizing public awareness of the movement in swirling, eccentric prose that everyone who was anyone was reading – or pretending to read. The young artists who became closely identified with the movement, willingly or not, became celebrities. Kerouac was the lion, but the poets Gregory Corso and Philip Lamantia, the painter Larry Rivers, who also fancied himself something of a saxophonist, and many others were added attractions in the jazz clubs when they turned up in the audience. Kerouac was even booked into the Village Vanguard to 'play' regular sets, reading poetry with jazz accompaniment, the brainchild of the television talk show host Steve Allen, who was also a jazz piano player. Allen could not salvage Kerouac's performances, however, and neither could the good musicians with whom he shared the stand, among them Zoot Sims and Al Cohn. Throughout the engagement, Kerouac began each evening with faltering barely audible recitations that degenerated as the evening wore on into boozy, incoherent rants; on his better nights, he dispensed with the poetry and took up scat singing, including a faithful rendering of a Miles Davis solo that, according to one of Kerouac's biographers, "was entirely accurate, and something more than a simple imitation."

Not the least conspicuous member of the audience at the Vanguard or the Bohemia on many nights, though she was hardly a beatnik, was Baroness Pannonica de Koenigswarter-Rothschild, an English aristocrat known to the New York press as the Jazz Baroness and to the black musicians for whom she was something of a patron simply as Nica. For her, Horace Silver wrote *Nica's Dream*, Gigi Gryce wrote *Nica's Tempo*, and Thelonious Monk wrote *Pannonica*. The baroness had left her husband at his post in the French embassy in Mexico City in 1951 and moved with her daughter to the more thriving after-hours atmosphere of New York, where she lived in the fashionable Hotel Stanhope on Fifth Avenue. Her apartment became a hospitality suite for some of the greatest jazz players of the day, whom she treated generously. Monk was her closest friend among them, and through Monk she came to know the others, including Charlie Parker. When Parker died in her apartment, the *New York Mirror* bleated in its headline: "BOP KING DIES IN HEIRESS' FLAT." Most of her good works for the musicians were less conspicuous, but there was nothing inconspicuous about the baroness herself, whose attendance at a jazz club was usually signaled by the presence of her Bentley parked at the curb in front of it. Up to a point, she participated in their lifestyles as well as in their audiences. Her Bentley seemed to them neither more nor less exotic than Miles Davis's Mercedes-Benz, the first in a series of European thoroughbreds that he would own over the years. Hampton Hawes, who arrived in New York from Los Angeles that summer on the familiar rounds that addicted jazzmen were always making, recalled one incident: "Monk and his wife and Nica and I driving down Seventh Avenue in the Bentley at three or four in the morning – Monk feeling good, turning round to me to say, 'Look at me, man, I got a black bitch *and* a white bitch' – and Miles pulling alongside in the Mercedes, calling through the window in his little hoarse voice cut down by a throat operation, 'Want to race?' Nica nodding, then turning to tell us in her prim British tones: 'This time I believe I'm going to beat the motherfucker.'" These were heady times for jazz musicians.

The undercurrent for self-destruction persisted, and it was never far from the surface. Heroin addiction remained rampant. Hawes's summer in New York, for instance, ended with his hitting bottom again and finally committing himself to a narcotics hospital in Fort Worth, Texas. "Last thing I remember when the money was gone," Hawes wrote in his autobiography, "was sitting alone in Nica's Bentley in front of the Café Bohemia and Miles poking his head in with his sly grin and asking in his raspy voice, 'You cattin' with Nica?' And I'm mumbling, 'Yeah, cattin' with Nica,' trying to smile with my head on the thousand-dollar wood dashboard." For most of the jazz musicians, heroin remained an occupational hazard. The Miles Davis Quintet were no exception. While Davis himself remained straight, he was all alone in that respect. "His musicians, to a man, were still shooting up," according to J.C. Thomas, "at least in part due to the pervasive influence of Philly Joe Jones, who was to drugs that W.C. Fields was to booze." The addictions were taking a heavier and heavier toll on the quintet's performances, causing one or another of the musicians to be late almost every evening and sometimes to be absent for the whole night. Sometimes when they did show up, they might have been better not to.

John Coltrane was suffering most conspicuously, and on several nights he spent an entire set leaning against the piano, nodding. On one such night, a major record producer sat in the audience, expecting to sign Coltrane to a contract, but he left without even approaching him when he saw his condition. Ray Draper, the tuba player who recorded with Coltrane in 1960, remembers going to the Village Vanguard as a high school student in the mid-1950s and seeing Coltrane on the stand "disheveled, with his shirt collar dirty, buttons missing from his shirt, and his suit dirty and wrinkled." Draper told C.O. Simpkins that Coltrane seemed "locked in a struggle, playing only snatches of phrases and spitting out jumbles of notes. There would be long pauses of silence followed by brief spurts of more notes. Miles appeared angry with him." Between sets, Draper went downstairs to talk to the musicians: "John was sitting down, sick and uncommunicative. Two members of the quintet ran out to find him some drugs, after which he was a different person, talking and looking much better." Red Garland, who was in better control, paid the rent for his room only when it became absolutely essential for him to get a change of clothes. Hawes remembers, "He was always drawing money from the club so he could get his door unlocked, go back in his room to put on his clothes and go to work." With drugs using up so much of their incomes, setting aside money for food and rent was a constant, and nearly impossible, task for all the sidemen. In St. Louis, Coltrane and Paul Chambers shared a hotel room, as usual, but by the end of the engagement neither of them had any money to pay the bill, and they had to leave by the fire escape with their suitcases in hand.

No one was more aware of their problems than Davis, who faced them musically on the stand and managerially off it. He was also aware of the limits of his own power to solve their problems. "I just tell them if they work for me to regulate their habit," he says. "When they're tired of the trouble it takes to support a habit, they'll stop it if they have the strength. You can't *talk* a man out of a habit until he really *wants* to stop."

Davis's patience was far from inexhaustible and by the fall of 1956, Coltrane had succeeded in using up what there was of it. Davis warned him, and when Coltrane continued to dissipate, he brought in Sonny Rollins to replace him for an October date at the Café Bohemia. Part way through the engagement Davis relented, and both Coltrane and Rollins were in the band for a few nights. Paul Jeffrey, the tenor saxophonist, says, "I saw Coltrane at the Bohemia in late 1956, and this was one of the times Sonny Rollins and Trane both played with Miles. I knew Sonny's style, but Trane really surprised me. I'd always thought of Rollins as a great tenor virtuoso, but Coltrane more than held his own. He followed Sonny's melodic solos with some of the strangest, most convoluted harmonies and chord progressions I'd ever heard." Rollins's presence no doubt helped Coltrane to straighten himself out and play as well as he was capable of playing, but it was only temporary. For the last nights of the engagement, Rollins was Davis's only tenor player and Coltrane had returned to his mother's house in Philadelphia.

Immediately after the Bohemia date, Davis disbanded the quintet. He traveled without the others to Europe as a featured player in a touring concert package in November. Lester Young, another featured soloist on the tour, had no band of his own at the time, and he played his solo spots in front of the René Urtreger Trio, a French group. Davis also used Urtreger's trio for his spots. The other featured players were the Modern Jazz Quartet and the European orchestra of Kurt Edelhagen. This was Davis's second trip to Europe, seven and a half years after his appearance at the Paris Jazz Festival. This time he arrived as a leader, sharing top billing with Lester Young, a venerable figure although he was, at forty-five, a taciturn alcoholic of unpredictable musical prowess. The itinerary was good, taking in not only the cultural capitals Zurich and Paris but also Freiburg, Germany, a medieval city in the heart of the Black Forest. The distances were short enough to allow some leisure for sightseeing and other tourist activities – Davis bought a camera in Germany – and some hanging out with the growing community of expatriate jazzmen. The concerts were low-pressure affairs through which the musicians could coast if they chose to without ruffling their highly appreciative audiences. Private tapes of several of the concerts exist, but only one of them, in Freiburg, has been issued on record. The details are as follows:

Miles Davis and the René Urtreger Trio
Miles Davis, tpt; René Urtreger, pno; Pierre Michelot, b; Christian Garros, dms. The
Stadthalle, Freiburg, Germany, 12 November 1956
Tune up and *What's New*
(both on Unique Jazz UJ 14)

All Star Jam Session
Miles Davis, tpt; Lester Young, ts; Milt Jackson, vbs; John Lewis, pno; Percy Heath, b;
Connie Kay, dms.
How High the Moon (issued as above)

All Stars and the Kurt Edelhagen Orchestra
Davis; Young; Jackson; Heath; Kay; Conny Jackel, Hanne Wilfert, Rolfe Schnoebiegel,
Klaus Mitschele, Siegfried Achhammer, tpt; Otto Bredl, Heinz Hermannsdörfer, Werner
Betz, Helmut Hack, tbn; Franz von Klenck, Helmut Reinhardt, as; Paul Martin, Bubi Ader-
hold, ts; Helmut Brandt, Johnny Feigl, bs; Werner Drexler, pno; Kurt Edelhagen, cond
Lester Leaps In (issued as above)

Davis's exposure on the four titles on which he plays here amounts to slightly less
than twenty-four minutes, but his featured spot with the Urtreger Trio normally
included four titles instead of the two released on this recording. Alun Morgan,
the English critic, attended both concerts at Salle Pleyel in Paris, and he reports
that Davis played *Four, How Deep Is the Ocean, Tune up* and an unidentified
fourth title at both concerts. Morgan enthused over what he heard of Davis, but
perhaps he expected too little from him because Davis's important quintet recordings were not yet available. "He played brilliantly, surpassing in quality anything
which I had heard before," Morgan says. "His playing had the tonal richness and
melodic elegance of Bobby Hackett at his best combined with a highly personal
approach to improvisation." The Freiburg performance does indeed reveal some of
the remarkable facility Davis had shown in his recordings with the quintet, at
least on his solo features.

The other two titles at the Freiburg concert are loose improvisatory romps,
where the featured players are thrown together on stage to see what might happen. If nothing else, they document the decline of Lester Young, catching him
pathetically on *How High the Moon* as he solos at less than half the tempo of the
rhythm section and overstays his turn at the end when he cuts in to trade bars
with the other soloists. Young performed less and less frequently throughout the
rest of the 1950s, his great talent smothered by his apparent indifference not only
to music but to life, and he died in 1959.

The stay in Paris gave Davis and the others a chance to renew their acquaintance with the many bop musicians who had made their homes there. When Alun Morgan caught up with Davis in the audience at Club St. Germain, where Don Byas was appearing with the French pianist Raymond Fol and drummer Jean-Marie Ingrande, he found him at ease and accessible away from the pressures of the New York scene and the problems of his quintet sidemen. "Sitting there at the bar Miles was completely relaxed," Morgan writes. "He spoke slowly and with a deep, hoarse voice. A throat ailment had impaired his speech and for the same reason he wore a cravat instead of a tie." Later in the evening, Milt Jackson, Percy Heath, and Connie Kay arrived with expatriates Kenny Clarke, the MJQ's original drummer, and Bud Powell and his wife Buttercup. Powell, who suffered from schizophrenia, was recuperating. "Their delight at meeting Miles was obvious," Morgan says. "They pummeled each other good naturedly, arms were thrown around shoulders. Bud stood slightly apart and looked sad. The conversation flowed and laughter came easily. Later the hum of conversation was stilled. Someone said, 'Bud's going to play,' in a kind of shocked half-whisper; there was Bud up on the stand with Pierre Michelot and Alan Levitt. No one had noticed him leave the circle around the bar. All talking ceased as Bud went into a fast *Nice Work If You Can Get It* which began to degenerate into chaos before the end of the first chorus. A kind of paralysis seemed to have seized the pianist's hands and the more he tried to fight his way free the more inaccurate became his fingering. Four choruses and it was all over. Bud stood up quickly, bowed, mopped his face with a handkerchief and began his uncertain walk back to the bar ... It was an age before Buttercup led her husband back to the silent circle of embarrassed musicians. Miles broke the tension by flinging a comforting arm around Bud's shoulders. 'You know, man, you shouldn't try to play when you're juiced like that.' Within a few minutes the room was normal." Later that night, around 3 a.m., Morgan and his friends met Davis again, "strolling along the pavement with Sinatra-like nonchalance." He was looking for his hotel, the name of which he had forgotten.

Back in New York at the end of the month, Davis re-formed the quintet with Coltrane as the tenor saxophonist. Davis recognized better than anyone the strength of the combination of talents he had put together, notwithstanding the extramusical problems. "I always liked Coltrane," he said a few years later. "When he was with me the first time, people used to tell me to fire him. They said he wasn't playing anything. They used to tell me to get rid of Philly Joe Jones. I know what I want though. I also didn't understand this talk of Coltrane being difficult to understand. What he does, for example, is to play five notes of a chord and then keep changing it around, trying to see how many different ways it can sound. It's like explaining something five different ways. And that sound of his is connected with what he's doing with chords at any given time." Davis was equally generous about Philly Joe Jones, whom many observers considered to be the root of the personal problems in the quintet. Davis was willing to ignore the hassles – up to a point – because of Jones's talent as a drummer. "Look, I wouldn't care if he came up on the bandstand in his BVD's and with one arm, just so long as he was there," he told Nat Hentoff, in a widely quoted statement. "He's got the fire I want. There's nothing more terrible than playing with a dull rhythm section. Jazz has got to have *that thing*. No, I don't know how you get that thing. You have to be born with it. You can't even buy it. If you could buy it, they'd have it at the next Newport Festival." (A later version of this statement, also from Hentoff, replaces the sentence mocking the Newport festival by these words: "You have it or you don't. And no critic can put it into any words. It speaks in the music. It speaks for itself.") The two men who thus posed the greatest threat to the stability of the quintet, Coltrane and Jones, were also its necessary foils musically, providing the intensity and power that counterbalanced the lyricism of the other voices, especially Davis's.

The quintet began a series of engagements in December 1956 that would take them across the country on a two-month road trip. The first stop was Philadelphia, the hometown of three of the sidemen, in early December. (Some tapes of the quintet's club date on Saturday 8 December apparently exist, but they have not yet been issued publicly.) They probably moved on to Chicago over the Christmas season, Davis's regular stop at that time of the year. In January, they moved on to a club called Jazz City in Los Angeles. While there, the rhythm section moonlighted by recording with the alto saxophonist Art Pepper on a Contemporary album released under the title *Art Pepper Meets the Rhythm Section*. Two-thirds of the rhythm section, Chambers and Jones, also made some recordings with an avant-garde group led by the french horn player John Graas, called *Jazz Lab 2*, for Decca. Philly Joe Jones's entrepreneurial instinct went beyond merely making extra money in the recording studios during his stay in Los Angeles. Sy Johnson, a composer and arranger who was then in Los Angeles studying law, attended several evenings of the quintet's performances and indulged his hobby of photography. "I shot pictures by available light with my Leica whenever I could get close to the bandstand," Johnson says. "That in itself was unheard of in the 50s, and when I made some prints, Philly Joe undertook to sell them to the customers."

The extended stay at Jazz City was broken by a two-week interval at the Blackhawk in San Francisco. While there, the members of the quintet often turned up at an after-hours club called the Streets of Paris. Jerry Dodgion, the alto saxophonist, was particularly interested in the music of John Coltrane, which he was hearing live for the first time at the Blackhawk, but he could never get

Coltrane to play after hours. Whenever he invited him onto the stand, Coltrane replied, "Not right now, I'd rather listen." "That's what he did," Dodgion says, "for three nights straight."

Back at Jazz City in Los Angeles, Sy Johnson was surprised to find that Davis began seeking him out. "Miles sat down at my table late one night and began to talk about the Leica he got in Germany, and how much he liked it. He said he had the clerk set the shutter speed and aperture at the store when he bought the camera, and hadn't changed them since." From that night until the end of the engagement, Davis used Johnson as a buffer between himself and the other fans. "He would motion me into the kitchen of Jazz City with a nod, usually on the first intermission, when the club was crowded with people who wanted to talk to him. He'd stand with his back to the kitchen door, talking about his Mercedes, other players, women, and pointedly ignoring musicians and fans who wanted to say hello. They would wait patiently or try to say something over his shoulder, and finally drift away. I remember Benny Carter in line once, and murderous glances at me from some of the younger black players."

Davis was developing various ploys, apparently, to shield himself from his fans, who were increasing in numbers. Most often, of course, he was simply not around – when his sidemen went to an after-hours club, he went somewhere else. But on many occasions it was impossible for him to hide, and then he had to find some other way of keeping people at the distance he seemed to require. As often as not, he chose ways that were construed as rudeness, as with Sy Johnson. Another way, observed by Ross Russell, could be construed as arrogance. "Once in St. Louis he was standing on a corner after an autographing appearance at a record store, surrounded by sycophants, talking in low, barely audible tones," Russell says. "Suddenly an old acquaintance came hurrying up like a lost puppy to shout out an enthusiastic greeting. Miles froze the man with a penetrating look. Realizing that he had committed a serious gaffe, one that might cost him his status and wreck his career in jazz, the other had the presence of mind to instantly withdraw and walk slowly around the block. He then approached the group from a new angle and stood at its edge for some time. Finally Miles' eyes met his and there was the briefest of nods. The other had been restored to grace, but it had been a very near thing."

The same kind of imperiousness also surfaces around this time in some of Davis's statements to the press, which were usually only made out of a sense of obligation upon his arrival in a city where he had an engagement. He kept such meetings short, when he put up with them at all, but often the reporter went away with a bona fide pronouncement on the state of the art in jazz. In one such pronouncement, Davis blasted the style of jazz associated with California at the time. "You know what's wrong with the music on the Coast?" he asked, and he supplied his own answer: "Smog!" He went on to declare, "I've heard a lot of bad music coming from the Coast. Some of the arrangements are good but they die because there are no soloists. You've got to have a good rhythm section and you have to have guys who fit together. Maybe the climate has something to do with the guys playing the way they do. I know it makes my eyes water." Pronouncements such as these fed Davis's reputation as a controversial figure now that he was squarely in the public eye. It was not as if he had altered his behavior noticeably in order to gain the new notoriety. As Jackie McLean had said, "Miles was arrogant when his heels didn't point in the same direction." The difference was not so much in anything that he did but in the number of observers that he now had whenever he did anything.

Complaints about Davis's stage manner grew until they became a kind of critical obbligato to the music he made. Davis, sagely, has usually paid no attention at all to the complaints and gone about his business of making music, but on a few occasions when the obbligato has threatened to drown out the music altogether he has spoken up about it. "Some critic that didn't have nothing else to do started this crap about I don't announce numbers, I don't look at the audience, I don't bow or talk to people, I walk off the stage, and all that," he told Alex Hailey in the interview for *Playboy*. "Look, man, all I am is a trumpet player. I can do one thing – play my horn – and that's what's at the bottom of the whole mess. I ain't no entertainer, and ain't trying to be one. I am one thing, a musician. Most of what's said about me is lies in the first place." Faced with the same charges when he arrived in England for a tour in 1960, Davis used the same defense, simply denying the charges outright. "I don't know anyone," he told one reporter, "who would turn his back on the audience." During that evening's performance, Davis played part of the concert, as always, with his back to the audience. Part of the time that he did not have his back to the audience, he was nowhere to be seen, having left the stage, as usual, during some of the others' solos.

A few times, he has answered the criticisms more plausibly. "Everything I do, I got a reason," he says. "The reason I don't announce numbers is because it's not until the last instant I decide what's maybe the best thing to play next. Besides, if people don't recognize a number when I play it, what difference does it make?" Of course it makes no difference at all, except that performances of jazz have traditionally been presented with all the trappings of popular entertainment rather than of serious symphonic music, including patter from the stage. The absence of the small talk jars some of the more hidebound fans and critics. But, as Chris Albertson says, "We don't, after all, expect Rostropovich or Casadesus to warm up their audiences with small talk, and Miles Davis is as serious about his music as were Brahms and Schubert." In his own defense, Davis continues: "Why I sometimes walk off the stand is because when it's somebody else's turn to solo, I ain't going to stand up there and be detracting from him. What am I going to stand up there *for*? I ain't no model, and I don't sing or dance, and I damn sure ain't no Uncle Tom just to be up there grinning. Sometimes I go over by the piano or the drums and listen to what they're doing. But if I don't want to do that, I go in the wings and listen to the whole band until it's my next turn for my horn."

The unwritten code at a jazz performance calls for a player to remain in place following his own solo and absorb himself in the music that follows. In removing himself from the stage, Davis breaks part of the code conspicuously, but he does not break it completely, for he does not simply detach himself from the music. Robert Altschuler, the publicity director for Columbia Records, says, "I have been with him on several occasions when he left the stage during a performance. He either crouches or ambles to the side of the audience, and you realize that he is deeply concentrating on everything that his musicians are playing – he is digging his own band, digging it in a way a Miles Davis fan would. He simply becomes part of his own audience." Davis adds: "Then they claim I ignore the audience while I'm playing. Man, when I'm working, I know the people are out there. But when I'm playing, I'm worrying about making my horn sound right ... When I'm working, I'm concentrating. I bet you if I was a doctor sewing on some son of a bitch's heart, they wouldn't want me to talk."

He draws a closer analogy with classical musicians and other jazz musicians – white ones. "The average jazz musician today, if he's making it, is just as trained as classical musicians," he points out. "You ever see anybody go up bugging the classical musicians when they are on the job and trying to work? Even in jazz – you look at the white bandleaders – if they don't want anybody messing with them when they are working, you don't hear anybody squawking. It's just if a Negro is involved that there's something wrong with him. My troubles started when I learned to play the trumpet and hadn't learned to dance." Whether or not the code differs for white and black musicians, no musician of either color has ever defied the code the way Davis has.

Davis's stage manner has contributed mightily to his public image as the solitary, defiant black man. But his demeanor seems to have a much homelier foundation. "Basically Miles is very shy, that's the whole thing," says Dizzy Gillespie. "You know, I know him probably better than he knows himself. I was talking to his daughter Cheryl in St. Louis, and I said, 'Did you know that your father is really a very bashful man?' and she said, 'Yeah, I've always known that, but nobody else can dig it; he puts up that front to cover up the shyness.'" Nat Hentoff agrees: "Miles's way of coping with shyness is to affect fierceness. 'Like all of us,' a musician who has known him for many years explains, 'Miles has only a certain amount of energy, and he finds it difficult to meet new people. Rather than subject himself to what is for him a tiring discomfort, he tries to create so forbidding an image of himself that he won't even be bothered.'" In spite

Philly Joe Jones and Miles Davis (Raeburn Flerage, courtesy of *Down Beat*)

Miles Davis and Gil Evans (Columbia Records, courtesy of *Down Beat*)

John Coltrane and Thelonious Monk at the Five Spot, with drummer Shadow Wilson (Don Schlitten, courtesy of *Down Beat*)

of all the print his stage manner has engendered and all the psychologizing it has sparked, the best comment on it – perhaps the only one that need ever have been made – comes from Davis himself, from the mellower viewpoint of 1981. "I'm not being vain or anything, but that's the way I am," he said. "I play for myself and I play for musicians."

In April 1957, a little more than a month after the quintet had returned to New York from their West Coast stay, the drug problems of Coltrane and Jones were again causing professional problems that Davis found intolerable. He fired both of them. This time there was a note of finality to the firings, especially in Coltrane's case. Thelonious Monk, according to J.C. Thomas, walked in on the firing of Coltrane when he went backstage at the Café Bohemia between sets one night. As he approached the musicians' room, he saw Davis slap Coltrane and then punch him in the stomach. Coltrane, characteristically, took it passively, but Monk was outraged. "As much saxophone as you play," he shouted at Coltrane, "you don't have to take that. Why don't you come play with me?" Not long after, Coltrane joined Monk's quartet at the Five Spot and Sonny Rollins again took up the tenor saxophone chair in the Miles Davis Quintet.

All of Davis's problems that spring with the quintet's discipline and with his own public relations were more than counterbalanced by a musical project with Gil Evans that fired his enthusiasm more than anything he had worked on since his first project with Evans nine years earlier. This one was not altogether unlike that one, involving orchestral elements such as french horns and tubas in a distinctive jazz setting, but there could be no comparison in scope. The new project was far removed from the youthful experiments conceived in the grimy 55th Street basement. It involved a nineteen-piece orchestra, and it was backed by the corporate weight of Columbia Records. Planning by Davis and Evans had started in the fall of 1956, probably inspired at least initially by Davis's role as the featured soloist with the Brass Ensemble of the Jazz and Classical Music Society, but the final result went well beyond the concerns of the third stream movement, melding the styles of Davis and Evans so forcibly and so compatibly as to create an invidivuality all its own. Several critics immediately drew parallels with Duke Ellington's consummate orchestrations of the early 1940s. André Hodeir proclaimed, "After so many years the Ellington spirit has come into its own again, with a persuasive power it has never known since Ellington's own masterpieces of 1940. For the first time since then we are presented with a consistent approach to the full jazz band." The details are as follows:

Miles Davis with Gil Evans and His Orchestra
Miles Davis, flugelhorn; Bernie Glow, Ernie Royal, Louis Mucci, Taft Jordan, John Carisi, tpt; Frank Rehak, Jimmy Cleveland, Joe Bennett, tbn; Tom Mitchell, bass tbn; Willie Ruff, Tony Miranda or Jim Buffington, frh; Bill Barber, tba; Lee Konitz, as;

Danny Bank, bass clnt; Romeo Penque, Sid Cooper or Edwin Caine, flt, clnt; Paul Chambers, b; Arthur Taylor, dms; Gil Evans, arr, cond. New York, 6 May 1957
The Maids of Cadiz; The Duke
(both on Columbia CL 1041)

Same personnel and place, 10 May 1957
My Ship; Miles Ahead
(both issued as above)

Same personnel and place, 23 May 1957
New Rhumba; Blues for Pablo; Springsville
(all issued as above)

Same personnel and place, 27 May 1957
I Don't Wanna Be Kissed; The Meaning of the Blues; Lament
(all issued as above)

Davis and Evans's selection of melodies is astonishingly eclectic, ranging from compositions by jazz players with Brubeck's *The Duke*, Jamal's *New Rhumba*, John Carisi's *Springsville*, J.J. Johnson's *Lament*, Evans's own *Blues for Pablo*, and Davis's *Miles Ahead* (now credited also to Evans as co-composer), to theater songs with Delibes's *The Maids of Cadiz* and Kurt Weill's *My Ship*, and taking in even the trite pop ditty *I Don't Wanna Be Kissed*. Yet all these diverse sources come together in Evans's orchestrations as if they are brief movements in an extended suite, one melody giving way to the next almost imperceptibly in a linking orchestral passage. The themes of the ten identifiable melodies are, as Max Harrison puts it, "a series of miniature concertos for Davis," but the effect of Evans's orchestration is to turn them into "a continuous aural fresco whose connective resonance and authority gain strength with each addition."

So cohesive is the music, which was released under the title *Miles Ahead* (CL 1041) in the fall of 1957 and has never been out of print since, that there has been relatively little critical comment on the individual melodies themselves. The arranger Quincy Jones, speaking of Evans's ingenious arrangement of Brubeck's *The Duke*, says, "Gil put Duke into *The Duke*."

Hodeir, who wrote the original notes for the album, later singled out Evans's *Blues for Pablo*: "Gil Evans can write music, there is no doubt about that! I know of no other jazzman who can compare with him as a harmonizer and orchestrator, but he may not have quite come into his own as a composer. His own *Blues for Pablo* is the weakest piece on a record on which all the other themes chosen are unusually fine; but then perhaps it only seems so weak because it does not go with the rest of the pieces. It was originally meant to be recorded by Hal McKusick's small ensemble, and Evans was probably wrong to include it in a set where it was bound to be out of place." And yet, obviously, *Blues for Pablo*'s provenance is no odder than any of the other themes, which come from all over the place. In his original notes for Columbia, Hodeir was enthusiastic about its arrangement, singling it out for the way in which "Evans breaks away here at a few points from the four-bar unit of construction and thus destroys the symmetrical form of the traditional blues, which is something that very few arrangers dare to do."

Hodeir's point about Evans's apparent weakness as a composer, which his criticism of *Blues for Pablo* seems to be in service of, raises the difficult issue of just where to draw the line between composing on the one hand and orchestrating and arranging on the other. Evans crosses that line and recrosses it freely in this music. As Whitney Balliett says, "Evans continually 'improvises' on the melodies in the ensemble passages and rarely presents them anywhere in straightforward fashion." His arrangements are, in a sense, compositions in their own right, as Charles Fox points out: "He establishes, one might say, a periphery of sound which acts as a container for his ideas, across which melodic lines are stretched, and which is disturbed by rhythmic devices. What he is striving for, perhaps, is a musical equivalent to James Joyce's theory of epiphanies, the awareness of an entire context of association and meaning existing within one clear image or (in the case of music) within one pattern or web of sound. It is ... action that has frozen into sound. The preoccupation may be reflected in the fact that Evans' work has largely been upon the plane of re-composition, the conversion of an existing tune into what is virtually a new and often much more exciting orchestral reality. It is, after all, a perfectly legitimate method of composing, analogous to the way a European composer uses folk-tunes or devises variations upon a predecessor's theme."

There is an extraordinary congruity between Evans's ensemble voice and Davis's solo voice, making a fusion in which it is almost impossible to separate the division of labor. "Gil has a way of voicing chords and using notes like nobody else," Davis says. "We work together great because he writes the way I'd like to write. In fact, years ago I used to do arrangements and give them to him to look over. He'd tell me my charts were too cluttered up, that I could get the same effect using fewer notes. Finally, I decided the best thing to do was let Gil do the writing. I'd just get together with him – sometimes not even in person, just on the phone – and outline what I wanted. And he always has such a complete feeling for what I mean that it comes out sounding exactly like what I had in mind." He put it more succinctly when he said, "I wouldn't have no other arranger but Gil Evans – we couldn't be much closer if he was my brother."

In turn, Evans lauds Davis's ability to exploit the tonal palette of the ensembles. "A big part of Miles's creative gift is the creation of sound," he says. "He arrived at a time when, because of the innovations of modern jazz, all new players had to find their own sound in relation to the new modes of expression. Miles, for example, couldn't play like Louis Armstrong because that sound would interfere with his thoughts. Miles had to start with almost no sound and then develop one as he went along – a sound suitable for the ideas he wanted to express. Finally, Miles had his own basic sound, which any player must develop. But many players keep this sound more or less constant. Any variation in their work comes in the actual selection of notes, their harmonic patterns, and their rhythmic usages. Miles, however, is aware of his complete surroundings and takes advantage of the wide range of sound possibilities that exist even in one's own basic sound. He can, in other words, create a particular sound for the existing context. The quality of a certain chord, its tension or lack of tension, can cause him to create a sound appropriate to it. He can put his own substance, his own flesh on a note and then put that note exactly where it belongs."

The collaboration could hardly have been more compatible. Even Davis conceded that he liked it. "I don't keep any of my records," he once said. "I can't stand to hear any of them after I've made them. The only ones I really like are the ones I just made with Gil Evans [*Miles Ahead*], the one I made with J.J. on by Blue Note date about four years ago [probably 20 April 1953], and a date I did with Charlie Parker."

Davis's own approval of the collaboration has been almost unanimously seconded. *Miles Ahead* was acclaimed immediately as a masterpiece of jazz orchestration, and it has held its place ever since. One of the few comments that was even mildly negative came in the *New Yorker* from Whitney Balliett, who conceded that the recording was "the most adventurous effort of its kind in a decade" and that "the playing throughout is impeccable," but found that, for his taste, the music lacked fiber, especially Davis's solos. "All the solos are by Davis, whose instrument sounds fogbound," he said. "Buried in all this port and velvet is Evans's revolutionary use, for such a large group, of structure, dynamics and harmony." He felt that the technical innovations were not sustaining enough in their own right: "There is, in fact, too much port and velvet, and Davis, a discreet, glancing performer, backslides in these surroundings into a moony, saccharine, and – in *My Ship* – downright dirge-like approach. The result is some of the coolest jazz ever uttered." Balliett's metaphor "port and velvet" was not unopposed, as Max Harrison picked it up and countered with a few metaphors of his own. "The scoring's effect is often that of light imprisoned in a bright mineral cave, its refinement such that at times the music flickers deliciously between existence and non-existence," Harrison wrote. "No matter how involved the textures, though, it is always possible to discover unifying factors as an altogether remarkable ear is in control, ruthlessly – and almost completely – eliminating clichés. Complaints that these Davis/Evans collaborations produced unrhythmic music were due to faulty hearing, and the widely quoted metaphorical description of the textures as 'port and velvet' is inept. Despite its richness, the orchestral fabric is constantly on the move, horizontally and vertically; it is unfortunate that some listeners cannot hear a music's pulse unless it is stated as a series of loud bangs."

Hodeir had some reservations, which he stated in an article published some time after he wrote the enthusiastic notes for the album. "I, for my part, wish that Evans's musical idiom took greater account of the blues spirit, and we may be sure that he himself would have liked to see his arrangements rehearsed as often as necessary and even performed publicly a few times before they were recorded. Now and then there are still a few rough spots, if not actual flaws, to be heard; a few solos were post-recorded – never a desirable procedure in any case – and it would have been well to replace one or two musicians (the flutist, for example, whose phrasing in *The Duke* shows that he simply did not understand the score). But even the sum of these reservations is of little weight compared with the amount of imagination, inspiration and sensibility that went into a record which, with all its faults, constitutes a remarkably successful achievement."

The release of *Miles Ahead* was greeted enthusiastically not only by reviewers but also by virtually all musicians and fans. Dizzy Gillespie, a musician far removed from port and velvet in most matters, said, "*Miles Ahead* is the greatest. I wore my first copy out inside three weeks so I went to Miles and said, 'Give me another copy of that dam record.' I tell you, everybody should own that album." For Tommy Flanagan, cryptically, "the *Miles Ahead* album was almost a copy of what Ahmad recorded with a trio." Art Pepper comments: "His [Evans's] writing for Miles on *Miles Ahead* to me was the most perfect thing I've ever heard done for a soloist with a band. Gil's understanding of Miles was perfect." And of Davis, Pepper adds: "His development has been phenomenal. I've listened to *Miles Ahead* by the hour and his warmth, choice of notes, and beautiful simplicity has touched my very soul." Few jazz recordings have met with, and sustained, the level of praise of this collaboration between Davis and Evans, which was the first of a series of splendid joint projects in these peak years.

While the *Miles Ahead* sessions were being recorded in the Columbia studios, Davis was again working at the Café Bohemia with his quintet, which now included Sonny Rollins and Arthur Taylor in place of John Coltrane and Philly Joe Jones. The new men seemed, at least on paper, fully adequate replacements, and both were at the peaks of their careers. Taylor was a steady, sensitive drummer, in some demand for recording sessions with pickup groups on such labels as Prestige and Riverside. Rollins had made a remarkable series of recordings for

Prestige in 1956, and the appearance of any new LP in his name was an event of more than passing interest. Nevertheless, the new men seemed to fit uneasily into the quintet, especially Rollins, and Davis never took this band into the recording studios, presumably because he reckoned that they had not gelled sufficiently. The only documents that survive are tapes of performances, of which a Saturday broadcast from the Bohemia has been issued on record. The details are as follows:

Miles Davis Quintet
Miles Davis, tpt; Sonny Rollins, ts; Red Garland, pno; Paul Chambers, b; Arthur Taylor, dms. Café Bohemia, New York, 13 July 1957
Four [*Four Squared*]; *Bye Bye Blackbird*; *It Never Entered My Mind*; *Walkin'* [*Roy's Nappin' Now*]
(all on Chakra 100)
Four Squared and *Roy's Nappin' Now* are the titles under which these tracks are listed on the record. Rollins does not play on *It Never Entered My Mind*.

All these titles except *Four* are incomplete. On *It Never Entered My Mind*, in the same Jamalesque arrangement that Coltrane sat out when it was first recorded for Prestige just as Rollins sits it out here, the missing material seems only to be the first four bars or so of Davis's introduction. The other two titles, however, are mere fragments, with *Walkin'* ending abruptly during Davis's opening solo, and *Bye Bye Blackbird* cut off early in Rollins's intriguing solo which sounds like Ben Webster playing bebop, after Davis has already soloed. On *Four*, the one complete performance, some idea of the developing group dynamics comes through, as Davis plays a cool, floating solo over the solid rhythm (in which Taylor's bass drum is overrecorded) and Rollins enters playing a hotter, busier solo after him. It affords a taste of what might have developed, but it is too little to do much more than whet one's appetite.

Later in the month the quintet appeared at the Great South Bay Jazz Festival in Great River, Long Island. Whitney Balliett, covering the festival for the *New Yorker*, mentions them only in passing, noting the presence of Rollins and Chambers among the sidemen and stating that their Sunday afternoon set "was notable for a languishing rendition by Davis playing a tightly muted trumpet, of *It Never Entered My Mind*."

Coltrane and the other members of the Thelonious Monk Quartet, which also included Wilbur Ware on bass and Shadow Wilson on drums, had taken up residence at the Five Spot for the summer, and they were suddenly the talk of the town. Monk had been unduly neglected for years, but a string of adventuresome recordings for Riverside was attracting attention to him, which would continue to grow over the next few years until he finally gained a measure of the respect with the fans that he had always been accorded by other musicians. The Five Spot engagement, which was eventually extended into the fall, made a perfect forum for his quartet, and Coltrane quickly developed into an ideal interpreter of Monk's beautifully quirky, idiosyncratic compositions. The Five Spot was packed throughout the summer, and one frequent visitor was Miles Davis. Joe Goldberg described the scene on one of those summer evenings: "A small, slim, graceful man, impeccably dressed in the continental style that was then a few years ahead of its time, leaned casually against the bar smoking a cigarette and listening to the music that Monk was making with one of his former employees. Everyone else in the audience – which was made up of collegians who at the time probably did not know who he was – was busy watching Miles Davis watch Monk." Davis could not help but notice that Coltrane was not only showing up regularly with Monk, and more or less on time (which was the best one could ever hope for from Monk, let alone Coltrane), but also that he was growing more confident with his restless, searching music as he conquered Monk's harmonic labrynths.

In September, Rollins quit the Miles Davis Quintet to form his own group. The time was ripe for him: his best recorded work had been in the company of rhythm trios rather than larger groups, playing his own repertoire. With the quintet, he had carried on playing Coltrane's parts in Davis's repertoire, and the comparisons of his playing with Coltrane's cropped up inevitably in the jazz press, leading to a lot of opinion-mongering which did neither saxophonist any good and fabricating a rivalry between the two men in which neither of them participated. For the rest of his career Rollins would work as a leader, often with just bass and drums accompanying him, and would continue to spell himself off with long periods of inactivity. To replace Rollins, Davis chose Bobby Jaspar, the Belgian flutist and tenor saxophonist who had been playing with J.J. Johnson off and on during the preceding year. Jaspar, at thirty-one the same age as Davis, had led his own quintet in France for several years, playing in a standard neo-bop framework in places such as Club St. Germain in Paris. A member of a patrician family that immersed itself in music and art, Jaspar had earned a university degree in chemistry before turning to music as a profession. In Paris, he met the expatriate singer Blossom Dearie, whom he married in 1955. The next year they moved to Greenwich Village, and Jaspar gained favorable notices wherever he played. His competence was hailed by the American jazz press as evidence that the present generation of European jazzmen had truly broken the barrier that until then had marked jazz as a music that could only be well played by Americans.

There were other changes in the quintet. Philly Joe Jones was back, replacing Art Taylor, but Jones's old running mate Red Garland was replaced by Tommy Flanagan. Paul Chambers remained on bass. Jaspar's tenure in the quintet lasted only about six weeks, and he may have been thought of by Davis as a temporary replacement from the beginning. No taped performances by this short-lived combination have come to light.

Whatever the conditions of Jaspar's appointment to the quintet, his term was inevitably limited by the availability of Julian (Cannonball) Adderley. Davis had begun talking to Adderley about the possibility of his joining the quintet during the summer, when Rollins was still his reed player. Adderley was then fronting his own quintet with his brother Nat Adderley, the cornetist, and had been doing so for over a year, since returning to New York after his summer of rave notices in 1955. Although he had quickly been accepted into the front rank of jazz musicians, he remained dissatisfied with the drawing power of his band, then earning $1,000 a week. "Nobody was really making it except for Miles, Chico [Hamilton] and Brubeck," he says. "I had gotten an offer from Dizzy to go with his small band. I was opposite Miles at the Bohemia, told him I was going to join Dizzy, and Miles asked me why I didn't join him. I told him he'd never asked me." It was not an opportunity that a shrewd assessor of talent such as Davis was likely to pass up. "Well, Miles kept talking to me for two or three months to come with him," Adderley says, "and when I finally decided to cut loose in October '57, I joined Miles. I figured I could learn more than with Dizzy. Not that Dizzy isn't a good teacher, but he played more commercially than Miles. Thank goodness I made the move that I did." He made no secret of his original motive in joining Davis. "I wanted to get the benefit of Miles's exposure rather than Miles's musical thing," he told Ira Gitler, but it was not long before the musical advantages outweighed the commercial advantages. "It was a commercial move but I noticed that Miles could do some things naturally that I had difficulty doing, and so we started finding out why, and it was easy, you know, more or less," he said. The main lesson showed in Adderley's ability to handle harmonics, and it served his purposes perfectly to learn his lessons while playing for larger audiences. For Davis, Adderley's presence restored to the quintet another perfect foil for his own more delicate, introverted sound. It was a pairing that could hardly be improved – except, perhaps, by the return of Coltrane.

The new quintet with Adderley made their debut in October in a concert package known as Jazz for Moderns which made a circuit around the United States and closed with a concert at Carnegie Hall the next month. Besides the Davis Quintet, the lineup included Helen Merrill, Gerry Mulligan's quartet, the Chico Hamilton Quintet, and two pop-jazz groups, the Australian Jazz Quintet and George Shearing's Sextet; at the Carnegie Hall finale, Shearing's group were replaced by an all-star swing group led by Lionel Hampton. Whitney Balliett's report singles out the new quintet for providing some of the few highlights of the evening: "The only indications that there was any life on-stage occurred during Hampton's performance, and during two of the four numbers by Davis's group, which included Julian Adderley on alto saxophone, Tommy Flanagan, Paul Chambers, and Philly Joe Jones. In *Walkin'* and *Night in Tunisia*, Davis, often a moody, hesitant performer, let loose a couple of belling solos that were spelled by some incisive drumming by Jones."

As soon as the tour ended, Davis traveled alone to Paris, where he was booked to play as a guest soloist for three weeks and to provide the soundtrack for a film entitled *Ascenseur pour l'échafaud* (released in Britain as *Lift to the Scaffold* and in North America as *Frantic*), directed by Louis Malle and starring Jeanne Moreau. French filmmakers had been experimenting with soundtracks by American jazz musicians for a few years and director Roger Vadim had come up with an impressive one earlier in the year when he had the Modern Jazz Quartet play John Lewis's score for his film *Sait-on jamais* (literally 'one never knows,' but released in English-speaking countries as *No Sun in Venice*). The experiments would continue for the next few years, notably with the Jazz Messengers' 1958 soundtrack for *Des Femmes disparaissent* (in English, *Girls Vanish*), directed by Edouard Molinaro. American filmmakers wasted little time catching on to the French trend, and for a few years at the end of the 1950s jazz musicians found themselves in some demand in the American film industry as well. Jazz figured prominently in, for example, Robert Wise's *I Want to Live*, a 1958 film with a soundtrack written by Johnny Mandel and featuring Gerry Mulligan, Art Farmer, Shelly Manne, and most of the other prominent West Coast players, and *Anatomy of a Murder*, a 1959 film by Otto Preminger with a soundtrack by Duke Ellington. Television went along too, notably in the soundtracks for hard-boiled private detectives such as *Peter Gunn*, an NBC series that began in 1958 with Henry Mancini's big band score played by the likes of Pete Candoli, Milt Bernhart, and Larry Bunker. The use of jazz and jazz-derived soundtracks became so predominant that jazz came to seem like the natural backdrop for high-speed chases, mass mayhem, and cold-blooded murder, because the films for which jazz players were enlisted were uniformly violent.

In *Ascenseur pour l'échafaud*, Davis's score accompanies a character named Julien as he murders his lover's husband and then is inadvertently trapped in an elevator while making his escape; it then accompanies a thief who steals Julien's car, goes joy-riding, and ends up killing a man with Julien's gun, with the result that Julien is arrested for the murder he did not commit after he emerges from the elevator the next morning. Fortunately, much of the music has a life of its own quite apart from the film which called it forth. The details are as follows:

Miles Davis Ensemble
Miles Davis, tpt; Barney Wilen, ts (on three tracks only); René Urtreger, pno; Pierre Michelot, b; Kenny Clarke, dms. Paris, 4 December 1957

Générique; L'assassinat de Carala; Sur l'autoroute; Julien dans l'ascenseur; Florence dans les Champs-Elysées; Dîner au motel; Evasion de Julien; Visite du vigile; Au bar du Petit Bac; Chez le photographe du motel
(all on Columbia CL 1268; reissued on Mercury [Netherlands] 6444 701)
Wilen is heard only on *Sur l'autoroute, Florence sur les Champs-Elysées,* and *Au bar du Petit Bac; Evasion de Julien* is a bass solo by Michelot; *Visite du vigile* is a duet by Michelot and Clarke; Urtreger does not play on these two tracks or on *Sur l'autoroute* and *Dîner au motel.*

Two of Davis's sidemen for the soundtrack recording, Urtreger and Michelot, were members of his backup trio on the tour with Lester Young and the Modern Jazz Quartet a little more than a year before. They are supplemented now by Bernard Wilen, known as Barney, a twenty-year-old tenor saxophonist already highly regarded in Paris, and by Kenny Clarke, whose uptempo brushwork figures prominently in the score.

The soundtrack preserves the edited version of the music recorded for it, keyed to the scenes of the film, rather than the masters from which the soundtrack was selected. Several of the titles are fragments, ending abruptly. The editing does some disservice to Wilen, who barely begins his solo on *Florence sur les Champs-Elysées* before he is cut off. But the tracks that end abruptly were probably never complete takes in the conventional sense, because of Davis's manner of scoring the film. Rather than devising a set of themes keyed to certain characters and elaborating them as the plot thickens – the normal compositional framework for film scores and one that John Lewis followed so ingeniously for *Sait-on jamais* that he ended up writing a suite that could be played thereafter in the MJQ's concerts – Davis viewed the film sequences for which he was to provide music, set the tempos and deployed the sidemen as he felt the scene demanded, and then improvised the soundtrack as the film sequence was replayed. It is a technique for film scoring that had probably never been used since the days of the silent films, when pianists and organists, Fats Waller among them, played live accompaniment to the films at every showing in the theater.

The entire soundtrack for *Ascenseur pour l'échafaud* was conceived and recorded in one sitting at a Paris radio studio after the day's broadcasting was finished. It is a tour de force in the art of improvising, and it shows as well as almost anything else Davis recorded the power and control he had over his art. Several of his solos have the unity of composed themes. On *Générique* and *Chez le photographe du motel,* his trumpet is distorted by the heavy-handed use of echo, but *Florence sur les Champs-Elysées* is a lush blues, *Au bar du Petit Bac* is a handsome simultaneous improvisation by Davis and Wilen (one of the simultaneous solo lines, probably Davis's, may have been added later by overdubbing), and *Dîner au motel*, is a muted trumpet solo accompanied by bass and drums that ranks with any of Davis's ballad solos for Prestige. On *Dîner au motel*, Davis's bell-like tone has an unusual wave motion, later explained as the result of a piece of loose skin from his chapped lip lodging in the mouthpiece. In spite of the stimulus for this music in the service of another medium, there is a great deal of it that deserves to be heard. The soundtrack recording won the Prix Louis Delluc the next year.

The soundtrack recording, though it forms the most interesting document to come out of Davis's Paris visit, was almost incidental in his busy three-week schedule. He started with a concert at the Olympia Theatre and continued with a three week stint at Club St. Germain, all with the same pickup band he used for the soundtrack recording. Michael Zwerin, the sometime trombone player who almost by accident played with Davis's nonet at the Royal Roost in 1948, was in Paris at the time "finding" himself (as he put it), and he kept tabs on some of Davis's public appearances. He was at the Olympia the first night, his sense of anticipation about the concert made all the keener by the fact that Urtreger's wife had spread the word among Zwerin's circle of friends that Davis had not yet shown up in Paris. "The Olympia Theatre was sold out that night, but by curtain time Miles' whereabouts were still a mystery," Zwerin recalled. "Finally the curtain went up, revealing Barney Wilen, René Urtreger, Pierre Michelot, and Kenny Clarke all set up. They started playing *Walkin'* and sounded fine. But no Miles Davis. Barney took a tenor solo, and as he was finishing, backing away from the microphone, Miles appeared from the wings and arrived at the mike without breaking stride, just in time to start playing – strong. It was an entrance worthy of Nijinsky" – or at least of Charlie Parker, who had occasionally choreographed similar entrances for himself in his younger days. Zwerin adds, "If his choreography was good, his playing was perfect that night."

Davis's Paris performances exposed a new audience to his stage manner and inevitably stirred up the controversy anew. André Hodeir, in his review of the concert, came down firmly on Davis's side. "He will not make concessions," Hodeir wrote. "When Miles cuts short the applause and moves efficiently from number to number, it's not from contempt of the public. On the contrary, he restores to the public its dignity by refusing it any concession in terms of choice of program or 'showmanship' on the part of himself and his musicians." Hodeir's point that Davis imposes his own recalcitrance upon his whole band proved true not only in Paris but elsewhere, somewhat to the chagrin of several American critics, who predicted that Davis's hiring of Julian Adderley, an effervescent showman with his own hands, was done partly as a concession to audience rapport. At no time did Adderley address Davis's audiences as long as he was in his band.

Zwerin also showed up in the audience at Club St. Germain nightly during Davis's first week there and occasionally during the other two weeks. One incident reported by Zwerin suggests that Davis was less than fully satisfied with his sidemen, although his displeasure did not seem to show in the music they made together. Zwerin says, "Once Wilen came over to me when I was sitting at the bar and said, 'You wouldn't believe what Miles said to me in the middle of my solo on the last tune. He said, 'Man, why don't you stop playing those awful notes?'" Zwerin was probably not nearly as surprised as Wilen expected him to be. After all, the only words Davis had said to him in Paris until then were, "Mike, you're putting on weight." Zwerin recalls that Wilen was not greatly upset by the insult: "Barney was a hot, confident young player at that time and, fortunately for him, was not inclined to paranoia. He thought it very funny and had just gone on playing." Davis's evaluation of his sidemen also became clear when the band made a television broadcast for Paris-TV, which is preserved on tape in some private collections. On Tadd Dameron's *Lady Bird*, Davis takes one and a half choruses for himself and allots Kenny Clarke one chorus alternating with the ensemble, but Wilen and Urtreger are given only half a chorus each.

Davis returned to New York in early December, and his quintet, with Adderley on saxophone, were installed again at the Café Bohemia, just as the Thelonious Monk Quartet with John Coltrane were finally ending their long engagement at the Five Spot. The tenor saxophonist Rocky Boyd had drifted onto the New York scene – he would play in Davis's quintet very briefly in 1962 before disappearing from jazz – and seems to have been acting as Davis's dogsbody, because Davis sent him over to the Five Spot with a message for Coltrane. He was to tell Coltrane that "a big, fat girl" from Boston (the description is C.O. Simpkins's), the thirteen- or fourteen-year-old daughter of a man who had hosted Davis and Coltrane when they played at Storyville in Boston, had arrived in New York in search of Coltrane. When Boyd passed along the message, Coltrane hid in the kitchen of the Five Spot and refused to appear on stage. Davis then had Boyd phone the girl's parents to come and get her.

The early progress of the Davis quintet with Adderley has not been documented on records or even apparently on private tapes of their performances. There is no reason whatever for suspecting that it was anything less than scintillating, given the talents of Davis and Adderley individually and their rapport with one another, all of which is abundantly documented starting just a few months later, in the spring of 1958. Still, Davis was restless, and the source of his disquiet had nothing whatever to do with Adderley's playing in the quintet but had something to do with Coltrane, whose work with Monk he had monitored carefully, however casual he tried to make it seem. Davis knew, as everyone else would soon know, that Coltrane had what Davis once called *"that thing,"* the indefinable spirit that "speaks in the music." And he wanted it back in his band, where he could hear it every night and nurture it and take his own sustenance from it. Late in December, as Monk's quartet were wrapping up their engagement, Davis phoned Coltrane and said, "I want you back." And Coltrane paused a few seconds, and said, "All right." The Miles Davis Quintet thus gave way to the Miles Davis Sextet, perhaps the finest small band in the history of jazz.

8

Fran Dance
1958–9

If you place a guy in a spot where he has to do something else, other than what he can do, he can do *that*. He's got to have something that challenges his imagination, far above what he thinks he's going to play, and what it might lead into, and then above *that*, so he won't be fighting when things change. That's what I tell all my musicians; I tell them be ready to play what you know and play *above* what you know. Anything might happen above what you've been used to playing – you're ready to get into that, and above that, and take that out.   Miles Davis

John Coltrane rejoined Miles Davis's band late in December 1957, in time to play the Chicago engagement that was the customary stop for Davis's groups during the Christmas season. Red Garland also returned, and Philly Joe Jones had been reinstated earlier, and so at first the new sextet were just the original quintet with Julian Adderley added. But the new group were considerably more than the sum of their old parts, and the multiplier in the equation was Davis's search for a musical foundation that would unburden his music of what he had come to consider mere clutter. That search found a ready exponent in Coltrane, who also, surprisingly, became its most articulate spokesman in an article published in *Down Beat* in 1960. "On returning, ... I found Miles in the midst of another stage of his musical development," Coltrane explained. "There was one time in his past that he devoted to multichorded structures. He was interested in chords for their own sake. But now it seemed he was moving in the opposite direction to the use of fewer and fewer chord changes in songs. He used tunes with free-flowing lines and chordal direction. This approach allowed the soloist a choice of playing chordally (vertically) or melodically (horizontally)."

Davis's new development was gradual rather than revolutionary, the natural outgrowth of the direction he had begun with the harmonic clarity of the nonet, the use of space triggered by Ahmad Jamal, and the reductions found in Gil

Evans's orchestrations. It was also, according to the jazz educator Jerry Coker, a theoretical response to the maturation of any good improviser. Coker put it this way: "Imagine a student who has heard many recorded solos and knows all the possible chord scales and progressions. Perhaps he can even play indefinitely without playing a 'wrong' note, but he still has many choices to make in each phrase he decides to play, and chances are he isn't ready to make them. Some of the 'right' notes are 'righter' than others, and only observation and experience will eventually enable him to make better choices, and fewer choices too, since good improvisers usually acquire a sense for economy (deleting unnecessary pitches) as they mature. Miles Davis is today perhaps the most skillful in playing economically – stressing fewer, but well-chosen, notes and also making better use of rests, a very potent musical device."

The great improvisers in jazz, like the best artists in any other medium, have always learned to do what Coker here praises Davis for doing, manipulating the formal framework of their art in ways that often startle their audiences and always earn the admiration of lesser artists. Cecil Payne, the baritone saxophonist in Dizzy Gillespie's big band, watched it happening among the bop musicians. "Dizzy and Bird would be playing six or seven choruses – and every one would be different – and creating different sounds," Payne remembers. "See, Bird and Dizzy and Miles too developed to the stage where they could actually 'play.' What they were playing was free. You have groups that play 'free' music now, like the 'space' music or something like that. They're playing free. Actually Bird and Dizzy were playing free too. In their minds they were playing free. They didn't have any hangup about this chord or that chord. In their minds they were playing anything they could play, freely. But they were playing correct. I mean they were playing according to what the song they were playing to implied." The main difference between the great improvisers of the past and Miles Davis at this point in his development is that Davis took the next logical step and rationalized the harmonic basis for what Payne calls "playing free," and built it into the group dynamics of his band.

In Coltrane, Davis's explorations found not only a champion but also an adventuresome alter ego. "In fact, due to the direct and free-flowing lines in his music," Coltrane says in his *Down Beat* apologia, "I found it easy to apply the harmonic ideas that I had. I could stack up chords – say, on a C^7, I sometimes superimposed on an E^7, up to an F^7, down to an F. That way, I could play three chords on one. But on the other hand, if I wanted to, I could play melodically. Miles's music gave me plenty of freedom. It's a beautiful approach." As Coltrane settled into the new approach, he showed less and less tendency to play what he calls "melodically" and became a resolute experimentalist. "I was trying for a sweeping sound," he explained. "I started experimenting because I was striving for more individual development. I even tried long, rapid lines that Ira Gitler termed 'sheets of sound' at the time. But actually I was beginning to apply the three-on-one chord approach, and at that time the tendency was to play the entire scale of each chord. Therefore they were usually played fast and sometimes sounded like glisses. I found that there were a certain number of chord progressions to play in a given time, and sometimes what I played didn't work out in eighth notes, sixteenth notes, or triplets. I had to put the notes in uneven groups like fives and sevens in order to get them all in. I thought in groups of notes, not of one note at a time. I tried to place these groups on the accents and emphasize the strong beats – maybe on 2 here and on 4 over at the end. I would set up the line and drop groups of notes – a long line with accents dropped as I moved along."

Davis's music was the catalyst for Coltrane's conception, but he had been given a boost in that direction when he was playing in Thelonious Monk's band, and it came about because of Monk's uncanny intuition about harmony. Coltrane said, "Monk was one of the first to show me how to make two or three notes at a time on tenor. It's done by false fingerings and adjusting your lip. If everything goes right, you can get triads. Monk just looked at my horn and 'felt' the mechanics of what had to be done to get this effect." Naturally, Coltrane's experiments had their pitfalls. One of them came about because of the group accompaniment. "Sometimes what I was doing clashed harmonically with the piano – especially if the pianist wasn't familiar with what I was doing – so a lot of time I just strolled with bass and drums," Coltrane says. Another came about because audiences were not ready for what he was trying to accomplish. An English critic complained that his playing showed "a surfeit of passion at the expense of subtlety," and other listeners savaged his playing as incoherent, chaotic, illiterate, or worse.

Coltrane persisted, mainly because his work was understood and appreciated by the audience he considered most important – the other members of the sextet, especially Davis, who told Coltrane's critics, "He's been working on those arpeggios and playing chords that lead into chords, playing them fifty different ways and playing them all at once. He's beginning to leave more space except when he gets nervous." Davis also gave Coltrane the playing time he needed to pursue his experiments, which frequently led him to play at what might have appeared to other leaders to be unconscionable length. Adderley reports, "Once in a while, Miles might say, 'Why did you play so long, man?' and John would say, 'It took that long to get it all in.'"

At least as important to his development as the supportive setting of the sextet was the self-discipline he finally imposed on his private life. Coltrane was obsessive, a trait seen not only in his addictions to narcotics and alcohol but in many smaller ways as well, such as his gorging himself with sweets even when his teeth – not the least important physical equipment for a saxophonist – were constantly aching and rotting. But before Davis invited him back into the band in December 1957, he brought at least the most debilitating of his addictions into some semblance of control – apparently less than complete abstinence – through an obscure mystical experience, the details of which remain unknown although its effects are clear. In the notes for his album *A Love Supreme* (Impulse A-77), recorded in December 1964, Coltrane wrote: "During the year 1957, I experienced, by the grace of God, a spiritual awakening which was to lead me to a richer, fuller, more productive life. At that time, in gratitude, I humbly asked to be given the means and privilege to make others happy through music. I feel it has been granted through His grace." In the delicate balance he sought between sensuality and spirituality, Coltrane became a touchstone for the artistic temper of the time. John Clellon Holmes, trying hard to explain the Beat Generation to an eager public in 1958, said, "Nothing seems to satisfy or interest it but extremes, which, if they have included the criminality of narcotics, have also included the sanctity of monasteries." More than any individual directly associated with the Beat Generation, Coltrane embodied those extremes.

Through his conversion, the silent, diffident Coltrane found the conviction and determination to pursue his own star even against the refractory opposition of a large part of the jazz audience. He pursued it, as he did all the other things in his life, single-mindedly, and his long, turbulent solos with the sextet became part of a superb spectacle. On watching the sextet in action, Joe Goldberg remarks, "One speculated on how much of some men's personalities are released only in music: the quiet, pleasant Coltrane played fierce, slashing lines in direct opposition to the gentle, delicate phrases of the often blunt, arrogant Miles." The contrast in their musical and personal styles did not symbolize antipathy between the two men and was probably the source of their mutual respect. When Coltrane was listening to Davis soloing, Teo Macero remembers, "He'd smile like a little boy when Miles would play something he liked." Still, the path that Coltrane was taking, which would soon make him one of the supreme improvisers in the history of jazz, was a tortuous one, which could only be explored through what Hentoff calls "the sheer will to creativity of Coltrane on his better nights."

He was a notoriously late developer, and even then a painfully slow one. "With Miles, it took me around two and a half years, I think, before it started developing, taking the shape that it was going to take," he told Frank Kofsky. Davis was essential not only because he provided the musical approach that set it in motion but also because he was the most influential figure, the 'boss,' in jazz. "It was important for Coltrane to work with Miles," Hentoff says. "For one thing, of course, he received attention, with the Davis imprimatur legitimizing Coltrane for some of those who up to that point had considered Trane either incompetent or a charlatan or both. Miles, it was agreed by nearly all, could not and would not be conned musically. If he hired the man, the man must have something to say. That imprimatur also gave Coltrane confidence. Feeling set upon by the critics, he had passed a far more severe test by being considered worthy of a place in the Miles Davis band." Jimmy Heath, the tenor saxophonist, goes a step further: "At the time Coltrane was playing with Miles he worked just about every week and he practised more than anybody I ever met. So, if he didn't play better than anyone else he would have to be a dumb man. I think anybody who was a pretty good musician, who had the opportunities that Trane had, would get better."

With the striking dialectic of Davis and Coltrane in the sextet, Julian Adderley's presence might seem to be diminished, but there were few performances by the sextet that did not send the audience away buzzing about Adderley's prowess as well as, and often with flattering comparisons to, his front-line mates. Adderley's career after he left the sextet in 1959 has perhaps made it easier to underestimate his abilities, especially by contrast to Coltrane's career in the same period. Adderley's talent emerged as precociously as Coltrane's did methodically. He seems to have had his musical gifts intact from the moment he arrived in New York to play professionally, and in the fifteen years of his career after he left the sextet until his death in 1975 he seemed to many observers to be merely replaying what he had played before. His reach seldom – some might say never – exceeded his grasp, and he worked the rest of his career as a respected and popular, but not widely honored, figure. The shape that his career thus took, from an early creative peak that was consistently maintained but hardly rejuvenated afterward, is not at all unusual even for the major figures in jazz. It is much more commonplace than the multiple peaks of creativity in careers such as Duke Ellington's and Miles Davis's, or the fitful rise to brilliance in a career such as Coltrane's, and one can easily name great players – Louis Armstrong, Thelonious Monk, and Dizzy Gillespie among them – who achieved the heights of their abilities early and spent the rest of their careers at best approximating the powers of their early years.

One difference between Adderley and the others whose careers took a similar shape, apart from the obvious fact that his peak was not as salient historically as Armstrong's or Gillespie's or Monk's, is that while all of them, Adderley included, passed through long periods when their contributions were taken for granted, the others all eventually received their due in a thorough and broadly based revaluation that revived enthusiasm for their early music and elicited interest in their current music. Adderley, in contrast, died quite suddenly just before his forty-seventh birthday, and he had not yet received the revaluation he deserved. He was simply taken for granted at the time of his death and remains so today, notwithstanding the evidence of his brilliance on recordings not only with the sextet but also notably as the featured soloist in orchestrations by Gil Evans (reissued as Blue Note LA461-H2) and Ernie Wilkins (Riverside 377) and with numerous smaller combinations on Riverside and other labels. What the evidence shows, for those who bother to listen, is a remarkably facile, blues-oriented melodist with one of the richest, most expressive tones ever heard on an alto saxophone, an instrument that has had more than its share of articulate players in jazz but very few who rank with Adderley.

Adderley's period with the Miles Davis Sextet marked a time of some growth in his playing. "Miles taught me about chords, and Coltrane did too," he said later. "Coltrane knows more about chords than anyone. John knows exactly what he's doing; he's gone into the melodic aspect of chords. He may go 'out of the chord,' so-called, but not out of the pattern he's got in his mind." Occasionally Adderley's playing in the sextet reveals his debt to Coltrane, prompting Zita Carno, in an early article praising Coltrane's style, to remark: "Cannonball Adderley is by now classic proof that you can't play with Coltrane without being influenced by him." Adderley knew what Coltrane was doing harmonically beside him and shared in its inception to some extent, just as he expanded his range and his originality as a melodic player by learning from Davis on the other side. But most of all, finding himself in what might have become an intolerable position by playing nightly beside two of the greatest innovators in modern jazz, Adderley had the good sense to stake out his own ground and make a personal contribution to the music of the sextet that is hardly less central to it than the contributions of his more celebrated colleagues.

The first recordings made after the sextet were assembled were not by the working group but by a pickup quintet nominally led by Adderley with Davis as the second horn. They were made for Blue Note, with Davis participating by a special arrangement with Columbia, perhaps as a concession in order to release Adderley for future recordings with Davis on Columbia. The Blue Note session probably reflects the music made by Davis's quintet at the close of 1957, when Adderley was the only other front-line player. The details are as follows:

Julian Adderley and the All Stars
Miles Davis, tpt (except on *Dancing in the Dark*); Julian Adderley, as; Hank Jones, pno; Sam Jones, b; Art Blakey, dms. New York, 9 March 1958
Autumn Leaves; Somethin' Else; One for Daddy-o; Love for Sale; Dancing in the Dark (all on Blue Note 81595)

That Adderley was the leader of this session in name only is abundantly clear in the music that resulted, both in the allotment of solo space and in the choice of tunes. Davis states the melody alone on *Autumn Leaves* and *Love for Sale*, and he and Hank Jones, a superior accompanist who plays beautifully throughout this session, fashion a long, apparently extemporaneous movement at the end of

Autumn Leaves that ignores Adderley altogether. Adderley gets a more equal share on the two blues numbers, Davis's *Somethin' Else* and Nat Adderley's funky *One for Daddy-o*, and he finally gets the spotlight on *Dancing in the Dark*, in which he is the only solo voice. *Autumn Leaves*, a popular hit of the year before in an instrumental version featuring endless arpeggios by the cocktail pianist Roger Williams, gets an ornate arrangement in the style of Ahmad Jamal; Davis told Leonard Feather, who wrote the notes for the LP, "I got the idea for this treatment of *Autumn Leaves* listening to him." *Dancing in the Dark*, although it is Adderley's showcase, was also selected by Davis. "I made him play this because I remembered hearing Sarah Vaughan do it like this," Davis told Feather. Even on *One for Daddy-o*, the one number distinctly foreign to Davis's repertoire though it features a neat abstraction of the blues by Davis as well as a gorgeous traditional blues solo by Adderley, it is Davis's voice that breaks in at the end calling to Alfred Lion, the producer, in the control booth, "Is that what you wanted, Alfred?" Davis was clearly in charge, and even though this recording stands slightly apart from the magnificent music he made with his working band and with Gil Evans in these years, it nevertheless shares many of its best qualities.

The sextet finally made their recording debut in early April, in two recording sessions that left no doubt that Davis had assembled a great band. The details are as follows:

Miles Davis Sextet
Miles Davis, tpt; Julian Adderley, as; John Coltrane, ts; Red Garland, pno; Paul Chambers, b; Philly Joe Jones, dms. New York, 2 April 1958
Two Bass Hit; Billy Boy (rhythm trio only); *Straight No Chaser; Milestones*
(all on Columbia CL 1193)

Same personnel but omit Garland on *Sid's Ahead*; Davis plays piano and trumpet; same place; 3 April 1958
Dr. Jekyll [*Dr. Jackle*]; *Sid's Ahead* [*Walkin'*]
(both issued as above)
Dr. Jekyll is a misspelling (*pace* Robert Louis Stevenson) of Jackie McLean's title, *Dr. Jackle*.

With the expanded instrumentation from the quintet to the sextet, Davis makes strategic use of the instrumental combinations. Red Garland's role as a solo voice almost disappears, except for the trio track, *Billy Boy*, the American folk song that Ahmad Jamal rearranged into a swinging vehicle for piano players. Garland's version was only one of dozens being played at the time, which later prompted Jamal to complain, "I was stupid enough not to copyright the arrangement, and then Oscar Peterson did it, Red Garland did it, Ramsey Lewis did it, everybody did it, and I didn't get paid for it." Garland's only other solo turn is on *Straight No Chaser*, and everywhere else the space conventionally taken by the piano player is given to Paul Chambers on bass, who solos on every track except *Two Bass Hit* and *Milestones*.

The unusual emphasis on bass rather than piano as a solo voice rankled Garland, who walked out of the studio during the warm-up for *Sid's Ahead*, leaving Davis to double on piano and trumpet on the recorded version of this track. But the emphasis not only reflects Davis's displeasure with Garland; it also, more positively, reflects his delight in his bassist's development. Soon after these recordings were made, Davis told Nat Hentoff, "Paul Chambers ... has started to play a new way whereby he can solo and accompany himself at the same time – by using space well." How that polydexterity might translate into performance is hard to guess, but Chambers was given ample opportunity to show his wares both arco and pizzicato.

The solo orders take some unconventional turns, too. Adderley is the first soloist on *Milestones* and *Straight No Chaser*, followed by Davis and then by Coltrane, an order that exploits the stylistic contrasts among the three horns magnificently and also preserves the dynamics of the superseded quintet by allowing Coltrane to charge in behind Davis. On *Sid's Ahead* and *Two Bass Hit*, Coltrane opens the solo round, with Davis again interposed between the two reedmen on the former but not soloing at all on the latter. On *Dr. Jackle*, Davis solos first, exercising the traditional privilege of the leader in jazz bands, but the round of solos turns out to be another innovation, as Davis shares his final three twelve-bar choruses with Philly Joe Jones, and then Adderley and Coltrane trade choruses in their turn.

Probably a more challenging problem for Davis than alloting solo space for the expanded band was working out the ensembles. Only *Dr. Jackle* seems cluttered in the ensembles, and that impression probably comes not from the lines played by the horns so much as the quick tempo at which they are asked to play it, which prevents them from giving full value to each note. Otherwise the arrangements are very effective, even on the complex *Two Bass Hit*, where each horn takes charge of a counter-theme in a glorious small-band adaptation of John Lewis's composition. Equally noteworthy are Adderley's lead on the ensemble of *Straight No Chaser*, with the other horns playing tight dissonances under him, and the startling fanfare of *Milestones* from which Davis's translucent tone rises at the bridge.

But despite all the attention to solo orders and ensembles that went into these recordings, they succeed only because of the improvisations that sustain the moods of the ensembles and cohere both individually and collectively. Benny

Golson, who reviewed this album for *Jazz Review*, remarks that in *Two Bass Hit* "Coltrane enters into his solo moaning, screaming, squeezing, and seemingly projecting his very soul through the bell of the horn," and he adds: "I feel that this man is definitely blazing a new musical trail." Perhaps the best evidence of that new trail, in retrospect, occurs on *Straight No Chaser*, where Coltrane stacks up chords in breathless runs of eighth-notes and sixteenth-notes, a solo that makes a textbook demonstration of the "three-on-one" approach he discussed in his *Down Beat* article.

Golson and most other reviewers noted that Adderley's playing here shows Coltrane's influence, but that influence is more apparent than real at the point where most listeners think they hear it. In *Dr. Jackle*, the seams between the alternating choruses by the two players are almost indistinguishable, and there is momentary confusion on a first listening as to where Adderley leaves off and Coltrane begins, and vice versa. But the confusion does not seem to be caused by similarity of phrasing so much as by similarity of tone, as Adderley's full, rich tone on the alto almost seems to be aping Coltrane's tenor in the transitions. Coltrane's influence comes across more clearly on Adderley's solo on *Sid's Ahead*, a series of sweeping glissandi worthy of Coltrane at his best. The two reedmen are balanced by Davis's sure, spare trumpet, characterized by Golson as "a sound psychological approach in that he never plays too much." Golson adds, "He leaves me, always, wanting to hear more."

The power of the sextet is thus clearly demonstrated in their first recordings. Apart from *Dr. Jackle*'s flawed ensembles, each composition crystallizes various aspects of that power as a self-contained miniature. The intricate, ingenious arrangement of *Two Bass Hit*, which is worthy of Gil Evans, was almost certainly put together with only a few gestures by way of instruction for the reallocation of parts. For Ian Carr, the British trumpet player, it is *Straight No Chaser* that wins the accolades. "With Miles Davis, everything *counts*," Carr told Lee Underwood. "Everything must count, and every note must be accountable. If there's no reason for its being there, then it shouldn't be there. And he swings. For me, he swings more than any other trumpet player, more than almost anybody – just listen to his solo on *Straight No Chaser* on the *Milestones* album. No other trumpet player swings like that." Benny Golson points out, among the more arcane delights of this music, that Red Garland ends his solo on *Straight No Chaser* with "a beautiful harmonization of Miles's original solo on *Now's the Time*." He states flatly that *Straight No Chaser* is "the best track on the album."

At least as many people would choose *Milestones* as the best track. This new composition by Davis, which recycles the title he first used in 1947 – it was obviously too good a title to simply abandon – but otherwise bears no resemblance whatever to the earlier composition, contains a remarkable unity. Michel Legrand remarks, "I love the way they approach this melody – everything is for the melody; the chords are very simple, like a carpet on which all the music is based. In other words, the whole thing is not based on complexity, but on simplicity and purity." (It is juvenile, of course, to speak of any work of art as 'perfect,' but it is somehow irresistible to come right out and say – at least parenthetically – that *Milestones* seems to be a perfect jazz performance. Its components are a simple, memorable, highly original melody, followed by three individualistic explorations of the theme, each one as memorable as the theme itself, by Adderley, Davis, and Coltrane, all buoyed by the brash but sensitive rhythm section, and then the simple, unforgettable melody again. There is nothing more, it seems to me, that one might hope for or ask for in a jazz performance.)

Amazingly, *Milestones*, which appears to be simple, highly accessible, and above all swinging, also represents a structural innovation of great consequence not only for the music of Miles Davis but also for jazz in general. It is Davis's first completely successful composition based on scales rather than a repeated chord structure. James Lincoln Collier, in his history of jazz, describes its structure this way: "The ability to place his notes in unexpected places is Davis's strongest virtue. It colors his work everywhere. His masterwork in this respect is his *Milestones* ... It is made up of the simplest sort of eight-bar melody – little more than the segment of a scale, in fact – which is repeated and then followed by a bridge made out of a related eight-bar theme, also repeated. After the bridge, the theme is played once more. The point of it all lies in the bridge, where the rhythm goes into partial suspension. Miles stretches this passage out with notes falling farther and farther behind their proper places. Indeed, in the reprise of the theme at the end of the record he stretches the bridge so far out that he cannot fit it all in and has to cut it short." Collier adds: "It is built not on chord changes but on modes ... For Davis, who was already making a point of simplicity, they were a perfect vehicle. He was not the first to see what could be done with them, but he was the one who brought the idea to fruition. *Milestones* uses one mode on the main theme, then switches to a second mode for the bridge."

Collier correctly points out that Davis was not the first jazz player to promote a modal foundation for jazz compositions – that distinction probably belongs to George Russell. During one of Russell's enforced absences from jazz activity due to tuberculosis, he formalized his thinking in a dissertation called *The Lydian Concept of Tonal Organization*, first published in 1953 and required reading ever since for jazz scholars, but well before that Russell had tried to use modes in his writing. The first composition in jazz to use a modal organization is probably Russell's introduction to the Dizzy Gillespie orchestra's *Cubano Be*. "Diz had written a sketch which was mostly *Cubano Be*," Russell says. "His sketch was what later turned out to be the section of the piece called *Cubano Be* except that I wrote a long introduction to that which was at the time modal. I mean it wasn't based on any chords, which was an innovation in jazz because the modal period didn't really begin to happen until Miles popularized it in 1959. So that piece was written in 1947, and the whole concept of my introduction was modal, and then Dizzy's theme came in and we performed it."

Davis's contribution was not in discovering the innovation but in making it work. He was fully aware of the breakthrough he was making in *Milestones*, as its title indicates, and he described its advantages to Nat Hentoff at the time. "When you go this way," he said, "you can go on forever. You don't have to worry about changes and you can do more with the line. It becomes a challenge to see how melodically inventive you are. When you're based on chords, you know at the end of 32 bars that the chords have run out and there's nothing to do but repeat what you've just done – with variations. I think a movement in jazz is beginning away from the conventional string of chords, and a return to emphasis on melodic rather than harmonic variation. There will be fewer chords but infinite possibilities as to what to do with them." This was the innovation that Coltrane described when he spoke of Davis's "new stage of jazz development" and of his compositions with "free-flowing lines and chordal direction." Hentoff draws the conclusion from his discussion with Davis that "Davis thus predicts the development of both Coltrane and, to a lesser degree, the more extreme, more melodic, Ornette Coleman."

For the ordinary jazz listener, Davis's modal breakthrough is meaningful not for its formal musical properties or for its historical importance but for the gain in expression it allows the musicians, which in the hands of individuals of the caliber of Davis, Coltrane, and Adderley is heard and felt powerfully. In *Milestones* and in the other modal compositions that follow it in Davis's repertoire, there is no feeling of self-conscious experimentation and no implication that these musicians are revising the structural foundations of their art. In this regard, Davis contrasts strikingly with the proponents of third stream music and even with the humbler innovators in his old nonet, and also with the avant-garde or free form musicians soon to follow, all of whom spent more than a little energy talking about the uniqueness of their contributions rather than making their music.

After the *Milestones* recording session, Red Garland was replaced as the sextet's piano player. In the next few years, Garland would occasionally return to the group as a fill-in but his tenure as Davis's regular pianist, which had lasted two and a half years with a few interruptions, was over. Davis was not replacing Garland as a disciplinary measure but because he had found a new man who was already deeply involved in modal composition and improvisation. His name was Bill Evans, and few jazz musicians have ever presented so unprepossessing an appearance. Evans was pallid, with owlish glasses and lank hair that, even in the close-cropped Ivy League fashion he favored at the time, became disheveled in the drafts he caused when he turned his head. He was painfully shy and taciturn, and his personality seemed to be expressed perfectly in his posture at the piano, which was S-shaped, with his narrow shoulders hunched and his nose almost touching the keyboard. He joined the sextet with characteristic trepidation. He later said, "I felt the group to be composed of superhumans."

Among all of Davis's discoveries, none better demonstrates his prescience than Evans. Probably only Coltrane had a greater long-term impact on the music. Like Coltrane, Evans was a late-bloomer. Born and raised in Plainfield, New Jersey, a commuter community for New York, in 1929, he was still virtually unknown when he joined the sextet, although he had led a trio on a Riverside recording in 1956. Although he was raised within hailing distance of New York, his personal roots seemed to be oriented more toward the southeast: his parents retired to Florida, his older brother, a sometime musician who had allowed Evans to play piano in his semi-professional dance band as a teenager, settled in Baton Rouge, Louisiana, and Evans himself earned an undergraduate degree in music from Southeastern Louisiana College, about a two-hour drive from New Orleans.

After college, Evans held down jobs in several bands, starting in 1950 with the ill-starred Herbie Fields, with whom Davis had made his own recording debut five years earlier. While Evans's talent stirred almost no interest among jazz fans, other musicians often caught on to the values of his understated ruminations. It was the guitarist Mundell Lowe, with whom Evans had played in Louisiana, who first recommended him to Orrin Keepnews of Riverside Records. Evans kept up his music studies as much as time allowed while he was playing professionally, and he was enrolled at New York's Mannes School of Music when he joined Davis.

Evans's academic work brought him into close contact with George Russell, at first as a student but later as a colleague in the modal developments. Russell was almost as unknown as Evans in the late 1950s, but he began to get a few opportunities as the third stream movement crested, and he included Evans in them. Most notable was Russell's commission for the Brandeis University festival in 1957, entitled *All about Rosie*, which provided solo space for Evans, as did Russell's best-known recorded work of that period, *New York, N.Y.* (Decca DL 9216), recorded while Evans was a member of Davis's sextet. Through Russell and Gunther Schuller, Evans was also loosely associated as a sessional instructor with the School of Jazz in Lenox, Massachusetts, where the other two were on the faculty. If Russell was little better known to the general public than Evans, there was still a quantum difference in their status in New York's jazz community, where Russell's credentials went back several years, and it was almost certainly through Russell that Evans came to Miles Davis's attention.

Both Evans and Davis benefited. To the sextet, Evans brought a solo voice capable of holding its own with the three great hornmen, making it perhaps the greatest aggregation of soloists ever to play side by side in a working band. He also served as a third important researcher, with Davis and Coltrane, in the nightly nonverbal seminars for extending jazz's modal foundations. Davis's enthusiasm was, for him, effusive. "Boy, I've sure learned a lot from Bill Evans," he told Hentoff soon after Evans joined the band. "He plays the piano the way it should be played. He plays all kinds of scales, can play in 5/4, and all kinds of fantastic things. There's such a difference between him and Red Garland, whom I also like a lot. Red carries the rhythm but Bill underplays, and I like that better." Hentoff played Davis a recording by Oscar Peterson, and his critical comments crystalized his predilections about music in general and piano-playing in particular. "It's much prettier if you can get into it and hear the chord weaving in and out like Bill Evans and Red Garland could do – instead of being so heavy. Oscar is jazzy; he jazzes up the tune. And he sure has devices, like certain scale patterns, that he plays all the time." Davis continued: "Does he swing hard? I don't know what they mean when they say 'swing hard' anyway. Nearly everything he plays, he plays with the same degree of force. He leaves no holes for the rhythm section." Asked to compare Evans with Ahmad Jamal, Davis said, "Bill plays a little like that but he sounds wild when he does – all those little scales." From Davis this is high praise indeed, the first time in at least four years that he had found a piano player he could compare favorably to Jamal. To cap it all, he went on to say, "If I could play like Ahmad and Bill Evans combined with one hand, they could take the other off."

If Evans's effect on Davis was considerable, then Davis's effect on Evans was inestimable. By the close of 1958, at the end of his eight-month tenure as the sextet's pianist, Evans was recognized in *Down Beat*'s international survey of critics as the new star on piano, and the next year he began anew his career as the leader of a piano trio that would bring him two decades of critical and popular success matched by very few musicians in the history of jazz.

Evans had been with the sextet about five weeks when they broadcast from the Café Bohemia one Saturday in May, which is the first documentation of his work in the group. For some unknown reason, Julian Adderley was absent for the broadcast, reducing the group to a quintet. The details are as follows:

Miles Davis Quintet
Miles Davis, tpt; John Coltrane, ts; Bill Evans, pno; Paul Chambers, b; Philly Joe Jones, dms. Café Bohemia, New York, 17 May 1958
Four [*Four Plus One More*] (Chakra CH 100); *Bye Bye Blackbird* (unissued); *Walkin'* (unissued)

Only *Four* has been issued, and it is the least interesting of the three titles. It is another run-through of Davis's favorite set opener, with solos by Davis and Coltrane only. Coltrane's solo sounds awkward, and Davis re-enters playing the theme rather suddenly, as if cutting off Coltrane's attempt to begin another chorus. Evans is inconspicuous. On the other two titles, Evans solos after Davis and Coltrane mainly using soft-spoken single note lines with lots of rests. His playing is tentative, and on *Bye Bye Blackbird* it inevitably suffers by comparison with Red Garland's showy accompaniments in all the extant versions; *Bye Bye Blackbird* was a tune that Garland obviously loved to play. However, Davis's playing, probably in response to Evans's presence, finds him toying with the melody, a distinct departure from his usual verbatim statement; he interpolates snatches of Leonard Bernstein's *Maria* in two of his choruses, and in *Walkin'* as well as in *Bye Bye Blackbird* he sustains many of his choruses by repeating short phrases for as long as eight bars at a time. Apart from the slight changes in Davis's style, no particular concession is made to accommodate the new member of the band. The same three titles had also been called in his last broadcast from the Bohemia ten months earlier, when Sonny Rollins was a member of the quintet. The absence of *Milestones* and the other new entries in the repertoire seems a lost opportunity, but it might be explained by the absence of Adderley, whose presence in the ensembles was essential.

The drug problems among the sidemen apparently continued. "In a way, I suppose, I was a kind of stabilizing influence on the band," Adderley said later. "Two of the men he had – fine musicians – weren't exactly on time or dependable." Finally, in May, Philly Joe Jones left the band and Davis replaced him with Jimmy Cobb, a disciple of Jones who had been the drummer in Adderley's quintet before he broke it up to go with Davis. In letting Jones go after more than two and a half years, Davis knew that he was giving up Jones's extra, ineffable quality, which made him the most respected drummer of the day. Cobb was excellent, and he did most of the things that Jones could do on the drums, so that even expert listeners have sometimes been unable to identify which one of them is playing on some of the more obscure tapes from this period, but no one could pretend that Jimmy Cobb had whatever it was that Davis had called, speaking of Jones's drumming, "that *thing*." Because of the stature he had earned working for Davis, Jones could form his own band almost immediately and have it booked into Birdland and other major clubs, often with Red Garland playing piano for him. For Cobb, replacing the top drummer added pressure wherever the sextet played, but Cobb, a mature and sensible twenty-nine-year-old, worried more about sounding right than about taking on the ghost of Philly Joe. He was given a boost, perhaps unexpected, by Davis, who fended off the inevitable questions about his drummers with some tact. "Jimmy makes me play in a different way from Philly," he told a British reporter. "Everyone's got their own way of playing. Philly gets some things out of me that Jimmy doesn't but it's the same the other way. I play with the rhythm section."

Still, the two changes in the sextet's personnel in April and May forced some changes in emphasis. Adderley recalls that Davis's instinct was to play more ballads. "Especially when he started to use Bill Evans, Miles changed his style from very hard to a softer approach," he said. "Bill was brilliant in other areas, but he couldn't make the real hard things come off. Then Miles started writing new things and doing some of Ahmad's tunes. When Philly Joe left the band, Miles at first thought Jimmy Cobb wasn't exciting on fast tempos, and so we did less of those." The new emphasis was realized brilliantly in the first recording session by the sextet with Evans and Cobb, which took place just a few weeks after Cobb joined:

Miles Davis Sextet
Miles Davis, tpt; Julian Adderley, as (except on *Stella by Starlight*); John Coltrane, ts; Bill Evans, pno; Paul Chambers, b; Jimmy Cobb, dms. New York, 26 May 1958
Green Dolphin Street; Fran Dance; Stella by Starlight; Love for Sale
(first three titles on Columbia CL 1268; *Green Dolphin Street* and *Stella by Starlight* reissued [1973] on C32025; *Love for Sale* first issued 1975, reissued [1977] on JP 13811 and [1979] on 36278)
Fran Dance was identified as *Put Your Little Foot Right out* on the liner of Columbia CL 1268 but as *Fran Dance* on the label; subsequent recordings of the same composition identify it as *Fran Dance*.

The first three titles were released almost immediately as one side of an LP coupled with Davis's soundtrack for *Ascenseur pour l'échafaud* and won an immediate popular response with their delicate lyricism but intense swing.

This rare combination of elements carries over less thoroughly onto the fourth title, because *Love for Sale* was simply a head arrangement at a faster tempo designed to give the musicians a chance to cut loose after working through the tight, controlled arrangements of the other pieces. Evans told Sy Johnson, who wrote the liner notes for its belated release in 1975: "Paul Chambers and Jimmy Cobb were getting edgy having to hold back, and wanted to cook on something. Miles just turned and said *Love For Sale*, and kicked it off." The result is a straightforward romp in 4/4 time featuring long solos, without any of the ornaments Adderley and Davis added to it in their Blue Note recording just ten weeks earlier. Evans's solo is a percussive essay with several tricks in the time, but all the others are just ebullient ad libs. Presumably the existence of the same title on the Blue Note recording led Columbia to withhold its release for seventeen years, but the two versions have little in common. The Columbia version also has little in common with the spirit and the form of the other three titles recorded on the same day, which are all thoughtful ballads.

Green Dolphin Street, best known in the annals of popular music because it became a hit after it was rejected for the background score of the 1947 movie by the same title starring Lana Turner and Van Heflin, ranks among the great ballad performances in jazz. Paul Chambers carries the entire arrangement by alternating a static eight-bar bass figure with eight bars of walking bass, creating successive currents of tension and release. Each of the soloists – Davis, Coltrane, Adderley, and Evans, in that order – must then cope with the alternating pulse in his own way. This tune was suggested by Adderley, and it is one of those rare discoveries that Ahmad Jamal then picked up from Davis's band rather than vice versa. But Jamal was not the only player who picked it up; Jimmy Heath recalls, "When Miles Davis started playing *Green Dolphin Street* everybody started playing it." For a while, it was as familiar in jazz clubs as *Salt Peanuts* had been ten years earlier.

Stella by Starlight gets a reverential, perhaps melodramatic, treatment, with Davis and Coltrane singing their roles as if performing an aria. The romanticism is blatant but not altogether ineffective, and this tune also became a favorite with jazz players.

The third piece, Davis's original *Fran Dance*, is based on a novelty dance number entitled *Put Your Little Foot Right out* which enjoined an earlier generation of Americans to form a circle on the dance floor and place one foot or the other in or out of the circle. Anyone old enough to remember the origin of *Fran Dance* might well have to face it with a supercilious grin, but fortunately few of Davis's listeners seemed to remember it and the tune was accepted in the form in which Davis presents it, as a haunting, romantic ballad. As such, it bears almost no resemblance to the original in mood, tone, or tempo, and little resemblance in melody, a fact that apparently occurred to Davis and his Columbia producers only after the notes for the original release were already printed, where it is identified by the novelty title.

The transformation of the source material into Davis's composition prompted Martin Williams to say, "Miles Davis, after all, can undertake some unspeakably mawkish material as *Some Day My Prince Will Come*, *Put Your Little Foot Right In* [sic] (which he calls *Fran Dance*), or *Spring is Here* and make it palatable by his intense involvement as he recomposes the melodies," and from that, Williams concludes: "In repertory, as in other obvious respects, Miles Davis's music often represents the triumph of an innate artistic sensibility over middlebrow taste." Williams's conclusion does not necessarily follow, of course. The banality of the lyrics or the dance steps associated with a particular melody does not in itself mean that the melody is also banal. Musicologists are just beginning to discover that American popular song has often obscured its artistry behind marketability, and most listeners can readily think of beautiful melodies with stupid lyrics. On at least one occasion, the transformation of a song has gone the other way, when Charlie Parker's *Now's the Time* was fitted with a lyric to become the boneheaded novelty dance called *The Hucklebuck*. By Williams's reasoning, whatever survives of Parker in *The Hucklebuck* must be mawkish, but clearly it is only what is added on to Parker that is mawkish, as Williams would no doubt agree. The appropriate conclusion, then, about Davis's ability at recomposition is not necessarily that it allows him to triumph over his "middlebrow taste" but that it reveals his ability to discern musical values beneath surfaces of such banality that most listeners miss them entirely.

Ironically, Davis's next recording venture was designed as an exercise in middlebrow taste. The record companies had discovered in the mid-1950s an untapped market for something they called mood music, an indefinable mélange somewhere between light classics and Hollywood production numbers. The original hit albums in the field, marketed by Capitol Records under the name of the television comedian Jackie Gleason and sometimes featuring the smooth cornet of Bobby Hackett, were apparently intended as boudoir music for the bourgeoisie, but when the marketing analysts discovered that the records were being played at reveille as well as at taps, and in the bathroom and kitchen as well as the bedroom, the race was on to supply a yawning populace with insipid soundtracks to accompany its most mundane activities. Into the gap rushed André Kostelanetz, Mantovani, Ray Conniff, and dozens of even less interesting orchestrators, with music not only to love by but also to eat by, drink by, and sleep by.

In 1957 Columbia imported the young Parisian arranger Michel Legrand to make a series of mood albums. The manager in charge of Legrand's projects may not have known that in addition to his successes as a songwriter and soundtrack arranger he was also a jazz piano player and an avid jazz buff. Certainly Legrand did nothing to tip his interest in jazz when he put together commercial albums with the titles *I Love Paris*, *Holiday in Rome*, *Vienna Holiday*, *Castles in Spain*, *Bonjour Paris*, and *Legrand in Rio*, all of which proved insipid enough to garner their share of the market and establish Legrand's name in the field. As his next excursion in mood music, he prevailed upon his producers at Columbia to let him make an album of jazz classics under the title *Legrand Jazz*. For the album, he enlisted a handful of good jazzmen, including Davis, Coltrane, Evans, and Chambers from the sextet. The details are as follows:

Michel Legrand and His Orchestra
Miles Davis, tpt; Phil Woods, as (except on *Django*); John Coltrane, ts (except on *Django*); Jerome Richardson, bass clnt (except on *Django*); Herbie Mann, flt; Betty

Glamann, harp; Eddie Costa, vib; Barry Galbraith, gtr; Bill Evans, pno; Paul Chambers,
b; Kenny Dennis, dms; Michel Legrand, arr, cond. New York, 25 June 1958
Wild Man Blues; Round Midnight; Jitterbug Waltz; Django
(all on Columbia 1250; reissued on CBS [French] 62 637)
Davis does not play on the remaining titles of *Legrand Jazz* (Columbia 1250).

Legrand's concept was to embellish the familiar jazz melodies and the improvisations in a framework of orchestral textures, and he succeeds nicely. His writing
makes particularly interesting and unusual use – at least for jazz – of the vibraphone in the ensemble, where it functions almost exclusively as a rhythm instrument. Evans is prominent in the introduction to Fats Waller's *Jitterbug Waltz*, in
which he and Davis, Coltrane, Herbie Mann, and Phil Woods all play full
choruses. On *Round Midnight*, Davis states the melody except for the first
bridge, which is taken by Mann, and he solos throughout, playing many of the
same phrases as he did in his quintet's performance of Gil Evans's arrangement.
Django is also given over to Davis almost exclusively, as he first plays obbligatos
around John Lewis's beautiful theme, stated by the guitar, harp, and vibraphone,
and then as he solos over the backdrop provided by that same combination and by
Bill Evans.

For Legrand, meeting these musicians on their own ground proved to be a
bit daunting. "I loved the way Miles Davis and John Coltrane played," he told
J.C. Thomas, "but I was also a bit afraid. I wondered how they would react to
my arrangements. Miles didn't say anything, but John asked me, 'How do you
want me to play my solo?' I was amazed. All I could say was, 'John, play
exactly the way you feel after you listen to what's happening around you.'
When it came time for him to solo, he integrated himself thoroughly into my
arrangements without sacrificing one note of his own conception." Legrand's
point also holds for Davis, and as a result, while this music is slight it cannot
be dismissed as uninteresting. Legrand drew on the individualism of his musicians as well as on his stockpile of mood music devices to make a listenable
middle ground.

The session with Legrand began a busy summer of work for Davis. The main
event was the recording of George Gershwin's music for *Porgy and Bess* with Gil
Evans's arrangements, an undertaking that would require four separate studio
sessions with a large orchestra in July and August. At the same time the sextet
were booked in and around New York as well. One engagement, inevitably, took
the band to Newport, Rhode Island, for the Friday concert at the fourth annual
Newport Jazz Festival. It proved, if nothing else, that even this band could have
an ordinary outing. Their performance was recorded by Columbia, and four of the
six titles they played were released as one side of an LP six years later. The details
are as follows:

Miles Davis Sextet
Miles Davis, tpt; Julian Adderley, as; John Coltrane, ts; Bill Evans, pno; Paul Chambers,
b; Jimmy Cobb, dms. Newport, RI, 4 July 1958
*Ah-Leu-Cha; Straight No Chaser; Fran Dance; Two Bass Hit; Bye Bye Blackbird; The
Theme*
(first four titles on Columbia CL 2178; *Fran Dance* reissued [1973] on C 32025; fifth title
issued [1982] on C2-38262)
All issues of this material by Columbia incorrectly list Wynton Kelly as the piano player.

Although Davis included the relatively new *Fran Dance* in his Newport program,
the repertoire otherwise consists of old favorites, and here they sound a little the
worse for wear. The sextet's performance is substandard. Davis's most conspicuous contribution comes in tapping out overzealous tempos on all tunes, including
a breakneck tempo on *Ah-Leu-Cha* that reduces the ensemble to a shambles. The
playing is pretty well left up to Coltrane, who plays the only solo on *Two Bass
Hit*, as usual, and an incredibly long one on *Bye Bye Blackbird* (on which
Adderley is not heard at all) as well as taking his regular turn on all the others.

Davis's apparent lack of interest has been matched by Columbia's: it released
approximately two-thirds of it in 1964 and waited eighteen years before releasing
more; identified the piano player as Wynton Kelly when the announcement at
the festival, which occurs on the tape immediately following the part it mastered,
identifies him as Bill Evans; and stated on the 1973 reissue of *Fran Dance* that the
sextet shared the bill with Thelonious Monk and Pee Wee Russell, when in fact
they shared it with the Dave Brubeck Quartet. (Monk and Russell played
together at Newport five years later, in 1963, and some of the material they
played is coupled with the Davis sextet material from 1958 on Columbia CL
2178.)

The festival appearance worked well for Jimmy Cobb as well as for Coltrane,
but is otherwise quite undistinguished. *Down Beat's* review in its 7 August issue
was duly critical but chose to lay most of the blame in Coltrane's lap. "Unfortunately the group did not perform effectively," the review said. "Although Miles
continues to play with delicacy and infinite grace, his group's solidarity is ham-
pered by the angry tenor of Coltrane. Backing himself into rhythmic corners of
flurries of notes, Coltrane sounded like the personification of motion-without-
progress in jazz. What is equally important, Coltrane's playing has apparently
influenced Adderley. The latter's playing indicated less concern for melodic structure than he has illustrated in the past ... With the exception of Miles' vital contribution, then, the group proved more confusing to listeners than educational."
These were complaints that Coltrane was to hear fairly often in the next few
years. In due course, he would impose greater consistency on his playing as he

became its master and the complaints would turn into almost universal praise, but now there were many nights when he communicated the search more than what it was that he sought, and the Newport festival of 1958 was one of these.

Maynard Ferguson often led his band opposite the sextet in clubs, and he recognized that Coltrane inevitably suffered by comparison to the other players on some nights. "In baseball, the more of a power hitter you are, the more often you miss, because you swing so hard," he explained. "I worked opposite Miles Davis when he had Cannonball and Coltrane, who admired each other very much. But Cannonball had the better average in the baseball sense. Because Coltrane was the *experimenter*. Maybe he had a minimal cult then, a tiny number of people starting to really love his music. And some that would resist it and then suddenly hear something in it. And it was a great education for me not to make judgements on people in the first ten hearings. Whereas some people make judgements on their *first* hearing." Coltrane always worked hard at his music; the same could not be said of his colleagues, and the festival concert was a performance at which Coltrane at least outworked the others.

The recording sessions for *Porgy and Bess* started on 22 July, but the day before the second of them took place, the sextet appeared in a Monday night engagement at the posh Plaza Hotel. The occasion was a command performance for the management at Columbia Records and its invited guests, to celebrate the jazz division's dominating position in the jazz market at a time when jazz was enjoying considerable popularity. The evening included, along with the sextet, sets by the Duke Ellington orchestra, Billie Holiday (a little less than a year before her death, and suffering), and Jimmy Rushing. Ellington and the vocalists appeared both before and after the sextet, which then had to work in a little clearing amid the orchestra's paraphernalia. The recording suffers from more than a few technical problems but the musicians were closer to the top of their form than they had been at Newport. The details are as follows:

Miles Davis Sextet
Miles Davis, tpt; Julian Adderley, as (except *My Funny Valentine* and *If I Were a Bell*); John Coltrane, ts (except *My Funny Valentine*); Bill Evans, pno; Paul Chambers, b; Jimmy Cobb, dms. Plaza Hotel, New York, 28 July 1958
Straight No Chaser; My Funny Valentine; If I Were a Bell; Oleo
(all on Columbia C 32470 [first issued 1973])
On the liner and label, the drummer is incorrectly listed as Philly Joe Jones, and *Straight No Chaser* is mistitled *Jazz at the Plaza*.

If Davis believed a few months earlier that Evans and Cobb were incapable of playing the hard swingers, he had obviously changed his mind by now. Both the

Plaza date and the Newport concert included fast pieces in proportions that were typical of his selections for sets prior to their joining the sextet. For Evans, the main concession is that *My Funny Valentine* has been turned into a feature for him to share with Davis. It gives him an opportunity to transform the simple melody in numerous complex variations, from his introduction unaided by the other rhythm players to his long, lyrical solo following Davis's. Evans receives some unnatural aid in taking the spotlight away from Davis on *My Funny Valentine* by the fact that Davis is under-recorded here, as he also is on *If I Were a Bell*. If the technical problems help Evans, however, they hinder Cobb; in making the technical adjustment to balance Davis, the engineers bring up Cobb's drums to the point where they are distracting. The best track, both technically and musically for the whole band, is *Straight No Chaser*, which, after an ensemble lapse where Adderley enters playing the lead before the other horns are ready, features long, facile solos by Davis, Coltrane, Adderley, and Evans, in that order. This title was probably the set closer at the Plaza even though it is placed at the beginning on the record, because it ends with a few bars of *The Theme* tagged onto it. But whatever the pleasures and the pressures of playing before the Columbia brass in an Edwardian setting that had never admitted jazz until then, for Davis they could only have been a momentary distraction from his real business at the time, which was taking place in Columbia's recording studios.

Porgy and Bess, the best-known American opera, was first produced in 1935, after nearly ten years of collaboration among George Gershwin, who wrote the music, DuBose Heyward, who wrote the libretto (based on his 1924 novel *Porgy*) and most of the lyrics, and Ira Gershwin, the lyricist for many of his brother's best-known songs, who helped Heyward with the lyrics. The thin plot revolves around a crippled black man who commits murder when he believes that he has lost his lover to another man, but most of the interest in the opera comes from its attempt at dramatizing the rich and colorful ghetto life of Catfish Row, a southern waterfront community. Gershwin's music self-consciously incorporates elements of black music – gospel, work songs, jazz – in a full-scale theatrical score. In 1958, *Porgy and Bess* was being produced as a motion picture directed by Otto Preminger and starring Robert McFerrin, Adele Addison, Sammy Davis Jr, and Pearl Bailey, and several record executives seized the occasion to commission jazz adaptations they could release amid the brouhaha that was certain to surround the release of the movie in 1959. *Porgy and Bess* offered a score that jazz players could potentially elucidate.

Jazz versions of Broadway musicals, movie and television themes, and the works of Tin Pan Alley songwriters had proven to be an unexpected boon to record companies in the wake of an enormously successful jazz version of some songs from the musical comedy *My Fair Lady* by the trio of André Previn, Leroy

Vinnegar, and Shelly Manne (*Shelly Manne and His Friends*, Contemporary C 3527), a best-seller on the pop charts for two years after its release in 1956. Jazz players – and pseudo-jazz players – had started cranking out versions of almost every imaginable score, from current Broadway hits such as *West Side Story* and *Li'l Abner*, to songbooks by Cole Porter and Harold Arlen, to the unpromising *Nutcracker Suite* and *Peter and the Wolf*, and even to school fight songs and national anthems.

Miles Davis and Gil Evans hardly needed the commercial boom to encourage Columbia's executives to finance their version of *Porgy and Bess* in high style because their collaboration on *Miles Ahead* left no doubts whatever about the commercial potential of further collaborations. Nevertheless, it must have done them no harm at all when they chose to work on Gershwin's score at such a commercially propitious moment. The details are as follows:

Miles Davis with Gil Evans and His Orchestra
Miles Davis, tpt, flugelhorn; Ernie Royal, Johnny Coles, Bernie Glow, Louis Mucci, tpt; Joe Bennett, Frank Rehak, Jimmy Cleveland, tbn; Dick Hixon, bass tbn; Willie Ruff, Julius Watkins, Gunther Schuller, frh; Bill Barber, tba; Julian Adderley, as; Phil Bodner (on 22 and 29 July), Jerome Richardson (on 4 and 14 August), Romeo Penque, flt; Danny Bank, bass clnt; Paul Chambers, b; Philly Joe Jones (on 22 July), Jimmy Cobb (on the other dates), dms; Gil Evans, arr, cond. New York, 22 July 1958
My Man's Gone Now; Gone Gone Gone; Gone
(all on Columbia CL 1274)

29 July 1958
Here Come de Honey Man; Bess You Is My Woman Now; It Ain't Necessarily So; Fisherman, Strawberry and Devil Crab
(all issued as above)

4 August 1958
Prayer (Oh Doctor Jesus); Bess Oh Where's My Bess; Buzzard Song
(all issued as above)

14 August 1958
Summertime; There's a Boat That's Leaving Soon for New York; I Loves You Porgy
(all issued as above)

Davis plays muted trumpet on *Here Come de Honey Man, Summertime,* and *I Loves You Porgy* and open flugelhorn on all other titles.

The extent to which Davis and Evans's *Porgy and Bess* is a recomposition of the original is truly remarkable; one can easily imagine the consternation of the Columbia executives when they realized – if they did – that moviegoers looking to this record for a recapitulation of the music they heard in the movie would discover, at most, a few scattered melodies and absolutely nothing else. Davis and Evans's work resembles the original opera no more than does Gershwin's own *Suite from Porgy and Bess* of 1936, perhaps even less.

The opera's most popular song – Gershwin always called it an aria – *I Got Plenty of Nuthin'*, is left out by Davis and Evans, as are several lesser numbers. A few are retained with their melodic lines more or less intact, especially *Summertime*, *It Ain't Necessarily So*, and *There's a Boat That's Leaving Soon for New York*, their melodies 'sung' by Davis quite faithfully over Evans's sonorous voicings. Others, notably *Bess You Is My Woman Now* and *My Man's Gone Now*, retain key phrases of the originals and build them into new songs. Still others are based on little more than the mood or the dramatic situation that Gershwin's music covered, as in the call-and-answer of *Prayer* and the dirge-like *Gone Gone Gone*.

Even more tangential in their relation to the original are *Fisherman, Strawberry, and Devil Crab*, apparently a free combination of elements suggested by Gershwin's *It Takes a Long Pull to Get There* and *Street Cries (Strawberry Woman, Crab Man)*, and *Here Come de Honey Man*, a march with a rapid crescendo and diminuendo suggesting a passing parade, perhaps inspired by the title of Gershwin's *They Pass by Singing*. One of the most effective pieces, *Buzzard Song*, which Davis later claimed sole credit for orchestrating, was not even used in the original production of *Porgy and Bess*. And the scintillating *Gone*, one of the most beautifully orchestrated drum features ever recorded and the showcase for which Philly Joe Jones was purposefully imported, has nothing at all to do with the music of George Gershwin but is Gil Evans's very own. Among the outpouring of jazz scores at the end of the 1950s and later, which were never more than jazzed-up versions of their Broadway or Hollywood originals, Davis and Evans's *Porgy and Bess* is a breed apart. It is a new score, with its own integrity, order, and action.

Davis's few comments on *Porgy and Bess*, all made during his interview with Nat Hentoff, which took place when the recording sessions for it were still very much on his mind, emphasize the recomposition from a different perspective by detailing the modal structure of Evans's score. Listening to the master tape that would later be released as *I Loves You Porgy*, Davis commented, "Hear that passage. We only used two chords for all of that. And in *Summertime* there is a long space where we don't change the chord at all. It just doesn't have to be cluttered up." Later on, he returned to the same theme. "When Gil wrote the arrangement of *I Loves You Porgy*, he only wrote a scale for me to play. No chords. And that other passage with two chords gives you a lot more freedom and space to hear things. I've been listening to Khachaturian carefully for six months now and the thing that intrigues me are all those different scales he uses. Bill Evans knows too what can be done with scales. All chords, after all, are relative to scales and certain chords make certain scales. I wrote a tune recently that's more a scale than a line. And I was going to write a ballad for Coltrane with just two chords." Davis's last comments almost certainly refer to his early efforts at composing the music he would record the following spring under the collective title *Kind of Blue*. For the time being, he was more interested in the state of the art. "Classical composers – some of them – have been writing this way for years, but jazz musicians seldom have," he said. "The music has gotten thick. Guys give me tunes and they're full of chords. I can't play them. You know, we play *My Funny Valentine* like with a scale all the way through."

Max Harrison, whose review of Gil Evans's music is probably the most comprehensive, stated flatly that "*Porgy and Bess* ... contains, at least in potential, the finest music Davis and Evans recorded together," singling out Davis's playing on *Prayer* and *My Man's Gone Now* as some of his most eloquent recorded work and Evans's orchestrations of *Fisherman, Strawberry and Devil Crab* and *Here Come de Honey Man* as "exquisite scoring." However, Harrison also expresses some reservations about the realization of Evans's charts for *Porgy and Bess*, stating that "the performances left even more to be desired than those of *Miles Ahead*."

Harrison's reservations apparently come not so much from his hearing of the recording as from the intelligence passed along to him by a member of Gil Evans's studio orchestra. In a personal letter to Harrison, this man, whom Harrison identifies only as "one of the musicians who played on the *Porgy and Bess* date," claims that Evans's charts were even more intricate and subtle than the recordings revealed, and that the members of the orchestra were prevented from realizing the full value of the charts because of the haste in which the sessions were conducted.

The musician's letter to Harrison is worth quoting at length not only because it documents his view but also because it offers an inside view of the recording sessions: "The crux of the matter is that Gil, on both sets of dates, did not rehearse carefully enough, as is evident already on *Miles Ahead*. I believe that this is mostly the result of the unfortunate conditions under which American recording is done. It is too costly for any project of more than average difficulty to be done well, unless the music in question is rehearsed before the date (which is illegal according to union rules), or has been previously performed. Under these, to say the least, less than ideal circumstances, both Miles and Gil have a too relaxed attitude about accomplishing the tasks they set themselves. In pieces which are scored as sensitively and as intricately as Gil's, it's a shame to let the performances cancel half of their effectiveness. Many details of scoring simply could not be – or at least were not – touched upon in the sessions I was on. Some things were left undone which *I* would not have let go. But, as I've indicated, the blame lies more with the conditions than the people. And I suppose one could say that it is remarkable that both LPs are as good as they are. If Gil were a better conductor it would also help: he sometimes confused the players. On the other hand, he is quite patient – perhaps too much so for his own good – and very pleasant to work for. Whatever excellence these recordings have I would attribute (apart from Gil's own magnificent scores, of course) primarily to the supreme abilities of some of the leading players, like Ernie Royal, Bill Barber, the very fine reed men (on all manner of flutes and bass clarinets), and in general the respect which all of us, in spite of what I've said above, have for Gil Evans."

This perspective on *Porgy and Bess* and also, incidentally, on *Miles Ahead* will stun legions of listeners, including many musicians, who have been struck by the subtlety and the intricacy of Evans's orchestrations in their received form. Whether Evans's charts can be executed with even more subtlety and intricacy will remain a moot contention until there are jazz repertory orchestras that perform scores such as Evans's *Porgy and Bess* publicly, rather than letting such flowerings of creative energy wither after a single performance in a studio.

If its performance is less than perfect, it nevertheless fuses sophisticated orchestrations and jazz substance so brilliantly that it is unmatched in the jazz canon. It found a large, appreciative audience as soon as it was released in 1959 and continues to find it today. Until 1971, when it was overtaken by *Bitches Brew*, an album of Davis's very different music of 1969, *Porgy and Bess* was his best-selling album.

After the summer's recording activities, the sextet returned to business as usual. Their tours to jazz clubs outside New York were eagerly anticipated and attended by capacity audiences. In Philadelphia, their usual venue was the Showboat, and Coltrane's hometown fans were enthusiastic supporters. Not the least enthusiastic were Earl and Carl Grubbs, cousins of his wife Naima and budding young saxophonists, who usually managed to get into the nightclub to hear him even though they were only sixteen and fourteen, respectively, in 1958. "Carl and I used to catch John at the Showboat here in Philadelphia, when he was playing with Miles," Earl remembers. "We were still teenagers, so we'd darken our mustaches to look older, and we'd get in most of the time. John would come over to our table and talk with us, and everybody else would wonder who we were and why he was talking with us. He used to do that a lot. He always took time to talk with us and show us things about his music and help us get our music down right."

Not all of Coltrane's visitors were so congenial. Jimmy Cobb remembers a near miss at the same club. "Coltrane and I were working at the Showboat in Philadelphia, and one night during intermission some guy came up to us and said, 'I'd like to see you both upstairs in the men's room.' I thought he was a faggot; I just said, 'So what?' Trane didn't say anything. Then the guy flashed a badge and said, 'Don't make a scene, I'm a narcotics officer.' We all went to the men's room, and he had us take off our shirts. He claimed some lady had told him we were on drugs. I showed him my arms and asked, 'Aren't they beautiful?' Then he looked at Coltrane's arms and said, 'What about those marks?' Trane looked sheepish and said, 'Those are birthmarks; I've had them as long as I can remember.' I almost cracked up, but Trane looked so boyishly innocent that the narcotics cop believed him, and he ended up letting both of us go."

A performance by the sextet at an unknown club sometime around the end of the summer has been preserved in private collections of tapes and shows what the jazz fans heard as part of a set on an ordinary working night. The three titles on tape are surprisingly familiar fare: *Walkin'* had been played by Davis's bands since 1954, and the two ballads, *All of You* and *Round Midnight*, were recorded at the same quintet session in 1956. To some extent, the perpetuation of the same old tunes was probably dictated by the fans, who, having bought the latest Miles Davis record, naturally expected to hear some of it played back to them, whether or not it had been recorded more than a year before and had been played for other fans in other cities scores of times. It was probably also a natural reaction for Davis and the others to perform material that was felt to be safe and comfortable. Most of the challenges for the sextet seemed to be left in the recording studio: in Gil Evans's scores, the 'new' ballads *Stella by Starlight* and *Green Dolphin Street*, the modal *Milestones*, and so on.

Each of the sidemen developed his own way of coping with the repetition of material. For Coltrane, of course, it was easy; he carried on with his restless search for new sonorities, leading him, for instance, to construct an impenetrable wall of eighth-notes on *Walkin'* that seemed to seal him off from the audience. For Adderley, besides studying Coltrane, there was the playful tinkering, as when he adds a new dissonance to the ensemble at the coda of *Walkin'* that gives it the sound of a train whistle. For Chambers, there was the challenge of humming along in unison with his bass solos, like some latter-day Major Holley or Slam Stewart, a gimmick first noticed in one of his solos at Newport and carried on in the clubs. For all of them, there was the challenge of playing *Round Midnight* with only the barest outline of Gil Evans's fatigued arrangement and all the notes altered a half-step here or an octave there. It was all in a night's work.

At least the rooms where they played changed – from night to night when they were playing concerts, and otherwise from week to week or from fortnight to fortnight. Sometimes they changed in a more irrevocable sense too, because jazz clubs have notoriously short existences and the sextet often went into a city after a year's absence to find that not only were they booked into a new club but that the available after-hours clubs were all new too. The clubs also changed when a competing club offered a better deal, a situation that very few other jazz bands ever experienced. A significant move had taken place in the spring of 1958, when Davis moved the sextet out of the Café Bohemia, where he had played regularly for over two and a half years, and into the Village Vanguard. The change took place just before Jimmy Cobb took over the drum chair, with the result that Cobb, who was with Davis for nearly five years, never played in the Bohemia. At the Vanguard, the sextet were usually paired with a soloist – often it was singer-pianist Blossom Dearie – or a small group.

No matter who shared the bill with them, the sextet's fans filled the room, a fact that was not easy to live with if one was in the other group. Jim Hall, the guitarist, remembers finding himself in that situation (although he may not remember Davis's drummer correctly): "I worked in a duo with Lee Konitz opposite Miles Davis at the Village Vanguard when he had Cannonball and Philly Joe Jones and Bill Evans, and the audience would listen to Miles as if they were in church, and then talk all the way through our set, which was about the way everything seemed to be going for me then."

By mid-1958, nearly everybody seemed to be listening attentively to Davis. David Amram, who paid Davis the compliment of adapting one of his phrases as a motif for his *Autobiography for Strings*, recalls an occasion when Dmitri Mitropolous inquired about Amram's activities and, upon finding out that Amram still worked at jazz sometimes, asked, "Who is the latest thing now, Dizzy Gillespie?" Amram told him no and named Sonny Rollins, John Coltrane, Bill Evans, and Miles Davis: "'Oh,' said Mitropolous, 'I've heard the music of Miles Davis, but I don't know much about the work of the other three. The only criticism I have of the jazz world is that every six months the heroes change.'"

Mitropolous chose his term well in including Davis among the "heroes." That was also the term being used by other people at the time. John Stevens, the English drummer, says, "A lot of things fall into place with Miles. Brilliant musician, coupled with hipness, his image. That's why he's a culture hero. For his work and the way he's handled the system." He was certainly being looked on as something more than a trumpeter and jazz composer, and not only by the hipsters who had lionized Charlie Parker. Even *Life* magazine, the voice of the American bourgeoisie, knew about him; it named him along with a handful of black politicians, professionals, and businessmen as individuals who were advancing the prestige of black people in America at a time when the world was horrified by the news of racial violence in Little Rock, Arkansas. Miles Davis, the silent, sometimes sullen, recalcitrant, always uncompromising leader of the second generation of bebop revolutionaries, had become a bona fide celebrity.

The mystique surrounding him did not begin in 1958, and it did not peak then either. Its sources remain a mystery, but it was not cultivated by Davis; few stars in any performing art ever put less effort into their public relations. That too became part of the mystique, though it was nowhere near its essence. The mystique begins with a talent for making music that is at once self-communing and perfectly articulate, introverted yet highly accessible. George Goodman Jr sees the trumpet sound as the key to a more complex symbol: "To worshipful fans, from Hollywood to Antibes, the sound of Mr. Davis became the perfect signature for his personality, the style and substance of the new archetypal man of jazz. The trumpeter added a quality of elegance to Bird's image of raw authenticity, and it was embodied in the sound that fit him as perfectly as his finely tailored clothes." Those clothes, as almost everybody knows, would eventually win him recognition on the annual best-dressed lists, a piece of social frippery that he neither sought nor acknowledged. He exchanged his Mercedes for a Ferrari. The clothes and the cars were the conspicuous consumptions of a man who was almost invisible except when he was on the bandstand – occasionally glimpsed perhaps in a New York club, or thought to have been glimpsed there, and the whisper spread throughout the room. "All the money, cars, clothes, the bitches – all that was to match my ego," he told Don DeMicheal in 1969, in a *Rolling Stone* article. DeMicheal reported that Davis was no longer smoking, was driving a van, and was eating vegetables, which sounded more like the lifestyle of a *Rolling Stone* subscriber than of Miles Davis; the next time he was in the news he had smashed up his new Ferrari. The mystique kept on growing.

At the heart of Davis's lifestyle is financial security, which he grew up with in East St. Louis, surrendered for long enough in his early days of independence to learn how much he missed it, and regained with interest in the late 1950s. "When I first left home as a musician, I used to spend all I made, and when I went on dope, I got in debt," he said in his interview in *Playboy*. "But after I got enough sense to kick the habit, I started to make more than I needed to spend unless I was crazy or something." The greatest exponents of jazz were for several generations dealt rejection and borderline poverty, but Davis is a phenomenon. The mystique grew among his colleagues as well as his fans. "It came to the point where he made some money and invested it in blue chip stocks," Duke Jordan, his colleague in the Charlie Parker Quintet, says. "In other words, every time they turn the lights on in New Jersey, Miles is collecting some money. So that makes him independent, and once you're independent you can demand this and you can demand that." For Davis, more often than not, the demands are met.

Late in 1958, he was still living in an apartment on Tenth Avenue near 57th Street. The building housed other jazzmen as well, with John Lewis living on the same floor as Davis and Michael Zwerin on the floor below. The space was comfortable, and the decor was elegant. "The largest area in his apartment is the living room," Nat Hentoff wrote, describing the setting for his interview. "Like the other rooms, it is uncluttered. The furnishings have been carefully selected and are spare. Miles has a liking for 'good wood' and explains thereby why his *Down Beat* plaques – and even his Four Roses Award from the Randall's Island Festival – are all displayed. He has a good piano and an adequate nonstereo record player." Comfortable it may have been, but it was hardly the place to park a Ferrari, and he moved soon after into a large brownstone on West 77th Street near the Hudson River. The house is a converted Russian Orthodox church, with four storeys and a gymnasium in the basement. The decor, according to Sy Johnson, who went there to interview Davis in 1976, is based on "a circle-in-a-cube motif that is repeated throughout the house." Thus, the music room includes "a circular upholstered seat built around the wall, and a built-in piano overlooking the space." The liking for good wood is carried over into the new place, apparently, because Johnson adds, "Poll-winner plaques hung on the walls." One of Davis's favorite tales, which has now gone through a couple of variations, involves his answering the door when a repairman comes around and being mistaken for the butler.

The brownstone was not so much for him as for Frances Taylor, the Fran named in the title of his *Fran Dance*, whom he married at this time. A tall, elegant former dancer, Frances Taylor Davis was by all accounts even less interested in being in the public eye than her husband, although she let him talk her into posing for the cover photos on three of his albums in the 1960s. Her striking beauty and quiet dignity complemented Davis's image perfectly. As the decade drew to a close, everything that surrounded him seemed to complement his image perfectly. He could well afford to sit back a minute, look around, and say, "Now I got a pretty good portfolio of stock investments, and I got this house – it's worth into six figures, including everything in it ... Then I got my music, I got Frances, and I got my Ferrari." His only problems were the ones that go along with success, and they were beginning to mount up.

The most obvious problems came from within the sextet, where the success of the sidemen was making it feasible for them to strike out on their own. Julian Adderley had led his own band before joining, and Davis had sensibly let him take over some of the leader's duties with his sextet, thereby increasing his pay and expending some of his personal ambitions to the advantage of Davis's band. But by October he had reached the end of the term that he and Davis had informally agreed on when he joined. It took some doing by Davis and Harold Lovett, his manager, to keep Adderley in the band, but in the end they succeeded by appealing to Adderley's practical nature. Adderley explained: "I had planned when I joined him to stay with Miles about a year. But I stayed longer. Miles was getting more successful, and there was the business recession. I was functioning meanwhile as a kind of road manager – paying off the guys, collecting money." He stayed, somewhat uneasily and ever more restlessly, for another year.

Bill Evans presented a different case entirely. He had been earning excellent notices wherever the sextet played since he joined the band eight months before, but unlike Adderley he had been something of a nonentity when he joined, and neither he nor anyone else was certain that he was ready to make it on his own as a leader. He felt worn out by all the traveling and by the constant pressure of performing before crowds of Davis's fans. The other players, whose professional training had largely taken place on the road, seemed to have more stamina than he did. On more than a few occasions, too, he had heard rumblings from black fans and some black musicians about being a white man in a black band, and even though he knew that the rumblings did not mean anything – certainly not to Davis, who would have told him if they did – they still left him with a kind of hollow feeling. And then there was the heat he sometimes felt about his playing being too restrained on the faster pieces. Adderley said, "Although he loves Bill's work, Miles felt Bill didn't swing enough on things that weren't subdued." It was not something that Davis harped on – he seldom said anything about the music one way or the other – but it bothered Evans as much as if he did harp on it. After eight months, Evans said, "I felt exhausted in every way – physically, mentally and spiritually."

Evans decided to leave, regardless of what the future might hold, and he could not be dissuaded. His immediate plans were crystal clear; he intended to get some rest. He left the sextet in November and headed for his brother's house in Baton Rouge, where he rested and practiced away from the New York winter. After that, he returned to New York and went about the business of putting together his career as a leader. He would return to the Miles Davis Sextet one more time, for two days only, one in March and one in April, to participate in the recording sessions that would be the culmination of the great sextet. By that time, he was leading his own trio and by the end of 1959, when he settled on Scott LaFaro as his bassist and Paul Motian as his drummer, listeners everywhere started to take notice. James Lincoln Collier calls Evans "the piano player who has had the widest influence in jazz since 1960 or so."

In the two decades before Evans's sudden death in 1980, the relations between Evans and Davis were distant, as indeed they always had been, and perhaps a little cool. In 1969 *Rolling Stone* reported Davis as saying about Evans, "I liked the way he sounded. But he doesn't sound now like he did when he played with us.

He sounds white now." That was not a surprising sentiment from Davis at the time because he was making pronouncements on racial matters to the press fairly regularly, even though he had three white sidemen in his band. Between 1963 and 1971, Evans won three Grammy awards from the National Academy of Recording Arts and Sciences for the best jazz album of the year. At the 1971 awards ceremony Davis was also a nominee, and when Evans was announced as the winner, Davis and his table of guests left immediately. Asked by a television reporter if Davis's leaving should be taken as a slight, Evans just smiled and said that he knew Davis well enough to know that he had probably left because there was no longer any reason for him to stay.

Evans's comment showed an astute grasp of Davis's logic, but then, Evans had shown that grasp of his logic for years, in his music, which was always filled with the virtues that Davis extolled. His mature style blossomed during his months in Davis's sextet and came to full fruition almost immediately after he left it. Some of his critics complained that Evans had not only learned about music in Davis's band but had also learned his stage manners there. "Evans doesn't tell his listeners what he is playing, which is doubly rude: the composer is erased and the audience is made to feel unworthy of such information," Whitney Balliett complained, adding, "It's like a minister neglecting to reveal his chapter and verse." (Balliett's complaint about Evans refutes Davis's contention that the critics would not complain about his stage manner if he were a white man. Obviously they would.) For a student as apt as Bill Evans, even eight months was long enough to learn all manner of things in the Miles Davis Sextet.

For the sextet, Evans's departure coincided with a slowing down of Davis's modal experiments and finally, less than a year after he left, in their curtailment for several years. The main reason for that probably had nothing to do with Evans's quitting the band, as we shall see, but his resignation may have had a small effect on it. As Adderley said, comparing Evans to his successors, "His imagination is a little more vivid so that he tries more daring things." Davis's bands could not help but miss that quality as they went about putting in their night's work.

Davis immediately asked Red Garland to fill in until he could find the replacement he wanted for Evans, and Garland ended up staying for three months, until February, when he left to form his own trio. The sextet did not record in this period, but tapes of two engagements, one at the Spotlight Lounge in Washington, DC, and the other at an unidentified club, document the stylistic changes that followed. The tapes catch the sextet playing *Sid's Ahead* and *Bye Bye Blackbird* at the Spotlight, probably late in November, and yet another version of *Bye Bye Blackbird* (this one with Adderley sitting out) at the other club. Although *Bye Bye Blackbird* had been played countless times after Garland first left the band, none of Davis's pianists ever played it so well, or with such relish, as Garland did. Even the familiar tempo at which it was usually played, the standard Jamalesque groove, is accelerated considerably, as if in celebration of the return of a piano player who ponders less before he pounces. When the Miles Davis Sextet played in a concert package at Town Hall on the last Friday of November, in the company of bands led by Jimmy Giuffre, Gerry Mulligan, and Thelonious Monk, not only was Garland back but so also was Philly Joe Jones, and Davis celebrated their reunion in his band by letting them dust off *Billy Boy* as a trio feature.

The return of Garland solved Davis's major problem at the end of 1958, and Adderley's decision to carry on in the sextet for a while longer postponed that problem, but he still had to deal with Coltrane, who was even edgier than Adderley about striking out on his own. He was taking more than his share of criticism in reviews of the sextet's performances but he was aware that at least part of that criticism was because the reviewers and the fans turned out primarily to hear Davis and the popular Adderley. They had little inclination to try to understand what he was playing. However, everywhere they played there was a growing nucleus of listeners who were there specifically to hear him, and they sought him out between sets and sometimes even followed him from club to club. Even the unassuming Coltrane sometimes dared to think that there was an audience out there for a band of his own. His problem was in bringing himself to discuss making the break with Davis.

After more than three years together the early problems between them were long gone. Davis did not say much, of course, but Coltrane knew he was happy with the way he was playing. He let him play at length, and he no longer asked him to sit out on ballads; more often he asked Adderley, a very fine ballad player, to sit out instead. There were lots of little indications too. When Davis left the stand during the others' solos in clubs, he often sat with Naima Coltrane, who was there gently riding herd on her husband's activities between sets, and Davis had taken to ribbing Coltrane about his weight, which ballooned as his addiction to sweets was allowed free rein, but he was so concerned that he sold Coltrane some of his exercise equipment, including a punching bag, boxing gloves, and weight bars, with the promise that he would show him how to use it. Coltrane was naturally pleased to think that he met the approval of the man he had taken to calling "the teacher," but it certainly did not make matters easier for him now that he felt he should go out on his own.

When Coltrane got around to broaching the subject to Davis, Davis put him off by telling him that he was not yet ready for the problems of leading his own group. When he brought it up again and seemed adamant, Davis compromised by proposing that he stay with the sextet for the time being and begin a kind of apprenticeship for the business end of the job. Coltrane agreed, a little reluctantly at first, and Davis quickly made good on his end of the arrangement. In January, Harold Lovett took over Coltrane's financial affairs and immediately helped him negotiate a recording contract with Nesuhi Ertegun of Atlantic Records – he had been recording for Prestige as a leader for two and a half years – that would bring him a bonus of $7,000 annually. Lovett also set up a publishing company for Coltrane's music, called JOWCOL (for John William Coltrane). Davis then lined up Coltrane with Jack Whittemore, who would book Coltrane in the periods when the sextet were laying off. As a result, Coltrane was launched on what was really a double career.

Coltrane celebrated his independence promptly by recording for Atlantic on 15 January, with a quintet co-led by Milt Jackson. The session was fitted into his schedule hurriedly because he had to leave for Chicago soon after, where the sextet were booked into their usual venue, the Lounge at the Sutherland Hotel. In Chicago, Coltrane immediately recorded again, this time for Mercury in a quintet made up of the sidemen from Davis's band, nominally led by Adderley.

Coltrane's visit to Chicago was memorable in other ways. He was fitted for an eight-tooth upper front bridge when his teeth finally caved in under the constant assault of sweets. More important in the long run, one of his fans at the Sutherland introduced himself between sets one night as Pat Patrick, the baritone saxophonist in Sun Ra's experimental band. Coltrane was interested to hear of the changes that were moving a growing number of musicians in Chicago's jazz community, and Patrick arranged for him to meet Sun Ra. According to C.O. Simpkins, Coltrane confided to Sun Ra that he was deeply dissatisfied with his work in the sextet because it interfered with his own goals, and Sun Ra encouraged him to play further out with Davis and thus to stop trying to compartmentalize his development into the two separate aspects of his double career.

Coltrane's double career was not the strain it might have been because Davis, for the past year and a half, had grown more and more selective about the engagements he accepted. "I never work steady," he said in 1959. "I work enough to do what I want to do. I play music more for pleasure than for work." It was an artistically liberating regimen with more than a dash of good business sense. Since he was always in demand, he could refuse to play unless the price was right, and since he was not constantly in the public eye, he was in greater demand than ever. The regimen also helped the sidemen, who were well paid even playing less than a full schedule, because it gave them the chances they wanted to get out on their own. On one such occasion, both Adderley and Coltrane assembled bands to play in Birdland on a Monday night. The engagement became something of a watershed in Coltrane's progress and in the progress of the new free jazz that was suddenly finding adherents among many of the best young players arriving in New York. One of these was the tenor saxophonist Wayne Shorter from Newark.

Five years later, in 1964, Shorter would join Miles Davis's band and prove to be the catalyst for what would be Davis's best band since the sextet, but now, at twenty-six, he was relatively untried and he leapt at the chance to play in Birdland on Coltrane's one-night stand. "We had a rehearsal at his house, and that night we were playing," Shorter told Julie Coryell. "Opposite us was Cannonball with his brother Nat. Cannonball and Trane were working with Miles then, but they had time off and they split up and got different bands. Elvin Jones was on drums that night. It was historic; everybody realized it – we tore that place up. Ten years later, when I went to California, people were still talking about it – 'Yeah, we heard about it out here, that memorable Monday night at Birdland.' That's when Trane started playing all the new stuff he had written. It was a new wave."

There was indeed a new wave being felt in jazz in 1959. Coltrane was destined to be its patriarch, and the nucleus of his fans at all the performances of the Miles Davis Sextet comprised the leading edge of its audience. Coltrane's memorable nights away from the sextet only made him more uneasy about his role as a sideman.

Davis, as usual, was keenly aware of what was happening in jazz. In the first months of 1959 he spent many nights in the audience at jazz clubs, apparently keeping an eye out for the piano player who could replace Garland in his band. One of the young musicians he encountered was a young trumpeter named Freddie Hubbard, recently arrived in New York. Hubbard, who was working at Birdland, recalled the scene for Leonard Feather: "I was working there with Philly Joe, and I had my eyes closed, as I often do during a solo. I opened my eyes and there was Miles, and it scared me to death. I had tried for months to summon up the courage to speak to him, and he never said a word to me. So everyone asked him how he liked the way I played, and over the next couple of years he said things about me that were pretty cool, even though I didn't really have it together then."

Another young musician who caught Davis's eye was Josef Zawinul, a piano player from Austria who emigrated to the United States in January 1959, quit the Berklee School of Music almost before he started, and began working professionally, first in Maynard Ferguson's band and then as Dinah Washington's accompanist. Although it seems improbable, since Zawinul had arrived in the country only six or seven weeks earlier, Davis may have invited him to join the sextet as Garland's replacement. Zawinul told Conrad Silvert in 1978 that Davis had offered him an opportunity to record with him in 1959, but he declined because he felt that he was not ready. Nine years later, after a long stint as the piano player in Julian Adderley's quintet, Zawinul would record some remarkable music with Davis.

Davis finally chose as the sextet's new piano player Wynton Kelly, who joined the band in February. For Kelly, joining Davis was a break that was long overdue, not so much because he was old – he was twenty-eight – but because he had been playing professionally for a long time. He started working as a musician when he was twelve, and he was a veteran of all kinds of bar bands when he attracted attention in Dizzy Gillespie's short-lived big band of 1957. Born in Jamaica and raised in Brooklyn, Kelly is the first cousin of another Brooklyn pianist, Randy Weston, who is five years older. "He was already a fantastic pianist at the age of fifteen," Weston recalls. "He was a young genius."

Julian Adderley believed that Kelly's arrival in the sextet was a real advance because he combined the strengths of Red Garland and Bill Evans. "When Bill left, Miles hired Red again and got used to swinging so much that he later found Wynton Kelly, who does both the subdued things and the swingers very well," Adderley said, and he added: "Wynton is also the world's greatest accompanist for a soloist ... Wynton plays with the soloist all the time, with the chords *you* choose. He even anticipates your direction. Most accompanists try to lead you." Another of Kelly's early boosters was Bill Evans, who said, "When I first heard him in Dizzy's big band, his whole thing was so joyful and exuberant; nothing about it seemed calculated. And yet, with the clarity of the way he played, you know he had to put this together in a very carefully planned way – but the result was completely without calculation, there was just pure spirit shining through the conception." For many horn players, Kelly's ability as an accompanist made him their first choice for pickup groups in recording sessions. His tenure with Davis's bands would last more than four years.

The main activity of the sextet immediately after Kelly joined it involved him only peripherally and Bill Evans centrally. The occasion was the recording of five modal compositions eventually released together under the title *Kind of Blue*. They were recorded in two sessions, the first on 2 March and the second on 22 April, with a television appearance by Miles Davis and the Gil Evans Orchestra – the first public performance ever of the *Miles Ahead* material – interposed between them. Of the five compositions recorded in the *Kind of Blue* sessions, Wynton Kelly plays only on the first, *Freddie Freeloader*, and Bill Evans plays on all the others. *Kind of Blue* constitutes the culmination of the achievements of the great sextet of 1958–9, a stunning condensation of its strengths. Davis probably intended it to be a beginning, a new direction that would challenge his musicians and perhaps slake their urges to move on. *Kind of Blue* did provide a beginning, but only for other musicians, among them John Coltrane. For Davis, *Kind of Blue* seemed, under the circumstances, to be another major recording project, like the orchestration of *Porgy and Bess*, that was not followed up outside the studio. Five years would pass before he would try seriously to extend the direction in which it pointed, and by then almost all the circumstances were different. And so it became a culmination instead.

The project had been fomenting for some time. Davis's impetus is clear in all his talk of scales and chords, Khachaturian, musical space and clutter, which for more than a year had been his main musical preoccupation. The summer before, he told Nat Hentoff that he had written "a tune recently that's more a scale than a line"; he might have been describing the preliminary draft for any one of the compositions on *Kind of Blue*. Bill Evans, who had not been in close contact with Davis for four months and was away in Louisiana for part of that time, was also involved in the planning. Although Davis is listed as the sole composer of all five pieces, J.C. Thomas claims that Evans composed *Blue in Green* and *Flamenco Sketches*, and Thomas says that Evans once claimed credit for arranging all five. These claims were never amplified or corroborated, and Davis remains the credited composer, although clearly Evans was not invited to participate in the *Kind of Blue* sessions just for old time's sake. He was deeply, if unofficially, involved in them.

The details for the first of the two recording sessions are as follows:

Miles Davis Sextet
Miles Davis, tpt; Julian Adderley, as (except on *Blue in Green*); John Coltrane, ts; Wynton Kelly, pno (on *Freddie Freeloader*), Bill Evans, pno (on *So What* and *Blue in Green*); Paul Chambers, b; Jimmy Cobb, dms. New York, 2 March 1959
Freddie Freeloader; So What; Blue in Green
(all on Columbia 1355)

The music is best discussed along with its companion session on 22 April. Apart from the musical innovations taking place in the Columbia studio at this session, a homelier innovation appeared in the form of a new face in the control booth. It was Teo Macero, the tenor saxophonist and third stream composer, newly appointed at Columbia as a record producer. Before Macero's promotion, all of Davis's Columbia recordings were produced by George Avakian, although the producer was never listed as such on the albums. Afterward, almost all of Davis's massive output for Columbia would be produced by Macero (and after Macero's first two albums, producer credit would never again be omitted). Macero spent part of his apprenticeship at Columbia working on the post-recording production of the *Porgy and Bess* album, but with the *Kind of Blue* sessions he assumed full charge of production – whatever that may mean when Davis is the artist being recorded.

Macero did not entirely surrender his aspirations as a composer or as a player to become a producer, although his activities as a player at least were sharply curtailed. Macero points out that his active career as a musician was important in working effectively with Davis. "You can go along with an artist like Miles, and encourage him – these are new directions, these are new changes, this is something new that hasn't happened before," he told Gregg Hall. "You can be as current as he is because you've been going through the changes in a different way. I'm going through them as a composer, Miles as a composer-musician-performer." Macero's work with Davis has certainly been productive, which may speak volumes for having a Juilliard graduate with good professional credentials as a record producer, a position too often filled in the jazz field by a businessman who also happens to be a jazz fan. Macero certainly agrees, and probably Davis would too. Macero says, "He knows I have a great pair of ears and I'm looking out for his interests and he's looking out for mine, and it's nice. It's comfortable but, at the same time, it's very exciting because it's very creative." It has not always been smooth, but Macero's career got off to an auspicious start with *Kind of Blue*.

One month later, Miles Davis and Gil Evans performed the public debut of three titles from the *Miles Ahead* album of 1957, on the Robert Herridge Theater Show, a local New York television program on the arts. On the same program, Davis led a quintet in a performance of *So What* from the *Kind of Blue* session. The details are as follows:

Miles Davis Quintet
Miles Davis, tpt; John Coltrane, ts; Wynton Kelly, pno; Paul Chambers, b; Jimmy Cobb, dms. Robert Herridge Theater Show, New York, 2 April 1959
So What (issued [1975] on Beppo BEP 502)

Miles Davis with Gil Evans and His Orchestra
Miles Davis, tpt, flugelhorn; Ernie Royal, Clyde Reasinger, Louis Mucci, Johnny Coles, Emmett Berry, tpt; Frank Rehak, Jimmy Cleveland, Bill Elton, Rod Levitt, tbn; Julius Watkins, Bob Northern, frh; Bill Barber, tba; Romeo Penque, Eddie Caine, woodwinds, Danny Bank, bass clnt; John Coltrane, as; Paul Chambers, b; Jimmy Cobb, dms; unknown harp; Gil Evans, arr, cond
The Duke; *Blues for Pablo*; *New Rhumba*
(all issued as above)

When the film of the orchestral portion of this telecast was shown at the 1979 Newport Jazz Festival among other historically interesting clips of jazz performances, Whitney Balliett referred to it in his review as "a long, apathetic sequence showing Miles Davis playing *The Duke*, *Blues for Pablo*, and *New Rhumba* with Gil Evans's band." He was presumably criticizing the cinematography rather than the music, for the music itself is hardly apathetic. These arrangements are given a much more robust reading than they received on the rather muted, delicate versions of the definitive recordings of 1957. One can more readily separate the individual voicings that make up Evans's palette, with Bill Barber's tuba lines uncommonly clear, perhaps partly because of miking differences between the two productions. The difference in the performance of the arrangements reveals in Evans's music overtones of a more traditional big-band sound and again raises the issue of the awful waste when music of this caliber is stashed away in a bottom drawer instead of being reinterpreted in public performances.

The quintet's performance on the same show is notable as one of the rare occasions when a composition entered Davis's working repertoire immediately, *So What* having been played for the first time in the recording studio just a month earlier. The fact that Paul Chambers leaves out a phrase of his opening theme is the only obvious flaw created by its novelty. Coltrane plays magnificently. His tenor line – he played alto in the orchestra, something he had not done in public since his days with Gillespie in 1949–51 – suddenly sounds like the Coltrane of a few years hence, when he was at the height of his powers in the early 1960s. Near the beginning of his solo he improvises a sequence that he later developed into the melodic line for *Impressions*, one of his landmark compositions after leaving Davis's employ. The direct line from the *Kind of Blue* sessions to Coltrane's new music is thus neatly encapsulated.

Less than three weeks later, the sextet including Bill Evans reconvened to complete the recording of *Kind of Blue*. The details are as follows:

Miles Davis Sextet
Miles Davis, tpt; Julian Adderley, as; John Coltrane, ts; Bill Evans, pno; Paul Chambers, b; Jimmy Cobb, dms. New York, 22 April 1959
Flamenco Sketches; *All Blues*
(both on Columbia CL 1355)

Of all the *Kind of Blue* compositions, probably *Blue in Green* and *Flamenco Sketches* are the most difficult to appreciate on only a few hearings, and for similar reasons. The other compositions are sharply defined and immediately distinctive, but both *Blue in Green* and *Flamenco Sketches* are insinuating and calm; their themes are ripples whereas the others are waves. Their differentness, however, disappears after a few careful hearings, and they too fill their own distinctive space.

Blue in Green has what Evans, in his notes for the album, calls "a 10-measure circular form," without further explanation. The circularity is apparent, though only after listening with the kind of concentration needed to solve a conundrum, in the movement of the piece as a whole: it opens with Davis's muted trumpet exploring a theme, continues with Evans exploring a second theme, and then introduces Coltrane playing yet a third theme, but after that Evans returns with his earlier theme and Davis then closes as he opened. Each of the three players thus has his own scale to play, and only when the overall structure is understood do the three parts connect.

Flamenco Sketches is less puzzling (although for many years Columbia issued the LP with *Flamenco Sketches* identified as *All Blues* and vice versa, which made it much *more* puzzling). It is a slow blues constructed over a latinate beat that seems to be implied rather than stated. One reviewer, Ronald Atkins, notes that "few recordings exude so hushed an air of solemnity – a feeling arising as much from the absolute perfection of the solos as from the slow tempo."

The other three compositions draw the listener's attention more insistently. *Freddie Freeloader*, a more traditional blues than *Flamenco Sketches*, played in 4/4 time, gives Wynton Kelly a star turn for his only appearance. He fills in the spaces between the simple, singing lines played in unison by all three horns and takes the lead solo as well, in which he gets away with more than a few old-fashioned clichés amid the new sounds. While it is unjust to single out individual solos on an album loaded with excellent ones, Julian Adderley's marvelous blues on *Freddie Freeloader* stands out even in superior company.

The remaining two compositions, *All Blues* and *So What*, are purely and simply masterpieces. Max Harrison calls *All Blues* "a good example of primitive jazz serialism," which he explains this way: "Here, instead of a chord sequence, the improvisations are based on a series of five scales, that is, five selections of notes from the twelve available. Davis constructed fragmentary tone-rows which replace harmony in giving the music coherence." The ensemble structure builds up layers of sound, starting with a repeated trill by Evans, stepping up to sing-song cadence by the saxophones, and topping off with Davis's muted statement of the melody, all built on 6/8 rhythm. The solos that follow are of unequal duration, apparently dictated by each soloist's progress from scale to scale.

The most complicated work formally, *So What*, has also had the greatest currency among other jazz players, no doubt partly because Davis's band began playing it regularly from the very start, but also because of its infectious construction, in which Paul Chambers's ostinato, the unifying line throughout, is answered first by the piano and then by the horns. Martin Williams observes that *So What*, "in a sense restricted as well as free in its outline, asks the improviser to make his melody from one assigned Dorian mode for sixteen measures, then a half-step up for eight measures, then back to the first mode for the final eight measures." Jerry Coker, illustrating the point that Davis "didn't merely change *with* the times (with regard to style) but was largely – if not completely – *responsible* for most of the changes," explicates Davis's particular use of the Dorian scale, the mode that was the subject of George Russell's dissertation, observing that *So What* "intro-duced a voicing for the Dorian mode that is now often referred to as the *So What* voicing. Actually it is one voicing used in two different places in the mode, so that the keyboard player has two vertical chord sounds for each mode occurrence, with each using only available tones from the Dorian scale."

Coker's explanation is intended for musicians, but whatever else a general audi-ence might take from it, it at least shows clearly a significant role that *So What* filled – and is still filling – in disseminating the use of modal structures among jazzmen. For the young players coming up in the years right after the recording of *So What*, formal instruction in the use of modes in jazz was simply unavailable. Young players struggling with *So What* eventually grasped its formal basis intuitively, and for the more thoughtful among them that was enough to start them working at extending it. Coker mentions McCoy Tyner, Herbie Hancock, Chick Corea, and Keith Jarrett among the prominent young piano players who make heavy use of its voicing in their own work. *So What*, and to some extent all the compositions on the *Kind of Blue* recording, provided informal lessons for jazz players emerging in the 1960s, but it did so only because of the masterful perfor-mance that introduced it to the public. It was a tune that young players felt they had to learn to play.

In any discussion of *Kind of Blue*, there is a temptation to belabor its formal aspects. While ignoring them is impossible, stressing them misrepresents the music and the intentions of the men who made it. Davis's major contribution to jazz form, of which *Kind of Blue* stands as the most influential example, involves a principled shift from the constraints of chordal organization to the different constraints of scalar organization. Instead of constructing melodies by selecting a few notes from each consecutive chord, Davis's music forced him and the other players to create melodies from a single scale for long stretches. In *So What*, only two scales are available in each cycle of thirty-two bars, forcing the improviser to find novel combinations by selecting notes from two sustained chords.

As a working musician, Davis showed no interest in the theoretical niceties of his innovation except as a means of relieving his music of the predictable chord progressions, creating an aural effect of lightness, and challenging his melodic ingenuity. Because his goals were functional rather than purely academic, he succeeded in bringing modal constructions fully into jazz where George Russell and others had not really succeeded despite years of diligent study. Davis's modal innovations have escaped entirely any allegations of obscurantism, formalism, ivory-towerism, and the like. On the contrary, the best of his modal composi-tions – *Milestones*, all of *Kind of Blue*, and some of Evans's recompositions on *Miles Ahead* and *Porgy and Bess* – met with an enthusiastic popular and critical response. His achievement was not merely in altering the formal basis of the music but in doing it in the service of some of the most affecting small-band and orchestral jazz ever played.

One of the most astute comments ever made about the *Kind of Blue* sessions came from Bill Evans. "We just really went in that day and did our thing," he told Lee Jeske twenty years later. In Evans's liner notes for the album, he says: "Miles conceived these settings only hours before the recording dates and arrived with sketches which indicated to the group what was to be played. Therefore, you will hear something close to pure spontaneity in these performances. The group had never played these pieces prior to the recordings and I think without exception the first complete performance of each was a 'take.'" That statement flatly contradicts J.C. Thomas's claim about Evans's role as a co-composer and jibes perfectly with everything we know about Davis's disdain for rehearsals and multiple takes. Valuing immediacy and spontaneity above polish and precision, Davis maintains that if a jazz musician were forced to respond to a situation he might otherwise have thought to be beyond his capacities, he might very well come up with an unexpected and stunning solution, perhaps even a moment of genius. "If you place a guy in a spot where he has to do something else, other than what he can do, ... he can do *that*," he told Leonard Feather. "He's got to have something that challenges his imagination, far above what he thinks he's going to play, and what it might lead into, and then above *that*, so he won't be fighting when things change."

Davis's belief in challenges lies behind his claim that "real" jazz records will have the "mistakes" left in them and also accounts for his disdain for rehearsing during the sextet years. Julian Adderley recalled, "As for rehearsals, we had maybe five in the two years I was there, two of them when I first joined the band. And the rehearsals were quite direct, like, 'Coltrane, show Cannonball how you do this. All right now, let's do it.' Occasionally, Miles would tell us something on the stand. 'Cannonball, you don't have to play *all* those notes. Just stay close to the sound of the melody. Those substitute chords sound funny.'" Adderley's five rehearsals in two years were a bonus that Bill Evans did not get during his eight months in the band. "We never had a rehearsal," he said. "Everything was done on the job. On the record dates, half or all of the material might be all new and had never been rehearsed before." Needless to say, that kind of regimen could work only with a cast of superior musicians. With the players in the sextet, especially on *Kind of Blue*, it worked magnificently.

The approach included potential pitfalls. If the group of musicians happened to be much larger than, say, six or seven, the lack of rehearsal time could be telling. It was also likely to pose problems for musicians who did not regularly work together or know one another's responses very well. Those problems cropped up two weeks after the second *Kind of Blue* session, on 4 and 5 May, when John Coltrane arrived at the Atlantic recording studios to make his second album under his new contract. The music he recorded was eventually released as *Giant Steps* (Atlantic 1311), and it is probably the first truly indispensable recording by Coltrane as a leader, so the method he used was hardly a complete failure. However, he arrived in the studio with a sheaf of completely fresh and unknown sketches for his compositions *Countdown* (based on Davis's *Tune up*), *Cousin Mary*, *Syeeda's Flute Song*, *Spiral*, and *Giant Steps*, all recorded in the two days, and several other pieces as well. He presented them, as Davis had done with him so many times before, to Tommy Flanagan, Paul Chambers, and Arthur Taylor.

As good as these musicians were, they found it impossible to handle all the material on such short notice. "As he explained to me, in this date he wanted to get a lot of things out of his system," Tommy Flanagan told Michael Ullmann. "He did a lot of songs with the same kind of chord progression as in *Giant Steps*. Some things didn't even appear on the record – we just couldn't play them. The tempos were too fast and we didn't have enough time to get it all down in one session." Then Flanagan reflected on the whole Davis-based process: "Why they like to do a whole album in one session I don't know. It almost kills you, to stay with that kind of playing – so intense – for eight hours a day. It takes a toll on you, unless you really know what you are doing. Trane knew what *he* was doing." Coltrane was also learning that there were other, perhaps better, ways of doing things than the ways that seemed to work so well for Miles Davis.

In the spring of 1959, Birdland revitalized its jazz policy after a period of wavering loyalties, and the Miles Davis Sextet moved in. Their engagement there is documented by a taped broadcast of *Bags' Groove*, which has not yet been released as a recording. (This performance has circulated among private collectors for many years mistakenly identified as *Walkin'*.) Its reappearance in Davis's repertoire for the first time since its extraordinary performance in the Christmas eve session of 1954 is almost certainly calculated to show off the strengths of Wynton Kelly. Although it is given an enthusiastic playing, it does not allow the sextet to show any of the subtlety of their recent recordings. It seems a little time-worn because it had been widely recorded after Davis's seminal recording of it, and it was also part of the Modern Jazz Quartet's working repertoire. Davis might better have started performing *Freddie Freeloader*, also within Kelly's métier, but unfortunately he never performed it beyond the studio walls.

Around the same time that Birdland reopened for jazz, an even more historic revival was attempted. The Apollo Theater in Harlem, for decades the most famous nightclub in uptown New York, was refurbished and reopened by some young black businessmen, in an attempt to revive its former glory. The revival did not work, but during the short-lived reopening the Miles Davis Sextet were one of its headline attractions, in a jazz slate that also included Thelonious Monk, James Moody, Eddie Jefferson, Betty Carter, and comedienne Moms Mabley. The Apollo performances, as C.O. Simpkins recalls them, featured John Coltrane playing in a kind of extraterrestrial frenzy. On one occasion, Simpkins says, he "got down on his knees, throwing off the fire of his improvisation," and on another, he "closed his eyes and continued over the twenty minute time limit the Apollo set for each group." In Simpkins's description, everyone backstage except Miles Davis seems to have ended up in a comparable frenzy: "The lights were blinking. Curtains were going back and forth. The stage manager shouted to Miles, 'Go get him, man! Go get him! We runnin' over the show! Stop him!' but John kept on playing."

The sextet spent the first three weeks of June in San Francisco at the Blackhawk, receiving an enthusiastic review from Russ Wilson in the *Oakland Tribune*. Wilson singled out their performances of *Autumn Leaves*, *Two Bass Hit*, and *Billy Boy*, as well as "several new originals by Davis," among them "a still-untitled blues that starts and ends in 3/4 time" and "another that employs an Afro-Cuban beat," probably *All Blues* and *So What*, respectively. Wilson also broke the news of Coltrane's desire to move out on his own. "There's nothing definite yet," Coltrane told Wilson, "but I have been seriously thinking of it." Wilson went on to say, "Coltrane has informed Miles of this, and should the parting come, it will be amicable. Davis understands Coltrane's viewpoint and will not stand in his way." The article mentions that Coltrane's most likely successor in the band was Jimmy Heath. (Heath did become Coltrane's immediate successor, but only for two months and not until another year had passed.) Of Coltrane, Wilson notes, "In the last year or so he has come to be regarded as one of the most exciting and influential tenor saxophonists in jazz, a factor that figures in his thinking."

Not the least of Coltrane's successes during this year was an adulatory article entitled "The style of John Coltrane," by Zita Carno, in the October issue of the *Jazz Review*. "Coltrane seems to have the power to pull listeners right out of their chairs," Carno said. "I have noticed this terrific impact on the various rhythm sections he has played with; he pulls them right along and makes them cook, too." Carno's illustration drew on the sextet. "Say Miles Davis is the first soloist," she says. "Notice the rhythm section doesn't push. They are relaxed behind him. Now Coltrane takes over, and immediately something happens to the group: the rhythm section tightens up and plays harder. The bass becomes stronger and more forceful, as does the ride cymbal beat; even the piano comps differently. They can't help it – Coltrane is driving them ahead." What Carno had noticed was the stylistic contrast between Davis and Coltrane that Davis had built into the group sound almost from the beginning of Coltrane's tenure.

For all his restlessness, Coltrane remained with Davis long after their tour of the West Coast ended. He stayed mainly because he lacked confidence in his own drawing power as a leader and because he enjoyed the financial security of working for Davis. *Down Beat* reported that the sextet were paid $2,500 a week for their engagement at the Seville at the end of this tour.

Summer arrived and the sextet, barely back from their spring tour, set off on a round of festival appearances. One of these, in early August, took them to Chicago for the first Playboy Jazz Festival, sponsored by the phenomenally successful business conglomerate that started out as a magazine featuring naked women and trendy fiction, and expanded into nightclubs, health spas, television and film production, and much else. The jazz festival at Chicago Stadium was its latest venture. Coltrane chose to stay behind in New York, working at his own commitments, but if his decision upset Davis and the others it certainly did not show in the makeshift quintet's performance of *So What* that was broadcast from the festival. It is taken at a quicker pace than usual, a familiar change in Davis's live performances of his standard repertoire, but there is no impression of his carelessness in the quickening of the tempo, as there so often is in his other live performances, such as the Newport festival performance. Davis himself plays a long, ebullient, driving solo, and he is followed by a beautifully swinging statement by Adderley. Although the overrecorded drums threaten to drown out Wynton Kelly's solo, enough of it is recoverable to hear in it a sparkling, basic romp, and when the horns riff behind him in the last choruses he rises above them and earns a burst of spontaneous applause. The large, enthusiastic crowd may well be the key to what turns out to be a great live performance by the band, perhaps the best unissued performance from this period.

Near the end of August the band settled into Birdland. They were happy to be back in New York, but the long stint on the road in the spring and the summer traveling had taken their toll. Coltrane was back in the band, but he continued to complain about being there. Wayne Shorter, who was playing with Maynard Ferguson's big band opposite the sextet, listened every night to Coltrane's talk about starting his own band. At one point Coltrane told him, "You want to be with Miles? You got it. I'm finished doing the Miles gig." Davis seemed to be grumbling much of the time too, although that was probably less surprising. One night he left the stand while the rhythm trio were playing their feature and sat down at the musicians' table with Michael Zwerin. "Miles seemed annoyed," Zwerin says. "He said, 'What the hell is Paul doing with the time?' The time seemed pretty good to me, but I didn't comment." Things were not going very smoothly for Davis at the moment. And then the roof caved in.

On the night of 26 August, a Tuesday, the kind of muggy day you get in New York before the summer starts making its long transition into fall, Davis came up out of the basement jazz club with a woman at his side. She was young, and she was white. He walked with her to the curb where a taxi was waiting and watched her ride off in it. He glanced at his watch, and then he dug a cigarette out of his shirt pocket, but as soon as he got it lit the policeman who patrolled that part of Broadway strolled up and stopped in front of him.

"No loitering," he said. "Move along."

"I work here," Davis said with a glance. The cop was by Birdland every night. He knew who Davis was and what he was doing there.

The policeman told him move along again. He seemed to be dead serious.

Davis got serious too. "I'm not going nowhere – I'm just getting a breath of fresh air."

"Move!" he shouted.

"I'm trying to dry off, get some air. It's smokey down there ..."

The policeman said he would arrest him if he did not get moving right away, and Davis said, "Go ahead, lock me up." Broadway was crowded and several people gathered around them now, gawking.

The policeman stepped closer and said, "Are you goin' peaceful, or am I gonna put handcuffs on you?" He reached for Davis's wrist and Davis pulled it away; he reached for it again and Davis pushed his arm away. The cop moved in fast and grabbed his shoulders and somebody else came toward him out of the crowd, and after that everything was just a blur.

He was in a police station and blood was dripping onto his shirt, the way it does when you get a cut on the scalp. The policeman was holding him by the arm and the other man, the one who had hit him with the nightstick, was there too. He was a plainclothes policeman.

They had asked him who he wanted them to phone, and he gave them his home number, but now that things were coming clearer he knew he should have got Lovett and left Frances out of it, but the blood was oozing down his face onto his shirt and by the time they finished booking him on charges of disorderly conduct and assault, Frances Davis was there. She took one look at him and was nearly hysterical.

At the hospital with the police still standing around and his wife fretful beside him, a doctor put in ten stitches to close the gash in his head. Some reporters arrived and a press photographer came in after them. And then he was taken back to the station and kept there overnight. His arrest made the front pages of the New York papers the next day.

When Harold Lovett arrived in the morning to post bail he was livid. Miles Davis said little but he was livid too, now that the blur was clearing away. When a reporter asked him if it was true that the policeman dropped his nightstick and

Miles Davis Sextet listening to a playback in the studio; from left, Red Garland, Davis, Paul Chambers, and Julian Adderley (Columbia Records, courtesy of *Down Beat*)

Miles Davis recording *Porgy and Bess* (Don Hunstein, Columbia Records, courtesy of *Down Beat*)

Miles Davis entering the police station after the Birdland incident (*New York Journal-American*, courtesy of *Down Beat*)

Davis had picked it up, he just pointed to the bandage on his head and said, "If I picked it up I wouldn't look like this."

That day a spokesman for the police department announced that Davis's cabaret card was revoked and until it was reinstated he was barred from working in New York clubs. Harold Lovett announced that Davis was suing the city for half a million dollars for illegal arrest. Those announcements made most of the front pages too. From then on, everything was in the hands of the courts and it looked as if it might take forever to get the whole thing settled. The newspaper accounts receded into the middle pages when they saw print at all.

In the cool world where Miles Davis was the undisputed champion, life went on pretty much as it always had. There were lots of whispers, naturally, and people who loved Davis's image more than his music saw the whole affair as another awesome act by their hero, taking on the whole NYPD, a real mystique-builder. Davis's closest associates, the men in his band, reacted the way jazzmen of their generation were expected to react. They went in and started the next set at Birdland without him, and they played their hearts out until closing time. Al Young, a novelist who went to Birdland that night to hear John Coltrane, came away thinking that Davis's absence had been a bonus for him. "Sure enough, there was Coltrane sounding totally different from the way he did on the latest recordings I'd gathered," he wrote. "It was the very night Miles Davis stepped outside between sets and got in an altercation with some cops about loitering. He had to be hospitalized. The band, winding up the evening without its leader, continued to smoke and burn until the very air crackled with flames scorching enough to warm the heart of even a plainclothes policeman. It was truly a Coltrane night."

In the larger world, the whole thing was forgotten almost as soon as the newspapers that reported it were thrown out. There were no editorials in the big dailies expounding on the right of a citizen to take a smoke break outside the place where he was working on a hot night, no law associations petitioning the revoking of a cabaret card because of a criminal charge that had not yet even come to court, no demonstrators marching to protest police brutality, and no riots in Harlem proclaiming the civil liberties of a distinguished member of the black minority. If the incident had happened five years later there might have been some response along those lines, and ten years later there might have been a whole program of responses along those lines, but this was 1959.

Davis's bitterness was undisguised. He stated immediately that the whole incident happened because the young woman he was escorting to the taxi was white.

The legal proceedings did nothing at all to assuage his bitterness either. His suit against the city had a reasonable legal basis but Davis was caught in a double bind with both the criminal charges hanging over his head and the police-controlled cabaret card revoked. (The constitutionality of the police issuing cabaret cards was strongly challenged at police commission hearings starting in late 1960 by a committee of entertainers and artists; as the committee piled up evidence of alleged irregularities in the issuing and withholding of the cards, police enforcement of card-holding slackened off and the city council finally abolished them altogether several years later.) In the end, Davis was enjoined by his lawyers to drop his suit altogether, evidently to fulfill his end of a plea bargain. On 24 October, almost two months after he had been hit on the head, a panel of three judges ruled that his arrest had been illegal and dismissed the charges against him.

The legal hassles ended around the time the gash on his head was fully healed, but the court's decision has not really had the same healing effect. Not surprisingly, he remains bitter. Also perhaps not surprisingly, he feels that he was attacked because he is a black man and that he was denied justice because he is a black man. Mary Lou Williams, the piano player who in her later years had a propensity for moralizing and spiritualizing, talked to Roland Baggenaes about the people she remembered from her days on 52nd Street, and when she came to Miles Davis she could not resist bringing his spiritual history up to date in her own peculiar terms. "Miles was terrific then," she said. "Miles was not like he is now. When I saw him in England he would try to be nice and everything, but, you know, something very bad happened to him when Birdland was open. Miles used to stand outside and he was beaten by the police and since that time he has been kind of – off. You know, I saw Miles in England and he just grabbed and hugged and kissed me, but I was afraid of him." Mary Lou Williams's impression of Davis is as unique as her impressions of dozens of other people; she seemed to see everyone with a singular eye. To her, Davis had withdrawn even further after the Birdland incident and had become vaguely threatening. But she was not the only one who saw that in him. Davis's idolators of the 1960s saw something of the same dark threat in his public image, and they took to calling him the "prince of darkness." Perhaps that is the image a man intends to leave people with when he drops ominous hints of malevolence, as Davis did when speaking to Joachim Berendt about the fate of the policeman involved in the Birdland incident. "The cop was killed, too," he said. "In a subway."

There can be little doubt that the incident remains for him an active ghost. When Sy Johnson interviewed Davis in 1976, seventeen long and eventful years after the incident, their conversation centered on music and musicians, but during a pause while they listened to a tape, completely out of the blue, there was a strange twist in the conversation:

"White people don't like me," Davis said. Johnson glanced over at him.

"'I mean, a policeman grabbed me around the neck.'

"'Why?'

"'Cause I was black. I'm not gonna say what no white man wants me to say.'

"He reassured me, 'I'm talkin' 'bout a policeman – "Are you goin' peaceful, or am I gonna put handcuffs on you?" I'm supposed to say, "Yes, I'll go down peaceful"?'

"'That's what I would have said' [says Johnson, and after a pause:] 'Is it gonna be o.k.?'

"He shrugs."

The scars definitely seem to go deeper than his scalp.

The incident at Birdland affected his professional activities immediately following it. With his cabaret card revoked so that he could not work even if he wanted to, Davis absorbed himself in the legal battles being fought over him, keeping abreast of events whenever there were any new developments and suffering impatiently when there was nothing happening. The sextet ceased to exist at the end of September when Julian Adderley left, as he had said he would after two years. Coltrane did not leave immediately, although he always acted as if he wanted to, his vacillation continuing for another ten months. Wynton Kelly, Paul Chambers, and Jimmy Cobb remained too and stayed long after Coltrane finally left. So Davis still had the men he wanted, the ones he had brought along with him, two of them from the days of the quintet, another of them, Cobb, from the days of the great sextet with Bill Evans, and the other one, Kelly, though a relative newcomer, as close as anyone could be, as Adderley had said, to combining the talents of Evans and Red Garland. There was no lack of high-class manpower.

If there was something missing, it showed most conspicuously in Davis's lack of interest in expanding his music. For the next four years, he explored no new modal voicings, tried no new settings, and wrote almost no new music. To be sure, the Miles Davis Quintet remained one of the finest bands around, and Davis continued to play ballads as effectively as anyone ever had. But the rich promise of *Kind of Blue* remained largely unfulfilled, at least by Davis's bands. Most of Davis's career is impelled by his search for new plateaus, but between 1959 and 1964 he seemed content to remain on the plateau he was already on. In the same period, there were changes coming fast in jazz in general, and for the first and perhaps the only time in his career he would not only not direct those changes but he would not even appreciate them. It was a bitter irony for the man who said of his musicians, "He's got to have something that challenges his imagination, far above what he thinks he's going to play and what it might lead into, and then above *that*, so he won't be fighting when things change." As Martin Williams said, "*Kind of Blue* was an influential record both in and of itself and because it paralleled other, independently conceived, events in jazz. But for a while it seemed a rather isolated event for Davis himself – one might say that it was more immediately important to John Coltrane's development than to Davis, and for the next few years the repertory of ballads and standards was resumed to a great extent." For some four years – a relatively short time in so long and productive a career – there was a pause, and though it was highly creative in many ways, it was definitely out of character. For part of that time, one cannot even know for certain what Davis's music was like, because he entered the recording studios on only three days between April 1959, when he completed the second of the *Kind of Blue* sessions, and March 1961. For the time being, the apostle of change became the prince of darkness.

Bibliography

Adderley, Julian (Cannonball) "Paying dues: the education of a combo leader" *Jazz Review*. Reprinted in Martin Williams ed *Jazz Panorama* New York: Collier 1964

Albertson, Chris "The unmasking of Miles Davis" *Saturday Review* 27 November 1971

Amram, David *Vibrations* New York: Macmillan 1968

Anderson, Jervis "Harlem IV: Hard times and beyond" *New Yorker* 20 July 1981

Baggenaes, Roland "Duke Jordan" *Coda* October 1973

— "Interview with Mary Lou Williams" *Coda* July 1974

— "Red Rodney" *Coda* February 1976

— "Interview with Marc Levin" *Coda* March 1976

Balliett, Whitney *The Sound of Surprise* Harmondsworth: Penguin 1959

— *Dinosaurs in the Morning* Philadelphia: J.B. Lippincott 1962

— *Alec Wilder and His Friends* Boston: Houghton Mifflin 1974

— *Improvising: Sixteen Jazz Musicians and Their Art* New York: Oxford University Press 1977

— *Night Creature: A Journal of Jazz, 1975–80* New York: Oxford University Press 1981

Berendt, Joachim *The Jazz Book* St Albans, Herts: Paladin 1976

Berg, Chuck "Interview with Dexter Gordon" *Down Beat* 10 February 1977

Bernstein, Leonard *The Joy of Music* New York: Simon and Schuster 1959

Birnbaum, Larry "Ahmad Jamal" *Down Beat* March 1981

— "Eddie 'Cleanhead' Vinson" *Down Beat* October 1982

Bosworth, Patricia *Montgomery Clift* New York: Harcourt, Brace, Jovanovich 1978

Brown, Richard "Ah! Unh! Mr. Funk" *Down Beat* October 1979

Brown, Ron Review of *Miles Davis: Blue Moods* (America 30 AM 6051) *Jazz Journal* July 1972

Burns, Jim "Miles Davis: the early years" *Jazz Journal* January 1970

Butcher, Mike "Modern jazz: the bopsters and beyond" In Sinclair Traill ed *Concerning Jazz* London: Faber 1957

Carno, Zita "The style of John Coltrane" *Jazz Review* October and November 1959

Carr, Ian *Miles Davis: A Biography* New York: Morrow 1982

Chadbourne, Eugene "Heard and Seen: Miles Davis" *Coda* June 1973

Chilton, John *Billie's Blues* London: Quartet 1975

– *Who's Who of Jazz: Storyville to Swing Street* Revised Time-Life Records Special Edition 1979

Choice, Harriet "Miles Davis, solo: brews concocted and broods begotten" *Chicago Tribune* (Arts and Fun section) 20 January 1974

Coker, Jerry *The Jazz Idiom* Englewood Cliffs, NJ: Prentice-Hall 1975

Cole, Bill *Miles Davis: A Musical Biography* New York: Morrow 1974

Collier, James Lincoln *The Making of Jazz: A Comprehensive History* Boston: Houghton Mifflin 1978

Coltrane, John "Coltrane on Coltrane" *Down Beat* 29 September 1960

– Liner note *A Love Supreme* (Impulse A-77) 1964

Coryell, Julie, and Laura Friedman *Jazz-Rock Fusion: The People, the Music* New York: Delta 1978

Coss, Bill. Liner note *Miles Davis: Blue Moods* (Debut DEB-120) ca 1956

Crawford, Marc "Miles Davis: evil genius of jazz" *Ebony* 16 January 1961

Crosbie, Ian "Claude Thornhill" *Coda* October 1975

Crouch, Stanley. Liner note *Thelonious Monk at the Five Spot* (Milestone M-47043) 1977

Dance, Stanley *The World of Duke Ellington* London: Macmillan 1970

– *The World of Count Basie* New York: Scribner's 1980

Davis, Miles "Self-portrait of the artist" Columbia Records Biographical Service 26 November 1957

DeMicheal, Don "Miles Davis" *Rolling Stone* 27 December 1969

Dorough, Bob. Liner note *Yardbird Suite* (Bethlehem Records BCP-6023) 1976

Evans, Bill. Liner note *Miles Davis: Kind of Blue* (Columbia CL 1355) ca 1959

Feather, Leonard. Liner note *John Graas: Jazz Lab 2* (Decca DL 8478) ca 1957

– *Encyclopedia of Jazz* Revised. New York: Bonanza 1960

– *Encyclopedia of Jazz in the Sixties* New York: Bonanza 1966

– "The modulated world of Gil Evans" *Down Beat* 23 February 1967

– "Blindfold test: Miles Davis" *Down Beat*. Reprinted in Feather and Ira Gitler *Encyclopedia of Jazz in the Seventies* New York: Horizon 1976

– "Blindfold test: Michel Legrand" *Down Beat* 28 December 1967

– *From Satchmo to Miles* London: Quartet 1974

– *The Pleasures of Jazz* New York: Horizon 1976

– *The Passion for Jazz* New York: Horizon 1980

Feather, Leonard, and Ira Gitler *Encyclopedia of Jazz in the Seventies* New York: Horizon 1976

Feather, Leonard, and Conrad Silvert "Jazz world remembers Bird" *Down Beat* August 1980

Feather, Leonard, and Jack Tracy *Laughter from the Hip: The Lighter Side of Jazz* New York: DaCapo 1979 (first published 1963)

Fox, Charles "Gil Evans: experiment with texture" In Raymond Horricks ed *These Jazzmen of Our Time* London: Jazz Book Club 1960

– Liner note *Cannonball and Coltrane* (Mercury [Netherlands] 6336 319)

– *The Jazz Scene* London: Hamlyn 1972

Gardner, Mark. Review of *Miles Davis* (UAS 9952) *Jazz Journal* March 1972

Garland, Red "Memories of Miles" *Musician, Player and Listener* 41, March 1982

Getz, Stan. Album notes *Stan Getz* (Book-of-the-Month-Club Records BOMC 40-5510) 1980

Gifford, Barry, and Lawrence Lee *Jack's Book: An Oral Biography of Jack Kerouac* New York: St Martin's Press 1978

Gillespie, Dizzy, and Al Fraser *To Be or Not to Bop* New York: Doubleday 1979

Gitler, Ira. Liner note *Miles Davis and the Modern Jazz Giants* (Prestige LP 7150) ca 1957

– Liner note *Miles Davis: Collectors' Items* (Prestige LP 7044) ca 1957

– Liner note *Sonny Rollins First Recordings* (Prestige 7856) 1971

Gleason, Ralph J. *Celebrating the Duke ... and Other Heroes* Boston: Little, Brown and Co 1975

Goddet, Laurent "Randy Weston interview" *Coda* 1 February 1978

Goldberg, Joe *Jazz Masters of the Fifties* New York: Macmillan 1956

Golson, Benny. Review of *Miles Davis: Milestones* (Columbia CL 1193) *Jazz Review* January 1959

Goode, Mort. Liner note *Basic Miles* (Columbia C 32025) 1973

Goodman, George, Jr "Miles Davis: 'I just pick up my horn and play.'" *New York Times* Sunday 28 June 1981

Gordon, Max *Live at the Village Vanguard* New York: St Martin's Press 1980

Gottlieb, William P. *The Golden Age of Jazz* New York: Simon and Schuster 1979

Grimes, Kitty *Jazz at Ronnie Scott's* London: Robert Hale 1979

Hailey, Alex "Playboy interview: Miles Davis" *Playboy* September 1962

Hakim, Sadik "My experiences with Bird and Prez" *Coda* 181, December 1981

Hall, Gregg "Miles: today's most influential contemporary musician" *Down Beat* 18 July 1974

– "Teo [Macero]: the man behind the scene" *Down Beat* 18 July 1974

Hamm, Charles *Yesterdays: Popular Song in America* New York: W.W. Norton 1979

Hammond, John, with Irving Townsend *John Hammond on Record* New York: Ridge Press 1977

Harrison, Max *A Jazz Retrospect* Boston: Crescendo 1976

Harrison, Max, Alun Morgan, Ronald Atkins, Michael James, and Jack Cooke *Modern Jazz: the Essential Records* London: Aquarius 1975

Hawes, Hampton, and Don Asher *Raise Up Off Me* New York: Coward, McCann and Geohegan 1974

Hentoff, Nat. Review of *Miles* (Prestige LP 7014) *Down Beat* 16 May 1956

- "Birth of the cool, parts 1 and 2" *Down Beat* 2 and 16 May 1957

- "An afternoon with Miles Davis" *Jazz Review* December 1958. Reprinted in Martin Williams ed *Jazz Panorama* New York: Collier 1964

- "Miles Davis: a story of Miles" *Esquire's World of Jazz* New York: Thomas Y. Crowell 1975 (from *Esquire* 1959)

- Liner note *The Piano Scene of Ahmad Jamal* (Epic LN 3631) ca 1961

- *Jazz Is* New York: Random House 1976

Hodeir, André *Jazz: Its Evolution and Essence* trans David Noakes. New York: Grove Press 1956

- *Toward Jazz* trans Noel Burch. London: The Jazz Book Club 1965

Hoefer, George "The birth of the cool" *Down Beat* 7 October 1965

- "Early Miles" *Down Beat* 6 April 1967

Holmes, John Clellon "The philosophy of the Beat Generation" *Esquire* 1958

Horricks, Raymond "Thelonious Monk" In *These Jazzmen of Our Time* London: The Jazz Book Club 1960

Jablonski, Edward "The making of *Porgy and Bess*" *New York Times Magazine* 19 October 1980

James, Michael *Miles Davis* New York: A.S. Barnes 1961

Jepsen, Jorgen Grunnet *A Discography of Miles Davis* Copenhagen: Karl Emil Knudsen 1969

Jeske, Lee "Bill Evans: trio master" *Down Beat* October 1979

- "Jimmy Knepper" *Down Beat*, August 1981

Jewell, Derek *Duke: A Portrait of Duke Ellington* New York: W.W. Norton 1980

Joans, Ted "Bird and the Beats" *Coda* 181, December 1981

Johnson, Sy. Liner note *Black Giants* (Columbia PG 33402) 1975

- "Miles" *Jazz Magazine* fall 1976

Katz, Dick "Miles Davis" *Jazz Review*. Reprinted in Martin Williams ed *Jazz Panorama* New York: Collier 1964

Kimball, Robert, and Alfred Simon *The Gershwins* New York: Bonanza 1973

Kofsky, Frank *Black Nationalism and the Revolution in Music* New York: Pathfinder 1970

Korall, Burt "Tal Farlow: Turning away from fame" *Down Beat* 22 February 1979

Lysted, Lars "Meet Benny Bailey" *Down Beat* 15 February 1973

McCall, Cheryl "Miles Davis" *Musician, Player and Listener* 41, March 1982

McDonough, Bob "Profile: Barrett Deems" *Down Beat* 5 October 1978

McRae, Barry. Review of *Early Miles* (Prestige PR 7674) *Jazz Journal* September 1975

Maher, Jack. Liner note *Miles Davis: Workin'* (Prestige 7166) ca 1957

Martin, John. Editorial *Jazz News* 1 October 1960

– "Miles out" *Jazz News* 1 October 1960

Martin, Terry. Review of *Miles Davis* (UAS 9952) *Down Beat* 22 June 1972

Meeker, David *Jazz in the Movies* New Rochelle, NY: Arlington House 1977

Mingus, Charles *Beneath the Underdog* ed Nel King. New York: Knopf 1971

Monk, Thelonious "What the performer thinks" *Esquire's World of Jazz* New York: Thomas Y. Crowell 1975

Moorhead, Arthur "Cedar Walton's major league play" *Down Beat* January 1981

Morgan, Alun "Miles Davis: Miles ahead" In Raymond Horricks ed *These Jazzmen of Our Time* London: The Jazz Book Club 1960

– Liner note *The Definitive Charlie Parker* Vol 4 (Metro Records 2356 087)

Morgenstern, Dan "Miles Davis" In George T. Simon et al *The Best of the Music Makers* New York: Doubleday 1979

Mulligan, Gerry. Liner note *The Complete Birth of the Cool* (Capitol M-11026) 1971

Nisenson, Eric *'Round about Midnight: A Portrait of Miles Davis* New York: Dial 1982

Nolan, Herb "Blindfold Test: Lenny White" *Down Beat* 14 March 1974

– "Helen Merrill" *Down Beat* 6 May 1976

O'Day, Anita, with George Eels *High Times Hard Times* New York: G.P. Putnam's Sons 1981

Pepper, Art, and Laurie Pepper *Straight Life: The Story of Art Pepper* New York: Schirmer 1979

Perla, Gene "Dave Liebman" *Coda* January 1974

Peterson, Owen. Letter *Jazz and Blues* March 1972

Porter, Bob "Talking with Teddy [Reig]" Album notes *Charlie Parker: The Complete Savoy Studio Sessions* (Savoy S5J 5500)

Priestley, Brian "Discography" Appendix C in Ian Carr *Miles Davis: A Biography* New York: Morrow 1982 pp 267–300

Primack, Brett "Drummers' colloquium III" *Down Beat* November 1979

Prince, Linda "Betty Carter: bebopper breathes fire" *Down Beat* 3 May 1979

Ramsey, Doug. Liner note *Julian Adderley: What I Mean* (Milestone M-47053) 1979

Reisner, Robert G. *Bird: The Legend of Charlie Parker* New York: Bonanza 1962

Renaud, Henri. Liner note *A Jazz Piano Anthology* (Columbia KG 32355) 1973

Rosenblum, Bob "Jimmy Heath" *Coda* June 1976

– Liner note *Chet Baker: Once upon a Summertime* (Artists House 9411) 1980

Ruppli, Michel "Discographie: Miles Davis" *Jazz Hot* February and March 1979

Russell, George *The Lydian Chromatic Concept of Tonal Organization* New York: Concept 1953

Russell, Ross "Bebop: Part III – Brass" *Record Changer* 1948–9. Reprinted in Martin Williams ed *The Art of Jazz* London: The Jazz Book Club 1962

– *Bird Lives! The High Life and Hard Times of Charlie (Yardbird) Parker* New York: Charterhouse 1973
– Liner note *Yardbird in Lotus Land* (Spotlite SPJ 123) 1975
Saal, Hubert "Jazz comes back!" *Newsweek* 8 August 1977
Saunders, Jimmy. Interview with Miles Davis *Playboy* April 1975
Shapiro, Nat, and Nat Hentoff *Hear Me Talkin' to Ya* New York: Dover 1955
Shaw, Arnold *The Street That Never Slept* New York: Coward, McCann and Geohegan 1971
Shera, Michael. Review of *Miles Davis-Tadd Dameron* (Columbia 34804) *Jazz Journal* April 1978
Silvert, Conrad "Herbie Hancock: revamping the present, creating the future" *Down Beat* 8 September 1977
– "Joe Zawinul: wayfaring genius" *Down Beat* 1 June 1978
Simmen, Johnny "George 'Big Nick' Nicholas" *Jazz Journal* September 1972
Simpkins, C.O. *Coltrane: A Biography* New York: Herndon House 1975
Smith, Bill "The Anthony Braxton interview" *Coda* April 1974
Spellman, A.B. *Black Music: Four Lives* (originally *Four Lives in the Bebop Business* 1966) New York: Schocken 1970
Stearns, Marshall W. *The Story of Jazz* New York: Oxford University Press 1956
Stern, Chip "Jack DeJohnette: South Side to Woodstock" *Down Beat* 2 November 1978
Stewart, Zan "Gil Evans" *Musician, Player and Listener* 39, January 1982
Sullivan, Patrick "Benny Bailey" *Jazz Journal* April 1977
Taylor, Arthur *Notes and Tones: Musician-to-Musician Interviews* New York: Perigee 1977
Taylor, J.R. Liner note *Charlie Parker Encores* (Savoy SJL 1107)
Thomas, J.C. *Chasin' the Trane* New York: Doubleday 1975
Traill, Sinclair "The Shelly Manne Story" *Jazz Journal International* August 1979
Tristano, Lennie. Liner note *Crosscurrents* (Capitol M-11060)
Ullmann, Michael *Jazz Lives* Washington, DC: New Republic Books 1980
Underwood, Lee "Profile: Ian Carr" *Down Beat* November 1979
– "Blindfold Test: Med Flory" *Down Beat* August 1980
Watts, Michael "Miles Davis" Ray Coleman ed *Today's Sound* London: Hamlyn 1973
White, Andrew. Liner note *John Coltrane: On A Misty Night* (Prestige P-24084) 1978
Wild, David. Review of *Miles Davis: Jazz at the Plaza* (Columbia C32 470) *Coda* March 1975
Wilder, Alec *American Popular Song: The Great Innovators, 1900–50* New York: Oxford University Press 1972
Williams, Martin *Where's the Melody?* New York: Minerva Books 1966
– *The Jazz Tradition* New York: New American Library 1970
Wilmer, Valerie *Jazz People* New York: Bobbs Merrill 1970

Wilson, John S. *Jazz: The Transition Years 1940–60* New York: Appleton-Century-Crofts 1966

Wilson, Russ. Review of Miles Davis Sextet at the Blackhawk *Oakland Tribune* 4 June 1959. Quoted in C.O. Simpkins *Coltrane: A Biography* New York: Herndon House 1975

Wisckol, Marty "Profile: Charles McPherson" *Down Beat* June 1981

Yanow, Scott "Columbia's Contemporary Masters Series" *Record Review* April 1978

– "Miles Davis: the later years" *Record Review* April 1978

Young, Al. Liner note *John Coltrane: Black Pearls* (Prestige P-24037) 1974

Zwerin, Michael "Miles Davis: a most curious friendship" *Down Beat* 10 March 1966

Index

Authors and composers are cited in parentheses following the titles of books and musical works, respectively.

COST
9400

CRC → NTN 9608

4 X
8/93